Power, Profit and Politics:
Essays on Imperialism, Nationalism and Change in Twentieth-Century India

Edited by

CHRISTOPHER BAKER, GORDON JOHNSON
and ANIL SEAL

CAMBRIDGE
UNIVERSITY PRESS

CAMBRIDGE UNIVERSITY PRESS
Cambridge, New York, Melbourne, Madrid, Cape Town, Singapore,
São Paulo, Delhi, Dubai, Tokyo

Cambridge University Press
The Edinburgh Building, Cambridge CB2 8RU, UK

Published in the United States of America by Cambridge University Press, New York

www.cambridge.org
Information on this title: www.cambridge.org/9780521133869

First published 1981
This digitally printed version 2009

A catalogue record for this publication is available from the British Library

ISBN 978-0-521-13386-9 Paperback

In Memoriam
John Andrew Gallagher
1919–1980

Acknowledgements

The essays collected together in this special issue of *Modern Asian Studies* are concerned with the ways in which Britain's imperial connection with India impinged upon the political, economic and social development of the sub-continent in the first half of the twentieth century. They have been written by students and colleagues of Professor J. A. Gallagher, whose death last year has robbed historical scholarship of a powerful and creative mind.

Editorial responsibility for the issue has been shared with Dr Christopher Baker and Dr Anil Seal, who, together with Professor Gallagher, first suggested that we explore in a publication of this kind some of the dominant themes relating to the last years of colonial rule in India. Much of the credit for the successful completion of this work must go to them.

Generous grants from the Master and Fellows of Trinity College, Cambridge, and from the Managers of the Smuts Memorial Fund, University of Cambridge, have made possible the publication of this much enlarged part of the journal.

I am grateful to Miss Livia Breglia, who, as for all issues of *Modern Asian Studies*, has laboured nobly to put typescripts in order and to read proofs; and it is a pleasure to record the work done for the journal by Mr Dennis Forbes, Mrs Hilary Moore, and Mrs Rosemary Tennison at the Press.

April 1981   GORDON JOHNSON

CONTENTS PAGE

Modern Asian Studies, **15**, 3 (1981), pp. 355–368.

Nationalisms and the Crisis of Empire, 1919–1922

JOHN GALLAGHER

University of Cambridge

ONCE the British Empire became world-wide, the sun never set upon its crises. The historian who studies any of these crises in isolation does so at his peril, for their consequences tended to interlock. In the astounding geometry which the British Government constructed across the map of tropical Africa, many of the lines they drew were guided by pressures far away, in Ireland, in Egypt and in India. During the years between 1919 and 1922 a new and more elaborate set of crises marched indefatigably on through the body politic of Empire, like gout through the enfeebled frame of a toper. By this time Britain was threatened by the rolling up of her old interests in East Asia as well as by the phasing out of her new interests in West Asia; while in the classical centres of disaffection Zaghlul Pasha, Gandhi and Mr de Valera pursued the old aims by new methods. No analysis of any of these crises will be complete without establishing its interplay with the others. Each joined in the rataplan which frayed the minds and the nerves of the policy-makers. But at a deeper level, each of them was part of a general problem; and there is much to be said for studying problems, not regions. In the case of underdeveloped subjects, such as African or Indian history, it is important not to study them as though they were merely the annals of the parish.

I

When the palace revolution brought Lloyd George into power in December 1916, he chose only four ministers to join him inside his War Cabinet. Bonar Law, the wistful plain man, was invited as leader of the Conservative Party, while the presence of Henderson was supposed to

Professor Gallagher died in March 1980, leaving much unpublished material. This article, written in 1968, was presented at seminars in Cambridge and London; some if its themes were later elaborated by the author in the Ford Lectures, 1974. It is hoped to publish more of Professor Gallagher's work in due course.

0026-749X/81/0406-0904$02.00 © 1981 Cambridge University Press.

symbolize the People's War. But the other two members sounded like
ancestral voices. Curzon and Milner seemed to be imperialists of the
traditional kind, men with a great future behind them, relics from the
froward old empire-building which had been quashed in 1906. Spurned
by the electorate, hobbled by the party system in the Commons—'that
mob', 'this rotten assembly', as Milner had termed them—they now
used the emergency of war to shin up the greasy pole once more. With
them a group of Milner's men also came into the government: Waldorf
Astor, Lionel Curtis and Philip Kerr who joined the Prime Minister's
Secretariat; L. S. Amery, who became Under-Secretary for European
and Far Eastern Affairs; Sir Mark Sykes, who became Under-Secretary
for Islamic Affairs. If the titles of some of these posts looked constitutionally bizarre, they showed that the ministry's thinking was likely to
be far-flung.

From the outset, these men decided to provide the ministry with its
light and leading. Managing the Commons seemed a fit task for the
humdrum talents of Bonar Law, while cozening the Trades Unions was
good enought for Henderson; but high policy was to be managed by the
gentlemen from Balliol.[1] They exploited to the utmost this uncoven-
anted mercy of power. One consequence was the effort to modernize the
British economy by firm State action, so as to fight a semi-total war.[2]
Another was their renewed attempt to integrate the Empire and to place
its future security beyond doubt. Already in January 1917 the Cabinet
was considering a policy of annexation or control of new regions, once
the war had been won. Why not the Middle East? On 1 March Sykes
told the editor of the *Manchester Guardian* that

... we should exercise a protectorate over Palestine and Mesopotamia and
give support to the new Arab Kingdom which would included the Arabian
Peninsula and extend as far north and include Damascus ...[3]

And why not throw in East Africa as well? When the Imperial War
Cabinet of Prime Ministers met on 20 March, they were able to ponder a
memorandum by Amery, calling for security in

... that great southern half of the British Empire which lies in an irregular
semi-circle around the Indian Ocean—South Africa, East Africa, Egypt, India,
Australia and New Zealand ... The retention of German East Africa, of

[1] Milner was 'just a typical product of Balliol'; Marquess of Crewe, *Life of Rosebery*
(1931), I, 215.
[2] A. J. P. Taylor, 'Politics in the First World War', *Proceedings of the British Academy*, 1959,
86–7; but Mr Taylor misses the connection between imperialism and modernization.
[3] Journal of C. P. Scott, 1 March 1919, quoted in L. Stein, *The Balfour Declaration*
(1961), 387.

Palestine and Mesopotamia, and of the German Pacific colonies, is the indispensable means of securing this end.[4]

These exponents of the new cartography found nothing to complain of in the attitude of the Dominions Prime Ministers, ardent sub-imperialists to a man. Consequently, the Imperial War Cabinet set up a committee to consider 'Territorial Desiderata', its members being Curzon, Cecil, Chamberlain, Long, Massey (because Australia wanted the German Pacific colonies), Smuts (because South Africa wanted German East Africa), and Amery as Secretary.[5] Deciding what to do with other people's colonies was agreeable work. The Partition of Africa should be readjusted. By giving way in Togoland, by giving up in the Gambia, they should obtain Tanganyika. Selling West Africa to buy East: here was the classical strategy of the Partition, now restated by Smuts:

General Smuts . . . declared that, if it were a choice between keeping German East Africa or the German West African colonies, he considered it much more important to make sure of the safety of the eastern route from South Africa, more particularly as the retention of German East Africa included the provision of a land communication with Egypt and also secured the Red Sea route to India.[6]

Here was the African thesis of a revived imperialism. But it had an Asian thesis as well, and it was unclear whether they could be reconciled. In March 1918, at Milner's prompting, Lloyd George set up an Eastern Committee, to study annexation policy in the event of a Turkish and a Russian collapse; and Curzon, Balfour, Smuts, Montagu (Secretary of State for India) and Wilson (Chief of the Imperial General Staff) were appointed as members. It was not so easy now to maintain the African thesis, for if Britain were to move into the Middle East how were the other Powers to be squared into giving her East Africa as well? And if they could not be squared, which of these regions should Britain buy, and which should she sell? When it came to settling priorities ministers were soon at odds. Montagu flew a kite for transferring East Africa to India: the idea was a non-starter. Amery's Cape to Cairo visions fitted well with Smuts' view of South African interests. Balfour thought as little of the Cape to Cairo route as his uncle had done and as Lloyd George now did. They both favoured launching into Palestine and Mesopota-

---

[4] Amery: 'Note on the Possible Terms of Peace'; Austen Chamberlain Papers.

[5] The Asquith ministry had already set up a Territorial Changes Committee; but that had been a low-powered affair made up of civil servants only.

[6] 'Committee of the Imperial War Cabinet on Territorial Desiderata, second meeting, 18 April 1917'; Austen Chamberlain Papers. It is gratifying to find Smuts in 1917 pursuing the same argument which has been advanced in R. E. Robinson et al., Africa and the Victorians (1961).

mia, and in return they were ready to see the U.S.A. in East Africa. For
their part, Amery and Smuts had no objection to an American presence
somewhere in Africa, but preferably at someone else's expense; they
could see great advantages for civilization if the Americans went into the
Belgian Congo or into Portugese Mozambique. It is curious to reflect
that if Washington had agreed to any of these plans, the First World
War might have led to a new Partition of Africa.[7]

The complex negotiations of the Peace Conference are not here our
concern. In the event the Americans refused to accept any mandates or
special positions anywhere, and, at the cost of a few more West African
trifles, Britain emerged with the gains desired by both her wings of
imperialists. But not only did she obtain German East Africa, Palestine
and Mesopotamia; during the war she had won effective control over
much of Persia and Arabia; and her interventions in the Caucasus and
Transcaspia had rolled Russian power still further from the frontiers of
India.

It would be hard to envisage a more heavily insured position than the
British Empire in India had achieved by 1919. The Indian Ocean was
now a British lake; and in addition a great new spur of control jutted out
from Egypt to Arabia, to Baghdad and to Teheran, linking at the eastern
frontiers of Persia with the westernmost bounds of India. At last the
policy launched by the younger Pitt, strengthened by Palmerston and
consolidated by Salisbury, seemed to have reached its goal. Now that
the last of the insurances had been taken out, security had been found.

II

But security, like love affairs or solvency, is here today and gone to-
morrow; and within a year of its apogee, the vast system so carefully
constructed in 1919 was in disarray. While the statesmen still sat at
Versailles, Asia was plunging into a series of contemporaneous revolu-
tions and wars as complex and at least as important as the General Crisis
of Europe during the seventeenth century. In March 1919 the British
were confronted with a rising in Egypt, in April they were grappling
with a rising in the Punjab. By the following month they were at war
with Afghanistan, and they were being gravely embarrassed by Mustafa
Kemal's defiance of the Sultan of Turkey. By the end of 1919 the
Persians were resisting the treaty which Curzon had forced upon their

[7] In which case we should doubtless have been regaled with books proving that this
second Partition was economically inevitable.

rulers. In July there was a revolt in Mesopotamia against the new British occupation. These events mainly affected the British; but there were many other turbulences in Asia at this time. 'The May Fourth Incident' of 1919 showed the depth of Chinese resentment against the West and Japan alike; the rising in Syria during July 1920 marked the beginning of the French mandate; and the upheavals of 1919 in the Bashgir and Tatar Republics, the fighting in 1919–20 in Kirghizstan, Georgia, Armenia and Azerbaijan showed the desire of her Asian borderlands to escape from Russia's control. Most of the continent was in crisis, and much of this crisis impinged upon British interests. It is instructive to follow the effects of this Asian backlash upon the plans which the British had so hopefully elaborated only a year or so earlier. So far, we have merely been considering British imperialism in the abstract. But, by examining the nature and style and weight of its reactions to these crises, we can pitch upon an earthier estimate of its real strength; and by observing its behaviour under pressure we may begin to see where its true priorities stood.

III

But for us the road to Asia lies through the swing doors of the Grafton Hotel in Dublin, one of the cover headquarters of the revolutionary Irish Government. By 1919 Gladstone's coming storm in the west had become for Lloyd George a hurricane. After the proclamation of the Republic by Dáil Eireann in January, and the first attacks on police stations in April, the country moved that winter into full guerilla war. By that time 30,000 soldiers of a much shrunken British Army had to be kept in Ireland; and in 1920 they were reinforced by another 7,000 regulars, as well as by the less phlegmatic Black and Tans. The Irish commitment was calling for more and more of an Army which was growing less and less. The more for Ireland, the fewer for Asia: in this way the end-game of the old Anglo-Irish struggle was to interact with the opening moves in the new Anglo-Asian struggle, while the political difficulty of settling the Irish crisis was to obstruct a settlement in India and Egypt.

Both the Indian and the Egyptian crises opened in the same way: administrative change led to political demands which weakened the moderates, whom the British Government then tried to rally by soothing Declarations. In spite of all the speculation by historians about the Montagu-Chelmsford reforms, their genesis was quite simple. A new

Viceroy and a weak Council were browbeaten by strong provincial Governors, who argued, unanswerably, that the strains which the war was bringing to India could not be properly handled from Delhi, and that Government must be decentralized. The India Office reluctantly accepted the principle of this administrative change, since the botching of the Mesopotamia expedition showed that the Government of India did not look like an organizer of victory. But already in 1917 it was clear that the Indian moderates were losing ground, and Montagu now saw his chance to tack on to these administrative reforms a poltical reform which would strengthen the moderates' hands. This decision looks portentous in retrospect, but at the time it gave little concern to the British Cabinet which had troubles of its own. In any case, by arranging that Montagu should carry out his plans under the supervision of Curzon and Austen Chamberlain, they could be sure that plenty of water would be poured into his wine. There were difficulties in 1919, Gandhi's *satyagraha* campaign in Gujarat, the Punjab disturbances and the Afghan War, but these shook Delhi more than Downing Street, where the Cabinet pushed ahead with the Government of India Bill. With Tilak, Mrs Besant and Vithalbhai Patel all lobbying M.P.s, there were still good hopes that Congress would agree to work the reforms when they came off the stocks.

Events in Egypt seemed more alarming. At the end of the war the Egyptians were pressing for an end to the protectorate which Britain had snapped on their wrists in 1914. When Zaghlul and three of his *Wafd* associates were deported in March 1919, there were vast demonstrations of protest. More interestingly, there were signs of an organized resistance network, and the British retaliated by declaring martial law. To get off this hook, the British Government in May set up a Commission of Inquiry under Milner. For various reasons the Commissioners did not reach Egypt until December, when they came, they saw, they declared. Their Declaration implicitly abandoned the protectorate in principle, and their report explained why:

Anti-British feeling is practically confined to the upper class and the *intelligentzia* and is strongest among the students, doctors, lawyers and the bulk of the official class . . . actual rebellion is less to be apprehended than the progressive weakening of authority and respect for Government . . .[8]

[8] There is an edited version of the Report in *Parliamentary Papers*, 1920, Cmd. 1131. Copies of the full text, which is rather less respectful to the *intelligentzia*, are in the Milner Papers and the Montagu Papers. For another statement of his view, see Milner to Lloyd George, 28 December 1919 (a letter full of candid Milnerisms); A. M. Gollin, *Proconsul in Politics* (1964), 590–1.

At first sight, this seems an oddly liberal attitude for Milner. But in fact
his plan was intended to give little away. He was reproached by

an anonymous correspondent, who concludes with the words: 'I fear, my Lord,
you are getting old.'
   This is unfortunately true. But I think that even in my hey-day I should have
regarded the proposed concessions to Egyptian Nationalism as just and politic,
and as calculated to strengthen and not to weaken our Imperial position ... The
security of our communications with India, and other parts of our Empire
beyond India, was the supreme object which led to our intervention [in 1882].
And certainly that object is more vital to us than ever today ... [Egypt] is truly
the nodal point of our whole Imperial system.
   But is it therefore necessary that we should own it? Is it not sufficient if we
have a firm foothold there? ... there will, at any rate at the outset, be a party
clamouring for still greater concessions and wishing to get rid of us altogether.
But as against these extemists we shall have, as I believe we already have, the
saner elements of Egyptian 'Nationalism' on our side.[9]

Evidently, the moderates were to be rallied in Egypt as well as in India.
   But the simplest proof that Milner's plan would make little difference
to the British presence is that the Egyptians themselves showed little
inclination to negotiate with him on these terms. Instead, they procras-
tinated, engrossed in the rivalries between Zaghlul and the Prime
Minister, Adly Pasha, with Zaghlul 'in such an exalted frame of mind
that it would not be beyond him to attempt a coup similar to that of
Arabi Pasha'.[10] But there was delay from the British side too. For one
thing, Milner had had enough. By January 1921, he was anxious to
retire, and two months later he managed to disentagle himself from
Lloyd George. This removed from the Cabinet the most powerful
supporter of the new Egyptian policy, since its other champions were of
small account, Montagu because he was manic, H. A. L. Fisher because
he was academic. Curzon had liked the policy, but he liked office more.
Lloyd George disliked it, but he disliked candour more; and until the
Prime Minister came into the open, Curzon's attitude was Laodicean, to
say the most of it. Admittedly, Lloyd George had good reasons for lying
doggo. There was open dissension in Cabinet over Egyptian affairs,
Churchill, for example, coming out with a preposterous scheme for
turning the protectorate into a Dominion. Again, the House of Commons was troublesome. The post-war election had made the Conservatives the preponderant party inside the coalition and had filled the

[9] Milner, Cabinet Memorandum, 'The Egyptian Proposals', Secret, 16 September
1920, Montagu Papers.
[10] Allenby (High Commissioner, Egypt) to Curzon, 8 April 1921; Lord Lloyd, *Egypt
since Cromer* (vol. II, 1934), 40.

House with 'Industrials' and hard-faced men who had little sympathy with lesser breeds without the vote. It is simply a waste of time to drum up large statements about British policy towards Egypt or towards India during these years without observing that Montagu and those other ministers who wanted some flexibility in these policies were trapped inside a partliamentary majority which wanted nothing of the sort.[11]

It was not that these unreconstructed back-benchers held trenchant views about Egypt; but the Egyptian problem was now becoming interlocked with the Irish problem, about which they were bitterly against surrender. It was becoming easier to treat the one as an awful warning about the other, to imply that one step backwards in Cairo would lead to a headlong retreat in Dublin. Attacking the Egyptian proposals in 1920, Churchill wrote:

> If we leave out the word 'Egypt' . . . and substitute the word 'Ireland', it would with very small omissions make perfectly good sense and would constitute a complete acceptance of Mr. de Valera's demands.[12]

The syndrome worked on the supporters of the proposals as well. At the end of 1921 Montagu wrote to one of Lloyd George's secretaries:

> I am much worried about Egypt. The fact of the matter is that we are going to have a row there . . . I drafted the enclosed [a Cabinet Memorandum urging concessions], then I came to the conclusion that with Ireland in its present position I ought not to worry the Cabinet . . .[13]

By this time India too had joined in the interplay. Here the crisis which had opened in the Punjab in April 1919 had transformed the Congress. Hitherto the movement had been controlled from the three Presidencies of Bengal, Bombay and Madras (for the benefit of whose educated classes it had largely been run). A triple revolution upset these comfortable arrangements. First, the movement spread geographically, so that fresh provinces were enlisted into Congress politics. Secondly, it spread downwards, so that lower strata of the population were mobilized. Thirdly, large groups of Indian Muslims moved against the *Raj* when they learned of the terms which Britain was trying to impose on Turkey. The Afghan War of 1919 showed how far disaffection had

---

[11] For an account of this captivity, see T. Wilson, *The Downfall of the Liberal Party, 1914–1935* (1966), 187–204. Many of the Coalition backbenchers made a dead set against Montagu, for example during the debates over the retiring of General Dyer after the Amritsar shootings.

[12] Churchill, Cabinet Memorandum, 'The Egyptian Proposals', 24 May 1920, Montagu Papers.

[13] Montagu to Griff, 17 November 1921, *ibid.*

gone in the North, where the Chief Commissioner of the North-West Frontier Province reported that

The people of the Punjab & N.W.F.P. are frankly hostile to us & would welcome the Amir . . . I have got the Peshawar people down just in time or we should have had an organised rising here . . .[14]

As Gandhi was working in 1919–20 to swing Indian politics towards a more radical course, he was powerfully assisted by another of the British Government's plans for the post-war world. Since the spoils belonged to the victor, it was clear that Turkey would lose by the Peace Treaty. But how much should she lose? Ministers who favoured a soft line wanted her losses to be confined to her European possessions; but the hard-liners went much further, demanding that Anatolia, Asia Minor and Arabia, as well as Constantinople, should also be wrested from the Ottoman Empire. In terms of the European power balance there were solid arguments in favour of the hard line. It would please the Greeks. It could spare the Italians. It might even conciliate the French. Yet, from the standpoint of British interests outside Europe, the arguments against it were unanswerable. In making war against the Sultan, in aiding the Arabs to despoil him of the Holy Places, Britain had gambled with the loyalty of Indian Muslims. The gamble had come off; but if the British went on to press their luck by turning the Commander of the Faithful bag and baggage out of Constantinople and the Holy Places, it was fairly certain that this luck would turn and that Indian Islam would move against the Raj. To do this in 1919 could only make the Indian crisis more critical; better by far to let sleeping Muslims lie. The initial plan of the British Government was to coax the Americans into rushing in where the Europeans feared to tread; for an American mandate at Constantinople would conveniently close the awkward option of turning out the Turk. When the option opened again, Lloyd George as usual kept mum; but the hard line was heard in the Cabinet. Montagu upbraided the Prime Minister for not quashing it:

. . . every single one of your colleagues, with the exception of Mr. Balfour and Lord Curzon, is in favour of leaving the Turkish Government the sovereignty of Constantinople and of the Turkish parts of Thrace. This is true of persons of such diverse opinions as Geddes, Long and Fisher . . . It is true of Bonar Law and of Barnes.[15]

Montagu cut little ice. Milner cut a great deal, and he held a similar view about the need for the soft lines: 'I know this would be best for us in

[14] Roos-Keppel to Harcourt Butler, 12 June 1919, Butler Papers.
[15] Montagu to Lloyd George, 8 September 1919, Montagu Papers.

Egypt &, I believe, in India. I think it would be best for us in the whole of
the Middle East.'[16] But Milner was out of England when he wrote, and
when he returned after five months of dealing with the Egyptians he
ached to put his old bones into retirement. In these circumstances, the
peculiarly personal diplomacy of Lloyd George went unchecked, and
the anti-Turkish policy flourished. So, too, did the Khilafat movement
in India. This Muslim enmity towards the Raj considerably widened the
base of Gandhi's Non-Cooperation Movement, and it also brought a
new quality of recklessness into its leadership. By May 1920 it seemed to
the Director of the Central Intelligence Bureau in Delhi that '. . .
Gandhi, in order to lead, has to follow . . . Gandhi is a retarding agent
and . . . Muhammadan extemists are adapting his programme to their
own purposes . . .'[17] Indeed, the Non-Cooperation movement cannot
be understood without realizing how far it was supercharged by this
Muslim alliance. Muslim votes went solidly for Gandhi at the vital
Nagpur Congress of 1920, and under the pressure of the Maulanas the
Congress-Khilafat alliance moved towards a demand for immediate
Indian independence. By the end of 1921 the Governor of the United
Provinces wrote that:

. . . the matter [Civil Disobedience] is now largely in the hands of Mussulmans,
and they are determined to go through with it . . . My ministers think that a
Mussulman rising is imminent.[18]

What concerns us is the strength of the Indian challenge and the
weakness of the British response. Even in late 1921, when the agitation
was running very high, the Congress–Khilafat grouping was so strong
that Government did not dare to arrest Gandhi: indeed, it even considered striking a bargain with him. In the indignant words of that
super-imperialist, George Lloyd, who was then Governor of Bombay:

On December the 19th . . . I got a long telegram from Reading [the Viceroy of
India] which showed clearly that he was little short of panic stricken . . . it was a
contemptible telegram. It asked me and my Government to concur . . . that if
Gandhi would call off all *hartals*, the Viceroy proposed to agree to having a
round table conference with Gandhi . . .[19]

We need not follow these Egyptian and Indian episodes to their
conclusion, to the ending of the Egyptian Protectorate and the collapse
of Indian Non-Cooperation in 1922. What matters to the argument is

[16] Milner to Montagu, 2 December 1919, Confidential, Montagu Papers.
[17] Government of India Records H[ome] P[olitical], 1920, June, 78, Deposit, Weekly
Report by Director, Central Intelligence Bureau, 10 May 1920.
[18] Butler to Reading, 23 November 1921, Butler Papers.
[19] Lloyd to Chamberlain, 24 March 1922, Private, Austen Chamberlain Papers.

simply to note how low the regimes in these countries had fallen, a mere three years after the British Empire had seemed to have reached its apogee.

IV

Ireland, Egypt, India: one by one these hammers beat upon the anvil of Empire. In December 1921 the British conceded Saorstát Eireann; in March 1922 they ended the protectorate over Egypt; between these dates they were at their wits' end how to deal with Gandhi. And yet it was the need to hold precisely these bastions which had induced them to retreat from other and less crucial positions. As early as April 1919 the War Office could not find the men to cover all the Cabinet's bets, and by 1920 the Chief of the Imperial General Staff was warning them that:

. . . our small army is much too scattered . . . in no single theatre are we strong enough—not in Ireland, nor England, not on the Rhine, not in Constantinople, nor Batoum, nor Egypt, nor Palestine, nor Mesopotamia, nor Persia, nor India.[20]

Consequently, the military advice given to the Cabinet called for retreats from the high points which British imperialism had scaled in 1918: the Army wanted to pull out of Persia and Arabia and to shorten the line in Mesopotamia, if all the British stakes in Ireland, Egypt and India were to be properly protected.[21] There were 'simply not enough troops'. And by late 1921, when Wilson was talking of the need for 100,000 or even 200,000 men in Ireland,[22] it was obvious that something had to give. If the formal empire in Ireland, Egypt and India was to be protected, then Britain had to cut her losses in the informal empire. Already in 1920 the General Staff had concluded that the British positions in China could be defended only with the help of troops sent by some other power.[23] They went on to doubt the credibility of those outer defences of India which had been constructed with such care only a few years ago. Of these new defences the new British position in Persia was the most important.[24] The Foreign Office was quite clear that this

[20] Wilson's Diary, 21 May 1920, C. E. Callwell, *Field Marshal Sir Henry Wilson* (1927), II, 240–1.

[21] E.g. Wilson's diary, 5 August 1920, 22 March and 31 May 1921, *ibid.*, II, 255, 281, 293.

[22] Wilson's diary, 13 September 1921; *ibid.*, II, 305.

[23] Memorandum by General Staff, 5 May 1920, *Documents on British Foreign Policy, 1919–1939*, 1st series, vol. XIV, 90–1.

[24] The history of Persia during these years is intricate and entertaining. During the years German agents lived dangerously, trying to stir up war against the British troops

position must be held for Indian reasons.[25] On the other hand, the War Office, short of troops, uneasily impressed by the rival case for holding on to Mesopotamia, plagued by the fears of the Government of India, longed for Britain to get out of Persia.[26] She got out. If the Foreign Office was grieved, the Government of India was delighted. Delhi was now very much on the defensive. The British interventions in Russia had stung the Bolsehviks into retaliating by fomenting trouble around the Indian frontiers,[27] and the Government of India were now coming to see their security in a Little Indian policy in Persia, as well as in Afghanistan and around the Persian Gulf:

It seems to us essential that we should seize every opportunity of working back to our old role of champions of Islam against the Russian Ogre. At present the roles are reversed ... British attitude in Persia is regarded in Moslem Asia, especially in Afghanistan and largely in Moslem India, as another example of Britain's crushing of Islam, thus providing Bolshevik propaganda with arguments ready made.[28]

From this time onwards these European rivals were to vie with each other for the support of Asian Muslims, Confucians and Hindus. Who was the hammer now? And who was the anvil?

V

Bismarck, in a memorable image, once described Polish noblemen as wearing sable coats with lice crawling under the collar. About the British Empire in Asia after 1918 there is a similar combination of splendour and misery. By 1918 that Empire had achieved the high-flying aims of guaranteeing Indian security by constructing two vast arms of power which encircled the Indian Ocean. But by 1922 much of this new system lay at risk.

How had this come about? It is clear that the Empire of 1918, like the Empire of 1763, was over-extended, and that the Empire which

there. The outbreak of peace saw a complex struggle between Persian Cossacks, officered by stateless Russians, and the South Persian Rifles, led partly by Swedes. Over all this wreckage the Shah presided with imperturbable lethargy.
    [25] Memorandum by Hardinge (Permanent Under-Secretary, Foreign Office), 20 May 1920, *Documents on British Foreign Policy, 1919–1939*, 1st series, vol. XIII, 487–8.
    [26] War Office to General Haldane, 23 December 1920, *ibid.*, 670–1.
    [27] This theme is discussed, rather disapprovingly, in *India and Communism*, compiled in the Intelligence Bureau, Home Department, Government of India (Simla, 1935, restricted); and more coolly in Harish Kapur, *Soviet Russia and Asia, 1917–27* (Geneva, 1966).
    [28] Chelmsford to Montagu, Telegram No. 107, S., 22 January 1921, *Documents*, 1st series, vol. XIV, 705.

emerged from the First World War, like the Empire which resulted from the Partition of Africa, was top heavy with the insurance it was carrying for India. But, while these statements may be formally correct, they do not carry us far into the inwardness of the process. How may we go further? In the first place, let us note how repeatedly and how success-fully the local crises combined to the detriment of imperial interests. This was clear to the men on the spot whose task was to combat them, to Allenby in Cairo, or to Cox in Baghdad. Casting around for the meaning of the Nagpur Congress, the Intelligence Bureau in Delhi thought they could see that: ' . . . the Congress have given up Egyptian methods in favour of Sinn Fein methods.'[29] But this interlocking was more palpable at the level of policy-making in London, for it was here that the plans devised to meet one crisis were immediately ruined by the onset of another. Montagu himself put the point perfectly:

The concessions which look likely to be necessary in Ireland harden public opinion against any new concessions in Egypt. Anything that is done as to complete independence of Egypt might appear to encourage Indian extremists.[30]

Even so, these events go much deeper than the ricochets from policies fired off by distracted ministers. What these withdrawals and adjust-ments point to is a growing weakness behind the imperial façade.[31] This is why Curtis, Amery and Kerr, the heirs of Milner, when they came to ponder over what had happended, drew the conclusion that the Empire could no longer go it alone. Since the League of Nations was anathema to them as a rival association, they concluded that from now on the best way of underwriting the Empire's liabilities was by contriving a special relationship with the United States. This would have the double advan-tage of saving the Empire from dissolution and of keeping Britain out of Europe. The preoccupations of 1968 are clearly foreshadowed in the 1920s.

The events of 1919-22 also seem to hint at another portentous shift in the priorities of British policy. While some of its exertions had been with a view towards strengthening Indian security, others worked against that aim. The anti-Turkish line followed by the Cabinet brought advan-tages in Europe, but it brought nothing but trouble in India. Hence it is

[29] H.P. 1921, May 19, Deposit, Memorandum by Director of Intelligence Bureau, 14 January 1921.
[30] Montagu to Reading, Telegram 5657, 4 November 1921, Montagu Papers.
[31] A similar argument might be made from the standpoint of the white Dominions. It was Smuts who warned the British that, unless these lands were given absolute self-government, they would go the way of Ireland.

tempting to move to the argument that India was beginning to lose pride of place in British calculations; that the trend already faintly signalled by the Anglo-Russian Agreement in 1907 was growing by the 1920s; or that since the interests which wanted the Indian connection were slowly losing importance in British society and in the British economy, then the case for retaining India was slowly going by default. There is probably something in this, although not when the case is made so sharply. We need to look cannily at it. After all, much of the apparent disregard for Indian interests at the time arose from the simple fact that Montagu himself was a light-weight minister, and that Lloyd George, who settled the options of policy, moved in an erratic way. It was still generally held that if India could be held without much trouble, then she should be held. But say that a time should come when she could not be held without much trouble, would she be worth the holding then? And if not, who would then struggle to hold the East African Empire either?

But while it is interesting to speculate about the priorities of Downing Street, there is a deeper level to dig into. Between 1919 and 1922, the British Empire in Asia, which had been held hitherto with an almost ridicuous ease, was at last confronted with the general crisis in Asia. In China, only the United States could underwrite its interests. In the Middle East and in South Asia it was now colliding with forces against which there was little chance of making headway through the techniques of formal empire. Moreover, Britain lacked the economic strength to develop the daunting expanses of Asia; so that there was little chance of holding by informal control the territories where her formal rule was being challenged. In any event, Zaghlul and Gandhi, Sun Yat Sen and Reza Shah, in their efforts to throw off western imperialism, were summoning dire and incalculable spirits. For what rough beasts was their hour coming round at last? Asia was on the move, lurching towards that time of troubles which would draw from its greatest figure a haunting judgement: 'The way to truth is paved with skeletons over which we dare to walk.'[32]

[32] Quoted in Pyarelal, *Mahatma Gandhi, the Last Phase* (Ahmedabad, 1958), I, 581.

Modern Asian Studies, **15**, 3 (1981), pp. 369–386.

'An English Barrack in the Oriental Seas'? India in the Aftermath of the First World War

KEITH JEFFERY

Ulster Polytechnic

DURING the last ninety years of British rule in India, the 'Jewel of the Empire' was, as Lord Salisbury remarked in 1882, easily regarded by many British imperialists as 'an English barrack in the Oriental Seas from which we may draw any number of troops without paying for them'.[1] In more prosaic terms India was seen as a permanent strategic reserve and the principal means by which British interests were secured throughout Asia, from Suez to Wei-hei-wei. As such, India was a central component in the British imperial system. The empire's matchless prestige, its wealth and apparent power all stemmed in large measure from India. In the second half of the nineteenth century the Raj, the East India trade and the Indian Army demonstrated a combination of power which Britain's imperial rivals might envy but never surpass. The central importance of India is illustrated by the Victorian conception of imperial defence, which was seen to depend on the twin pillars of naval supremacy and the defence of India. The only serious military commitment which British planners admitted before the turn of the century was the possibility of meeting a Russian invasion of India across the North West Frontier. This threat existed mostly in the minds of British generals. Britain and Russia came closest to war on the Frontier at the time of the Penjdeh incident in 1885, but even then the likelihood of a Russian expedition against India was hardly more than remote. Nevertheless, the threat of invasion was the principal rationale for the nature and size of the Army in India and this consideration guided Lord Kitchener's reforms of the Indian Army during his time as Commander-in-Chief from 1902 to 1909. Every effort was made to ensure rapid mobilization and to enhance mobility so that a 'Field Army' could be marshalled on the Frontier in the shortest possible time. Kitchener also made fantastic estimates of the numbers of troops required to defend the sub-continent. In 1904 he calculated that the War Office would immediately have to supply 160,000 men to reinforce

[1] Sir Charles Lucas (ed.), *The Empire at War* (5 vols, London, 1921–26), I, pp. 56–7.

0026-749X/81/0406-0904$02.00 © 1981 Cambridge University Press.

the 200,000-strong Army in India, and another 300,000–400,000 troops in a second year of war.[2] The real effect of these calculations was to startle the British cabinet into seeking a diplomatic solution to the military problem. This they did with the Anglo-Russian Convention of 1907 which aimed to ease the burden of imperial defence by securing the frontiers of India and lifting Russian pressure from parts of the Middle East. Along with the Anglo-French entente from 1904, this marked the beginning of Britain's military 'continental commitment' and a move away from the more specifically imperial strategy of the nineteenth century.[3] But so far as GHQ Delhi was concerned, this shift might never have occurred. Since the Russian agreement was regarded as a snare and a delusion, Indian military planners continued to treat Russia as their principal threat. After all, armies need enemies to justify their existence. Even the most plausible Indian general could hardly explain away an army of some quarter of a million men by referring to a potential Afghan threat or the need to police restive Pathan tribesmen. Thus, in 1913 the Army in India remained specifically organized to meet the needs of a major war on the Frontier. Nearly two-thirds of the entire force were set aside to act as a Field Army; the remainder being earmarked for internal security. Out of a total 234,000 men, 152,000 served in the Field Army.[4] The war briefly interrupted this concern, but following the Bolshevik revolution there were renewed fears of Russian expansion. After the armistice in 1918 the Indian General Staff automatically returned to their plans for the defence of the Frontier, no more questioning the principles upon which they were based than they had done before the war.

The second principal function of the military forces in India was internal security. These forces—the 'Army in India'—comprised two parts: British units stationed temporarily in India on the 'Cardwell' system, and the British-commanded Indian Army. The Army in India was treated as a coherent whole and managed by the High Command in Delhi. The Indian Army had been established after the Mutiny, as had a proportion of approximately one British soldier to two Indian, which was generally adhered to until the outbreak of the Great War. In 1914, for example, there were 81,000 British and 152,000 Indian troops.[5] 'The ratio' was a central tenet of the Indian military administration and a crude index of mistrust. Before the Mutiny the proportion of British to

---

[2] Michael Howard, *The Continental Commitment* (Harmondsworth, 1974), pp. 19–20.
[3] For an account of this, see Howard, *ibid.*, ch. 2.
[4] Government of India, *The Army in India and its Evolution* (Calcutta, 1924), pp. 221–2.
[5] *Ibid.*, p. 219.

Indian had been almost one to nine, but following it no-one had been prepared to risk continuing such a low ratio. For fifty years it remained high and unchallenged. Although by 1914 it had become well-nigh immutable, such was the demand for British units during the war that the ratio was dropped and they were drafted out at will. By November 1918 there were more than six Indian soldiers to each British.[6] There is little evidence to suggest that this constituted much of a security risk. After the war, nevertheless, the Indian high command spontaneously worked to restore the pre-war ratio. Despite the fact that soldiers might excuse it not only on the grounds of internal security but also of military efficiency, Indian political opinion was unlikely to be convinced. A military organization which implied that Indians were either untrustworthy or inefficient, or both, can hardly be expected to inspire confidence or loyalty among Indians. Yet this was precisely the aim of successive Indian governments. British administrators consistently asserted the specifically *Indian* nature of the Indian Army and British officers strongly rejected any notion that Indian troops were mere mercenaries. These admirable attitudes were to be put to the test in 1919–22.

Another legacy from 1857 was the pattern of recruitment. It was concentrated among the 'martial races' of north India which had largely remained loyal during the Mutiny. The most favoured recruiting area was the Punjab, where Sikhs, Jats and Rajputs joined up in increasing numbers during the years leading up to the war. Between 1914 and 1918 the Punjab supplied over forty per cent of the total combatants enlisted during the war.[7] Regional recruitment of this sort, initially encouraged for security reasons and later increased because northern Indians were allegedly more 'martial' than southern, was not entirely to the British advantage. The Punjab bordered on the intermittently unsettled Baluchistan and North West Frontier Province. It was also crucial to the army. So great was its strategic importance that civil administrators had to guard against straining the loyalty of their local Indian collaborators. This was particularly true after the war when Muslim unrest swept through the Punjab. Localized recruiting also provoked Indian accusa-

---

[6] 11 November 1918: British, 64,023; Indian, 388,599. War Office, *Statistical Abstract of Information Regarding the Army at Home and Abroad*, Public Record Office (PRO) W.O.161/82. Quoted by kind permission of Controller of H.M. Stationery Office.

[7] From a population approximately 15% of the Indian total. This figure was doubtless enhanced by the fact that 'Indian soldiers . . . were . . ., to face the matter quite frankly, persuaded with great vigour, in certain places, particularly in the Punjab, to join His Majesty's forces during the war'. Memo. by Montagu, 15 October 1920, PRO CAB. 24/112 C.P.1987.

tions that the British were pursuing a policy of 'divide and rule' in India. As with the ratio, it raised questions concerning the real nature of the Indian Army and, indeed, the Indian Empire itself. If the British aim was a united Raj with common political, bureaucratic and military institutions, why then was the army not 'all-India'? Did not the fact that the army was drawn largely from a limited constituency prove it to be little more than a mercenary occupation force; an instrument of British repression?

A third function of the Army in India—perceived more abundantly in London than in Delhi—was as an imperial military reserve. India provided not only an immense reservoir of manpower but also a convenient, and cheap, repository for a quarter of the British army. The 75,000 or so British troops in India were paid for by the Indian taxpayer. The Secretary for War in London had to provide for them neither in the Annual Army Act nor in his departmental estimates. Few ministers were so fortunate. As for the Indian troops, they were employed in numerous colonial expeditions during the nineteenth century. But from almost the very beginning there was friction between the Indian and British governments over the question of paying for these soldiers. Although it was generally accepted that expeditions on the Frontier or in Burma should be borne upon the Indian establishment, the position was much less clear in the case of operations in Africa or China. The despatch of Indian troops to reinforce the British garrison in Malta in 1878 raised the whole constitutional question of Indian Army service overseas and inflamed Liberal anti-imperialists in parliament. W. E. Forster, from the opposition benches, questioned a policy which relied 'not upon the patriotism and spirit of our own people, but upon the power of our money bags, to get Gurkhas and Sikhs and Mussulmen to fight for us'.[8] Even the popular parodists had a word to say on the matter:

We don't want to fight; but, by Jingo, if we do,
We won't go to the front ourselves, but we'll send the mild Hindoo.[9]

Imperial necessity, nevertheless, prevailed over tender Liberal consciences. In 1882, after Gladstone had returned to power for his second administration, Indian troops were employed to augment the British forces in Egypt. Finance, however, continued to cause difficulties between Britain and India until in 1895 a Royal Commission was appointed to examine the problem. In April 1900 the Commission proposed a solution which was finally accepted by both governments in

[8] Lucas, *The Empire at War*, I, p. 54.
[9] *Oxford Dictionary of Quotations* (2nd edn, London, 1953), p. 11, n. 9.

1902. Apart from such 'special cases' as might arise, it was proposed that India should bear primary financial responsibility for those geographical regions in which she had a 'direct and substantial interest'. Included among such regions were Egypt 'so far as the security of the Suez Canal is affected', Persia, the Persian Gulf and Afghanistan.[10] Thus the matter rested until after the Great War when the Indian government once more began to question the financial basis upon which Indian troops were employed outside India.

Despite the extensive use of the Indian Army overseas during the later nineteenth century, it was not until 1898 that Indian troops were first employed in colonial garrisons. The strains which the South African War, a white man's war in which Indian troops were not used, made upon the imperial military system confirmed these early arrangements and by 1914 the Indian Army was being regularly employed for garrisons in Egypt, the Indian Ocean, Singapore and China. There was, however, an older tradition of recruiting soldiers in India for service in special local forces in colonies and protectorates both in Asia and Africa. Sikh contingents saw service in the African protectorates, and the Malay States Guides regiment was largely recruited in India. From 1892 to 1903 special service battalions were raised in India for service in Hong Kong and a battery of artillery was specially recruited for employment in both Hong Kong and Singapore.[11] Although these special units for service in the empire comprised only a very small part of India's total contribution to imperial defence, after the Great War the Indian government was to put up a scheme for colonial garrison regiments, distinct from the Indian Army, to be raised in India. From the Indian point of view such a scheme made rendering charges to the imperial exchequer, for 'imperial' rather than Indian defence, more straightforward than British proposals simply to continue seconding battalions from the Indian Army proper.

There were, however, no financial quibbles when the empire went to war in August 1914. By the end of October 1914 two Indian infantry divisions were fighting in Flanders. At London's request six battalions were sent to East Africa and a rather larger force went to Egypt. In the early autumn a brigade was despatched to the head of the Persian Gulf in order to defend British interests in the area, especially the Anglo-Persian Oil Company's installations in south-west Persia. With the declaration of war against Turkey at the end of the same month, this

---

[10] 'Copy extract report of the Indian Expenditure Commission', India Office Records (IOR) L/F/7/783. Quoted by kind permission of Controller of H.M. Stationery Office.
[11] Lucas, *The Empire at War*, I, pp. 123–4, 255.

force was soon increased to a division.[12] By the end of the war there were
to be more than a quarter of a million Indian native troops in what
became known as the Mesopotamian Command, covering Mesopotamia itself, Persia and detachments in the Caucasus and Transcaspian
regions of south Russia.[13] This figure was greater than the total number
of Indian ranks serving in August 1914.[14] During the war nearly
1,200,000 Indians were recruited for service in the army.[15] In October
1918 the Military Secretary of the India Office estimated that in the year
ending 1 June 1919 'the normal pre-war recruiting figure for the Indian
Army of about 15,000 men will have been increased to 500,000'.[16] As
well as providing manpower the Indian government agreed early in the
war to continue to bear 'the ordinary charges of the troops sent out of
India which she would have had to pay had they remained in India',
and subsequently agreed also to make a substantial contribution towards the 'ordinary' charges for the extra troops raised for the war.[17] In
1917, moreover, India made an outright gift of £100 million towards the
cost of the war—'nearly twice India's whole net revenue before the
war'.[18]

India's greatest part in the war was played in the Middle East. In
October 1918 over half the troops in Mesopotamia were Indian and
rather more than a third in Palestine.[19] Throughout the war, moreover,
India was exclusively responsible for providing all supplies and stores
required by the troops, both British and Indian, in Mesopotamia.[20] But
the Mesopotamian campaign also revealed serious administrative weaknesses in the Indian military machine. Kitchener's reform of the Indian
Army a decade or so before the outbreak of war while enormously
improving the mobility of the army had sacrificed administrative efficiency to this end,[21] and nowhere was this to be more apparent than in

[12] Lucas, *The Empire at War*, V, p. 180.
[13] 261,067 soldiers (combatants only). 'Strengths by arms of the expeditionary
forces', 16 December 1918. Milner MS. (Bodleian Library, Oxford) dep. 145.
[14] Regular troops, 159,134; Reservists, 34,767; Non-combatants (Labour Corps etc.)
45,660; Total, 239,561. 21 November 1919, 'Memo. on the total contribution in men
made and casualties suffered by India during the war'. PRO CAB. 24/70 G.T.6341.
[15] Combatants, 757,747; Non-combatants, 404,042. *Ibid.*
[16] 2 October 1918, 'Note on India and the war' by Gen. Sir H. V. Cox. Montagu
MSS. AS/I/2/65 (Trinity College, Cambridge).
[17] *c.* October 1918, 'Note on finance'. Montagu MSS. AS/I/2/56.
[18] *Ibid.*
[19] *c.* October 1918, 'Note on military aspects'. Montagu MSS. AS/I/2/57.
[20] Govt of India, *India's Contribution to the Great War*, p. 107.
[21] Philip Mason, *A Matter of Honour: An Account of the Indian Army, its Officers and Men*
(Harmondsworth, 1976), p. 399.

Mesopotamia which for the first two and a half years of the war was an exclusively Indian theatre of operations. From the beginning there were administrative difficulties and it was an almost total breakdown in support services which was in the most part responsible for the surrender in April 1917 of General Townshend's division at Kut. Such was the Indian failure that for the rest of the war the control of military operations in Mesopotamia was transferred to the War Office in London,[22] and so it was to remain following the Armistice. Thus, while India continued to supply much of the manpower and all of the matériel for Mesopotamia, the direction of military policy lay in London.

   In the spring of 1919 the War Office took advantage of this agreeable state of affairs to canvass the idea that they should take over complete control of the entire Indian Army and incorporate it into a single imperial force. Edwin Montagu considered the scheme so 'idiotic' that he hardly thought it worth refuting.[23] But the disasters of Mesopotamia had left their mark and Lloyd George appointed a committee, chaired by the veteran strategist Lord Esher, with a wide-ranging brief to examine the *post bellum* Indian Army. It reported in the summer of 1920 that 'the military resources of India should be developed in a manner suited to imperial necessities'. That being so, along with a number of much-needed internal administrative reforms, Esher recommended that the running of the Indian Army should be placed directly under the authority of the Chief of the Imperial General Staff (CIGS) in London.[24] This dovetailed neatly in with the War Office opinion that 'the only sound and economical method of imperial defence is to regard the forces of any portion of the Empire as being available for use in any other'.[25] But the idea was an anathema to Delhi. However successful War Office control had been in war-time Mesopotamia, by 1920 the concept was already archaic. It had been overtaken by events in India. No Indian government, let alone one struggling to introduce constitutional reforms, could accept such an outright subordination of Indian to imperial interests. In any case, the proposal foundered on the rock of finance. Chelmsford had pin-pointed the problem early in 1919 when he insisted that 'so long as India pays,—and I do not suppose the War Office are going to propose to the English Treasury to take over the

[22] *Ibid.*, pp. 432–3; Lucas, *The Empire at War*, V, pp. 290–6.
[23] 28 May 1919, Montagu to Chelmsford, Montagu MSS. IOR D.523, vol. 3, pp. 120–1.
[24] 22 June 1920, 'Report of the Army in India committee, 1919–20', PRO CAB. 24/112 C.P. 1980.
[25] 2 June 1920, War Office to India Office, IOR L/MIL/7/19323.

charges of the Indian Army,—India must control its own Army'.[26] It was an understandable, if un-imperial, attitude.

At the same time as the War Office were proposing to assume overall charge of the Indian Army, they also unquestioningly assumed that India would continue to provide most of the men and material for the post-war imperial acquisitions in the Middle East. The Indian government, however, did not share London's happy confidence and soon began moving to reduce their commitments in the region. Early in December 1918 the Army Department in Delhi informed the India Office that 'in view of the extreme difficulty of our financial position and our own urgent needs', the 'drain both in money and material on the resources of India cannot any longer be met without the gravest embarrassment'.[27] Throughout 1919 the Indian attitude hardened. In September Austen Chamberlain complained to Lord Curzon that at a recent meeting concerning military expenditure in Mesopotamia, the India Office's contribution 'was limited to a warm support of whatever the military desired, coupled with the condition that no part of the expense was to fall on Indian funds!'[28] Montagu for his part saw things rather differently and told Chelmsford in October:

I cannot rid myself of the obsession that a good many people here are trying to establish a routine of running up a heavy bill of costs over whatever item of Imperial policy happens to suit them at the moment, and sending in the account to India as an afterthought.[29]

From India the Viceroy moved to the offensive. 'You have of course by this time realised', he wrote to Montagu in December 1919,

that one of our great difficulties is the keeping of some one hundred and eighty thousand Indian troops in Mesopotamia, the Black Sea, Palestine, France, East Persian Cordon, Bushire and elsewhere. It will be extremely difficult for our Army authorities to reorganise our Army in India so long as such a large proportion of the Indian Army is maintained outside India. I must point out also that India in this way is being exploited by the War Office because they find that they can maintain Indian troops abroad without those extremely objectionable questions in Parliament which would be asked if they were British and not Indian forces.[30]

[26] 12 February 1919, Chelmsford to Montagu, Montagu MSS. IOR D.523, vol. 8, p. 26.
[27] 2 December 1918, Viceroy to Secretary of State for India (S. of S.), Chelmsford MSS. IOR E.264, vol. 9, pp. 467–8.
[28] 17 September 1919, Chamberlain to Curzon, Curzon MSS. IOR F.112/209.
[29] 17 October 1919, Montagu to Chelmsford, Montagu MSS. IOR D.523, vol. 3, p. 218.
[30] 31 December 1919, Chelmsford to Montagu, *ibid.*, vol. 9, pp. 413–14.

This was the rub, for the Montagu-Chelmsford reforms then being introduced aimed to introduce an element of popular sovereignty into India. The Government of India Act (1919) provided for the establishment of an Indian legislative assembly which would certainly give Indian politicians an ample opportunity to ask 'extremely objectionable questions'.

Delhi's unwillingness to meet what London saw as justifiable military obligations in the Middle East was also confirmed by unrest, both internal and on the frontiers. Until early 1922 domestic security posed serious problems. The largely bi-communal Congress agitation, the Muslim Khilafat movement and the Moplah rising in August 1921 all served to restrict the imperial manoeuvrability of the Indian Army. General Dyer's Cromwellian peacekeeping methods at Amritsar in the Punjab, and their subsequent approval by many Britons in India and at home, did much to exacerbate Anglo-Indian relations. In its turn this made the Indian government yet more nervous of inflaming domestic political opinion by committing Indian revenues to expensive imperial military co-operation. On the Indian periphery the problems were more specifically military. The Kuki-Chin rebellion in Burma, which had broken out in 1917, was not finally quelled until the spring of 1919,[31] while across the sub-continent the Frontier was far from quiet. The 'Third Afghan War' from May to August 1919 imposed substantial strains on an Indian Army whose resources had been 'depleted by a long war' and came at a time when internal disturbances had necessitated 'the temporary redistribution of troops'.[32] In October 1919 Delhi was reluctantly forced to consider operations against hostile Waziri tribesmen. Despite their wish to keep the action as limited as possible, they found it necessary to undertake 'extended operations' and the area was not pacified until the beginning of September 1920.[33]

It was against this background of internal and peripheral disorder that London seemed incessantly to call for Indian troops to serve in imperial garrisons. These demands reached a peak in the summer of 1920 when the Mesopotamian rebellion broke out. Although there were already some 50,000 Indian troops in Mesopotamia, following the outbreak of violence in August the War Office arranged for an addi-

---

[31] June 1919, 'Despatch on the operations against the Kuki tribes of Assam and Burma', PRO W.O.106/58.
[32] 20 August 1919, Viceroy to S. of S., Chelmsford MSS. IOR E.264, vol. 11, pp. 188-9.
[33] 6 October 1919 and 23 March 1920, ibid., pp. 321-2 and vol. 12, pp. 274-5; 4 September 1920, ibid., vol. 13, pp. 214-15.

tional nineteen battalions to be sent as reinforcements from India.[34] In view of the emergency these troops were not begrudged by Delhi. London, indeed, had been assured on 7 July that 'in the event of a Mesopotamian crisis arising, and the despatch of reinforcements becoming absolutely necessary, you may rely on us to do our utmost to render such military assistance as we are able from the resources at our disposal'.[35] The demands made by the imperial government in respect of the Mesopotamian crisis, however, were of such magnitude that they seem, for the first time, sharply to have brought home to the Indian government the full extent of the imperial military burden which London expected them to share. From this point on the Indian government began to back-pedal strongly on the supply of overseas garrisons from the Indian Army and to argue forcefully that their military and financial responsibilities extended little further than the frontiers of India itself.

On 3 September 1920, Montagu circulated to the cabinet an important telegram from the Viceroy:

> Recent demands received by us for reinforcements for Mesopotamia on a large scale [it read] have forced us to consider the whole question regarding supply of overseas garrisons from Indian Army.
> It would appear that His Majesty's Government is counting on India to provide a quota of the permanent garrisons of the mandatory territories in addition to certain colonial garrisons, including Aden, the Gulf ports and consular escorts in East Persia. We have received no direct information that His Majesty's Government desires us to undertake this liability: but have received an estimate which shows that, on present figures, this force will include, among other details, 4 cavalry regiments, 1 cavalry troop, 10 Sappers and Miners Companies, $39\frac{1}{2}$ Infantry and Pioneer battalions, 1 signal troop and 4 signal companies. It is possible that this estimate is not final. We invite attention to the fact that we have not been consulted as to probable political effects in India of accepting an engagement of this magnitude. It appears advisable to us, however, to warn you at once of our views on this aspect of the question.

Chelmsford went on to describe that public opinion in India generally opposed the extensive use of Indian troops overseas and regarded India as being exploited, especially since no similar request for troops had so far been made on the dominions.[36] The Indian government, moreover, was at pains 'definitely to emphasise' that they 'could not accept an obligation to supply permanent overseas garrisons to mandatory territories' and they did not consider that 'the Indian Army should be

---

[34] Sir Aylmer Haldane, *The Insurrection in Mesopotamia, 1920* (Edinburgh and London, 1922), p. 64; 26 August 1920, 'Military policy in Mesopotamia', copy of telegram from S. of S. for War to GOCinC Mesopotamia, PRO CAB. 23/111 C.P. 1814.

[35] 7 July 1920, Viceroy to S. of S., Chelmsford MSS. IOR E.264 vol. 13, p. 24.

[36] The dominions were to be approached on 18 September 1920.

required to provide large overseas forces'.[37] Later the same month Montagu circulated a paper containing a selection of articles culled from Indian journals, each one quite opposed to the extensive use of the Indian Army overseas. 'I fear that the position is very bad', he noted, 'because they can be taken to be the first mutterings of a storm'.[38] As had been the case before the war, the Indian government displayed a marked reluctance to slip easily in with London's plans for the imperial disposition of the Indian Army. This prudence was particularly under-standable in the immediate post-war period, preoccupied as Delhi was with introducing domestic political reforms.

The telegram of 3 September was a straightforward reversion to India's pre-war position, arguing as it did that the Indian Army had no obligation to supply troops for permanent and extensive overseas garri-sons. The principle, moreover, that India should not pay for such garrisons had, in Indian eyes, long been established. In January 1919, Montagu told Chelmsford: 'I have pointed out by law and practice Indian revenues are not called upon to maintain an army in excess of Indian requirements on a reasonable estimate of same, and as at present advised I am strongly opposed to any alteration of this principle'.[39] The principle was applied frequently. In April 1920, Chelmsford noted that 'in order to meet the overseas requirements of His Majesty's Govern-ment', especially in the Army of the Black Sea, extra units might need to be maintained in India. 'We assume', he added, 'in that case the cost of additional units . . . will be charged to His Majesty's Government'.[40] In December 1920 the Indian government announced that it would cease contributing towards the cost of the South Persian Rifles (an irregular force with British officers) at the end of the year since 'we have consis-tently protested against payments being made from Indian revenues on account of South Persian Rifles, and have maintained that this expendi-ture cannot in fact legally be met from Indian revenues'.[41] When the question arose of sharing the costs of the Malleson Mission in east Persia in February 1921, the Viceroy objected to India taking any share in the expenditure on the grounds that the Mission 'had a definite military objective of a purely Imperial character'.[42]

The problem of Indian Army service 'ex-India' was accentuated by

[37] 3 September 1920, 'Supply of overseas garrisons from the Indian Army'. CAB. 24/111 C.P.1844.
[38] 16 September 1920, ibid., C.P.1871.
[39] 29 January 1919, S. of S. to Viceroy. Chelmsford MSS. E.264, vol. 10, p. 39.
[40] 7 April 1920, Viceroy to S. of S., ibid., vol. 12, p. 311.
[41] 17 December 1920, Viceroy to S. of S., ibid., vol. 13, p. 511.
[42] 19 February 1921, Viceroy to S. of S., ibid., vol. 14, p. 168.

internal political pressures to such an extent that by 1921, 'owing to political changes in India', Delhi declared that the 'standing arbitration agreement' of 1902 was no longer in force. 'The determining factor', they averred, 'in any . . . dispute under present conditions must be the state of native opinion and feeling'.[43] In February 1921 the Montford reforms were inaugurated, providing Indians with a new opportunity to influence decisions in Delhi. In addition to creating a legislative assembly, three-quarters of which were elected, the reforms established a convention that three of the eight-member Viceroy's Council should be Indians, who were thus admitted to the highest echelon of the administration.[44] But although a measure of representation had been introduced into the central government, the Viceroy and his council remained responsible to the British cabinet and constitutionally London retained the final say in major matters of policy. Despite this the CIGS, Sir Henry Wilson, was not reassured by the changes. Montagu and Chelmsford, he felt, had 'lost control' and they 'now *dare* not impose the extra taxation necessary' to maintain the size of the British garrison in India. 'The . . . Council will, before long', he continued, 'refuse to allow Indian Native troops to serve outside India! And then!'[45] He was not altogether wrong. Although military expenditure was excluded from legislative vote under the 1919 Act, the levying of taxation was not. The legislature could therefore exercise an indirect influence on military affairs. In addition to reforms at the centre, the 1919 Act devolved considerable powers—including budgetary ones—to new provincial assemblies. But Delhi had to fund these additional power-centres, and fund them generously if Indian politicians were to be kept sweet. This meant retrenchment in central expenditure. To the civil administrators of the Raj, military spending—'rather more than 32% of the whole revenue of the Country'[46]—was an obvious area for economy. Either the size of the army had to be cut or an imperial subsidy gained for ex-India commitments. Neither option appealed to London. India's strategic value to the empire depended to a very great extent on its being a military milch cow. The Indian Army was only a genuine imperial asset so long as it was cheap. This, then, was the dilemma facing Delhi. Political control in India could only, it seemed, be bought at the cost of

[43] February 1921, Report of committee on Indian charges for forces in east Persia, PRO W.O. 32/5808.
[44] Percival Spear, *A History of India*, vol. II (Harmondsworth, 1970), pp. 185–8.
[45] 11 January 1921, Diary of Sir Henry Wilson, Wilson MSS. Quoted by kind permission of the Trustees of the Imperial War Museum.
[46] 9 January 1921, Lord Rawlinson (CinC India) to Sir Henry Wilson, Wilson MSS. File 13C.

the imperial fire brigade. But this was a price which London was reluctant to pay.

When Lord Rawlinson became Commander-in-Chief in India during the late autumn of 1920, he was immediately presented with this dilemma. 'As we both foresaw before I left', he wrote to his old friend Sir Henry Wilson, 'there is bound to be a pretty severe fight over finance. Certain of my honourable colleagues on the Viceroy's council are endeavouring to bring pressure on me . . . to reduce the strength of the army and thus avoid the necessity of imposing further taxation'.[47] A few days later he told Wilson that he was determined not to take

the responsibility for making sweeping reductions in the fighting forces in India . . . All the members of the Viceroy's council that I have seen so far are terrified at the idea of imposing further taxation. They say that the matter will have to be brought before the new Legislative Assembly when it meets and that to start with a demand for raising further monies for the army would be a fatal political step, for it will put in opposition not only the present extremists in this country but also a large proportion of the moderates.[48]

During the winter of 1920–21 the Indian government scoured the military budget for possible savings. In January 1921 Rawlinson reluctantly suggested a reduction in the British establishment of 6,000 troops to 59,000 in all. But this would not be possible before 1922. As it was, the British contingent was under strength and required an actual increase of 7,000 men even to reach the proposed reduced total.[49] His proposal provoked an immediate response from London demonstrating clearly that imperial considerations still took priority over Indian. 'Recruitment and organisation of British Army', wired Montagu, 'takes account of fact that India has for many years maintained certain minimum strength of British troops'. The question of reducing the British garrison raised a vast number of difficult and complex problems and would take years to sort out.[50]

So the government went to the assembly with little to offer other than an assurance that they had been pressing London for the early return of Indian troops serving overseas. But their anxieties were not realized. When the assembly came to debate military affairs during its inaugural session in March 1921, although there was some general criticism of the high level of military spending, by and large their opinion coincided

[47] 25 November 1920, Wilson MSS., *ibid.* Rawlinson had landed at Bombay on 21 November.

[48] 3 December 1920, Rawlinson to Wilson, Wilson MSS., *ibid.*

[49] 18 January 1920, S. of S. to Viceroy, Chelmsford MSS., E.264, vol. 14, p. 50.

[50] 22 January 1920, Viceroy to S. of S., *ibid.*, p. 33.

with that of the administration. The underlying assumption of the Esher
report that a unified imperial command be established was repudiated
and the assembly affirmed that 'the purpose of the Army in India must
be held to be the defence of India against external aggression and the
maintenance of internal peace and tranquility'.[51] The Viceroy was
agreeably surprised by the moderate tone of the debate and reported to
London (in contrast to his views of the previous September) that 'there is
strong feeling in country in favour of employment of Indian troops on
garrison duty over-sea with Government of India's permission', but
subject always to the important condition 'that no additional expense is
caused thereby to Indian revenues'.[52] Rawlinson thought the assembly's attitude one of 'pleasing moderation' and the budget, including
some extra taxation to fund army spending, passed through 'without
much serious difficulty.'[53]

One of the factors regarding internal security which the British rulers
of India never considered was that whatever 'war games' the general
staffs in Delhi or London might play, to plan for a major rebellion in
India was quite unrealistic. This is not at all to suggest that such an
occurrence was either unlikely or unanticipated—Rawlinson regarded
it as 'a practical certainty' that there would be a war 'either within or
without our frontiers during my term of office'[54]—but simply to note
that the British had not the power to defeat a serious all-India rising.
Two-hundred-and-thirty thousand troops and one-hundred-and-
ninety thousand police—more than three-quarters of which were Indians themselves—would not go far in a country of 319 million people.
Lord Salisbury had been of the opinion that British rule in India rested
not on force but on consent[55] and this was just as true in 1921 as it had
been in 1874. When considering the possibility of internal unrest
Montagu warned the cabinet in October 1920 that

if any of my colleagues think of the isolation of Europeans in India, of the
smallness of the British force in India, and realise that a campaign comparable
to the Sinn Feinn campaign in Ireland would be almost impossible to deal with
except by punishment and revenge, certainly not by prevention, they will
understand the danger of the situation which has been caused [in the Punjab]

---

[51] 30 March 1921, Viceroy to S. of S., *ibid.*, pp. 293–4; *Legislative Assembly debates*, vol.
I, no. 15, enclosed in IOR L/MIL/7/10822.
[52] 6 May 1921, Viceroy (Army dept.) to S. of S., pt II, IOR L/MIL/3/2513, p. 958.
[53] 30 March 1921, Rawlinson to Lord Derby, Derby MSS. IOR D.605/5.
[54] 21 September 1920, Rawlinson to Gen. Sir Charles Monro (CinC India 1916–20),
Rawlinson MSS. 5201/33/22. Quoted by kind permission of the National Army
Museum.
[55] S. Gopal, *British policy in India 1858–1905* (London, 1965) p. 65.

by the assertion of a force we do not in reality possess in preference to the doctrine of goodwill.[56]

It is to his credit that Lord Reading, who became Viceroy in April 1921, recognized the futility of unambiguous repression and that throughout his first year in office, the 'peak year' of Hindu–Muslim agitational unity,[57] he displayed such admirable restraint towards the nationalists, flying frequently in the face of advice from London, Army headquarters and the majority of the provincial governors.[58] The mistakes of the Punjab in 1919 were not repeated, Delhi courted the moderate Indian politicians who were prepared to work the new constitution and the non-cooperation campaign was left to run out of steam on its own, unprovoked by any official over-reaction. In February 1922, when the national protest threatened to descend into violence itself, Gandhi called off the campaign and mass political action in India ceased for half a decade.[59]

Despite the Legislative Assembly's compliant attitude, the Viceroy still believed that Indian military policy needed to be re-assessed in view of the changed political circumstances. In May 1921 he appointed a committee under Rawlinson to examine 'Indian military requirements'.[60] The four Indian members of the committee demanded a substantial reduction in the number of British battalions earmarked for 'internal security'. Rawlinson had reluctantly to concede some reductions and thereby raise the proportion of Indian to British troops in India:

I was unable to resist the pressure when it came to weighing the fact that we had 28 Brit. Battns and only 21 Indian in Internal security. [He wrote in his journal.] It was impossible to defend these proportions—I have agreed to abolish the Ratio. There is no need for it nor can you defend such a basis of arrangements in present Indian conditions, though after the Mutiny there may have been something in it—Now there certainly is not for we have decided to trust the Indians to lead them to self governt. and we cannot therefore justify an Army of occupation.[61]

The final recommendation of the committee was for a reduction of three British cavalry regiments and five battalions of infantry, more than

---

[56] 15 October 1920, 'The state of India'. CAB 24/112 C.P.1987.
[57] R. J. Moore, *The Crisis of Indian Unity 1917–40* (Oxford, 1974), p. 21.
[58] D. A. Low, 'Government of India and the First Non-co-operation Movement 1920–22', in R. Kumar (ed.), *Essays in Gandhian politics* (Oxford, 1971), pp. 305–16.
[59] *Ibid.*, pp. 315–18.
[60] 10 May 1921, Rawlinson to 'Douglas' (Haig?), Rawlinson MSS. 5201/33/22.
[61] 10 July 1921, 'Indian journal', *ibid.*, 5201/33/23.

KEITH JEFFERY

Rawlinson would ideally have wished,[62] but subject to the proviso that any 'deterioration in the internal or external situation' might necessitate a modification of this proposal. The committee also favoured the 'adoption and publication . . . of a definite policy of Indianisation of Indian Army'.[63]

The Rawlinson committee's proposals for troop reductions were modest enough, but within a fortnight of their first being sent to London, disturbance among the Muslims of the Madras Presidency—the 'Moplah rebellion'—obliged Delhi to postpone consideration of the committee's report.[64] Although mopping-up operations continued until the second half of 1922, the back of the rebellion was broken by November 1921[65] and the military authorities could once more concentrate their attention on the problem of economy. This gave Rawlinson no pleasure because demands for retrenchment had escalated since the summer and it seemed likely in November that the Legislative Assembly would be satisfied with nothing less than a reduction of twenty or twenty-five British battalions. 'We cannot possibly accept any decision of this kind', wrote Rawlinson to Wilson, 'for the Viceroy and I fully realize that it would endanger the safety of the country'.[66] But some concession was necessary if only as a gesture towards Indian opinion in order to ease the passage of the budget in the spring. In February 1922, therefore, Delhi told London that they hoped not only to implement the reductions in British troops recommended by the Rawlinson committee but also to buy off the Indian politicians through adopting its Indianization scheme.

We have, [they telegraphed] in any event, a very difficult situation to meet. With political situation you are familiar. On top of this we are confronted with necessity of imposing, for the second year in succession, very heavy additional taxation. That taxation will inevitably be challenged as being due to heavy expenditure connected with maintenance of our Army. It is our considered opinion that, in order to avoid a complete breakdown, it is essential that we should be allowed to make the two announcements [of reductions and Indianization] . . . Unless we receive your permission to do so, consequence must be, we consider, grave, involving serious risks of complete breakdown of the Reform Scheme, and rendering administration of this country most difficult.[67]

[62] 12 July 1921, Rawlinson to Wilson, Wilson MSS. File 13E.
[63] 21 July 1921, Viceroy (Army dept.) to S. of S., pts 1 and 2. IOR L/MIL/3/2513 p. 1512.
[64] 4 August 1921, Viceroy (Army dept.) to S. of S. IOR L/MIL/3/2513 p. 1631.
[65] Sir Percival Griffiths, *To Guard my People: The History of the Indian Police* (London & Bombay, 1971), pp. 288–92; A. C. B. Mackinnon, 'The Moplah rebellion 1921–22', in *Army Quarterly*, viii (1924), pp. 260–77.
[66] 23 November 1921, Rawlinson to Wilson, Wilson MSS. File 13F.
[67] 6 February 1922, Viceroy (Army dept.) to S. of S., IOR L/MIL/3/2514 no. 1121.

There was little sympathy for the Indian position in London. A cabinet committee met to discuss the Viceroy's requests on 10 February and came out very strongly against any reduction in the British garrison but was less unanimous on the question of Indianization. Lloyd George declared that he thought all the Englishmen in India had got 'cold feet and that they must be cured of their feeling of discouragement'.[68] Montagu had little to offer when he sent the cabinet's reply to Delhi. No 'further reduction' of the British troops in India could be sanctioned. The general feeling in London was that taking into consideration 'the frontier of India, its size, the importance of its communications and the political conditions', the Indian government had 'no troops to spare'. The Rawlinson committee's Indianization proposal could not be accepted and, finally, the cabinet absolutely forbade the publication of any part of the committee's report for 'it could not fail to reveal differences of opinion between your Government and His Majesty's Government which at all costs must be avoided'.[69] On the same day, Montagu sent Reading a second telegram on 'the fundamental principles of Indian Government':

Reports are constantly reaching England of a widely held belief, not only among Indians but among Englishmen, that we regard our mission in India as drawing to a close that we are preparing for a retreat. If such an idea exists, it is a complete fallacy, and its continued existence can only in itself lead to a decline in morale among the services and to intensified challenges to our authority . . . The security of the country from dangers without and within upon which depends the capacity of its Government to fulfil its primary duties can only be ultimately guaranteed by the Army in India. With regard to it we cannot take any steps which would compromise our position. If therefore we find it impossible to reduce the size of the Army or to accept a programme of Indianisation which we are compelled to believe would be prejudicial to its efficiency, it is because we believe that an acceptance of such proposals would not only lend colour to the dangerous belief in a policy of retreat, but must directly hamper us in the exercise of the functions with which we are entrusted.[70]

The Cabinet, of course, were in a good position to demand a thoroughgoing application of 'empire' in India since they could safely leave its primary application to their agents in Delhi and perhaps not necessarily be implicated in the possible failure of such a policy. Besides, to take an imperial 'hard line' with Delhi could scarcely do any harm to Lloyd George's flagging reputation on the Unionist backbenches.

[68] 10 February 1922, diary of H. A. L. Fisher, Fisher MSS. (Bodleian Library, Oxford), Box 8A.
[69] 14 February 1922, S. of S. to Viceroy, IOR L/MIL/3/2534 M.1348/1922 no. 1.
[70] *Ibid.*, no. 2.

Lord Rawlinson, although he had reluctantly come to the conclusion
that Indianization must eventually happen 'whether we like it or not',[71]
was not displeased with London's refusal to allow any reduction in the
British garrison. In July 1922 he told the Viceroy that there was 'the
strongest argument of all for not reducing the British garrisons in India,
and nothing will induce me to agree to it even with bankruptcy staring
us in the face. But', he added, 'we must both reduce expenditure and
increase taxation if there is to be any hope of balancing our next
budget'.[72] The army vote, moreover, still offered the richest field for
economy. 'We cannot get away from it', wrote Reading to Peel,
Montagu's successor at the India Office, 'that no substantial reduction
can be made in expenditure unless military expenditure is tackled'.[73]
But to cut military expenditure meant reducing the number of troops—
preferably British from Delhi's point of view—and that was generally
unacceptable in London, not only for internal security reasons. When
Worthington-Evans was considering the Rawlinson committee recommendations in the summer of 1921 he noted that the reduction of British
units in India would throw those units

on to the Imperial Budget, or, as the only alternative, force us to disband them
and so to weaken the armed strength of the Empire as a whole without any relief
to the British taxpayer . . . It is in my opinion a question for special consideration whether the Indian taxpayer is to be endowed with this priority of
right to the savings to be made by weakening the Empire as a whole.[74]

Clearly the Secretary for War still regarded the Army in India as a
subordinate imperial military organization, free to be ordered about the
world at will by London—as had been the case during the war. But
Worthington-Evans was wrong. It was as nasty a case of *hubris* as one
might encounter for him to believe that the British taxpayer, or even the
British cabinet, was better qualified than the Indian to direct Indian
military expenditure. He was foolish also to assume in 1921 that Britain
still had the power (if indeed she had ever been so graced) fully to control
her Indian empire, and arrogance without power is just the sort of thing
which gives *hubris* a bad name.

[71] 21 July 1921, Rawlinson to Wilson, Wilson MSS. File 13E. A scheme of limited
Indianization was introduced in March 1923. See V. Longer, *Red Coats to Olive Green*
(New Delhi, 1974), p. 194; Mason, *A Matter of Honour*, pp. 453–66.
[72] 28 July 1922, 'Indian journal', Rawlinson MSS. 5201/33/22.
[73] 3 August 1922, Reading to Peel, Reading MSS. IOR E.238, vol. 5, p. 112.
[74] August 1921, 'Future military expenditure'. PRO CAB. 27/164 G.R.C.(D.D.)8.

Modern Asian Studies, **15**, 3 (1981), pp. 387–414.

Britain and India between the Wars

JOHN GALLAGHER and ANIL SEAL

University of Cambridge

I

In the nineteenth century, the British succeeded in deriving growing benefits from their Indian territories. With dominion firmly established, and the colonial connection beginning to take its modern shape, India came to fit less awkwardly with British economic interests. India now became Britain's best customer for her most important industry, a useful supplier of raw materials, a safe field for capital investment, a crucial element in her balance of payments and key to the multilateral system of settlements which sustained the continued expansion of her world trade.[1] The pattern of trade and investment, which brought such signal benefits to Britain, depended upon dominion over India. Dominion had given Britain the levers of power to open up Indian markets to her trade, knock down the internal barriers to the free flow of her goods, and prevent the erection of external tariffs to protect the Indian product. Dominion enabled Britain to build, at Indian cost, a system of transport by rail and road which linked the ports, themselves the creation of British rule, to their hinterlands, and to tilt the advantage in favour of her own nationals who dominated India's foreign trade; it helped to give British shipping, banking and insurance a virtual monopoly over the invisibles of Indian trade and it imposed upon India a currency and banking system which protected the ratio of sterling to the rupee. But these balance-sheets of imperialism do not reveal the full importance of

This article was planned as a joint venture before Jack Gallagher's final illness; unfortunately he could not turn to it. But it draws largely on unpublished papers he gave to seminars at Cambridge in 1973, which we hope to publish in due course. Some of the themes of this piece have been admirably treated by B. R. Tomlinson in two articles, 'India and the British Empire 1880–1935' and 'India and the British Empire 1935–1947', *Indian Economic and Social History Review*, XII, 4 (October–December 1975) and XIII, 3 (July–September 1976), and in a book, *The Political Economy of the Raj, 1914–1947* (1979).

[1] See A. Redford, *Manchester Merchants and Foreign Trade* (Manchester, 1956), II; A. H. Imlah, *Economic Elements in the Pax Britannica* (Cambridge, Massachusetts, 1958); A. K. Cairncross, *Home and Foreign Investment, 1870–1913* (Cambridge, 1953); and S. B. Saul, *Studies in British Overseas Trade, 1870–1914* (Liverpool, 1960), esp. Ch. 8.

0026-749X/81/0406-0904$02.00 © 1981 Cambridge University Press.

the Raj to the British world system. Just as India's growing foreign trade helped to push British influence into east and west Asia alike, so her growing military power underwrote that influence, whether formal or informal, in those regions. An oriental barracks, where half of Britain's world force was billeted free of charge, India was the battering ram of British power throughout the eastern arc of its expansion. Before the First World War, India seemed triumphantly to have justified the efforts of generations of empire-builders.

Yet this convenient symbiosis of profit and power was vulnerable to change. Here was a captive market lulling Britain's captains of industry into a false confidence that British was best when this was no longer necessarily the case; an expanding trade and a system of settlements which depended critically on a particular pattern of Indian imports and exports, which was already beginning to shift against Britain's advantage;[2] and there were awkward signs that India was becoming the soft underbelly of imperial defence. But for most of the nineteenth century the assets of Indian empire had clearly outweighed the liabilities. International constraints upon British expansion in the east had been few; local resistance had not been serious.[3] Of course, the protection of the routes to India and the defence of its frontiers had meant that Britain could not ignore the European balance or avoid a more or less continuous friction with Russia. But if the Tsar and Queen Victoria were the only potentates as yet seriously committed to expansion in Asia, there was still room for them both.[4] In the last two decades of the century, however, a wider rivalry between the powers hinted at the price that Britain might have to pay for the security of India in a world where she was being forced upon the defensive.[5] The Russian threat now came

[2] For example, British exports to India of cotton yarn reached their peak in 1888; thereafter Indian, and later Japanese yarn won an increasing share of the market. By now British dominance of the Indian market for the cheaper and plainer cottons had begun to be challenged by Indian mill production, foreshadowing the sharp decline of cotton exports after the First World War.

[3] Just as the collapse of the Mughal empire had given the British their opportunity in India in the eighteenth century, so in the nineteenth the Turkish polity had been thrown back upon extreme decentralization in the vilayats; the Quajar dynasty in Persia had begun to break down; the crack-up of Rangoon and Mandalay, of Spain in Manila, and Johore in Malaya, and the distraught condition of the Ching Government in Peking, all had given British expansion in the east a remarkably free run.

[4] The Great Game opened in the eighteen-forties; it grew sharper in the eighteen-sixties; from the seventies, there was friction over Sinkiang. But as yet these Russian pressures were little more than inhibitions; only later in the century was there to be standing room only.

[5] The case for Indian security brought about the large, perhaps preposterously large, insurance of founding an empire in east Africa; see R. E. Robinson and J. A. Gallagher, *Africa and the Victorians* (1961).

to dominate Britain's strategic preoccupations. If India had to fight off a Russian invasion, she was liable to be a source of weakness to Britain.[6] For the time being diplomacy rescued the British world system from international pressures which were mounting against it, and covered bets which power itself could not win,[7] but long before the First World War, the question had been raised whether defending India was worth a shilling on the income-tax or the lives of fifty-thousand street-bred Englishmen.

The British were anxious to pull resources out of India, not to put them into it. So a cardinal rule was that India was not to be a burden on the British tax-payer; she had to be self-supporting, secure and at peace. After the Mutiny, the British never again questioned that the main task of the army in India was to serve as an internal garrison force. Yet this army, which swallowed up such a large part of Indian revenues, could not by itself make British rule secure. Just as every foreign rule in India before it, the Raj depended upon the collaboration, active or tacit, of powerful local interests which had to give a share of the resources which government might claim. For much of the business of extracting tribute and keeping the peace, the British always relied upon the acquiescence of influential Indians prepared to work with the régime. By accepting these men as their local collaborators, the British were in fact striking a political bargain. Its terms were that they could expect their cut of the revenue, provided that they did not enquire too officiously who paid it; and they could take the façade of public order for granted, provided they themselves did not play too obtrusive a part in enforcing it. Local bargains of this sort were of great advantage to the British; they reduced Indian politics to the level of local haggles between the Raj and small

[6] Defending India against Russia required more troops than Britain possessed. By March 1904 Calcutta gloomily estimated that a war with Russia would call for a 100,000 troops from Britain (Cabinet Papers [henceforth CAB] 2/1, Minutes of the Committee of Imperial Defence [CID], 2 March 1904); only 30,000 could be found right away (*ibid.*, 24 March 1904), although 100,000 might be rustled up within a year of the outbreak of war; by November 1904, the Committee noted 'the progressive demands for reinforcements made by the Indian Government . . . have now reached the total of 158,000. . . . The Adjutant-General stated that if we comply with the demands to the extent even of 100,000 men, there will be no troops left for any imperial purpose' (*ibid.*, 16 November 1904); as late as 1907 the Committee saw that 'the needs of India are the key to [imperial defence] . . . War, on our Indian land frontier, they would make the largest demands upon our military resources' (CAB 2/2, CID Minutes, 30 May 1907).

[7] The Anglo-Japanese alliance, and the ententes with France and with Russia, meant that India no longer dominated British thinking about defence before the First World War. There may have been something Venetian about being forced to use diplomacy in this way, but, whatever the long-term effect of these changes, the British empire was able to come through the war at least ostensibly unscathed.

pockets of its subjects; they kept Indians satisfactorily divided inside a set of local societies, occupied with the scrabble for resources around the parish pump. But in return the British had to acquiesce in arrangements where strong local intermediaries blocked them from meddling too much in their affairs. In practice they had to wink at the existence of an administrative underworld, where the play of local faction settled the distribution of resources and the resolution of conflicts, without much reference to the Raj or its book of rules. By necessity the British had to be a laisser-faire régime; it could not have been otherwise. In the mythology of empire, the British engaged in heroic social engineering. But the rhetoric of their proconsuls disguised a ground-floor reality where they governed in name but Indians ruled in practice. The hard facts of local circumstance often buckled and sometimes broke the larger purposes of the Raj, which were always curbed by the doctrine that low-taxation and 'salutary neglect' were the keys to the quiet enjoyment of the political kingdom.[8]

But throughout the century and a half of British rule, the Raj was being worked in the service of interests larger than India herself, since they bore upon the British position in the world. If India was to make imperial sense, it was not enough that it should be ruled without too much effort and expense. Empires are not conquered to be kept in glass cases; and the Raj was not able merely to be a nightwatchman and receiver of tribute. India had to contribute positively to British power and profit. If the British were to bend India to imperial purposes, they could not let it remain balkanized and the autonomy of its localities undisturbed. In the Indian setting, the British had to be unifiers, not dividers. Imperial purposes called for metropolitan control over the Indian empire. It also called for a control by the Government of India over its subordinate administrations in the provinces. London needed a strong central government in India obedient to it yet capable of keeping the lesser administrations in line with metropolitan purposes. As London's authority over Calcutta grew during the nineteenth century, so also did Calcutta's powers over its provinces; this growing centralization was a dominant trend in Victorian India. Step by step the British imposed upon India an interconnected structure of government which stretched from its summit at Whitehall to the districts and taluks at the base, an administration close at the top, however lightly it rested upon the base.

[8] The argument here, and in the paragraphs which follow, has been developed in Anil Seal, 'Imperialism and Nationalism in India', in Gallagher, Johnson, and Seal (eds), *Locality, Province and Nation* (Cambridge, 1973), pp. 1–27.

But as imperial interests expanded, so did their demands upon India. Indian revenues had to support an army, with its costly white contingents, which was liable to defend British interests outside India, but which also had to maintain internal security and defend the frontiers. They had to meet the growing overheads of an administration whose managerial services expanded under the inexorable pressure of imperial requirement; they had to guarantee loans for the railways, built in the imperial interest, heedless of economy. These demands were harder to meet for a government which relied upon so regressive a system of taxation. Land revenue was inelastic; the notables in the countryside could not safely be shaken down. Customs duties were kept low by Lancashire's interests; income tax was obstructed by Indian interests. Locked in these fetters, the Raj had to create more resources in India and to take its cut. Driven forward by financial need, the Government of India strove towards the ideals of progress, more material than moral, conscious that it could set aside more for its British masters only by leaving less to its Indian clients.

London and Calcutta were parts of one and the same imperial system, but more and more their priorities tended to be different. Anxious to make ends meet, and to keep its Indian collaborators content, Calcutta could see the merits of taxing as lightly and spending as generously as possible inside India, whereas London in its own interest was prepared to be more lavish at India's expense. Time and again, viceroys and finance members in late-Victorian India protested at London's dictation of Indian policy;[9] the relationship between the metropolis and India was described by one old India hand as 'that of the wolf and the lamb in the fable', the former consuming everything the latter saved.[10] The Government of India would have liked London to pay more of the costs of using the Indian army overseas; and a customs duty on Lancashire's cottons would greatly have eased its financial problems. But London would have none of it. Even the complaints of its most imperious proconsul were swept aside, leaving Curzon vainly to protest: 'Govt. at home cannot go on treating the Government of India as

[9] Already in 1861 Samuel Laing had tried to get London to pay its fair share of Indian costs: 'The day is past when England can consider India as a sort of milch-cow. . . . Strict and impartial justice must be the rule in all money matters between England and India, if England wishes to get a return for her capital . . . and if she wishes to see India become, everyday, more and more the best source of supply for her raw produce and the best market in the world for her staple manufactures'. (Financial statement, 27 April 1861 in P. J. Thomas, *The Growth of Federal Finance in India* (Madras, 1939), p. 84). But the day was not past; it was to drag on for another three-quarters of a century.

[10] Richard Strachey, 1878 quoted in B. B. Misra, *The Administrative History of India, 1834–1947* (Bombay, 1970), p. 37.

though we were a negligible quantity. . . . Of course, we are subordinate and the S. of S. and Ministry are ultimately supreme. But there are two ways of doing things—a wise and unwise. . . .'[11] But when imperial interests were at stake, London's wisdom often seemed folly to the Guardians who had both to serve their metropolitan masters and to appease their Indian subjects.

Raising revenues inevitably meant a greater administrative intervention, going deeper into the affairs of Indian society than the previous system had done. If the administrative costs of intervening were not to overtake the returns, and if security was not to be put at risk, the British had to adjust the systems by which they enlisted the collaboration of their Indian subjects. In part this was done by inducting more Indians into the bureaucracy, particularly into its lower reaches; in part by introducing a measure of local self-government, designed to restore local autonomies threatened by these interventions. The heavier the interventions, the greater the risks. Mindful of the lessons of the Mutiny, when sepoy grievances and civil discontents had caught it off its guard, the Raj sought to make its legislation a little less arbitrary, its administration less olympian and the involvement of Indians more patent. As government intervened from above in spheres which previously it had left alone, it was brought into more direct contact with interests, once safely insulated in the localities; they now had to shift their attention to the higher levels from where the intervention was coming in order to protect their franchises and immunities. The modest representative bodies which the British created were themselves an incentive for Indians to build a matching structure of political organization, connected from the centre to the periphery, capable of negotiating with the British at the top in the name of constituents at the base. Thus one largely unintended result of these greater interventions into Indian society, and the steps taken to soften their impact, was to edge Indian politics out of their local arenas. These hesitant moves began to hint that the dictates of empire and the requirements of security inside India were not always compatible. Imperial interests dictated that India had to be treated as a whole by a unitary and active government; it could not be left as a set of sleepy hollows. But the requirements of safe government inside India called for a more self-denying policy of leaving things alone and not carelessly rupturing the autonomy of discrete localities.

Before the First World War, the Raj seemed to have deflected the main threats to its security, whether internal or external. But squaring

[11] Curzon to Godley, 5 August 1903, Kilbracken Papers, MSS EUR.F.102, quoted in *ibid.*, pp. 37–8.

the Russians was easier than solving the Indian problem. By bringing Indians into the reformed councils of 1909, Morley and Minto hoped to rally the conservative and weighty elements in Indian society, their old friends and allies. The reforms themselves did not add up to much: the legislative councils, both at the centre and in the provinces, were made larger and given an indirectly elected element; but their powers remained narrow.[12] The principle was laid down that interests, not mere numbers, were to be represented, and this was to be achieved through the devices of separate electorates, reserved seats and nomination as well as by the system of indirect election. But these apparently innocuous arrangements, using institutions which had been about for some time, failed to shepherd political ambitions back into the safe local pastures from which they had begun to stray. Unintentionally they helped to create powerful new links between the different arenas of Indian political activity, the locality, the province and the nation. If a politician wanted to get elected to the council in the province, he now had to win support in the local municipal and district boards; if he wanted a seat in the legislature at the centre, he had to secure the votes of the elected members in the provincial council. In either case politicians were now forced beyond the narrow boundaries of their own factions, and, by a converse process, Indians with larger concerns, the provincial politicians and the still small band of all-India men, had good reasons now to pay greater attention to local affairs. More and more was being decided by the central government, less and less by the provinces and the districts. Conscious that their local autonomy had been eroded, and unable to influence Leviathan at the base as they had previously done, Indians now strove to organize to reach the higher levels, whether the district headquarters, the provincial capitals, or Calcutta itself, which previously they could afford to ignore. The reforms of 1909 had shown favour to landlords, Muslims and other special interests defined by the broad categories laid down by the Raj. Unexpectedly, this provided an enormous incentive for politicians to stand forth as representatives of these groups, however imperfectly the categories themselves reflected social fact, and would-be spokesmen of yet other categories could see the advantage of winning special representation on the same lines. This led to a competitive flurry of activity among politicians to seek out their newly-defined constituents, and to get the British to accept them as their rightful representatives. This entailed a change larger than the archi-

---

[12] They did not hold the purse strings; in law-making they had little power of initiative; but they now had the right to comment on financial and administrative matters.

tects of the reforms had anticipated. In its classical policy, the Raj had dealt with local interests at local levels, leaving itself a relatively free hand in the all-India matters which were its imperial concern. But step by step a centralizing administration had hoisted these local interests to its higher reaches, and when the political reforms of the later nineteenth century and early twentieth century tried to smuggle in the old benefits of an atomized polity through the back door of the new-fangled representative systems, the plan went awry. Imperial self-interest demanded a measure of Indian unity and central authority; but the more India was unified politically, and centrally administered, the more vulnerable became the position which the rulers of that empire were trying to defend. From Britain's point of view this was the vicious circle of her imperialism in India. A united India with a strong centre made good imperial sense, but a divided and atomized polity was obviously easier to govern.

The First World War brought these problems sharply into focus; it did not create them. It was hardly the case that the war unleashed new aspirations in Indian Politics, only recently lulled into quiescence by the reforms of Morley and Minto. Indian politics had been developing in new directions before the war; the war simply accelerated these trends. But the war proved emphatically that India was still an imperial asset.[13] Its defence never became a liability during the war,[14] even if ensuring its future security became a preoccupation after it.

The war put great strains not only upon India's finances, but also upon its administrative and political arrangements. In 1909, the Decentralization Commission had called for the centre's grip to be relaxed over the provincial administrations. The disastrous mismanagement of the Mesopotamia campaign proved conclusively that Delhi's[15] powers would have to be curbed; the provincial governors, almost to a man, insisted that their administrations should have greater control over their own affairs. To these proposals for decentralization, Montagu and Chelmsford were to tack some political concessions, intended, in the time-honoured way, to rally the moderates and to damp down the

[13] More than a million Indian troops were recruited for duty overseas; by 1920, the Indian tax-payer was paying three times more for the army than he had a year before the outbreak of the war; in addition India made a free gift of £100,000,000 to Britain's war effort.

[14] Until the 1917 revolution, the Russians were Britain's allies; after 1917, the Bolsheviks had troubles of their own. The Germans and the Turks signally failed to push their offensive to the western frontiers of India; the Amir of Afghanistan held to his treaty obligations, and the Japanese alliance effectively covered India's eastern flanks.

[15] The seat of the Government of India was moved from Calcutta to Delhi in 1912.

agitational politics which had been given a spur during the war. Faced by the old problem of reconciling imperial interests with the political facts of India, the Montagu-Chelmsford report suggested a resolution worthy of Solomon on a bad day. British rule, unitary, indivisible and centralized, was to be spliced into parts, and one of the parts was to be cut into two. At one end, Delhi would remain responsible only to London, even though in its Assembly Indians were now to have the loudest voice; its authority in essential matters would remain 'indisputable'. At the other end, local self-government would be much extended. The provinces, as their governors had demanded, would have a larger measure of autonomy both financial and legislative, but their business would now be divided into subjects reserved to the governor and his officials and subjects transferred to Indian ministers responsible to elected majorities in the legislative councils. This was the famous principle of dyarchy. By these devices the British hoped to turn Indian politics into the provinces and localities, while keeping for themselves a free hand at the centre. But changes in Britain and in India worked against the resolution of the dilemma without upsetting the delicate balance of profit and power.

II

The First World War provided a vast bargain-basement for empire-builders. The downfall of the Second Reich placed African, Pacific and Chinese colonies on the market; some of the vilayats of the Ottoman empire became available after its collapse;[16] Russia's provinces in the Baltic, Siberia and South Russia, together with the old Russian interests in Persia, Turkey and China, all awaited a take-over. Lloyd George's cabinet seemed to have gone prospecting in the mood of H. G. Wells's Mr. Britling who remarked: 'now everything becomes fluid; we can re-draw the map of the world'.[17] Out of these opportunities it tried to guarantee the security of India once and for all. Britain emerged from the peace negotiations with German East Africa, Palestine and Mesopotamia. In Persia and Arabia she settled for a large measure of control

[16] British forces controlled from Egypt and India had pulled down the southern vilayats; Cairo's armies had conquered Palestine and Syria and helped to liberate Hejaz; Delhi had occupied Mesopotamia, overawed Persia and encouraged Ibn Saud in Arabia.
[17] H. G. Wells, *Mr. Britling Sees it Through* (1916), p. 197, quoted in B. Porter, *The Lion's Share: A Short History of British Imperialism 1850-1970* (1975), p. 235.

and her interventions in the Caucasus and Trans-Caspia had rolled Russian power still further from the frontiers of India; a great new spur of control jutted out from Egypt to Arabia, and beyond to Baghdad and Tehran, linking the eastern frontiers of Persia with the western-most bounds of India. But within a year of its apogee this vast system, so carefully constructed in 1919, was in disarray, and Britain was quickly forced to pull back from these high-tides of empire and retreat from the outer defences of India to an inner line drawn through Egypt, Palestine and Iraq.[18] During this retreat from empire to influence, some politicians, among them Smuts, had raised the question whether these new territories which Britain had snatched up in the Middle East needed to be retained at all.[19] Behind that question lay even more fundamental issues. These new eastern territories had been acquired to ensure Indian security. But there were signs that India was already a wasting asset in British trade, and might become more of a liability than an asset in British strategy. Yet a great deal of imperial policy in the east was designed to guarantee the security of that doubtful asset.

Behind these gloomy perspectives lay changes both in Britain and in India. Britain won the war but in the long run she was bound to lose the peace. To retain her options in a world-wide strategy, and to keep her far-flung empire secure, Britain had to have naval supremacy as well as the services of the army in India. But as Lloyd George explained to the Committee of Imperial Defence on 14 December 1920, Britain after the war faced 'two formidable new powers in the world, formidable today and possibly overwhelmingly so in a few years time', the United States of America and Japan. To retain naval supremacy would mean entering into an expensive competition with the United States in building battleships and cruisers, and this—'the biggest decision . . . since 1914'—might, as Lloyd George bluntly remarked, 'in the end ruin us'. The ardent imperialists in his Committee were reminded that 'in 1914 the resources of the British Empire were greater than the resources of our opponents. Today this was not the case'.[20]

Behind this lay the simple fact that after 1918 the efforts to move back to the normality of 1913 never succeeded and among the failures was the

---

[18] See J. Gallagher, 'Nationalisms and the Crisis of Empire, 1919–22', above, pp. 353–66.

[19] See CAB 32/2, Minutes of Imperial Conference, 6 July 1921.

[20] Warning the Committee to exercise extreme care, Lloyd George said 'He was unwilling to use the word "bankruptcy", but that word . . . might be applicable to Great Britain should she embark on this devastating competition.' Here, in the Prime Minister's opinion, was 'the most difficult [problem] which any Government in British history had to solve'. CAB 2/3, CID Minutes, 14 December 1920.

deadening of the expansive impulses of Britain's economy. The signs of this were soon clear. From now on the volume of her exports was pitched well below the pre-war level,[21] although less was now invested abroad.[22] Her capital went on migrating in the nineteen-twenties, and London did not recover its role as provider of financial services to the world; during the nineteen-thirties foreign investment became much smaller. The dwindling of exports was connected with the slump in the old industries such as textiles, coal, shipbuilding and iron and steel which had been the staple exports.[23] The countervailing growth in the 'new' dynamic industries did not make up the loss. Generally the British economy performed poorly,[24] and unemployment was high, particularly in the old industries.[25] These trends in the economy threw up new imperatives in British politics. Political futures in Britain in any case were unsure. Both Conservatives and Liberals, who had shared power throughout the nineteenth century were troubled by the prospect that Labour might come to power. More than three-quarters of those now entitled to vote in Britain had never voted before.[26] The old parties saw the strategic need to counter Labour by a tactical recourse to moderate politics. One way of dampening down the discontents of the working-class was to spend more on the social services. So the accepted line was to prune public expenditure, while spending more to conciliate the poor. But if more of the smaller budget[27] was to be spent upon social services, there was going to be less for defence. Paying for domestic necessities meant cutting out imperial luxuries. Politicians of all colours now

[21] *Volume of British Exports*: 1913 = 100

1919	54.9	1930	65.9
1922	68.1	1934	54.9
1926	67.0	1938	57.1

Source: London and Cambridge Economic Service, *The British Economy: Key Statistics, 1900–1966*, 1967, Table K.

[22] See D. A. Aldcroft, *The Inter-War Economy* (1970), p. 262.

[23] *Ibid.*, Table 23, p. 156 (cotton), pp. 150–55 (coal), Table 25, p. 164 (shipbuilding), pp. 169–74 (iron and steel).

[24] See C. M. Feinstein, 'Production and Productivity, 1920–1963', *London and Cambridge Economic Bulletin* (1963), Table 1. The annual growth rate was little more than 1.5 per cent between 1924 and 1937.

[25] Between 1920 and 1925 the work force of the old industries dropped by one million; by 1929 the workless from these industries amounted to nearly half the total number of the unemployed.

[26] By 1924, 5,800,000 more voters were to turn out than in 1918. See M. Kinnear, *The Fall of Lloyd George: the Political Crisis of 1922* (1973), pp. 21, 30.

[27] After the Geddes axe fell in 1922, government expenditure, exclusive of local government spending, never rose as high again until 1936. See A. J. Peacock and J. Wiseman, *The Growth of Public Expenditure in the United Kingdom* (Princeton, 1961), Appendix Table A-5, pp. 164–5.

worked against constraints which obliged them to hold unswervingly
to the primacy of domestic interests against those of the empire overseas.[28]

 Already by 1919 the cabinet's remembrancer was arguing that a
successful war against the Americans was 'quite out of the question'.
Since Britain could not beat the Americans she should join them in
disarming.[29] Accepting these axioms the cabinet on 15 August 1919 laid
down the Ten Year Rule which assumed that Britain would not have to
fight a major war for a decade.[30] This was to make very deep cuts in all
three armed services;[31] and was one reason why the new empire constructed after the First World War was faltering. In July 1920 the
General Staff's survey of the military liabilities of the empire made
gloomy reading[32] and in addition there was the need to check strikers in
England and the dissidents in Ireland. During 1920 it was the British
generals who did more than anyone to pull British soldiers out of Russia
and Persia. In 1921 these strains grew heavier, with the Chiefs of the
Imperial General Staff talking of the need to find 100,000 or even
200,000 troops for Ireland.[33] Once the British had sold their alliance
with Japan in order to buy naval disarmament from America in 1922,
the Geddes axe fell even more heavily upon the service estimates. From
the early nineteen-twenties the picture is clear: policy had to fall in line
with weakness; entrenchment meant contraction; Curzon's extrava-
ganzas of 1918 had to give way to Bonar Law's announcement that
Britain could no longer be the policeman of the world. Economic and

---

[28] Of course, the general agreement of the politicians to pay for social services by
cutting back on the armed services rested on the assumption of strategic security. By the
middle of the nineteen-thirties that assumption was exploded.
[29] CAB 21/159, Memorandum by Hankey, 17 July 1919.
[30] CAB 23/15, W. C. 616A, 15 August 1919: Service estimates to assume 'that the
British Empire will not be engaged in any great war during the next ten years'.
[31]   *Expenditure on armed forces*: (£ millions)

	1919–20	1920–21	1921–22	1922–23
Army	395	181	95	45
Navy	157	88	81	56
RAF	53	23	14	9

Source: *Parliamentary Papers*, 1924, XXIV, Cmd. 2207.

[32] Before the war, the military needs of the empire had called for sixteen and
two-thirds infantry divisions, three and one-third cavalry divisions, and four squadrons
of aircraft; in 1920, they required twenty-nine and two-thirds infantry divisions, five and
two-thirds cavalry divisions, and thirty squadrons of aircraft (CAB 4/7, 'Military
Liabilities of the Empire', Memorandum by General Staff, 27 July 1920, Appendix A,
CID255-B).
[33] Diary of Sir Henry Wilson, 13 September 1921, quoted in C. E. Callwell, *Field
Marshall Sir Henry Wilson* (1927), II, 305.

political constraints at home compelled every government to move towards a Little Englander position.[34]

But another constraint upon British policy was the growth of political activity in the colonies. From now until the end of empire, political change in overseas regions was to put an increasing pressure upon the operations of the British system, and set limits to its policy-making. The Government of India Act of 1919 had been planned as a way of diverting Indian political attention from the all-India stage to provincial affairs. There were to be Indian ministers in the governments of eight of the nine provinces. Indians were also to be in a majority in the Legislative Assembly in Delhi. Five million electors were given the vote. Somehow or the other, this constitution had to be worked. 'A reversal of the policy in India ...', Montagu wrote to the viceroy, 'would mean the end of the Indian Empire.'[35] To work the reforms, clearly the British would have to rely on the grace and favour of Indian politicians. Accordingly they had to be given a hand to play; and so they could also make their terms with the British. The First World War had put an enormous strain upon Indian finances; India had been bled 'absolutely white', the viceroy reported to London.[36] It came out of the war with a national debt of £370 million and a bad financial headache. Long before the Montagu-Chelmsford reforms were launched, the Government of India had begun its desperate search for new sources of revenue. When it had squeezed whatever it could from other sources, the government turned to a tariff on imports. In 1917 London reluctantly had to allow Delhi to impose a tariff of seven and a half per cent upon Lancashire cottons, whose imports into India had already been hit hard by the war.[37] The war had also stimulated industrial activity in India, mainly in areas where import substitution was possible, such as cotton, iron and steel, cement, sugar, engineering and chemicals. One side effect of these changes was that Indians who had profited from these new industries now wanted the temporary protection of war to be continued after it. These pressures for a change in the tariff policy, both financial and

[34] The Labour ministry of 1924 did not establish a new trend; rather it followed an existing trend which had been evident under the Conservative or Conservative-dominated governments before it.

[35] Montagu to Reading, 23 February 1922, Reading Papers, vol. 4.

[36] Quoted in B. R. Tomlinson, 'India and the British Empire, 1880–1935', *Indian Economic and Social History Review*, XIII, 4 (October–December 1975), 349.

[37] During the war, Lancashire's exports to India dropped drastically. By 1918, India was importing only 1,300 million yards, a decline which accounted for three-quarters of Lancashire's war-time losses. Indian mill production, and imports from Japan, captured a market which had for so long been dominated by the Manchester men.

political, were greatly increased once the reforms took shape. Dyarchy meant separating central and provincial revenues; the Meston Award gave the provinces all the revenues from land, irrigation, excise and stamps, while the centre kept income-tax, opium, salt and customs. So if the centre needed more money, it now had to raise it either from income-tax which was bound to be politically sensitive in India, or from customs which would hit interests in Lancashire. The reforms had also given India a measure of fiscal autonomy; and from now on whenever the Government of India was in financial straits, it inevitably looked to raising the tariff, especially upon imported cottons.[38] The reason why it had to be Lancashire and not Indian taxpayers who bore the brunt of this need for more money, was the primacy of the Government of India's domestic interests, the political priority of making a success of the Montagu-Chelmsford reforms.

By devolving some power from the centre to the provinces, and by grafting upon this decentralization concessions to Indian politicians, the reforms of 1920 aimed to place the Raj upon a broader base of Indian political support. But if this strategy was to work, Indian politicians in the provinces had to be given funds with which to buy votes and to build stable ministries. This was the Indian version of the constraints which forced politicians in Britain to spend less on the armed forces and more on social services. Under the new constitution, the centre had to transfer about £6 million a year to the provinces. Between the wars Indians were demanding a larger and larger slice of a cake which was getting smaller and smaller. Inevitably, they looked upon the use by Britain of Indian troops abroad not only as exploitation but also as a frittering away of resources which would turn out the voters at home. By pushing up the income-tax during the war, and by failing to return to pre-war levels of direct taxation after it, the Government of India had made a breach in its traditional policy of keeping direct taxes low. Now the cry of no taxation without representation could be raised in India; moreover the government had tied itself to powerful monied interests in India more closely than before by large borrowings on the Indian market during the war. Indians who had invested in government loans might have had an interest in the continued stability of British rule; but they also had more reason than before to influence the raising and spending of money. Expenditure on field armies in France, the campaigns in Mesopotamia, the drives to Damascus and adventures in Persia and South Russia

---

[38] 'When additional revenues are required', Sir Malcolm Hailey told the Assembly, 'the first heed to which one's thought naturally turns, is customs', Budget Statement (1922–23), p. 11, quoted in Thomas, *Federal Finance in India*, p. 336.

might be in the defence of large imperial interests, but they had little to do with Indian interests more narrowly construed. London knew this; Delhi knew this; and so did the Indian politicians. So if these politicians were to be satisfied, less would have to be spent upon the Indian army, the heaviest burden upon Indian finance. By 1920 more than forty per cent of the government's total expenditure was upon military costs.[39] As the Secretary of State for India told the Cabinet on Christmas eve, 1920:

> it is ... definitely impossible for us to make any contribution to Imperial Defence ... it is definitely impossible for us to embark on any grandiose schemes of military expansion .... So far as India is concerned, all idea of initiating as a normal peace measure a scheme, whereby she is to become the base for vast military operations in the Middle and Far East must be definitely abandoned; if public opinion in India would tolerate it, Indian revenues cannot bear the charge. Even more modest schemes, under which India is to be asked to furnish large military garrisons in the Middle East in times of peace, will have to be modified. In short, we must definitely get out of our heads the vague idea too often entertained that India is an inexhaustible reservoir from which men and money can be drawn towards the support of Imperial resources or in pursuance of Imperial strategy.[40]

Yet British expansion had always depended upon the Indian army as its main striking force in the east. Now London's interests were clashing directly with those of the Government of India in Delhi. Facing a run-down of the armed forces in Britain, the Esher Committee which had been set up to look into the Imperial role of the Indian army, argued in 1920 that the new post-war conditions had 'enhanced the importance of the Army of India relatively to the military forces of other parts of the Empire, and more particularly to those of the British Isles'. So not only should the Indian Army be reformed, it should be brought more directly under London's control by being put under the command of the Chief of the Imperial General Staff whenever it was used in an imperial role.[41] But neither Delhi nor the India Office could accept this. There was the problem of cost; there was the problem of working the new constitution, and finally there was the problem of maintaining peace and order inside India. 'The political situation in India', wrote Montagu during the

[39] CAB 6/4 Memorandum by Finance Department, India Office, circulated by Montagu, 7 December 1920. *Estimate of Indian Military Costs* (£ million: rupees £1 = 15)

1915–16	22.3	1918–19	24.5
1916–17	25.0	1919–20	52.9
1917–18	29.0	1920–21	60.0 (estimate)

The current revenue of the Government of India was £134.8 million.
[40] CAB 6/4, 'Indian Military Expenditure' Memorandum by Montagu, 24 December 1920, CID 118-D; also quoted in Tomlinson, *IESHR*, XII, no. 4, 360.
[41] CAB 6/4 'Report of the Army in India Committee, 1919–20 Part I', 115-D, *idem*.

non-cooperation campaign, 'indicates no possibility of setting free more troops from internal defence duties to increase the field army'. So in overseas duties 'India must now play a humble part'.[42] Here the Secretary of State was voicing the demands of the Government of India; and in its turn, the Government of India was voicing the demands of the Indian politicians. In 1921, the Government of India's despatch to London put its weight behind the resolution of the Legislative Assembly in Delhi that

... the purpose of the Army in India must be held to be the defence of India against external aggression and the maintenance of internal peace and tranquility ... [it] should not as a rule be employed for service outside the external frontiers of India except for purely defensive purposes or with the previous consent of the Governor-General in Council in very grave emergencies.[43]

The following year the Government of India fell still deeper into this new political trap. Now the Assembly wanted to cut the size of the Indian army. Constitutionally debarred from touching the army vote, it attacked the Government's revenues, such as the salt tax and the excise upon cotton. Delhi itself pressed hard for lightening the military burden.[44] These combined pressures could not be ignored. In January 1923, the Cabinet had to approve the view of the Committee of Imperial Defence that the

Indian Army cannot be treated as if it were absolutely at the disposal of His Majesty's Government for service outside India ... except in the gravest emergency, the Indian Army should be employed outside the Indian empire only after consultation with the Governor-General in Council. ... The view of the Government of India that the Indian Army should not be required permanently to provide large overseas garrisons is supported. Units required for such purposes should be maintained in addition to the establishment laid down for the Indian Army and the whole cost, direct or indirect, of recruiting and maintaining such units should be borne by His Majesty's Government, or by the dependency or colony requiring their services.[45]

Here the position was to rest until the nineteen-thirties. The Indian army was to be pegged at 228,000 men. Internal Indian security demanded twenty-eight British and twenty-two Indian infantry batal-

[42] CAB 6/4, Memorandum by Montagu, 24 December 1920, 118-D.

[43] CAB 6/4, Viceroy's Army Dept. to Montagu, 30 March 1921, 122-D, also quoted in Tomlinson, *IESHR*, XII, no. 4, 361. On the Indian army after the war, see Keith Jeffery, ' "An English Barrack in the Oriental Seas?"—India in the Aftermath of the First World War', above, pp. 367–84.

[44] Montagu to Reading, telegram, 22 February 1922, Reading Papers, vol. 11.

[45] CAB 6/4 'Report of the sub-committee on Indian military requirements' 22 June 1922, 'amended and approved by His Majesty's Government', 26 January 1923, 130-D; also quoted in Tomlinson, *IESHR*, XII, no. 4, 361–2.

lions. But as Churchill remarked in 1921, an army of internal garrisons simply required sabres and bayonets, not sophisticated weapons, so during the nineteen-twenties the Indian army lagged behind the times until it became a force of screw-guns and mules, incapable of taking on any serious opponent. It was held back by the poverty of the Government of India and by the demands of Indian politicians.[46]

Now of course this did not entirely strip the Indian army of its tasks as an imperial fire-service. In 1925–26 there were plans for sending Indian troops to Iraq. In 1927 the Indian army sent a mixed brigade to Shanghai on condition that London met the bill;[47] there were contingency plans for sending troops to protect the Persian oil fields, but on the express understanding that 'no financial liability whatsoever will fall upon India'.[48] By 1928 the Indian army was committed to sending a division to Iraq, and two infantry brigades to Singapore.[49] But the old days of getting the support for next to nothing had gone. Now the Indian army was a fire-service which worked on the contract, which turned out only in an emergency, and which was bound first to its own rate payers in India.[50]

Against a background of declining trade between Britain and India,[51] and the fall in British investment there, the recurrent financial crises of the Government of India were forcing it to raise the tariff,[52] cut the army, and curb its role overseas. These devices began to erode the

[46] Throughout the nineteen-twenties, Indian politicians went on protesting against the army. As the Finance Member admitted, 'the existing scale of military expenditure is a disastrous burden upon India. There is a crying need for more and more expenditure upon the betterment of the conditions of life for the people of India and since the reforms there is at last the beginnings at any rate of an effective popular demand for such expenditure'. (Memorandum by B. P. Blackett, 4 July 1927, Irwin Papers, 3.)

[47] See Hirtzel to Irwin, 15 January 1927, Irwin to Birkenhead, 16 January 1927, Birkenhead to Irwin, 3 February 1927, Irwin Papers, 3.

[48] See CAB 5/5, Memorandum by Hankey, 15 February 1924, 222-C; Report of sub-committee, 7 July 1924, 237-C and CAB 2/5 CID, Minutes, 29 June 1931.

[49] CAB 5/7, Memorandum by India Office, 3 May 1928, 318-C.

[50] These retrenchments in the Indian army, and the restrictions upon its use as an imperial task force, had a crucial bearing upon the first crisis of empire that the British faced soon after the First World War. See Gallagher, 'Nationalisms and the Crisis of Empire, 1919–22', above, pp. 353–66.

[51] In the nineteen-twenties, Lancashire's exports to India were relatively stable. In 1920, Lancashire exported 1,272 million yards to India; and in 1929 1,248 million yards, but in the nineteen-thirties this fell drastically. By 1939 Lancashire exported only 145 million yards to India (see Tomlinson, *IESHR*, XII, no. 4, Table II, 379). The more dynamic sectors of British industry found little outlet in India for their goods (see Tomlinson, *The Political Economy of the Raj*, Table 2.8, p. 48).

[52] Between 1923 and 1929, India flouted most of London's traditional taboos over the tariff. In 1924 an openly protectionist tariff was imposed upon iron and steel; in 1926, the countervailing cotton excise which helped Lancashire was abolished.

centre of that system of profit and power to which India had contributed in the past. India could be held in the empire, her politicians placated and her army paid for only by taxing the profits of the connection and cutting back the army's role as the enforcer of British wishes. The dwindling of India's contribution to the exercise of British power outside India was linked to political changes in India itself; a shift there in the basis of British rule had left Britain more dependent upon its Indian collaborators and this in turn weakened the British grip upon other countries far away. Giving more to Indian politicians in the provinces in turn deprived the centre of the resources to drive a way out of these difficulties. As usual it was Lloyd George who saw most clearly into the dilemma of British imperialism. He knew, as Cromer had known before him, that the secret of successful government in the east lay in low taxation. But he saw, too, that

the tradition of government in India with regard to finance and development [has] been the over-cautious one of an old family solicitor. We must increase the wealth of India if we are going to make a success of the new system of government. To attempt progress on the basis of the present revenue, must be to march straight towards turmoil and failure.[53]

This was an admirable insight. But increasing the wealth of India meant more trade and investment and there was little chance of this in the conditions of the British economy in the nineteen-twenties.[54] Since the British empire did not have to face any serious challenges for the rest of the nineteen-twenties, the acuteness of the dilemma tended to be disguised. But it came to the fore as soon as the next stage of constitutional advance came to be considered.

The reforms of 1919 had been based upon the strategy of locking Indian politics into the provinces and, by the device of dyarchy, of restricting the Indian share of government to matters which did not directly compromise imperial interests[55] and the British control at the centre which safeguarded them. As in Canada or in Malaya, this was a move by which British rule began to pull out of the provinces and came to be concentrated at the centre. The constitutional reforms of 1919 represented a change in technique; they did not mark a change in aims. But they did attempt to place the collaboration of Indians upon a wider

---

[53] Lloyd George to Reading, 26 July 1922, Reading Papers, vol. 21.

[54] Not until the period from 1941 to 1945 was the Indian economy to be driven hard, and then only through heavy government intervention. And for that there would be a heavy political price to pay.

[55] Indian ministers were given safe subjects such as education and local government, the 'nation-building' departments; the civilians kept the departments which mattered.

and more formal basis. Since 1922, the decline of agitation had left the British free to rally the moderates and the constitutionalists. Admittedly, they had hoped that the reforms would produce a party system in the provinces, and these hopes were usually frustrated. The elected members of legislative councils tended to switch their votes in response to the demands of patronage, not party; Indian politics in the twenties would have been more familiar to the Duke of Newcastle in the eighteenth century than to the men in Westminster in the twentieth century. But from another point of view, the strategy seemed to be working tolerably well; the policy-makers had reason to be sanguine about the prospects of placating Indian opinion in the next round of reforms sufficiently to keep themselves in the saddle at the centre.

The Act of 1919 envisaged a review of the workings of the reforms after ten years. Paradoxically, the Conservative victory at the polls in 1924, and Birkenhead's appointment as Secretary of State set the ball rolling earlier than the schedule had laid down. Birkenhead thought that the 1919 Act had been unnecessary. He was determined to keep in Conservative hands the appointment of the Statutory Commission which would review its working. In November 1927, he jumped the gun because

We could not run the slightest risk that the nomination of the 1928 Commission should be in the hands of our successors. You can readily imagine what kind of Commission would have been appointed by Colonel Wedgwood and his friends.

As it turned out, this was an error. Birkenhead wanted to slow down the pace of constitutional advance; in fact, he probably speeded it up. But British thinking, both in London and New Delhi, was still quite flexible about the tactics of its future policy in India. The aims of the policy remain clear enough; as Irwin put it to Birkenhead's successor at the India Office in May 1930, 'The big stake for which we are playing . . . [is] the retention of India within the Empire'.[56] Already in December 1928 the viceroy had seen that the British would have 'so to change the approach to the problem as to give us some hope of getting a substantial portion of Indian political opinion to accept the degree of control that Parliament is likely to deem essential'.[57] Early in 1929 his enquiries suggested that Gandhi and his Lieutenants 'would not make difficulty about an accommodation of the Dominion Status idea by

---

[56] Irwin to Benn, 8 May 1930, Irwin Papers, 6.

[57] Note by Irwin, signed and dated December 1928 (shown to Simon 21 December), Simon Commission Collection, Box 34, quoted in R. J. Moore, *The Crisis of Indian Unity, 1917–1940* (Oxford, 1974), p. 43.

which Foreign Affairs, Political and possibly Defence' would be reserved to the British,[58] and that nationalist opinion could be persuaded to accept Dominion Status to mean, not full independence, but a lesser arrangement by which the British might concede a degree of responsibility at the centre, while continuing to reserve control over the crucial portfolios. On 31 October 1929, Irwin made his historic statement which described 'the attainment of Dominion Status' as 'the natural issue of India's constitutional progress'. Of course there were ambiguities in what Dominion Status meant.[59] But Irwin was less concerned with 'the exact definition of Dominion Status worked out by ingenious disciples of the law'[60] than with persuading the political leadership to come to the Round Table Conference. Indeed, the viceroy exploited the ambiguities in his declaration, saying one thing to his critics in Britain and another to the Indians he was trying to win round.

Throughout Irwin's term as viceroy, his chief strategic aim was to keep India in the empire and so he had to settle 'the real question, whether all this Indian nationalism that is growing and bound to grow, can be guided along imperial or will more and more get deflected onto separatist lines'.[61] To win the big stake, and to keep British control over what mattered, Irwin's scheme was to give Indian politicians power in the provinces. Under the Montagu-Chelmsford reforms they had already achieved a measure of this control. But Britain had to remain in command of the centre so as to ensure control over defence, foreign policy and internal security. After all, these were the keys of the political kingdom. Hanging on to New Delhi was worth a few declarations about Dominion Status. If Indians wanted power, he was ready to let them have all they wanted in the provinces. But 'at the centre we come to matters which touch Great Britain',[62] and here Irwin's policy envisaged a share of responsibility for Indians at New Delhi, tempered by a determination to hold firmly onto the vital attributes of sovereignty. So

---

[58] Note on conversation with Patel, 11 January 1929, Irwin Papers, 5, quoted in *ibid.*, p. 46.

[59] The statement, described by Jawaharlal Nehru as an 'ingeniously worded announcement which could mean much or very little' (J. Nehru, *Autobiography* (1936), p. 196), was made at a time when Dominion Status had no fixed meaning. Constitutional lawyers have debated whether Dominion Status was compatible with external control, as Irwin believed it was, or whether it could be achieved only after full responsible government had been granted, as the Home Department in Delhi argued in 1929.

[60] Earl of Halifax, *Fulness of Days* (1957), p. 122, quoted in Moore, *The Crisis of Indian Unity*, p. 93.

[61] Irwin to Davidson, 5 December 1929, R. R. James, *Memoirs of a Conservative* (1969), p. 311.

[62] Irwin to Wedgwood Benn, 26 April 1931, Irwin Papers, 6.

the plans for political change which Irwin imposed upon the Labour Government in 1929, and which was continued by the National Government in 1931, were meant to revise the workings, but not to weaken the realities of British power in India.[63] As a later viceroy put it in 1939, 'After all we framed the constitution as it stands in the Act of 1935, because we thought that way the best way—given the political position in both countries—of maintaining British influence in India.'[64] Historically, the 1935 Act may have been a milestone in the passage back to Blighty; at the time it was past it was intended to secure tenure at viceregal lodge.

But these purposes had to be paid for. The strategy of keeping India in the empire depended upon Britain's ability to conciliate important sectors of Indian opinion, and in the crisis of the early nineteen-thirties, it became clear the political calculations in India clashed irreconcilably with London's construct of British commerical and financial interests. After 1919 there had grown up a fiscal autonomy convention that London should not in general interfere in Indian fiscal affairs.[65] First it had been gingerly applied. But the world slump hit India hard and slashed the value of her exports. Agrarian unrest, bad harvests, a falling exchange and yet another financial crisis forced the Government of India progressively to raise the tariff on imported cottons in 1928, in 1931 and 1933,[66] and awkwardly enough, the duties fell upon British imported cottons, at a time when Lancashire's markets in India were contracting rapidly. What was sweet for Bombay, was dire for Lancashire, and measures which brought easement to New Delhi brought agony to Whitehall. For Lancashire was not without defences. It had more than sixty members of Parliament and this is what caused concern to British cabinets, Conservative, Labour and National alike

[63] Most of the viceroy's provincial governors opposed his Plan. But a viceroy could override governors. More important, Irwin's viceroyalty was one of the rare periods in the later history of the Raj when policy was made more in New Delhi than in London. During the second Labour Government it was Irwin who dealt most of the cards which Ramsay MacDonald and Wedgwood Benn played. By the end of December 1930, MacDonald and Benn were at Chequers working on a scheme to give responsible government with safeguards to a native Indian government (see Benn to Irwin, 26 December 1930, and 10 January 1931, Irwin Papers); more than that, Irwin converted Baldwin as well. On 26 January 1931, the leader of the opposition stated that a Conservative Government would also follow such a policy.
[64] PREM 1/414, Linlithgow to Zetland, 21 December 1939.
[65] See Thomas, *Federal Finance in India*, p. 331.
[66] In these commercial matters, New Delhi was trapped inside its political calculations. Needing all the help it could get against agitational politics, it did not dare to embitter the Bombay millowners who might hit back by financing the agitators.

when they heard of each new tariff demand from India.[67] But the Labour and National Governments pushed the Indian reforms ahead, in spite of Lancashire's political leverage. The Indian plans were much disliked both by the employers and by the Trade Unions, but the politicians were resigned to the need to force them through. The constitutional plan for India made trouble in domestic politics back in Britain; but it made sense in imperial terms. Indeed in these terms it was a necessity. British governments were dragged into the risks and tedium of Indian constitutional reform by the need in India to ride the range upon politicians who might otherwise stray along separatist trails. So London had to agree to India's proposals over the tariff. There was worse to come. In 1932 the Imperial Economic Conference treated India in the same way as any other dominion. The 1935 Act ended the fiscal autonomy convention but it also deprived London of all say in India's tariff policy. Meanwhile India continued to buy less and less from Lancashire, and in return for a grudging and ineffective preference for British cottons, London had to agree to buy large quantities of short-staple Indian raw cotton for which it had no use. Indeed the Cotton Clause of the 1939 Agreement suggests that it was Britain who capitulated, sacrificing most of her own preferential advantages to win a doubtful benefit for her own cotton trade. One historian of British economic policy enquires whether by now India was not exploiting Britain rather than the other way round.[68]

In the nineteen-thirties another axiom of the British empire in India was challenged and this was the principle that London must control Indian finance. In 1930 Whitehall was not minded to budge on this point. As the Secretary of State put it, 'Hitherto the stability of Indian finance, official and unofficial, has been dependent upon the control of

[67] In 1929 there was 'a general feeling of consternation' in Baldwin's Cabinet; in 1931 'another tiresome tussle in the Cabinet this morning', reported Wedgwood Benn; in 1934, his conservative successor at the India Office, Sir Samuel Hoare, was deep in depression; 'If the moderates in Lancashire go off the deep end ... I shudder to think of the results on my Party in the House of Commons'. See Peel to Irwin, 30 January 1929, Irwin Papers, 5; Benn to Irwin, 27–28 January 1931, Irwin Papers, 6; Hoare to Willingdon, 2 November 1934, Templewood Papers, 10; Hoare to Willingdon, 3 February 1935, ibid. Also see R. A. Butler, The Art of the Possible (1971), p. 52.

[68] For the early operation of the fiscal conventions, see CAB 27/229. The dramas of the cotton duties are summarized in I. M. Drummond, British Economic Policy and the Empire, 1919–1939 (1972), pp. 121–40. This account describes Britain's mauling at the hands of the Indians in terms reminiscent of Ali Baba and the Forty Thieves. But in fact these were political not business transactions, and even Sir George Rainy, Commerce Member of the Viceroy's Council 'feels very strongly' that Indian politicians had to be given control of Indian trade; see Irwin to Wedgwood Benn, 2 August 1930, Irwin Papers, 6.

the Secretary of State. . . . There appears to be no practicable means of ensuring confidence in the future of Indian financial administration if Parliament is divested of control'.[69] The Treasury steered India through the financial crisis of 1931, keeping a firm hand on the helm. But New Delhi saw that more than ever before Indian finance now needed public support in India and this meant London's dictatorship had to go. Reluctantly in December 1932 the Cabinet agreed that control of India's external finance must be taken from the India Office and given to the viceroy in New Delhi. This decision was embodied in the 1935 Act.

But the more that government in London tried to reconstruct its hold over India the more it found itself losing support at home. Already in 1930, Baldwin's attachment to Irwin's plans had provoked discontent among the diehards of the Conservative Party. As Baldwin remarked, 'No Party is so divided as mine . . . it ranges from Imperialists of the Second Jubilee to young advanced Democrats who are all for Irwin's policy'.[70] By 1933, Churchill was able to organize a serious and protracted opposition to the White Paper which had been put forward by the National Government in which the Conservative Party was the preponderant group. This opposition, led by Churchill, Lord Lloyd and Salisbury, all figures living in the past, was never able to imperil the White Paper, or the Government of India Bill that came out of it. At their strongest they never assembled more than eighty Conservative votes against it in the House of Commons.[71] Yet the continuous nature of the opposition forced the government to lessen the liberalism in the Bill; and this new hardness was clear for all to see in the proceedings of the Joint Select Committee which did something to revise the powers of the Governors of the provinces. But above all it delayed the passage of the Bill until June 1935, some eight years after the constitutional review had been launched. For all that, the Bill went forward despite the strictures of deaf Jim Salisbury and three Dukes, the combinations of

---

[69] CAB 27/470, Memorandum on Indian Finance by Secretary of State, 8 December 1930, DDG(30)17, quoted in Tomlinson, *IESHR*, XII, no. 4, 371.

[70] T. Jones, *A Diary with Letters, 1931–1950* (1954), entry for 11 March 1931, p. 5.

[71] See Hoare to Willingdon, 13 February 1935, Templewood Papers, and R. A. Butler, *The Art of the Possible* (1971), p. 52. Some of this opposition was grounded on a general desire that the imperial flag of Britain should still fly high above the citadels of India; but there were other grounds, lying inside the factions of the Conservative Party. Some Conservatives joined in because they disliked the Party's captivity inside the National Coalition, and saw the Bill as a handy stick with which to beat it; others, because they supported the take-over bid for the Party, made by Churchill and his cronies, and others because they were swayed by the pressures from Lancashire. At most, thirty Conservative members liked the Bill.

Fenner Brockway, and the disingenuous solicitude of Churchill for the
Indian ryot, the obvious dislike of the party workers in the constituencies, the attacks of the elderly proconsuls such as O'Dwyer and some of
the spear-carriers in the later crusade against the axis powers. It went
forward despite the monstrous load that pushing this legislation through
had come to be upon British politics. It was under consideration from
1931 to 1933, and on the stocks from 1933 until 1935. Between 1934 and
1935, the Government had to fight through Commons and Lords what
became a gargantuan statute of 473 clauses and sixteen schedules. Its
passage was embellished by six hundred speeches by Hoare and his
answers to many thousands of questions. All this wrecked the time-tables
of Westminster and dammed the course of British politics. Indeed, as
long as the Bill's fate was uncertain, so was the leadership of the
Conservative Party. Until it became a statute, the Government could
not call a general election. All sorts of hazards beset the Bill. 'It has been
incredibly hard work doing day after day all this complicated Bill',
complained Hoare, 'made all the heavier by Winston's alarms and
excursions'.[72] In this war of attrition, some of the opposition had arisen
out of domestic issues, the rest out of the Indian situation.[73] But for those
in the councils of government, the imperialist criticisms of Churchill had
come to seem obsolete. 'Sensible men', Irwin concluded, 'do not any
longer think along these lines'.[74]

A double crisis for the empire lay behind this determination to push
ahead with what was obviously an unpopular reform. In India, the
growing militancy of some politicians on the left, the challenge of
Gandhi's civil disobedience movements which were designed above all
to impose a unity upon the divided factions in Congress, and the
imperious need from the British point of view to rally its collaborators,
made it vital to get the reforms settled. But outside India, the British
world system which had survived the nineteen-twenties by default of
serious challenge now faced challenges in plenty. Ever since Britain had
scrapped her alliance with Japan at the behest of the Americans, her
interests in the Far East had been at risk. Nothing much had been done
about building a British base at Singapore. When the Japanese attacked
Manchuria in 1931, and when they moved into the Treaty Ports, the
nakedness of the British position east of Calcutta was made plain. This
crisis led to the scrapping of the Ten Year Rule;[75] at long last it forced

[72] Hoare to Willingdon, 12 April 1935, Templewood Papers.
[73] In this way the growth of politics in India was exacting its revenge upon the
development of politics in Britain.
[74] Irwin to Benn, 13 December 1930, Irwin Papers, 6.
[75] CAB 2/5, CID Minutes, 22 March 1932.

the Government to press ahead with building a base at Singapore.[76] But the strategy of sending the Main Fleet to Singapore was put at risk when Rome turned towards Berlin, threatening to transform the Mediterranean into hostile waters and to block the short route to the east.[77] In 1933 Hitler took power in Germany and in 1935 Mussolini invaded Abyssinia. In 1936 the Spanish Civil War began, and the axis powers supported Franco. In 1937 full-scale war between Japan and China broke out. One by one these political mines detonated through the nineteen-thirties, wrecking most of the foundations upon which the security of the British empire was based, and destroying the assumptions which had guided its policies since the end of the First World War. By 1937, all these crises had begun to interlock to Britain's disadvantage.[78]

Faced by a triple threat of Germany, Italy and Japan, Britain had to swing back to a continental strategy; but this did not weaken the new emphasis on the defence of the empire. In fact, the revival of the imperial commitment became stronger in 1939, certainly stronger than at any time since 1919. Even when Chamberlain and his advisers recognized that there was no going back to the days of the Elder Pitt and that a field force would have to go to Europe, they pressed ahead with forming heavier garrisons outside Europe. By 1938 the Government was clear that a field force had to be built up in Egypt.[79] By 1939 these plans broadened into large schemes for military action in the Mediterranean, Egypt, Palestine, Malta, Gibraltar and Cyprus, as well as in the Red Sea and in East Africa. These operations were intended to attack the Italian empire in Africa and the Italian presence in the Mediterranean.[80] In a word, the Chiefs of Staff explained with relish in April 1939, the plan was 'to knock out the weaker partner in the Axis as soon as possible'.[81] By July they came to recognize that Mussolini could not be shoved down the trap-door so easily and that the possibility of war with Japan was likelier. So troops would be urgently needed in Burma and Malaya as well.

Reinforcing all these garrisons was not easy politically. In Egypt, few of the Pashas welcomed the prospect of Mussolini entering Cairo on his

[76] CAB 2/5, CID Minutes, 6 April 1933.
[77] See CAB 4/26, Memorandum by Eden, 15 June 1937, 1332-B; and memoranda by Chiefs of Staff, 28 July 1937, 1346-B, and 12 August 1937, 1347-B.
[78] See CAB 4/26, report of Chiefs of Staff, 26 October 1937, 1364-B; CAB 4/27, report of Chiefs of Staff, 24 November 1937, 1371-B; memorandum by Inskip, 19 November 1937, CP 283 (37); CID minutes, 18 November 1937.
[79] CAB 16/182, memorandum by Inskip, 8 February 1938, DP(P)16.
[80] CAB 16/183, memorandum by Chiefs of Staff, 20 February 1939.
[81] Ibid., memorandum by Chiefs of Staffs, 13 April 1939.

white horse, but they were nervous about the political repercussions of more British troops being tucked around the Suez Canal. Iraq was difficult too; so too was Iran; so obviously was Palestine. But much more serious was the question, where all these troops were to come from. Of course they would have to come from India. In spite of the constitutional folderols of the nineteen-twenties the imperial crisis of the late nineteen-thirties was so terrible that the British had to cut the constitutional corners in India. By 1938 in the event of a war with Italy, India was to be billed for two Brigade Groups and four Air Squadrons to go to Egypt, one Brigade Group and two Squadrons to go to Singapore, a Brigade to Persia and a Battalion to Aden as well as a force of idefinite size to Iraq.[82] These were promissory notes. Next year in 1939 they came up for payment. By now, everything was going wrong. There was fear of an imminent war in Libya and in East Africa. The Egyptian Garrison needed to be strengthened by moving a Brigade from Palestine. But Palestine was in the middle of a rebellion. All these maddeningly intractable questions fitted into each other like Chinese boxes.

By 1939 the Chief of Staff wanted to give up these off-the-peg arrangements and to pursue a policy of self-sufficiency in the Middle East.[83] They had in mind an imperial strategic reserve. This plan demanded that troops should somehow or other be disengaged from Palestine and that more troops must be sent to Egypt from India. By 1939, then, the military commitments in India were formidable. The promissory notes issued in 1938 have already been listed. To them must be added that Force 'Heron' was summoned from India to Egypt; Force 'Wren' was scheduled to go to Burma; Force 'Emu' was on call for Singapore; and Indian artillery had to go to Kenya. Once more the Indian army was to be moved around the world in British interests. But in 1939 we are not in Curzon's time. Indeed the wheel has spun past full circle. Assuredly India could still be persuaded into providing troops, but they would not be supplied on the old terms.

But the implications behind Britain's use of the Indian army from now and until the end of the Second World War were grave. Between the

---

[82] CAB 2/7, CID Minutes, 25 March 1938.

[83] These Middle Eastern tangles meant that a colonial division had to be formed ready to deal with them. Fifteen years before, Haldane had considered Britain's growing strategic interest in the Middle East and had noted: 'since the War the Empire's most serious commitments appear to be rather in the Near and Middle East than in Western Europe; the situation in Iraq, Egypt and Persia was such that demands might be made for troops in any of these countries'. CAB 2/4, Memorandum by Haldane, 4 November 1924, CID. These troops, Haldane had then hoped might come from India. In 1939 India remained the only source.

wars, this army had lagged behind the times, held back by poverty of Government and the requirements of Indian politicians who were working the constitution. Both had called for parsimony in military affairs. Step by step the army became obsolescent. Beyond internal security its main role was seen on the North West Frontier, against Afghanistan, a fantasy worthy of Kitchener. But if the army was to take on Germans, Italians and Japanese, and in the end it took on all three of them, then it had to be purged and had to be re-equipped in a modern form. Nodding plumes and gleaming lances were no longer enough. Once the world-wide scale of British commitments in the face of international pressures had become plain, then it would have to be the Indian army which provided much of the imperial mobile reserve. That meant that this army had to be dragged out of the Old Curiosity Shop, modernized and mechanized.[84] This had political implications. The better the Indian army, the higher the costs. Who was going to pay for them? Even the obsolescent army was costing more than half the budget of the Government of India. Now the Generals wanted more; at first their plans called for another £16 million, twenty-one crores of rupees. There was small chance of raising this from Indians. Since 1937, Indian politicians were working the constitution in most of the provinces. The stability of their ministries depended upon their keeping most of the taxes they raised and giving the central government as little as possible. If the viceroy tried to raise the sums needed for rearmament, then the Congress ministries in the provinces would not stand for it. Sir James Grigg, Finance Member in India, set out the alternatives. In the first place there was a political argument: 'I cannot tax for these extra demands . . . if I raid the Sinking Fund not to give the provinces more revenue but to provide more money for less troops there will be a storm . . . such that the Congress Governments would seize the excuse for walking out . . . . India should be relieved of this new burden.' If this was not done, the 'new Constitution' in India would fail. But there was a strategic argument as well. As Grigg put it,

Now that the stategic centre of the new Empire has moved eastwards India is going to be a source of weakness unless you are prepared to help it maintain a higher standard of defence than ever before. We [India] are at the end of our

[84] In 1938 the Auchinleck Committee castigated the Indian army for 'showing a tendency to fall behind the forces of such minor states as Egypt, Iraq and Afghanistan. Judged by modern standards, the *Army in India* is relatively immobile and under-armed and unfit to take the field against land or air forces equipped with up-to-date weapons'. See S. T. Das, *Indian Military—Its History and Development* (New Delhi, 1969), p. 117, quoted in Tomlinson, 'India and the British Empire, 1935–1947', *IESHR*, XIII, no. 3, 334.

resources . . . and so what is required is that India's lot in the scheme of Empire Defence should be re-determined . . . on the basis of the U.K. bearing everything that can reasonably be accounted imperial.[85]

So this is what it came to. In the interests of imperial defence and security the Indian army was to cost more. But in the interest of Indian political security, most of the additional cost was to fall on Britain.[86] There was to be a motorized division in India. Britain would pay for it. The rest of the Indian army was to be thinned down and re-equipped.[87] The British Treasury hoped that the British taxpayer would not have to pick up the bill for this too, and it said so, but the burden was inescapable. During 1939 an expert committee, the Chatfield Committee, was suggesting that Britain should pay for over £34 million of Indian military costs.[88] Under the threat of war, the empire was being revived at last. But for the first time since the eighteenth century, it was the British taxpayer who would have to pay for it. Here, then, would be a way of testing his will for empire.

[85] PREM 1/339, Grigg to 'H. J.' Sir Horace Wilson, 16 January 1938.

[86] *Ibid.*, Government of India to Secretary, Military Department, India Office, 9 February 1938.

[87] CAB 27/653, Interim Report by Committee on Defence of India, 18 July 1938, CP 174(38), Second Report, 29 July 1938, CP 187(38).

[88] CAB 27/65A, Draft Report of sub-committee of Committee on the Defence of India, 7 June 1939, ID(38). Of course there was to be no stopping there. By an agreement between London and Delhi in 1940, the division of Indian defence expenditure was settled. India was to pay only the cost of specifically Indian defence. In 1940–41 Britain's contribution to India's defence was Rs 53 crores, while India's contribution to Indian defence was Rs 73.6 crores. But by 1941–42 Britain's contribution to India's defence was Rs 297.9 crores and India's contribution was 103.9 crores. Britain's contribution to Indian defence continued to rise. By the end of the war, Britain owed India £1000m, a sum which was soon to rise to £1500m. (See Tomlinson, *IESHR*, XIII, no. 3, Table 1, p. 350.) Certainly this was defence at bargain prices. As Sir John Simon sarcastically put it, 'India was fortunate indeed in having us behind her'. (CAB 27/653, Minutes of sixth meeting of Committee on Defence of India, 7 June 1938.)

Modern Asian Studies, **15,** 3 (1981) pp. 415–454.

Alternative to Partition:
Muslim Politics Between the Wars

AYESHA JALAL and ANIL SEAL

University of Cambridge

WHEN the British came to power in India, it was certainly not in the face of the organized resistance of Islam. Yet the British Raj came to its end among political and social convulsions in which Hindus and Muslims cut each other's throats and large populations were shunted across the new frontiers of a sub-continent, now divided into two nations on the basis of religion. Events of such magnitude have encouraged historians to seek explanations of matching significance which may account for the growth of Muslim separatism. This article is concerned with the period of the nineteen-twenties and -thirties, before the onset of the end game when the communal quarrel burst out in deadly earnest. Explicit rivalries between the communities tended to exist at two main levels, the level of organized politics at the top where Hindu and Muslim élites were rivals for influence with government and eventually for the control of government itself, and the level of mob violence in the streets. This article is concerned with organized politics at the top, although it does not deny the existence and importance of tensions at the base. Its main emphasis will be upon the provincial stage, in particular the Muslim majority province of the Punjab. In the period before 1919 the development of Muslim politics suggested that a specifically Muslim separatism orchestrated by the United Provinces had emerged upon the all-India stage. But the coming of the reforms reversed the situation of the preceding decades, and there was less incentive for Muslim politicians in the United Provinces to claim to be the spokesmen of Muslims in the nation. The article will seek to demonstrate the rise of an alternative strategy for Muslim politics which developed in the Punjab, a strategy which qualifies any notion that the rivalries of Muslims and Hindus can

The authors wish to acknowledge their debt to John Gallagher, whose unpublished paper 'From Civil Disobedience to Communalism' was the first to stress the importance of the Punjab alternative; and to David Page, whose research he supervised. Page's doctoral dissertation, 'Prelude to Partition: All India Moslem Politics, 1920–1932', 1974, is due to be published in the Oxford University South Asian Studies Series.

be simply explained as the clash between separate but homogeneous political communities.

Inevitably, the argument will be grounded upon a number of assumptions about the nature of the Muslim community and its politics. The premise that Indian society as a whole was cast into two distinct communities, let alone two nations, will not be taken for granted; nor will it assume that communalism was a fundamental organizing principle of Indian political society, and that Indian Muslims have always seen themselves as a clearly identifiable and separate community, with a distinct set of political interests of their own. Since time immemorial, a great deal of Indian political life was organized in ways which cut across community, so that political choices, particularly in the localities, were determined by solidarities and interests other than those of a specifically religious sort.[1] No doubt the role the British played in the process was important but the main purpose of this article is not to investigate the inwardness of British policy. By coming to recognize community as the organizing principle of the greatest importance, the British themselves contributed to the distortion of social fact. Whatever may have been their experience in Europe, or in the colonies of white settlement, or of Islam in other parts of the world, there was no obvious reason why these experiences were relevant to India, where the religious affiliations of the people tended to be bounded by innumerable small localities and the scramble for resources within them. The communities which the British were supposed to have divided and ruled were at least in part the invention of the rulers.

I

Surveying Muslim politics in the nineteen-twenties, Choudhry Khaliquzzaman commented:

The history . . . of Muslim India is a mass of confusion and a chapter of political benightedness. . . . To try to find any consistency, sound reasoning or logical method in Muslim politics during that period, would be utterly futile.[2]

---

[1] This is not to deny that the hold of traditional Islam was powerful, particularly at the level of popular religion. But Hindus and Muslims had frequently to co-operate with each other in the affairs of local society, and networks of patron and client, and their factions often cut across the apparent solidarities of religious affiliation. However much of it may have been susceptible at the base to the cruder appeals of religion, Indian Islam had made its accommodations with the local environment.

[2] Choudhry Khaliquzzaman, *Pathway to Pakistan* (Lahore, 1961), p. 74.

Here was a striking contrast to the record of the previous decades in which organized Muslim opinion seemed to have achieved substantial gains. In 1906 Minto accepted the claim of the organizers of the Muslim League to speak for the community as a whole, and the Morley-Minto reforms had taken the momentous step of giving separate representation to Muslims in the provincial legislative councils, not simply in accordance with their numbers but also in line with their 'political importance'. In 1916 these advantages were hammered home in the Lucknow pact between the Muslim League and the Indian National Congress, the terms of which were to have a large impact on the Montagu-Chelmsford reforms. Since 1919 the Khilafat movement had swamped the politics of the Muslim League. Religion had overwhelmed politics, and the alliance of priest and politician had smashed the moderate line of the League and had given Gandhi support which was powerful, and possibly crucial, in his bid for leadership over the Congress at Calcutta in September 1920. During the non-cooperation, the Khilafatists, spurred on by the ulema, were in the van and until 1923 their influence continued to grow.[3] But once Gandhi called off non-cooperation and the Treaty of Lausanne in July 1923 settled the fate of the Holy Places, the Khilafatists lost the main justification for their cause and a general movement inside which to place it. Everyone was now ready to cut the ulema down to size, and by the end of 1923 not only had the Khilafat movement begun to collapse, but also the alliance between priest and politician which had given the Muslims in Congress their particular leverage. With the Khilafatists now rebels without a cause, Congress Muslims in disarray, and the Muslim League moribund, the method in Muslim confusion during the nineteen-twenties is to be found not in all-India organizations, but in the manoeuvrings of Muslim politicians in the provinces.

The Montagu-Chelmsford reforms swung the political pendulum back into the provincial arena, just as their authors intended. The Government of India Act of 1919 had given the provinces a much larger measure of autonomy, legislative, administrative and financial. It divided the business of government in the provinces into reserved subjects, which continued to be controlled by the Governor and his official executives, and transferred subjects which were now run by ministers responsible to elected majorities in the Legislative Council. This was the famous principle of dyarchy, the brainchild of the Indian Study Group

---

[3] See F. C. R. Robinson, *Separatism among Indian Muslims: The Politics of the United Provinces, 1860–1923* (Cambridge, 1974), chs 8 and 9.

of the Round Table, elaborated by Lionel Curtis, adopted by Montagu and eventually incorporated into the Government of India Act. So it is in the provinces that the key to the apparent disintegration of an overall Muslim strategy can be discovered. The reforms had given politicians some power in the provinces; it gave them nothing at the centre. So all-India organizations, critically important when the new constitution was being negotiated with the Raj, were less relevant once it was a question of working the concessions. Not surprisingly, in the nineteen-twenties there were few issues of any sort to breathe life into such organizations. The debacle of non-cooperation had persuaded many Indian politicians, Muslim as well as Hindu, that Gandhi and his Muslim allies had been using the wrong instrument for the wrong programme. Instead of tightly controlled all-India parties, with agitational programmes, they would substitute looser groups which would allow the provinces to go their own way, extracting what they could from the concessions that had already been won. So not only Jinnah and his handful of Independents but also Motilal Nehru were unable to make a unified movement against the resistance of the political bosses in the provinces. For most of the nineteen-twenties, the British saw little reason to take either the Indian National Congress, and mush less the Muslim League, seriously. They had succeeded in locking politics out of the centre; and in their new constitutional arrangements, by ensuring wherever possible that no community had an unquestioned majority in the provincial councils, they took some of the sting out of communalism in organized politics at the top. To achieve ministries with working majorities, politicians in the reformed councils had to rediscover the traditional arts of wheeling and dealing, of making alliances which cut across community and learning to work with government in a more formal manner. Rooted in actual local conditions, the issues which now dominated provincial politics did not pour easily into a communal mould. Moreover, these trends altered the balance inside the embryonic Muslim community. Since the later nineteenth century Muslim politics had been dominated by men from the United Provinces. But after the 1919 reforms they had less incentive to pursue a separatist line, and they lost the solid base upon which to place it.

Since the time of the Muslim invasions, the centre of Muslim power and opulence had been in Hindustan, the great tract of territory in North India from the eastern bounds of the Punjab to the western borders of Bihar, the provinces of Agra and Oudh which came to be known as the United Provinces. Here the Muslim population was a small minority, but in some districts, the home counties of the old

Mughal empire, they were more than a third of the population.[4] Here many Muslims lived in towns; and the higher orders, the *ashraf*, were a much larger proportion of the Muslim population than in other parts of India. In upper India, much of the old order had survived the vicissitudes of British rule, and not only did Muslims continue to have a large share of government posts but many of the big landowners in the region were Muslims.[5] Despite their successful propaganda to the contrary, Muslims enjoyed a solid educational base both in the old learning and in the new secular instruction. But these notables of north India belonged to an élite which by tradition was not exclusively Muslim. In the heartland of the Muslim dynasties, the Faithful lived among a sea of unbelievers, who were not to be converted by persuasion or by the sword. Accordingly, their systems of rule had to be tempered to fit the necessities of peoples beyond the range of Muslim doctrine, whether at the summit of society or at its base. The ruling groups around the courts of northern India embraced a striking medley of peoples, Muslim as well as Hindu, for the most part more committed to their own fortunes than to the integrity of their creeds. Muslim rule had always depended critically upon the collaboration of Hindu service groups ready to work for any government. From these accommodations, there emerged an Urdu-speaking élite with its famous syncretic culture, neither wholly Muslim nor Hindu, but a creative combination of influences from both, confined to the happy few, recruited from several communities, floating upon society like an oilslick upon the water, but destined to be broken in modern times by the waves of populism from below.[6] In the later nineteenth century, it was still the case that the most impressive unities in upper India were not those which flowed along the lines of religion but those which cut across them, the unity of men of whatever religious persuasion who saw themselves as the leaders of society and the guardians of its traditions.

Yet once the British had elevated the category of Muslims into a factor which was bound to influence the distribution of its patronage and favour, it was natural enough that those members of this Urdu-speaking élite, who happened to be Muslims, could see advantages in stepping forward as representatives of the communal interests which the British

[4] *Ibid.*, pp. 11–15; in 1921 there were 6,481,032 Muslims in the U.P. in a total population of more than 45 millions, or 14.28 per cent, *Census of India, 1921*, Pt II (Calcutta, 1923), pp. 40–3.

[5] See Robinson, *Separatism among Indian Muslims*, pp. 15–23.

[6] This is not to deny that the hold of traditional Islam was strong, particularly at the level of popular religion, among men of a lesser sort, the artisans of the townships of northern India.

believed to exist.[7] But there were also tactical advantages for the Raj to be derived from this development. By the later nineteenth century, when the most vocal critics of the Raj were literate Hindus from the maritime Presidencies, the Guardians found it convenient to counter their claims by pointing to the loyal Muslims of northern India and the well-advertised decision of Syed Ahmed Khan and his Aligarh coterie to break away from the Indian National Congress. In 1906 when Minto listened to the Muslim delegation, he was in fact accepting the dubious claims of a small group of Muslim notables, mainly from the United Provinces, to speak for the community throughout India. It was these Muslim leaders who gained most from separate representation and weightage in the provincial councils which the Morley-Minto reforms gave them. They consolidated these advantages in their localities by negotiating favourable terms in the U.P. Municipal Act; and the Lucknow Pact, concluded in 1916 between the Muslim League and the Congress, was unashamedly pitched in the interest of U.P. Muslims.[8] In all these measures, the men purporting to speak for Muslims throughout India, including the large communities in Bengal and the Punjab, designed their programme specifically to the advantage of the Muslim members of the Urdu-speaking élite of north India.

Yet even in the United Provinces themselves, which dominated Muslim affairs until the nineteen-twenties, there was no recognizably separate, and certainly no solid, political community of Muslims. Paradoxically, the genuine communal awareness which existed in the less rarified levels of ward and mohalla, was not faithfully reflected at the top. Quarrels over the killing of cows and music before the mosque, battles for the control of lesser neighbourhoods and resistance to militant Hindu revivalism, all suggest the importance of religious issues at these lower levels. As the Cawnpore mosque incident and the Khilafat agitation showed, a formidable religious frenzy could be unleashed, whether to protest against the demolition of a lavatory attached to a mosque or to rise in defence of the Holy Places of Islam. But inevitably, communalism at the base tended to throw effective control of the neighbourhood into

[7] Treating religious communities as separate political interests followed naturally from the British view of the Indian past. When the passion for social enumeration was exported to India, the censuses came to lump together, into artifically broad categories, people who often had next to nothing in common. But once the category of being a Muslim (or indeed any other category such as a landlord) had been raised to importance in the distribution of government favour and patronage, it was natural enough for men to step forward to claim to represent the interests the British believed to exist.

[8] See F. C. R. Robinson, 'Municipal Government and Muslim Separatism in the United Provinces 1883 to 1916', in John Gallagher, Gordon Johnson and Anil Seal (eds), *Locality, Province and Nation* (Cambridge, 1973), pp. 69–121.

the hands of rather more uncompromising men of religion, their opportunist political allies and footloose agitators. So far from welcoming these intrusions of populist religion into politics, most Muslim notables, just as many of their Hindu counterparts, actively deplored them, because these strident communal passions undermined their fragile hold over their rank and file, as well as endangered the cross-communal understandings in day-to-day matters which were the necessary complement to their separatist and mendicant stance towards their rulers. However much the U.P. Muslim leadership may have had to pretend to be heart-broken about the fate of the Khalifa, this specifically religious agitation led by alims and freebooting opportunists had undermined its expedient separatism and, by one of those quirks of Indian history, had put the Mahatma into the saddle of the Indian National Congress. In the circumstances of the United Provinces, communalism was a high card in the safe game the Muslim members of the élite played with their rulers in government house and council chamber, but was a wild card when placed on the mat in the dangerous realities of the base.

After the Montagu-Chelmsford reforms had come into effect, U.P. Muslim politicians had reason to alter their tactics which had stressed an apparently separatist line. In the United Provinces the reforms had given the vote to a broad range of substantial rural interests and had tilted the political balance back towards the countryside. The urban politician received much less than he had asked for. Under the new constitution, twenty-five out of twenty-nine Muslim members were returned by rural electorates, and, much as had been expected, the voters tended to choose the big landowners, the zamindars and talukdars who had been wooed by British policy ever since the Mutiny.[9]

In the United Provinces, land tended to be held by large holders.[10] In Oudh the great barons, with their huge incomes and control over the tenantry, were both Hindu and Muslim, and their common interests cut across communal divisions.[11] So Muslim landlords now had good reason

---

[9] Muslim landlords, men such as Kunwar Jamshed Ali Khan, the Nawabs of Baghpat, and of Chhatari, Khan Bahadur Kunwar Inayat Ali Khan, Fazlur Rahman Khan, and from the Eastern Divisions and Oudh, Talukdars, such as Nawab Mohamed Yusuf and the Rajas of Salempur and Pirpur and Jehangirabad were elected throughout the twenties and early thirties. See Page, 'Prelude to Partition', unpublished Oxford D.Phil dissertation, 1974, pp. 8–10.

[10] In Oudh, for example, there were only about 268 Talukdari estates, but they covered two-thirds of the area of Oudh, and paid about one-sixth of the total revenue of the United Provinces, i.e., more than a crore or ten million rupees.

[11] See Report of the Indian Statutory Commission, Vol. 1, Survey (London, 1930), p. 64, The Zamindars of Agra were less well organized, and there were fewer Muslims among their ranks, but they too began to organize, specifically as landlords, and since 1914 they had

to stress their landlord interests and to underplay their specifically Muslim status in the council and in their dealings with the Government. Their Agriculturist Party, which was in a majority, formed the ministries. But the Government, troubled by the agrarian disturbances in these provinces through the nineteen-twenties decided to try to do something for the protected tenantry, particularly in Oudh.[12] The result was the Oudh Rent Bill, the Agra Tenancy Bill and the District Boards Bill, all of which threatened landlord interests. Hindu and Muslim landlords alike were anxious to join together to protect their privileges. Consequently, many who had been specifically Muslim politicians during the first two decades of the century became landlord politicians in the third, sometimes with remarkable consequences.[13] Indeed, there was only one occasion when Muslim landlords voted as a communal bloc in the early nineteen-twenties. Since their community was a minority in the United Provinces, Muslim landlords had little hope of achieving power in the reformed council as leaders of a specifically communal party. To gain office, as they successfully did in this period, they had to ally with Hindu landed interests and this meant playing down their communal affiliations. This they successfully managed to do throughout the period.[14] But the conditions for doing well in the province disqualified the Muslim politician from the U.P. from claiming, as in the past he had sometimes done, the leadership of Muslims in India as a whole. The coming of the reforms in the nineteen-twenties had reversed the situation of the preceding decade.[15] In the changed circumstances of the nineteen-twenties, such spokesmen as

an Agra Zamindars' Association, with headquarters in Allahabad. But Peter Musgrave's work suggests that historians need to be as critically alert about the category of 'landlords' in discussing U.P. politics as they are beginning to be about the category of Muslims.

[12] See G. Pandey, *The Ascendancy of the Congress in the Uttar Pradesh, 1926–34* (Delhi, 1978) ch. 2, for a general survey of conditions in the U.P.

[13] During non-cooperation, the Raja of Mahmudabad as Home Member had the job of jailing many of his former Young Party associates. Jehangirabad helped Government to rally opposition to Abdul Bari, his wife's spiritual leader or pir. Many Muslim magnates in the U.P. threw their weight behind the Aman Sabhas or security leagues to combat non-cooperation; and many of the big landlords devoted themselves to organizing a landlord's lobby.

[14] So Chhatari became a minister from 1923; was Home Member in 1926 and in fact acted as Governor of the Province in 1928. Another leading Muslim landlord, Nawab Yusuf was a minister without a break from 1926 until the election of 1937. See Page, 'Prelude to Partition', p. 12, fn. 1.

[15] In the latter nineteen-thirties Jinnah and the Muslim League attempted, by other means, to return to the position that had existed before the reforms of 1919, when U.P. Muslims had successfully pretended to speak for Muslims in India as a whole. Jinnah's strategy between 1939 and 1947 will be studied in Ayesha Jalal's forthcoming work.

there were for Muslim interests had to come from provinces where politicians did not need to play down their communal stance to such an extent. Naturally this swung the emphasis away from the United Provinces to the Muslim majority provinces, particularly to the Punjab.

The Punjab, the other great base of Muslim populations in India, had never been a centre of Muslim imperial rule or civilization in the same way as the Muslim heartlands of upper India. In the districts west of Lahore where the Muslims were more than three-quarters of the population, the pattern was quite different from the centres of Muslim imperial power. Since the time of the Ghaznavids, Muslim settlement in the west had come from migration of Muslims from outside India, whether Turkish Afghans, Iranians, Arab fugitives from the Mongols, or the Afghans themselves who entered this frontier zone during its chequered past. These patterns of settlement and rule were in marked contrast to the central and eastern districts of the Punjab, which had been tenuously held as outposts of the Delhi Sultanate and more strongly controlled in Akbar and Jahangir's time, and which more closely resembled the western districts of the United Provinces.[16] Hence there were more Muslims in the towns and they had a less massive presence in the rural localities than in the western Punjab.

In the fluid conditions of this marcher region, no single religion, whether Islam, Hinduism or the militant syncretic creed of the Sikhs, had been able to impress its unchallenged stamp. Yet in the Punjab as a whole the position of the Muslim notables had stood up well against the pressures not only of the kingdom of Ranjit Singh but also of the British annexation. Its rural notables, especially powerful in the western districts, had prospered from the British connection. So, too, in their way did Muslims of the lower sort, whether by farming or joining the British Indian Army with the same enthusiasm as they had responded to the call to arms from Ranjit Singh, that Sikh leader with a popular touch. For the most part Punjab Muslims were not urban men, and the province as a whole was not noted for its letters. It was slow to come under the influence of western education, and according to the powerful tradition of the Punjab School of Administration, character, not erudition, was required of its notables, as was appropriate in the land of Ranjit Singh who ruled it without knowing how to read or write. Anxious to keep this province as a powerful buffer against threats from the north-west, British policy sought to insulate the Punjab from some of

[16] Under these Mughal emperors, Lahore for a time was the capital of the empire and the base from which the Mughal armies looked towards central Asia. See P. Hardy, *The Muslims of British India* (Cambridge, 1972), p. 4.

the centralizing and unifying trends of Victorian India. After its annexation, not only did the Punjab escape many of the uniformities of the Regulation Provinces, it also benefited from the self-denying ordinance, by which the British kept the pitch of the taxation low in a province, to begin with a poor cousin but later the beneficiary of a growing market for its agricultural produce.

There were three main communities in the Punjab,[17] but they had little tradition of internal unity, even in relation to their rivals. Rather, the Punjab had for long been marked by a powerful tradition of local particularism which inevitably cut across the grain of communal solidarity. Even in the supposed Sikh nation, devoted to Guru Nanak and the Khalsa, Ranjit Singh had smacked down rival Sikh chieftains, disciplined the Akalis and come to terms with some Muslims as well as Hindus, who not only helped him rule his kingdom, but also afforded the Sikh contingents in the army which was the foundation of his power. Just as there was no Sikh nation, so also it would be anachronistic to suppose that before the British annexation the Punjab had developed a nationalism based upon a territorial principle. In fact, Ranjit Singh's kingdom was built around the army, and the army was built around small platoons, or *deras*, recruited from separate villages and led by local bosses or *deradars*.[18] None of this suggests that the factions at the apex of Punjab society, or the British after them, had to face in the Punjab a polity characterized either by the principle of territorial nationality which cut across its three communities, or, conversely, by the rivalries of these embattled communities whose differences they sought to exploit to their own advantage. What distinguished the Punjab was the atomized and localized nature of its political concerns, a tradition insulated in the nineteenth century from the interventions of Calcutta, and one which in great measure survived and prospered into the twentieth century. Not surprisingly, the debates about Indian Muslims and the right political strategy for them in the later nineteenth century and the early twentieth century, took hardly any account of the province which was to assert itself between the two world wars, and was to be the main victim of the partition of India.

In the Punjab, the Montagu-Chelmsford reforms of 1919 had been

[17] In 1921, Punjab's 20.6 million people were divided into 11.4 million Muslims, 6.5 million Hindus, 2.3 million Sikhs, *Census of India, 1921*, Pt I, Vol. II, pp. 40–3.

[18] Indeed it was the failure of Ranjit Singh's successors in the Lahore Durbar to keep control over an army, popularly recruited, democratically run, and powerfully rooted in the rural localities, which was the main reason why the British reluctantly were forced to fight and beat this army and to annex the Punjab—at least in part at the invitation of its notables.

consciously used by the Government to call in the old world to redress the balance of the new, to shift the political centre of gravity away from the towns back to the rural areas, especially to those districts of the western Punjab where Muslims happened to be in a strong majority and where Muslims owned many of the larger estates. Urban politicians from Lahore, Jullundur and Ambala, who had begun to be a thorn in the side of an administration which, in the Punjab tradition, preferred rural simplicity, were given only four seats on the reformed council. Twenty-nine seats went to the rural areas and of these twenty-three were in the Muslim-majority districts, west of Lahore. The Punjab tradition had been to rely upon the landed interest; the British Army recruited many of its troops, whether Punjab-Muslims, Jats or Sikhs, from the countryside. So the 1919 reforms were unashamedly pitched against the urban politician and in favour of the rural vote.[19] At the same time, urban qualifications were pitched high and men from the towns had to prove a residence of four years in a rural constituency before being admitted to stand for election there. Those who did well out of the reforms were landlords and the agriculturalists; and this meant the dominance of the Rawalpindi–Multan tracts, where Muslims were most powerful. The result was that politics in the reformed councils of the Punjab tended now to divide along the lines of interest, not simply those of community. Urban interests, whether Muslim or Hindu were left in the cold, and the Sikh and Hindu Jat landed interests, represented by the Punjab Zamindar Central Association, found common ground with the big landed interests represented by the Punjab Muslim Association. so Hindu Jats from the Ambala Division[20] co-operated closely with Muslim zamindars.[21]

The architect and leader of this agriculturalist interest, which came to be known as the Punjab National Unionist Party, was a Muslim politician, Fazl-i-Husain, whose urban and rather humble origins and record

[19] Those who paid Rs 25 or more land revenue had been enfranchised and so also were the officially appointed *Lambardars* which added some 58,000 to the Punjab rural vote; the veteran sepoy, that most loyal of collaborators, was also given the vote and this added another 160,000 to the electorate.

[20] Men such as Chaudhuri Lal Chand who was Minister of Agriculture in 1924, and Chaudhuri Chothu Ram who replaced him in the post.

[21] Men such as Umar Hayat Khan Tiwana whose son was to become prime minister of the Punjab in 1942; Feroz Khan Noon, who was educated at Wadham, later married a young Australian, and was successively minister for local self-government in 1927, for education in 1931, Indian high commissioner in London in 1936, and chief minister for the Punjab after Partition in 1953, and Sikander Hayat Khan, revenue member in 1929, acting governor in 1932 and the first premier of a self-governing Punjab in 1937. This survey of Punjab after the 1919 Act is based on Page, 'Prelude to Partition', ch. I.

of sympathy with the Congress made him an unlikely person for this role. Yet urban Muslim politicians, whether they belonged to Husain's breakaway Muslim League or to Mahomed Shafi's branch, had no political future in the Punjab after the reforms, except as spokesmen for the dominant agriculturalist interest. Fazl-i-Husain seized on the chance of becoming a minister in 1921 to consolidate his personal position. He became the leader of the Muslim bloc and managed to get himself re-appointed as minister for education and local self-government in 1924. The legislation he introduced, which cut down the official control of district and municipal boards, was in line with what the Jat Zamindar Association had demanded. When he told the Punjab council in March 1923 that he stood for 'the principle of helping the backward community, irrespective of their religion, be they Muslim, Hindu or Sikh,[22] he may have exaggerated the backwardness of the community he was supporting but it was not mere propaganda. Fazl-i-Husain was able to point to the introduction of compulsory primary education and the building of schools and dispensaries in rural areas as evidence of his supra-communal record. But since the Muslims were the majority in the Punjab, and had most of the votes, it made good political sense for the Unionists to find ways of consolidating their support. This they did by giving them a protected quota in the educational and medical services, where they had few jobs, but by leaving alone the police where they already had most of the places. Also the terms of the Municipal Amendment Act of 1923 were tilted to Muslim advantage.[23] In the last resort there was merit in the Statutory commission's argument that 'The most striking feature of the [Punjab] Council remains ... its deep communal cleavages'.[24] In the nineteen-twenties, the Unionist Party must be seen not merely as a successful party of agriculturalists in the Punjab, but also as the single most powerful Muslim constitutional party in British India.

In Bengal, the other main Muslim-majority province, the situation was in stark contrast to that of the Punjab. In some ways, it was a mirror of the United Provinces, with the Hindus of Bengal in the dominant position of the Muslims in northern India. Here, most of the Muslims were poor peasants; nearly all of them were descended from converts,

[22] *Punjab Legislative Council Debates*, IV, 15 March 1923, p. 1318, quoted in Page, 'Prelude to Partition', p. 43.
[23] When Fazl-i-Husain's policies were censured in council in 1923 the vote split, uncharacteristically, on communal lines, with Muslims and officials supporting Fazl-i-Husain, and the Hindu Jats who usually worked with him joining the Hindu and Sikh members in voting against him. see Page, 'Prelude to Partition', pp. 46–7.
[24] *Statutory Commission, Vol. I, Survey*, p. 208.

contemptuously dismissed as 'little better than a mongrel breed of circumcised low-caste Hindus'. The educated Muslims, belonging to the élite, had always been a mere handful in Bengal, where most of the land and jobs in government or the professions were increasingly held by the Hindu *bhadralok*. In Bengal, as in no other part of India, it can fairly be asserted that the Muslims as a whole were a backward community. But they had always been so.[25]

In 1911, the reversal of the 1905 partition of Bengal had kept together in one province regions and peoples whose interests were hard to reconcile. In the east, Muslims were a majority; in the west, Hindus. Overall the Muslims had a bare but clear preponderance upon numbers, but in both east and west the socially dominant were Hindus. But of course the Muslims of Bengal were in no sense a homogeneous community; the interests of a handful of influential Muslim zamindars in the east were diametrically opposed to those of the mass of their Muslim tenantry; and the interests of the small number of Muslim-educated in Calcutta were not the same as those of either group. Yet in Bengal, the Montagu-Chelmsford reforms were less an insurance policy for the dominant than an invitation to the aggrieved to challenge that dominance. Before 1919, there had been only five Muslims among the twenty-eight elected members of the Legislative Council, chosen by a mere 6,346 voters. After 1919 Muslims had thirty-nine out of eighty-five territorial constituencies. Thirty-three of these seats were for rural areas, mainly in the eastern districts of Bengal. Of the million and a quarter new voters in the provinces, more than four hundred thousand were in the Muslim rural constituencies. Having forty-five per cent of the territorial constituencies, the Muslims of Bengal now had the means, if they were minded to deploy them, to promote their interests in the districts.[26] But the Muslim members of the council, described by one historian as clumsy, naive and self-seeking'[27] and as they themselves admitted, torn by 'personal jealousies and rivalries [which] bulk largely in Bengal Moslem Society',[28] were easily split by the leaders of the Bengal Congress.

Yet Chittaranjan Das, 'the most brilliant opportunist in Indian

[25] It was an error for W. W. Hunter to argue in his account of *The Indian Musalmans* of 1871 that Muslim backwardness was a consequence of British rule, and that the condition of the Bengali Muslims applied equally to Muslims in other parts of India.

[26] John Gallagher, 'Congress in Decline', *Locality, Province and Nation*, p. 280.

[27] *Ibid.*

[28] *Central National Mahommedan Association, Octennial Report, 1917–1924*, p. 61, quoted in J. H. Broomfield, *Elite Conflict in a Plural Society: Twentieth-century Bengal* (Berkeley and Los Angeles, 1968), p. 255.

politics, virtuoso of agitation, broker between irreconcilables, gambler for glittering stakes',[29] saw that the future of the Bengal Congress, of the Bengal Hindu *bhadralok* and indeed of Bengal itself, depended critically on the success with which the divisions among the Muslims of Bengal could be exploited and on the support that could be won from some of them. So Das offered them a deal, and showed that he was ready to pay a high price to get it.[30] Here was a breathtakingly audacious piece of opportunism. It was not the last chance of the old system but proof rather that the days of the old system were numbered. Das' alliance with the Muslims, with its high promise of arresting the decline of Congress in Bengal, and preventing the growth of communal politics, which in the end was bound to break the pre-eminence of the Bengali Hindus in their undivided province, was inherently unstable. Many of his Hindu supporters short-sightedly felt that Das had paid too high a price for this vital Muslim alliance. To attract Muslim support, he was giving away jobs which his Hindu constituents presently occupied, and to keep that support he would have had to make concessions to pressures for tenancy legislation which would have been regarded by his Hindu supporters in the east Bengal districts as anathema. There were problems also of reconciling the interests of the Swarajya Party as a legislative group with its interests as spokesmen for the districts, or the interest of Hindus in eastern Bengal who did not relish the prospect of becoming a permanent minority with the interests of Muslims, not to mention the problem of reconciling the interests of Bengal with those of all-India. Congressmen in other provinces were not prepared to give all-India's blessing to a Pact which made sense for the Bengal Hindus, but little sense for those in Hindu majority provinces.

So it is not surprising that this effort at a communal accord which seemed to have revived an alliance between the communities, did not long survive C. R. Das' death. In a combined operation, Government and a number of wily Muslim politicians, notably Sir Abdur Rahim,

[29] Gallagher, 'Congress in Decline', *Locality, Province and Nation*, p. 275.

[30] According to the agreement, known as the Bengal Pact, Muslims would be represented in the legislative council; they would keep their separate electorates and get representation in line with their population, which was more than the Lucknow Pact had given them. Muslims had less than a third of the appointments in the public services. So Das promised them that when Congress ruled Bengal they would get more than half—fifty-five per cent—of the jobs and up to eighty per cent until they had reached that level. In local bodies, Muslims would get sixty per cent of the seats, they would be allowed to kill cows, and they would not have to put up with Hindus playing music outside their mosques. The Bengal Pact of 1923 won Das and his Swarajists twenty-one Muslim seats when they entered the second council, enough reinforcements to make dyarchy unworkable.

began to build up a communal Muslim party in time for the 1926 elections. Relations between Hindus and Muslims rapidly deteriorated, with the impetus coming from politicians at the top, and the fire and the fury from below. In any event the result was the collapse of the alliance between Muslim factions and the Swarajists, who did not even bother to put up Muslim candidates in the 1926 elections. All the thirty-nine Muslims except one were returned on communal tickets, pledged now to work in the communal interest. From January 1927 until December 1936 there were six ministries in Bengal, all led by Muslims, and all dependent on the Muslim vote, supported by Europeans and the nominated official members. Politicians in Bengal now were taking office and holding it by a double policy of stressing their Muslim affiliations and at the same time of setting up as the defenders of peasant rights, both Muslim and lower-caste Hindu, against landlords.[31] The lines of communal division in Bengal were now being drawn over divisions by class. In the U.P. and in the Punjab the old social order had been bolstered by the Muslims who took charge; in Bengal it was being challenged and changed. This was one factor which militated against an alliance between the politicians of Bengal and their counterparts in the U.P. and the Punjab, whether at this time or later on when an all-Muslim strategy became more urgent.

So in the nineteen-twenties there was no longer any all-India party whose leaders could define Muslim demands at a national level. Under Gandhi's prompting, the Congress clung to the view that it was a party of the Hindus and Muslims alike and it exaggerated both the greatness and the goodness of the few surviving Muslims in the Congress ranks although by this time, after the failure of non-cooperation and the collapse of the Khilafat, they represented no Muslims but themselves. As for the Muslim League, it seemed now at death's door. Jinnah, that ambassador of Hindu–Muslim unity, that nationalist anxious to win a say at the centre by constitutional means, tried to resuscitate the League in 1923 when Nehru and Das plumped for council entry, but his non-cooperating enemies blocked his efforts. Jinnah's only base was now in the central legislative council, as the leader of a small body of Independents who, after 1923, held the balance between the Govern-

---

[31] In its turn the Swarajist Party in Bengal not only took on a more Hindu but also a more aristocratic, high caste, zamindari colouring: big zamindars now rallied in force to the Congress to meet the threat of an amendment of the Bengal Tenancy Act which would have given occupancy rights to their tenants. In contrast the Muslim ministries forced through a Rural Primary Education Bill in 1930; they brought in communal reservation of seats on local bodies and introduced legislation to relieve peasant indebtedness.

ment and the Swarajists. But the Independents were in no sense a Muslim party, since only three of its members happened to be Muslims. In 1924 Jinnah again attempted to revive the League but the resolutions passed at the 1924 session show where Muslim leadership had now come to lie. Under the overweening influence of the Punjabi Muslims, the League resolved that India's future lay with a federal form of government, in which the centre's function would be restricted 'to such matters as are of general or common concern'; it also resolved to protect the Muslim majorities in the Punjab, in Bengal and in the Frontier Province, demanding that neither territorial adjustment nor representation for minorities in these provinces should be allowed to affect them. This was the Punjabi view of Muslim interests with a vengeance. With no all-India Muslim party to act as a counter, the politicians of the Muslim majority-provinces could now step forward. Since the Muslim masses of Bengal were no more organized than they were advanced, and their politicians no more irreplaceable than they were incorruptible, in practice the leadership fell to the Muslims of the Punjab who inspired a ministry which ruled continuously and successfully at Lahore throughout the nineteen-twenties in contrast to most of the gimcrack experiments in dyarchy which were going on in British India throughout that decade.

II

In November 1927, the Simon commission was appointed to look into the workings of the reforms. The prospect of further reforms swung the pendulum of Muslim politics away from the provinces, where they had been firmly placed during the nineteen-twenties, and back to the centre. By the later nineteen-twenties it was clear that whatever Lord Birkenhead and the Old India Hands might proclaim, constitutional change was on its way. By announcing that the constitution would be reviewed, at a stroke Birkenhead had jerked up the carpet under which the all-India questions had so conveniently been swept since dyarchy had begun. Intended by the Conservatives as a pre-emptive strike against more radical reform by its Labour successors, the Statutory Commission inevitably raised the very aspirations and fears which it had hoped to damp down, by bringing the prospect of full provincial self-government closer. When it reported in 1930, the Simon Commission spoke of

the anxieties and ambitions aroused in both communities by the prospect of India's political future. So long as authority was firmly established in British hands, and self-government was not thought of, Hindu–Moslem rivalry was confined within a narrower field. . . . But the coming of the Reforms and the anticipation of what may follow them have given new point to Hindu–Moslem competition.[32]

London was ready to give more responsible government to the provinces, while hanging on to the vital attributes of sovereignty at the centre. But the biggest stumbling block to constitutional advance, whether in the provinces or the centre, seemed to be the communal problem. So it became urgent again for politicians of all colours, Hindu and Muslim alike, to think of coming to terms at a national level. But the fate of Jinnah's efforts to unite Muslims behind a League and then to negotiate with the Congress, as well as the fate of the All-Parties Conference and of the Nehru Report, show how intractable the communal problem had become in all-India terms.[33] In particular, they show how the interests of the Muslim majority provinces, and of the Punjab in particular, worked against Muslims coming to terms with the Congress at an all-India level.

As soon as the Simon Commission had been set up, Jinnah set to work to produce a united national front. Earlier in March 1927 his proposals had shown the lines of his strategy. In return for the creation of a separate Muslim province of Sind, raising the status of the North West Frontier Province and Baluchistan and winning representation on the basis of population for Bengal and the Punjab, as well as a guaranteed one-third of the seats in the central legislature for Muslims, Jinnah was ready to give up separate electorates, for so long the ark of the Muslim convenant. But this was clearly a strategy which appealed mainly to Muslims who had little chance of winning power in their own provinces. But Muslims with a stronger position in their own provinces soon vetoed these all-India initiatives by Jinnah. Certainly the lukewarm response from the Congress was not enough to keep his proposals alive. Once the Commission had been announced, Jinnah was given another chance but it was clear that the Punjab leaders were wholly opposed to his plans. Although Jinnah managed to secure that the League's session in 1927 be held in Calcutta (where the climate was mildly more favourable to his point of view than in Lahore) it was an unreal victory, since the Punjab Muslims held a rival League meeting of their own in December under Muhammed Shafi's presidentship, and attracted to it some of the important Muslims from the United Provinces, foreshadowing the

[32] *Report of the Indian Statutory Commission, Vol. I, Survey*, p. 29.
[33] See Mushirul Hasan, *Nationalism and Communal Politics in India, 1916–1928* (New Delhi, 1979), ch. 8.

powerful alliance which was to emerge as the All-India Muslim Conference.

This initiative by Muslims of the Punjab showed that they were already beginning to hammer out a distinctive strategy of their own for the coming reforms. As Sir Malcolm Hailey, who knew his Punjab well, wrote in December 1927, the Punjab Muslims

see that they can never quite the same interest as the Moslems in the provinces with large Hindu majorities and they seriously think of breaking away from the All India Moslem League and starting a Federation of their own. This will seek to embrace the Punjab, part of the U.P., the North West Frontier, Baluchistan and Sind, . . .[34]

Interestingly enough, Hailey added that the Punjabi expected little from the Muslims of the other main majority province, Bengal:

. . . the dream of the future to which I had alluded does not include Bengal. For the moment, the North India Moslem has given up his co-religionist in Bengal as hopeless and seems to expect no assistance from Bengal in the cause of Islam.[35]

But all this was for the future; here and now the Punjabi Muslim saw that his best course was to stand pat on what he had and to co-operate with the government, much as the Old Punjab Hands had predicted to Irwin and Birkenhead that he would.

For another year, Jinnah tried to patch together a working Hindu–Muslim alliance on the all-India stage. But by May 1928 Jinnah had failed to persuade anyone, whether the viceroy, the Congress or Muslims who mattered, to move in his direction. With his influence rapidly and visibly collapsing, Jinnah pulled the League out of the All-Parties Conference in Delhi and retreated to London. In the end, it was the Congress which attempted to sketch out a solution. The Nehru Report of 1928 dealt with the thorny communal problem by driving a coach and horses through the difficulties, but it paid scant regard to Muslim opinion, even the opinion of the hand-picked Muslim members who joined with Nehru in producing this Report. The Report advocated a unitary government at the centre, and called for all the departments of the central Government, including defence, finance and relations with the Indian States, to be made responsible to Indian legislatures. Separate electorates, weightages for minorities, the Muslim demand for a protected status for minorities, and for a guaranteed one-third share of power at the centre were all to go. However, Sind was to be made into a

[34] Sir Malcolm Hailey to Sir Arthur Hirtzel, 15 December 1927, Hailey Papers, 118 quoted in Page, 'Prelude to Partition', p. 148.
[35] *Ibid.*

separate province, and the North West Frontier was to be given full provincial status. This was clearly unacceptable to Muslim opinion of all colours. Even that old Khilafat stalwart, Shaukat Ali, denounced it and attacked those Congress Muslims who supported the Report as Hindu stooges. But since the Report was ratified by a carefully selected All-Parties Conference, and since the Congress now nailed its colours to the Report, an accord between the Congress and Muslims became improbable. Once Muslim politicians in the provinces and Congressmen at the centre had reached this parting of the ways, the entire Jinnah strategy of pressing for Nationalist advance at the centre, backed by a large body of Muslim opinion whose interests had been duly safeguarded, collapsed. Since Jinnah possessed no solid political base of his own, his effectiveness depended upon his ability to act as a broker between Muslim interests in the provinces and the rival Congress politicians at the centre. So Jinnah now was banished into a political wilderness. His career in the nineteen-twenties shows that at every step he had been forced to bend his policies, and alter his objectives, to try to suit the dominant provincial Muslim demand; but that his efforts, even at the cost of bending over backwards, had failed to succeed.

The dominant Muslim provincial demand found its spokesman not in Jinnah, nor in the League, but in Fazl-i-Husain and the All-India Muslim Conference which he organized. By the end of the nineteen-twenties Fazl-i-Husain was no longer merely a provincial politician but had become a leader with an Indian standing. In 1929 he organized the Muslim Conference; in 1930 he was appointed a member of the viceroy's executive council and he used this position to become the informal strategist and director of Muslim policy during the great constitutional reappraisals of these years. While Congress launched civil disobedience, boycotted the councils and kept away from the First Round Table Conference, Fazl-i-Husain called upon his followers to co-operate, pushed forward the Muslim Conference to represent the Muslim interest, and worked effectively from behind the scenes on the viceroy's council for a policy which was clearly stamped with the Punjab Muslims' construct of their particular interest.

The Nehru Report had tried to win the support of Punjab Muslims for a unitary central government by offering them a secure majority on the basis of joint electorates and an adult suffrage. But whatever the attactions of this bait for some of the Punjab's urban-based Muslims, Fazl-i-Husain wrote:

The Nehru Report is nothing else but a make-belief and flashes the Indian autonomy before the applauding Swarajists, while it takes no account of the real India which lives in the provinces and has its hopes, aspirations, difficulties and troubles. What does the Imperialist in charge of the Indian Empire care how the constituent provinces with their parochial interests get on. He is after the big game. The mere trifles of duck shooting or fishing have no attraction for him.[36]

So he encouraged the Muslim Council members in the Punjab to formulate their own proposals for the next stage of political advance. The proposals built upon what the Punjab Muslims had already achieved. The distinction between urban and rural constituencies would have to remain; and so would separate electorates for Muslims. There were, no doubt, some attractions in an adult franchise for a majority community, but here and now the Muslim members were content for the franchise merely to be extended. As for joint electorates, these were dismissed for the time being as impracticable. Provincial autonomy was what they wanted; they were ready to think of responsibility at the centre only after the provinces had been given a full autonomy, and then they preferred responsibility at the centre in the form of a weak federation of autonomous provinces rather than a strong unitary centre.[37]

At each stage of the constitutional negotiations as the reforms were slowly hammered out, British proposals bore the stamp of this Punjab construct of Muslim interests. In the Simon Commission's Report, published in May 1930, the provinces were to have full responsible government. But they were not as yet to be brought under a responsible (and so probably a Congress-dominated) centre. An all-India federation of British India and the native States put the prospect of changes at the centre into the indefinite future. Fazl-i-Husain liked some of the Statutory Commission's recommendations. Provicial autonomy was good for the Muslims in the Punjab, provided there was no question of the provinces being subjected to a non-British centre, and the Commission was obviously minded to uphold British control in Delhi. The Report had doubts about setting up Sind as a separate province, and giving the somewhat unreconstructed region of the North West Frontier Province the benefit of the reforms. But most serious of all, from Fazl-i-Husain's point of view, were the Simon Commission's doubts about retaining separate representation, particularly in the Muslim majority provinces. What the Report offered Muslims was the choice between

[36] Fazl-i-Husain to Sir Malcolm Hailey, 22 September 1928, Hailey Collection, MSS. EUR. E220/23, I.O.L., and quoted in Waheed Ahmad (ed.), *Letters of Mian Fazl-i-Husain* (Lahore, 1976), p. 57 (henceforth: *Letters*).
[37] *Ibid.*, pp. 56–9.

separate electorates everywhere on a population basis or general electorates in the Punjab and in Bengal, with separate electorates and weightage in the minority provinces.

This was less than the Punjab Muslims wanted and so Fazl-i-Husain took a hand; his intervention was decisive. In the majority provinces, Muslims had reason to be satisfied with the electoral provisions as they stood. The Simon Commission's proposals would make things worse; once the officials lost their votes, Muslims would no longer have a safe preponderance in their majority provinces. So Fazl-i-Husain's response was to advise Muslims to hold firmly on to their percentages and reservations in the majority provinces of Punjab and Bengal. As he bluntly stated in August 1930, Indian Muslims 'prefer the present position and no political advance to the political advance outlined in the Simon Report'.[38] He told the viceroy that the British could count upon Muslim co-operation in the constitutional negotiations on the condition that Muslims were given secure majorities in the Punjab and Bengal, Sind was separated from the Bombay Presidency and the North West Frontier Province was elevated to the status of a Governor's province.[39]

From behind the scenes, Fazl-i-Husain in Delhi directed the Muslim delegates at the First Round Table Conference to hold tightly on to their existing constitutional safeguards. As one commentator lamented, 'The real control rests with the younger section' who were 'understood to be in close touch with the Muslim Member of the Viceroy's Council'.[40] The Conference was a strange affair; it was rather like *Hamlet* without the Prince—indeed it was *Hamlet* not only without the Prince but also without the ghost of Hamlet's father. There were no Congress spokesmen at the Conference and the officials were told by the prime minister

[38] Note by Fazl-i-Husain, enclosed in Irwin to Wedgwood Benn, 28 August 1930, Halifax Papers 6, quoted in Page, 'Prelude to Partition', p. 203.

[39] Fazl-i-Husain's influence over Irwin is shown by the tenor of the Government of India's Reform Despatch of September 1930. It conceded much more of the Punjab's demand than Simon had. It proposed to retain separate electorates and weightage for Muslims in the Hindu majority-provinces, but also to give the Bengali and Punjabi Muslims the majorities to which their population entitled them. It did not recommend outright statutory majorities, but favoured a scheme by which the Muslims would get a predominance in line with their numbers, if not an actual majority of the seats. Muslims should be encouraged to secure their majorities by winning some of the special seats allotted to such interests as labour, the universities and the landholders. Here was Delhi's attempt to rescue some of the benefits of a supra-communal stance which had worked so well in the Punjab and elsewhere during the nineteen-twenties.

[40] Note by Gilbert Laithwaite, 6 November 1931, Templewood Collection, MSS. EUR. E240/65., I.O.L. Among these 'younger section' were such men as Mian Mohammed Shafi, Shafaat Ahmad Khan, and the Aga Khan, all leading lights of the All-India Moslem Conference.

to sit as 'judges', to find the facts rather than enunciate policy. This was just as well because London at this time had no clear policy at all. In the circumstances, it is not wholly surprising that this Conference came out with a curious brainchild of its own. This was the notion that there should be a federal solution to the Indian problem. The princes have been credited with the notion—it bears all the marks of their powerful constitutional intelligence. But the idea of a federation did have some attractions from the British point of view. It gave them the chance of creating the semblance of a 'safer' form of central government which would mollify opposition in Parliament and in India. Moreover, the complications of Dominion Status could conveniently be forgotten with this new alternative before them. It also had some attractions for the Muslims. But the warmest support for the federal idea came from that group, beloved of constitutional historians and of the policy-makers, the Indian Liberals led by Sir Tej Bahadur Sapru, who saw in the federal idea a possible way of patching together an alliance with the Muslims and the princes.[41] But the Indian Liberals suffered from the minor inconvenience of representing no-one but themselves. Impressed by their sincerity (and their elegant constitutional patter) some of the Muslim delegates, the Aga Khan, Jinnah and Muhammed Shafi among them, agreed in November 1930 at least to consider the federal idea and leave the question of safeguards for their community until later. Here were shades of the standard nationalist line which was 'First settle swaraj, then settle the communal issue'. But for the communities, the Indian minorities, and the Muslims in particular, the correct strategy was quite different. If they were to become citizens of self-governing provinces, then it was obviously prudent to get guarantees of fair treatment from the majority before the constitutional bargain was signed, sealed and delivered. Therefore, according to the Muslim Conference, the priorities have to be the other way round: 'First settle the communal issue, then settle swaraj'. So Fazl-i-Husain brought his dogs to heel, back to the narrow path of the Conference's established policy. He directed the Muslim delegates at the Round Table Conference to hold firm:

Now what is it the Labour people [*sc.* the Second MacDonald Government] offer? 'We give you responsibility at the Centre if you settle your communal

---

[41] The Hindu Mahasabha and the 'tyrannical method' of the Congress during the civil disobedience movement had led Sapru to doubt whether there was any 'true Nationalism in India', and whether India was ready yet 'for the rule of numbers'. Sapru to Iswar Saran, 12 November 1930, Sapru Collection, I, S.18, quoted in R. J. Moore, *The Crisis of Indian Unity 1917–1940* (Oxford, 1974), p. 146.

disputes'. Now who will benefit more by responsibility being introduced at the Centre at this stage? Undoubtedly the Hindus. Therefore who should be anxious to settle communal differences in order to secure the promised gain? Naturally the Hindus. Then why should Muslims, who are politically, educationally and economically weaker in the country, pretend that by ousting the British power from India and by introducing responsibility they stand to gain so much that, for it, they are prepared to sacrifice communal interests.[42]

The message from their leader was clear. The delegates were to stick to the communal safeguards and to leave the initiative at the centre to others. After all, the Simon Commission, the governors and the Government of India had all agreed on separate electorates for Muslims as well as the amount of Muslim representation both in the central legislature and in six provinces other than Punjab and Bengal. Agreement was now needed only on the critical question of Muslim representation in the Punjab and Bengal and even here promising signs could be read in the Government of India's despatch of September 1930 which came out in favour of giving the Muslims in both the Punjab and Bengal a majority representation of not less than 51 per cent.[43] What lay behind this were Fazl-i-Husain's largely successful efforts inside the executive council to improve the Muslim position, mainly by securing the interests of the Muslim majority provinces, first by pressing for as much provincial autonomy as was compatible with retaining firm Muslim control, and secondly for a central government with as little power over the provinces as possible. Significantly, the only real bone of contention between the rulers of India and the Punjab Muslims was the future relationship between centre and provinces.

Indeed, by the end of the First Round Table Conference, Fazl-i-Husain had reason to be satisfied with the results. His views had prevailed. The Muslim delegates had decided not to co-operate with any move towards responsibility at the centre until their safeguards had been assured. Indeed, the Round Table Conference itself had begun to move away from the traditional commitment to a strong unitary centre for British India, the big prize for which the Congress was playing. Instead there was talk of a federation, with two chambers, in which provinces and princes would have a say. This was much closer to what the Muslim majority provinces wanted; their aim in the long term was to get away from a strong unitary centre. Their strategy was to consolidate their position in the majority provinces and then, perhaps voluntarily,

[42] Fazl-i-Husain to Shafaat Ahmad Khan, 22 December 1930, Fazl-i-Husain Papers (Shafaat File). The authors wish to acknowledge the courtesy of Mr Azim Husain who gave access to these papers. Also quoted in *Letters*, p. 116.
[43] See note 39.

enter into a more equal partnership with the Hindu majority provinces in a loose federation. In preparation for the next round of negotiations, the All-India Muslim Conference which met in April 1931 worked out its strategy along these lines: it decided to press for the fullest autonomy of the constituent units of the federation. The provinces were to be given all the residuary powers, and they were to be on an equal footing with other units in the federation, the Indian States. No subject should be given to the federal centre without the prior consent of all the federating units. And as a further safeguard, the provinces would have the right of secession at all times. Not only would they be able to play states rights against the centre, like the once solid South in the United States of America, but they would have the right to secede without suffering the inconvenience of a civil war. This was the provincial thesis with a vengeance, and it meant putting back the historical clock to pre-British times.

Now of course such a plan cut across the grain of British imperial interests. By devolving power to the provinces, the Montagu-Chelmsford reforms had successfully postponed for the time being the nationalist challenge at the centre. But if the provinces were to be given autonomy, and little change was made at the centre, as both the Simon Commission's Report and the Government of India's Despatch seemed to propose, then the danger was that Delhi's powers would have to fall increasingly to the provinces. As the Reforms Commissioner could see, what was at stake was not simply the question of who should control the central government in the future, but whether there should be a strong central government at all. An irresponsible centre, with no concessions made to the nationalist demand, would find it increasingly more difficult to control provinces that had been granted full responsibility, and who could claim to have a mandate from their electors. If Muslim fears were appeased by accepting their extreme demands, this inevitably would lead either to an impossibly weak federal centre, presiding over almost wholly autonomous provinces, or to a strong centre still under British control which might find it difficult to rule provinces which were dominated by politicians not as committed as the Muslim majority provinces to the British cause. This is why the British in India could not go all the way with their Muslim collaborators in backing the Punjab strategy of 'standing fast at the Centre'. This policy, later to be described by the Aga Khan, as making India 'what she really is, i.e. a United States of Southern Asia', was one where the Muslims would work the state rights of their majority provinces for all they were worth against an emasculated federal centre. This is why the British could not simply

leave the communal question in the state of satisfactory deadlock produced by the First Round Table Conference, satisfactory at least from
the Punjab Muslim point of view. This is why London pressed New
Delhi to come to terms with Gandhi. This is why a pact was made
between Irwin and Gandhi in 1931, which offered the chance of another
Round Table Conference, this time with the Congress represented. It
was this which enabled the Second Round Table Conference to come
seriously to grips with the issue of communalism.

Fazl-i-Husain and the All-India Muslim Conference may have been
the dominant Muslim voice in India at this time, but they were not the
only one. In readiness for the next, and possibly the decisive, stage in the
negotiations, all manner of strategies were being put forward in Muslim
circles. The only thing these schemes, some more colourful than others,
had in common was that they were all trying to counter the potential
threat of a permanent Hindu majority at the centre, whether unitary or
federal. Best known was the strategy of Sir Muhammed Iqbal, Fazl-i-
Husain's most vocal opponent in the Punjab.[44] Time and again in
Indian politics, men defeated on their local or provincial arenas, sought
to hoist their efforts upon a larger stage. In much the same way, the
non-Unionist Muslims in the Punjab, making no headway against the
stranglehold of the Unionists, now attacked them for their parochialism
and 'narrow-visioned sacrifice of Islamic solidarity in the interest of
what may be called "Punjab Ruralism" resulting in a proposal which
vitually reduced the Punjab Muslims to a position of minority'.[45]

In his efforts to rally Muslims from other parts of India, Iqbal called,
in his 1930 presidential address to the All-India Muslim League, for
nothing less than the creation of a Muslim India, a state in the north-
west which would consist of the Muslim majority regions of the Punjab,
Sind, the North West Frontier Province and Baluchistan. This was not
the first statement of the demand for Pakistan, or for the division of India
since the proposal was firmly placed within the context of an all-India

[44] Sir Muhammed Iqbal, the famous poet-philosopher turned politician, spoke for
the urban Punjabi Muslims who had been given short shrift under the régime of the
agricultural oligarchs of the Unionist persuasion. The All-India Muslim League, of
which he was the president, was as yet not in a position to press its own independent line.
To maintain the semblance of Muslim unity, throughout the late nineteen-twenties and
the early nineteen-thirties, the League's sole contribution to Muslim politics appears to
have been its reluctant endorsement of resolutions passed by the Muslim Conference.
However, it was already becoming the organ of those discontented with the Muslim
conference, a trend which Iqbal hoped to encourage.

[45] See Sir Muhammed Iqbal's speech at the Twenty-first Session of the All-India
Muslim League, 29 December 1930 in Jamil-ud-Din Ahmad (ed.), *Historic Documents of
the Muslim Freedom Movement* (Lahore, 1970), p. 132.

federation. Indeed, Iqbal sought to reassure not only the British but also the Hindus that the 'life of Islam as a cultural force in this country very largely depends on its centralisation in a specified territory'. He went on to argue that by bringing together into one political unit the 'living portion of the Muslims of India whose military and political service has, notwithstanding unfair treatment from the British, made the British rule possible in this country', would 'eventually solve the problem of India as well as of Asia'. Moreover, only by recognizing the requirements of communal solidarity, would a true patriotism emerge in India.[46] Once Muslims had been given the opportunity to develop 'within the body-politic of India, the North-West Indian Muslims will prove the best defenders [of] India against a foreign invasion, be that invasion one of ideas or of bayonets'.[47] So there was something in this for the Hindus. But what about the Muslims in the minority provinces? Here Iqbal maintained that Muslims in the Hindu majority provinces would be assured of fair treatment because there would be Hindu and Sikh 'hostages' in plenty in the Muslim areas, a thesis which was to have a lively future for the next seventeen years until partition exploded its credibility.[48]

Fazl-i-Husain was not impressed by this 'epidemic of confusion' in which everyone seemed to be interested in finding difficulties to every solution. By difficulties, Fazl-i-Husain of course meant challenges to his own particular strategy. Hindu and Muslim differences, he argued, had never been worse, and Gandhi was mainly to blame.[49] Yet the problem was simple enough; reiterating his particular thesis, Fazl-i-Husain maintained that the real crux of the problem was the amount of repre-

[46] *Ibid*, p. 127. Iqbal maintained that only by conceding the importance of communalism could Muslims get a proper sense of responsibility, and this would help 'deepen the patriotic feeling'.

[47] *Ibid*.

[48] Iqbal's speech tended to be ignored by the Muslim politicians, but it did inspire a student at Cambridge to coin the word 'Pakistan'. The student, Chaudhri Rahmat Ali, yet another Punjabi Muslim, sketched out a scheme for an independent Muslim State in north-western India to the Muslim delegates at the Round Table Conference. Capital 'P' for the Punjab: 'A' for Afghanistan or for those whose interest in Afghan was understandably weak, 'A' stood for the Indian Afghans, in other words the North Western Frontier Province; 'K' for Kashmir. Others thought of it as a land of the pure or the holy. The University of Cambridge in its time has produced many peculiar theoretical concepts, ranging from Cranmer's Theology of the English Reformation to the Jesus style of rowing; among its concepts is the idea of Pakistan. But not surprisingly Chaudhri Rahmat Ali, who is buried in an unmarked grave on the Newmarket Road, was brushed aside and his scheme dismissed as a 'student's scheme' which was 'chimerical' and 'impractical'.

[49] Fazl-i-Husain to Irwin, 6 July 1931, *Letters*, p. 159.

sentation for Muslims to the provincial and central legislatures. In the six minority provinces, Muslims already had an assured representation; but since the officials were to be deprived of their vote, the Muslim position was going to be weakened. As for Bengal, Fazl-i-Husain had little time for the problems of his co-religionist on the other side of India. In Bengal, European interests were so large that the balance of power must, Fazl-i-Husain conceded, remain in their hands. However keen the Bengali Muslims might be to have an overall majority, 'they might be made to reconcile themselves to the inevitable' provided they were given the lesser advantage of a majority over the at least all other Indian representatives in the legislature. But in the Punjab, which was nearer to home, Fazl-i-Husain wanted Muslim representation on the basis of their population, even if Muslims were not actually given an overall majority. By getting some of the seats in the special constituencies under joint electorates, the Punjab Muslims were bound to improve their position.[50] But time was of the essence; delay would lead to complications. So he urged government to shoot from the hip, and make an award on its own terms. 'Personally I see no difficulty why Government should not decide straight away'.[51] A government award was more likely to favour Punjabi Muslims than a settlement negotiated between the communities. And this is the way it was to be. Despite efforts by Congress Muslims to negotiate a settlement in 1931 and despite Gandhi's apparent willingness to go to some lengths to gain Muslim support, the Second Round Table Conference made no headway on the communal question.

Before the Communal Award of 1932, a number of interesting proposals were made to settle the question. From the Sikhs came the idea of dividing the Punjab. This Fazl-i-Husain immediately repudiated as 'monstrous' an ironic comment in the light of what was to happen in 1947. Another idea was to bundle the Punjab into a union with some districts of the North West Frontier Province. But since the British would never have agreed to put the clock back to the situation before 1901 when the troublesome border had been the Punjab's responsibility, Fazl-i-Husain did not have to chase this hare. A more ominous suggestion was to add Sind to the Punjab, while taking away the Ambala Division where Hindus and Sikhs were more numerous than Muslims.

[50] Even though this did not meet the full Punjab Muslim claim, and although it was likely to be condemned by other interests, this, after all, Fazl-i-Husain philosophically commented, was the 'fate of all efforts at a fair settlement'. Fazl-i-Husain to Irwin, 24 August 1931, *ibid.*, p. 185.

[51] Fazl-i-Husain to Nawab Sir Muhammed Ahmad Said Khan of Chhatari, 2 November 1931, *ibid.*, p. 199.

This suggestion, Fazl-i-Husain reluctantly conceded, had some merit, but no Punjab Muslim, whatever his colour, would be prepared to accept it. Indeed, Punjab Muslims were 'satisfied with the Punjab as it is'. If Ambala was to be taken away and Sind was to be given to the Punjab in its stead, Punjab Muslims might reluctantly put up with it, 'but they have not asked, and will not ask, for it'.[52]

But the idea of amalgamating the Punjab with Sind had several attractions. It would be, Lord Lothian, the Liberal delegate at the Round Table Conference, argued, a 'permanent solution' to the difficulty in the Punjab of keeping the Hindus and Sikhs happy at the same time as giving Punjabi Muslims a decisive majority in their province. What was more, the two provinces together made up a natural unit since their populations had much in common, their territories were traversed by the waters of the Indus, and were welded together by rail and canal. But Lothian, who was learning something about India, and about its Muslims, recognized that the 'Sindhis are jealous and afraid of the Punjabis and are attracted by the "izzat" of being an independent Province.' More importantly, Sind was bestially poor; its finances were always in deficit; the Punjab on the other hand was comparatively rich and it did not want to take on the liability of its poor cousins to the west.[53] Fazl-i-Husain rejected this solution since he denied that the union with Sind would resolve the communal problem in the Punjab, at least not to the advantage of his constituents. It was more likely to make the problem worse since 'in these days of economic depression and financial bankruptcy, one cannot afford to be generous even to a starving relation or friend'. Moreover the Sindhis were 'very touchy' on this point and would see 'some Machiavellian device on my part to make the Punjab extremely strong'; and would suspect that this was a piece of Punjab imperialism, an effort to create a new 'Muslim Empire' of the Punjab all the way from the borders of Russia to Karachi and on to Lahore.[54] As usual, Fazl-i-Husain had a cannier view of the realities of Muslim politics; the Muslims of western India, the nucleus of modern Pakistan, were hardly a nest of singing birds, or a band of brothers, wanting to live in an ecstacy of Islamic solidarity and egalitarianism.

Brushing aside these alternatives, Fazl-i-Husain returned to the scarcely veiled threat that if the British did not give their friends and allies, the Punjab Muslims, the majority they demanded 'they may rest

[52] Fazl-i-Husain to Dr Alma Latifi, 14 October 1931, *ibid.*, p. 194.
[53] Lothian to Fazl-i-Husain, 27 May 1932, *ibid.*, pp. 222–4.
[54] Fazl-i-Husain to Lord Lothian, 6 June 1932, *ibid.*, p. 226.

assured that in the political struggle that was to follow the Muslim support will not be forthcoming'.[55] By sticking to the Punjab line at the Second Round Table Conference, the Muslim delegates managed to secure a complete deadlock. Afraid of losing the support of their Muslim allies, and mindful that the Hindu moderates were rapidly losing all credibility, London decided to make its communal award.

The 1932 Communal Award, delivered by MacDonald, was every much Fazl-i-Husain's creation. It left the Muslims of the Punjab and Bengal in a strong position.[56] Not only did they receive more seats in their provincial council than any other community, but they kept their separate electorates as well. In the Punjab, the Muslims had forty-nine per cent of the reserved seats; in Bengal, forty-eight.[57] So Fazl-i-Husain's strategy to secure the dominance of the Punjab Muslims had been outstandingly successful; and he had achieved this not by negotiating with the Congress but by making the British pay the price for his support. Even the Sikhs, so important an element in the British Indian Army, and thirteen per cent of the population of the Punjab, were given only 18.3 per cent of the seats, although they had demanded between twenty-four and thirty per cent. The Secretary of State would have liked to give the Sikhs more, but it is easy to see why he could not do so. The Muslims wanted an absolute majority; they had been given one per cent short of this and would hardly have accepted any further reduction. The Hindus of the Punjab with their thirty per cent would be bitter enough. Therefore there was no room to give extra to the Sikhs. With eighty-six seats in a house of 175, and with the expectation of winning at least three seats reserved for the landholders and one labour seat, the Punjab Muslims had got their majority. With the Communal Award out of the way, the reforms which were finally to emerge as the Government of India Act 1935 promised self-government to the provinces, a pleasing prospect for the Muslims in provinces where they had hopeful majorities, in the Punjab, in Bengal, in Sind and the North West Frontier Province.

This seemed the triumphant conclusion of the Punjab strategy. In

---

[55] Fazl-i-Husain to Shafaat Ahmad Khan, 2 November 1931, *ibid.*, pp. 202–3.

[56] See *Communal Decision 1931–2* (Cmnd 4147 of 1931–2), p. 7, reproduced in B. R. Tomlinson, *The Indian National Congress and the Raj, 1929–1942, The Penultimate Phase* (London, 1976), p. 19.

[57] London had wanted to give the Bengali Muslims less than the Award actually gave them, and the Governor of Bengal had agreed. But the Viceroy had told the Secretary of State that all-India interests demanded that the majority-province Muslims, even those of Bengal, be appeased. If they were not satisfied, he feared the spectre of non-cooperation by Muslims would be added to the threat of civil disobedience by Congress.

part it had been achieved by the convenient symbiosis of interest between the British on the one hand and the Punjab leadership on the other. But of course what was a pleasing prospect for Muslims in provinces where they had hopeful majorities was a gloomier prospect for Muslims in provinces where they had hopeless minorities. So there were dangers of dissension in the Muslim ranks here. At best, Muslim political unity at an all-India level was a new and fragile development, painfully brought about by the constitutional discussions since 1929. Now that these were giving more to those provinces which had much, and less to those which had little, how was this unity to be preserved? The Aga Khan, chief Muslim spokesman in London, and architect of this unity, was haunted by the fear that the grievances of the Muslim minority provinces against the Award might now wreck the whole Bill and the shaky unity of Indian Islam.

The most striking proof that Fazl-i-Husain's real interests were not these uncertain unities among Indian Muslims, or indeed the future of the Government of India Bill, but in strengthening the position of the Unionists in their own back yard, can be seen by his manoeuvrings after the Award had been made. London had stated that it would not itself make any changes or variations in the Award; nor would it take part in any negotiations to change it; but it would accept changes in the Award agreed to by the various Indian communities themselves. Fazl-i-Husain wanted icing on his cake. Stripped of its threadbare all-India weeds, the Muslim conference revealed the nakedness of its Punjab provincialism. For the time had come, Fazl-i-Husain decided, to reassure the Hindus and Sikhs in the Punjab that the door was not closed to cross-communal agreements which had served the Unionist Party so well. If the Award was to work satisfactorily in the Punjab, without being wrecked by the opposition, not only of Fazl-i-Husain's own dissidents but, more importantly, of his traditional allies among Hindus and Sikhs, an accommodation with them had to be reached. Hindus and Sikhs were naturally incensed by the provisions of the Award. So when in 1933 some leaders of the Hindu and Sikh communities made tentative moves to come to terms with the Muslims on joint electorates, the Unionists were ready to meet them half way, and they did so with Fazl-i-Husain's blessing. Writing to Jogendra Singh the Sikh leader, Fazl-i-Husain hinted that, despite Muslim prejudice against joint electorates, he was willing to consider the notion if the Punjab Hindus and Sikhs gave it their support. In an elegant variation of a tactic that had worked so well with the British, he now told the simple Sikh, 'The Punjab Muslims are quite satisfied with the existing position and, therefore, proposals for change must emanate from Hindus and Sikhs . . . '[58] In the event, these efforts in 1933 to make a pact between the communities, a striking reversal in the Muslim Conference's policy, but clearly in the Unionist interest, came to nothing. It broke on the oppositon of urban Muslims and the Hindus and Sikhs.

But the most telling commentary on Fazl-i-Husain's provincial tactics came from the Aga Khan, who had been struggling to create a common Muslim policy to press the reforms forward. A deal in the Punjab with the Hindus and Sikhs would be flagrant departure from the 'Principles we have been fighting for in the last four years'; Muslims in the minority provinces, already aggrieved by the terms of the settlement, might now withdraw their support from the Muslim Conference which would

. . . break up the solidarity of Muslims in India. It is only after a great deal of work that we have been able to build up a united program for Muslims which is supported by every Province throughout India. Our community will then be disorganised and split into innumerable fragments. . . . It will be difficult to prevent every part of the Communal Award being topsy turvy [sic], and Muslims in minority provinces will be dragged into discussions of percentages to which they would be entitled as a result of this Pact. . . . The Punjab question does not and cannot stand alone, it is a part of the all-India question and however strongly and persistently we may try to localise this issue it will be found that the whole question of communal proportion throughout India will be re-opened for discussion.[59]

Fazl-i-Husain's reactions to these criticisms from his old friend and supporter merely underly the fact that the Aga Khan had uncovered the inwardness of his tactics. The flurry of excuses that Fazl-i-Husain now put forward,[60] were all part of the smoke-screen that he laid around his real purpose. That came out clearly enough when he wrote to Shafat Ahmad Khan, that he could not see 'how Punjab Muslims can be deprived of the chance of improving their position by accepting this proposal.' In Punjab terms, it would clearly be a 'great mistake' for the Muslims there to 'miss the chance of establishing their position, for such a chance is not likely to recur'.[61]

And of course Fazl-i-Husain knew his Punjab. As far as the Punjab Muslims were concerned, the majority community could only secure its future by maintaining some semblance of co-operation with Hindus and

[58] Fazl-i-Husain to Jogendra Singh, 8 May 1933, Letters, p. 284.
[59] The Aga Khan to Fazl-i-Husain, 10 May 1933, ibid., pp. 285–6.
[60] In fact he was trying to safeguard the Communal Award by allowing negotiations with the Hindus and Sikhs to go forward, much as the Award had hoped; he thought a communal agreement in the Punjab was in line with Muslim Conference policy.
[61] Fazl-i-Husain to Shafaat Ahmad Khan, 19 June 1933, ibid., p. 305.

Sikhs. Fazl-i-Husain argued that the all-India Muslim Conference had left the majority provinces entirely free to improve their position; he restated the Punjab thesis:

The Punjab has stood by the minority provinces. . . . It will be a very poor return indeed of Punjab's courageous stand by the minority provinces, for you people now in your own interest to stand in the way of Punjab improving its position. If the All-India Muslim Conference takes up that attitude, then it will be doing what the Congress was not able to do—effecting disruption of united Muslim India.[62]

Fazl-i-Husain was now ready to discipline his own creature, the Muslim Conference, in the interests of a powerful Punjabi particularism.[63] Musing in the privacy of his Diary, Fazl-i-Husain could see the advantages of the abortive pact:

Indian Nationalism or Punjab Nationalism? For the present Punjab National-ism, Hindu and Sikh threat regarding Reforms and communal Award. If Punjab Hindus and Sikhs persist in not playing the game—Punjab Muslims should not insist, but let the Reforms be the establishment of autocracy and make sure that this happens all over India—Long-live John Bull![64]

In other words if his arrangements were put at risk by a failure to keep the Punjab communities in working harmony, Fazl-i-Husain would have preferred to ditch the reforms and to invite the British to continue to rule in India, because in this way his party would remain the real governors of a united Punjab. His entire strategy was based on the view that the Punjab Muslims' position was 'sound' and 'safe if not impreg-nable', ingenious devices by 'keen witted politicians' such as Iqbal were liable to bamboozle the unsuspecting Punjabi.[65] The Aga Khan learnt to his cost that the Punjab Unionists were simply interested in getting

[62] Fazl-i-Husain to Shafaat Ahmad Khan, 28 June 1933, *ibid.*, 312.

[63] Treated in a favoured and distinct way by the British, the Punjab had maintained a strong sense of identity throughout the century of British rule. This emerged clearly in the policy of the Unionist Party, in Fazl-i-Husain's attitude in the critical constitutional negotiations of the nineteen-thirties; it was to appear again in the attitude of the Punjab political leaders towards Jinnah and the League; and it is clear that this distinctive and strongly particularist attitude had dominated the politics of Pakistan since its creation.

[64] Fazl-i-Husain, 30 August 1935, in Waheed Ahmed (ed.), *Diary and Notes of Mian Fazl-i-Husain* (Lahore, 1976), pp. 168–9.

[65] Fazl-i-Husain to Aga Khan, 16 December 1933, *Letters*, pp. 331–2. Nor was Fazl-i-Husain impressed by the Aga Khan's warning that the Conservatives in Britain, particularly the Diehards such as Churchill and Salisbury, would welcome signs of Muslim discontent with the Award and that Samuel Hoare 'would be disgusted at us for letting him down by our incompetence and inability to leave well alone'. Aga Khan to Fazl-i-Husain, 21 January 1934, *ibid.*, p. 342.

power in their own province, and then going their own sweet particularist way.

But the Punjab strategy had inherent flaws which its architect and his British allies had failed to realize. They underestimated the strength of the opposition from the Muslims in the minority provinces, especially those of the United Provinces who had carried the baton of Muslim leadership before Fazl-i-Husain had snatched it away and locked it up in the Punjab. Moreover, the strategy which had been safe in the nineteen-twenties was unlikely to be safe in the later thirties once power at the centre was seriously at risk. The Punjab wanted nothing to happen at the centre, and to let sleeping safeguards lie in British hands. But of course the Punjab was not alone in India; and the Congress, admittedly negligible in the Punjab and absent from the critical negotiations in London, had seemed to be a less formidable factor in Indian politics at this time than they soon were to prove to be. But this was evidence of the provincial myopia which may have been Fazl-i-Husain's great strength inside his own region, but which the British could not afford to share in the broader perspectives of all-India.

During the long negotiations in London, the Muslim Conference improvised by Fazl-i-Husain in 1929, had proved an excellent instrument for his stone-walling tactics which proved so effective against the Congress and the British alike. But the Punjab provincialism of Fazl-i-Husain and his All-India Muslim Conference had serious weaknesses. The Conference itself was an oligarchical body, bristling with knights and nawabs. Its take-over bid for the Muslim League had failed, and the very unevenness of the Muslim gains under the Award and the new reforms left plenty of scope for provincial grievances to be exploited. What would happen to the Muslims in the minority provinces? Again, the Government of India Bill intended to federate India. What would happen to the Muslims even in the majority provinces, on the day when the larger Hindu community captured the centre? And how appropriate an organization was the Muslim Conference to steer the community through the elections under the new Act and to orchestrate its policies thereafter?

The year 1935 saw the Act on the statute book at last. But all these other questions still needed urgent attention from Fazl-i-Husain and the Aga Khan, the leaders of the Muslim Conference. It was plain to the Aga Khan at least that Indian Muslim politics would need to be reshaped to suit the new electorate of thirty millions, and that merely clinging to the letter of the 1935 Act would not suffice. Its constitutional safeguards were: '... all too unnatural and artificial; besides they weaken our natural strength in the North and in Bengal while they give us no advantage where we are in a minority.' The Aga Khan could see that 'the kind of politics that we have been thinking of in the past will not need the circumstances of the future'. This raised the question of 'what should be the future policy of the Moslems of India?'.[66] Shafaat Ahmad Khan, the Muslim Conference leader from the western United Provinces, had immediately realized the dangers of 'isolation and provincialism', he feared that the Muslim majority provinces beguiled by the provincial autonomy they had gained, would forget about the feelings of all-India solidarity and unity which had 'inspired all of us for four long years'.[67] The Conference now needed a general policy and a common ideal, at once 'practicable and inspirational', to prevent Muslims getting lost in the 'internecine struggle for power, ministerships, jobs and leadership'. But while Shafaat Ahmad Khan could see the need for such a policy and ideal, he admitted that he had been like 'a blind man groping in the dark' in his search during the past two years for such a programme. He called upon Fazl-i-Husain to 'serve as a beacon of light to all of us'.[68] But Fazl-i-Husain felt that he had done what he could for the Muslims, losing in the process 'what little was left to me of health'. 'Neither Islam nor my principles approve of suicide', he bluntly told Abdullah Khan. Taking on the mantle of leadership of Indian Muslims throughout the sub-continent was 'tantamount to committing suicide'. He encouraged the United Provinces, 'rich in leaders' to find its own helmsmen.[69] The appeal to Fazl-i-Husain to work out a new all-India programme to keep the Muslims from being 'smothered up by provincialism' fell upon deaf ears.[70] By now Fazl-i-Husain had served his province's interests well at Delhi and felt he could return to the Punjab, where he continued to manage the Unionist affairs until his death in 1936.

From his London home at the Ritz, the Aga Khan thought he could see a way forward. The Muslim strategy should now be to take advantage of their 'impregnable position' in the north-western tracts and in Bengal; at the centre, the Muslims should be 'out and out Federalists'.[71]

---

[66] Aga Khan to Fazl-i-Husain, 13 August 1935, Fazl-i-Husain Papers (Aga Khan File); also quoted in *Letters*, pp. 429–30.

[67] Shafaat Ahmad Khan to Fazl-i-Husain, 7 November 1935, *Letters*, p. 470.

[68] *Ibid.*

[69] Fazl-i-Husain to Abdullah Khan, 23 September 1935, *ibid.*, p. 467.

[70] Shafaat Ahmad Khan to Fazl-i-Husain, 30 November 1935, *ibid.*, p. 474.

[71] This meant demanding a status for the Muslim majority provinces at least as autonomous as the Indian States would have under a federation; and the Indian Army should be changed from an all-Indian to a territorial force.

But there remained the problem of hitting upon a rallying cry for the vastly increased Muslim electorate. The Aga Khan believed that

In self-interest . . . our attitude should be hardest possible political work on the lines of moderate State Socialism, a policy that will get for us the sympathy of many depressed and poor Hindus. . . . Our members in all the provinces (and especially in Bengal) should always be on the side of putting as many taxation burdens as possible on the upper and middle classes and reducing as much as they can indirect taxes, which fall generally on the poor. . . . With the realization of our policy in Pakistan and Bengal we could do away with all our props in a few years, and we would be in a strong position because in Pakistan we would only have to whistle and rule, and in Bengal (if this policy is carried out with adult or manhood suffrage and moderate State socialism—by the State here meaning the provincial resources to be used for the benefit of the poor and the public)—with such a policy even Bengal would become a second Pakistan.[72]

At first sight, this seems to point to 1947 and partition. But this was not the connotation of 'Pakistan' in the nineteen-thirties. For the Aga Khan and Fazl-i-Husain the plan involved not separate sovereign states, but rather to 'make India what she is, i.e. a United States of Southern Asia', where the Muslims would work for all they were worth the majority provinces against the new federal centre. But 'our Indian patriotism, of course, should never leave any doubt and our Hindu countrymen must realise that the welfare of India as a whole . . . is as dear to us as it is to them. . . .[73]

It was all very well for the Aga Khan to doodle at these federal blueprints and to advocate state socialism at the expense of the well-to-do in Bengal. Applying these ideas to the harsh complexities of India was a different matter. That Muslim pirs and zamindars, nawabs and talukdas would rush cheerfully into a future glowering with supertax and socialism, was not especially plausible; and in any case the Muslim Conference with its provincial counterparts, whether in Bengal or the U.P., was too stiff, too oligarchical, too reliant on influence and defer-ence for the mass electoral campaigning, called for by the wider fran-chise. Under the old state of things, the Unionist Party of the Punjab had been a sort of Oriental Whiggery:

People who had to make up their minds to support one or other of the candidates were influenced by personnel or tribal considerations, and were not at all swayed by the consideration to which Party the candidate belonged. To what extent these conditions will continue to operate under the new Constitu-

---

[72] Aga Khan to Fazl-i-Husain, 13 August 1935, Fazl-i-Husain Papers (Aga Khan File), and *Letters*, pp. 431–5.
[73] *Ibid.*

tion and under a better-defined party system, it is not possible to determine at this stage.[74]

Some of the urban discontents among the Muslims had urged Fazl-i-Husain to call in the real Muslim talent of the province, who were 'engaged in gathering wool' and who were 'passing their time in the wilderness'. Malik Barkat Ali wanted Fazl-i-Husain to ditch his oligarchs and to call in the young and the able who were pining 'at the meagreness of the opportunity to serve and advance [their] province under the awful conditions that your leadership have brought about'.[75] But Fazl-i-Husain, the 'prop and mainstay' of the rural notables, 'the favourites of the bureaucracy' was unwilling to drop them through the trap-door of history.[76]

And yet the question of how the old politics of deference would fare under the new electoral conditions, had to be determined. If the leaders of the old oligarchical system were unsure of their way, there was a newcomer who was not. In 1930 Mohamed Ali Jinnah had left India, supposedly forever. But four years later he was induced to come back, for the purpose of resurrecting the Muslim League to face the new electoral system and the new structure of politics. To the old guard of Muslim leaders, these innovations came as threats, but to Jinnah who had failed badly in the old-style politics, they came as opportunities. In 1936 he organized a parliamentary board designed for the central control of Muslim candidates throughout India, instead of leaving their selection to the whims of provincial bodies; and to emphasize this control he decided that these candidates should run on entirely communal tickets, thus cutting themselves adrift from the old parties of Muslim landowners such as the Punjab Unionists and the Agriculturists of the United Provinces, which had always found it tactically expedient to include Hindu members. Such a programme was anathema to the Muslim provincial oligarchs and they set to work to fend off the intruder. Significantly, they achieved this both in Bengal and in the Punjab, and the latter case illustrates how they did it.

Fazl-i-Husain was determined to keep his province as a private empire, insulated from central control. With funds provided by the Aga Khan[77] he wished to dislodge Jinnah, who then came to Lahore, saying

[74] Sir Zafrullah Khan to Fazl-i-Husain, 15 April 1936, Fazl-i-Husain Papers (Zafrullah File).

[75] Malik Barkat Ali to Fazl-i-Husain, 4 April 1936, *Letters*, pp. 509–10.

[76] *Ibid.*

[77] 'Your know perfectly well that the Punjab is the key of the Indian Muslim politics', Fazl-i-Husain told the Aga Khan; '[h]ence the importance of strengthening the Punjab

he was going to smash Fazl-i-Husain. But he found the Punjab organization too strong for him, and while he sat in Lahore waiting for visitors, no one of consequence dared to call. Sikander Hayat had warned Jinnah of 'keeping his finger out of the Punjab pie'; 'we cannot possibly allow "provincial autonomy" to be tampered with in any sphere, and by anybody be he a nominee of the powers who have given us this autonomy or a President of the Muslim League'[78] 'I shall never come to the Punjab again' Jinnah said as he was leaving in a rage, 'it is such a hopeless place'.[79]

Jinnah was to do better in the United Provinces. Slow to be caught up in the national movement, these provinces had more and more come to dominate it. The size of the provinces, the political potential of their peasant unrest, the strong Congress machines in Allahabad and Benares, the central position of the U.P. in the Hindu-speaking regions of the country: all these factors had led to the United Provinces' predominance, and this meant that Congress, the Muslims and the British alike all strove hard to control their politics. Here the Montagu-Chelmsford constitution had been worked by coalitions of landowners, organized into the Agriculturist Party by a succession of governors, Harcourt, Butler, Muddiaman, and Malcolm Hailey. With the prospect of a new constitution and a wider franchise, the British interests had everything to gain by keeping this group together. Since it was conservative, it would not exploit provincial autonomy. Since it was made up of notables, it could control the new electorate—or so it was hoped. Since it was inter-communal, it might steer clear of religious politics. But the obstruction of the Bill in London worked against the calculations of Government House in Lucknow. Already in 1933, Hailey foresaw what was to follow:

At one time I hoped that the early institution of provincial autonomy would monopolise public attention. But if we are not to have the Report of the Select Committee till February or March, it is not likely that we may see a Bill passed during 1935, and there will be a period of stagnation during which all sorts of

with a view to give a lead to Muslim India'; to break Jinnah's parliamentary board, Fazl-i-Husain needed election funds; and the Aga Khan, who had recently had some winnings at Ascot, immediately sent money to his old Unionist ally. See Fazl-i-Husain to the Aga Khan, 22 June 1936, *Letters*, pp. 596–7.

[78] Sikander Hayat Khan to Fazl-i-Husain, 1 May 1936, *Letters*, p. 528. Although Fazl-i-Husain feared that Jinnah had 'blundered into the [Punjab] arena very much to our prejudice' in fact, Jinnah failed to get any support from any section of the Unionists and even the discontents in the Ittihad-I-Millat, refused to co-operate with him and in fact withdrew from the League's parliamentary board.

[79] Quoted in Azim Husain, *Mian Fazl-i-Husain: A Political Biography*, 1966, p. 311.

452   AYESHA JALAL AND ANIL SEAL

issues may be taken up, and during which efforts made to consolidate a stable party will lose interest.[80]

In fact the time was lost, and the 'stable party' turned out to be a wasting asset. This harmed the British and the old leadership, and since the only beneficiaries turned out to be the new Muslim leadership of Jinnah, in time it was to harm the Congress, as well. Since the Agriculturist Party was so loosely organized and since it had marked time in the early nineteen-thirties, Jinnah's foray into the U.P. found all manner of dissident landowners waiting to be comforted and ex-Congress Muslims to be recruited.[81] More important than that, the United Provinces contained the ablest, the best educated, the most ambitious Muslims in India, socially superior to those in Bengal, educationally superior to those in the Punjab. But only one Indian in seven in the United Provinces was a Muslim, and so they had little to gain and much to fear from the coming of provincial self-government with a wider franchise. There was nothing for them in the Punjab programme of Fazl-i-Husain. Such people were ready to give sympathy to a party promising them a full-blooded communal programme and which could offer them national, and not merely provincial support. So it was in the United Provinces that the new type of mass politics, based on bitter excoriation of the Hindus, began to emerge. The contempt of the old Muslim politicians for this new movement and its new leader was pungently expressed by Sir Shafaat Ahmad Khan, the Conference's man in the United Provinces: He described Jinnah's parliamentary board as 'fantastic'; here was Jinnah's first attempt to organize Muslims outside the legislature and it would be his last. His tactics were characterized by 'a crudity which would do credit to the President of [a] school debating society';

. . . Jinnah has never done a solid day's political work in his life and 'organisation' is foreign to him. . . . This is an example of his pyrotechnics and inordinate desire for stunts. Hollywood atmosphere and methods, graceful poses and elaborate gestures are all right for boys of 18, but Jinnah's sole contribution to the present controversy, is an attack on 'reactionaries'.[82]

[80] Hailey to Jagdish Prasad, 12 September 1933, Jagdish Prasad Papers, New Delhi, quoted in Gallagher, 'From Civil Disobedience to Communism'.
[81] As one influential U.P. Muslim had written to Fazl-i-Husain in 1931, the impact of the civil disobedience movement and the increasing politicization of the U.P. peasantry, had shown that the old policy of relying upon Government to protect Muslim property was no longer enough, 'so even those Muslims who have so far been with the Government will go against it or lose all influence with the public.' (Mushir Husain Kidwai to Fazl-i-Husain, 3 April 1931, Letters, p. 129.)
[82] Shafaat Ahmad Khan, Fazl-i-Husain, 15 June 1936, Fazl-i-Husain Papers (Shafaat File); also in Letters, pp. 586–7.

Somehow or the other the Agriculturist Party would have to be raised up to crush the League, but Shafaat himself went on: '. . . the Agriculturist Party, it must be confessed, cannot command the allegiance of the Muslim electorate'.[83] Even though the Aga Khan consoled himself that he had never 'looked upon Aligarh or U.P. as the leadership of Islam', the United Provinces, standing as they did between the north-west and Bengal made it vital that the Congress (and equally the League) 'should not capture our "Centre" '.[84]

And there was the rub. When the last the elections came in 1937, the Muslim majority provinces stayed loyal to their old leaders. Fazl-i-Husain had died the previous year, but his successor, Sir Shikander Hayat Khan, brought the Unionists to power in the Punjab and became chief minister. Out of eighty-four seats, the League won only one in the Punjab. In Bengal, Fazl-ul-Huq formed a coalition ministry and in Sind and in the North West Frontier Province, the other Muslim majority provinces, the League won no seats at all. But in the United Provinces, the Agriculturists did badly and the League did well, and it was noticeable that in other Muslim minority provinces they made advances too.[85] This was to become the pattern. The League was to spread outwards from the United Provinces where most of its political talent was bunched; and one by one the Muslim parties in the minority provinces were to fall under Jinnah's control. But he did not win the leadership of Bengal Muslims until 1943 and of the Punjab Muslims until 1946.[86] The last two provinces to fall to the Muslim League were the two where Muslims were most powerful. They were also the two which were partitioned.

By now Jinnah's strategy was becoming a little clearer. It did not augur well for the provincialism of the Punjab. At the Round Table Conferences, Jinnah had been impressed by how powerfully Congress had been able to deploy its claim to speak with one voice for the nation. He also had seen how effectively the Congress High Command imposed its choices and its disciplines over the heterogeneous groups that had fought the 1937 elections under its flag. The contempt with which the Congress dealt with the Muslim League's hopes of a share of office in the Hindu majority provinces where the League had scored its only electoral successes rammed home these lessons. Congress, flushed with their

[83] *Ibid.*
[84] Aga Khan to Fazl-i-Husain, 14 January 1936, *Letters*, p. 481.
[85] In the U.P. the League won twenty-seven seats; in Bombay it won twenty and in Madras, ten.
[86] Even then, Jinnah had far less control over these provinces than is usually assumed—a theme to be developed in Ayesha Jalal's forthcoming work.

success at the polls, decided to launch a bold attack upon the Muslim problem and encouraged the League to disband and be absorbed in its ranks. By its programme of mass contacts and policy of agrarian and social reform, the Congress hoped to bring the Muslim villager into its fold. So Jinnah had now to rally support for the League and, under his unquestioned leadership, make it the only voice of Muslim India, and get the British to accept his claim; he had to counter the Congress mass contact campaign in the rural areas and he had to find a programme by which he could try to bring to heel the leaders of the Muslim provincial parties.

In 1936, Fazl-i-Husain had sent one of his followers to warn Jinnah to keep out of the Punjab. The messenger reported the failure to keep his mission and he added, 'my prayer is that those who have made efforts to raise Mr. Jinnah in the Punjab's estimation may not be placed in a position where they may have to repent'.[87] Perhaps there were some repentances in the summer of 1947, when nearly 200,000 Hindus and Muslims were slaughtered and nine million refugees stumbled fearfully across the burning plains of the Punjab.

[87] Ahmad Yar Khan Daultana to Fazl-i-Husain, 13 April 1936, Fazl-i-Husain Papers (Daultana File).

Modern Asian Studies, **15**, 3 (1981), pp. 455–486.

Colonial Firms and the Decline of Colonialism in Eastern India 1914–47

B. R. TOMLINSON

University of Birmingham

THE spectacular decline of the expatriate business houses of eastern India in this century is one of the many underdeveloped areas of Indian economic history. The extent of the decline itself seems hard to exaggerate. In 1900 almost all the commanding heights of the colonial economy appeared to be dominated by expatriate and foreign firms, most of them British. Not only was the foreign trade of Bengal almost exclusively in their hands, but so was the industrial and banking structure. In addition, most historians of the period have stressed that the expatriate sector was able to dominate internal trade, operating in a monopsony position in regard to cash crop production and marketing and also, thanks to its contacts with government, the railways and the port trusts, to enjoy hegemonic powers that impeded the development of indigenous rivals. Thus, as A. K. Bagchi has stressed, 'social discrimination was complemented and supported by political, economic, administrative and financial arrangements which afforded European businessmen a substantial and systematic advantage over their Indian rivals in India.'[1] The fate of the expatriate groups since 1950 has been very different. Many suffered considerable depredations during and after the second world war, losing important sectors of their business to Indian rivals, and even being bought out entirely by native enterprise. Such expatriate interests as survived after Independence have generally failed to perform well. Their recent history has been a gloomy one of a steady erosion of profitability and viability, so that most of those that still remain are now taken seriously only by a new generation of indigenous speculators and asset strippers.

The question which this article seeks to answer is why this decline occurred. To do this we must first investigate the chronology more closely. A simple outline which compares the 1900s with the 1950s may be misleading, for to stress this contrast suggests that it is the

---

[1] A. K. Bagchi, *Private Investment in India 1900–1939* (Cambridge, 1972), p. 166.

0026-749x/81/0406-0904$02.00 © 1981 Cambridge University Press

coming of political independence, the collapse of the colonial administration and its replacement by a national government in India, that was the vital factor. This argument has its attractions, not the least of which is the virtue of apparent simplicity. If the 'mystic bond of racial affinity with the rulers of the land' was the key to the strength of the expatriate sector in the colonial period,[2] then a change in the racial composition of the ruling élite must be seen as crucial. It is not necessary to see the 1940s as a great climacteric in this respect; new trends can be noted as early as the first world war. An awareness of the increasing pressure that Indian businessmen, and their allies in the nationalist movement, could exert on the colonial government in the inter-war period can add a degree of sophistication to the argument. Changes in tariff policy, in stores purchase rules, in the climate for decisions about government intervention and in expectations about the political future can all be used to suggest that the colonial government was being forced to withdraw from its mutually-supportive pact with expatriate enterprise some time before the final demise of the Raj. If the expatriates are given some credit for foresight, it can be argued that—despite continuing to fight energetic and acrimonious rearguard actions on politically sensitive subjects such as discriminatory commercial legislation in the 1920s, 1930s and 1940s—they were also planning a smooth retreat for the last thirty years of British rule, repatriating profits and restraining enterprise. The most recent study of industrial growth in Bengal, Dr R. K. Ray's *Industrialization in India*, is based on just such an analysis, stressing political unrest and uncertainty, and more favourable opportunities elsewhere, as factors inducing expatriates increasingly to repatriate rather than invest their Indian profits after 1914.[3] A small difficulty with this hypothesis, however, is that Dr Ray has no direct evidence to support it, except for a very general point about the total amount of expatriate investment which is itself based on a misreading of his sources.[4]

[2] The remark quoted was used by the All-India Manufacturers' Organization in 1944 and is cited in *ibid.*, p. 166.

[3] R. K. Ray, *Industrialization in India: Growth and Conflict in the Corporate Private Sector 1914–47* (Delhi, 1979), esp. pp. 356–8.

[4] *Ibid.*, pp. 13–14, 36, 357–8. Dr Ray claims support for his argument from a work by D. H. N. Gurtoo, *India's Balance of Payments (1920–1960)* (Delhi, 1960), which concludes that there was a 'sudden, massive and persistent withdrawal of capital from India' in the 1930s (p. 96). Unfortunately, Gurtoo's case for private foreign investment is based on a comparison of G. D. Birla's estimate of Rs 585 crores in 1929 (*Economic Journal* September 1932) with B. R. Shenoy's estimate of Rs 565 crores in 1939 (*Eastern Economist* October and November 1945) (Note: one crore is ten million, usually written 1,00,00,000). Gurtoo assumes that these two estimates are comparable because they use

This argument can be both modified and extended by setting it in a wider context. The decline of expatriate enterprise can be linked to a larger structural shift in the Indian and international economies in the inter-war period. As the old nineteenth-century world economy, into which the expatriates had integrated their activities so well, ran into difficulties after 1914, so their traditional sources of mercantile strength became weakened. The structural shift in the colonial economy that took place in the 1920s and 1930s is well known, although its extent and significance are still subjects for debate. With the rise of new industries behind tariff walls in India in the 1930s and 1940s, new opportunities for building corporate structures were presented to entrepreneurs. The expatriate firms seem to have been reluctant to participate in this process fully, leaving simple consumer goods such as sugar and cement to indigenous rivals, and advanced technology fields such as chemicals and pharmaceuticals to overseas manufacturers. By 1945 Indian businessmen had emerged as the only important rivals of, or potential collaborators with, multinational firms in the development of capital goods industries such as machine tools, automobiles and fertilizers. This is not to say that no expatriate firms expanded in the inter-war years. Some Calcutta-based companies co-operated with British firms in establishing subsidiary manufacturing plant in this period.[5] Others expanded into new lines on

much the same categorization of investment types (p. 100); however, if Shenoy's estimates are read carefully it is clear that this assumption is not valid. Shenoy, although dating his survey at 1939, was in fact using averages of earlier estimates with no allowance for the passage of time. His figures for capital of rupee companies registered in India and for capital invested in partnerships and private firms in 1939 are derived from comparisons between various estimates made in 1929-30. Shenoy's aim was to provide a more accurate alternative to Birla's estimate, not a later comparison with it (see A. K. Banerji, *India's Balance of Payments 1921-22 to 1938-39* (London, 1961), pp. 161-9).

The only modern estimate of private foreign investment is that made by Dr Banerji in the work just cited. He puts the figure for foreign private investment in trade and industry at Rs 302 crores in 1921 and Rs 413 crores in 1938 (pp. 171, 175, 183). His figures for rupee investments controlled by the expatriate sector (based on issued shares and debentures) suggest declines in such investment between 1921 and 1938 (in Rs crores) in jute mills (− 2.53), cotton mills (− 3.03) and coal mines (− 1.43), with rises in electricity and telephones (+ 9.14), engineering (+ 3.32), tea plantations (+ 2.04), railways (+ 0.74), sugar mills (+ 1.93) and miscellaneous enterprises (+ 0.72). Overall, he estimates a rise in British-held rupee investments from Rs 139.36 crores in 1921 to Rs 155.33 crores in 1938 (pp. 101, 125, 210-23). Dr Banerji also estimates that the dividends paid by Indian companies in which British capital was invested were higher, on average, than the returns on investments made in the United Kingdom (p. 87).

[5] The best example of this trend is the partnership between Gillanders Arbuthnot, a Calcutta-based expatriate group, and Goodlass Wall, a British manufacturing group, in establishing subsidiary companies in India to manufacture paint and chemicals. Other similar cases are the alliance of Octavius Steel with G.E.C., Turner Morrison with

their own, chiefly into electricity supply, transport and engineering.[6]
Yet it is remarkable that in eastern India the activities of most expatriate firms remained centred around their traditional core of jute,
coal and tea.[7]

The failure of the expatriate firms, by and large, to move into new
fields opened up by the events of the 1930s and 1940s is an important
phenomenon. But it is not clear whether it should be regarded as a
cause or a symptom of their larger decline. On the one hand, as Dr
Ray has pointed out, one might expect the expatriate houses to have
been in a good position to exploit new opportunities had they wished
to do so.[8] They had the advantages of good marketing networks, a
reputation for financial soundness and, perhaps, contacts with the
bureaucracy to aid them in any new venture. That they failed to take
full advantage of these might suggest that there was an underlying
failure of will, or decline of expectations, brought about by fears for
the political future. Yet, on the other hand, it is clear that the Indian
entrepreneurs who did move into the new consumer goods industries
of the 1930s—especially sugar and cement—were able to use the
exceptionally high initial profits secured to finance expansion into
other assured fields, such as paper, as well as more speculative ones

Pinchin Johnson, and Barry & Co. with Jensen & Nicholson. In all these cases the
expatriate group contributed some capital and management skills (see B. R. Tomlinson,
'Foreign Private Investment in India 1920–1950', in *Modern Asian Studies*, 12.4 (1978),
Appendix II).

[6] See M. M. Mehta, *Structure of Indian Industries* (Bombay, 1961), p. 333.

[7] According to the breakdown in Mehta, *Structure*, pp. 346–7, of the companies
managed by 17 leading expatriate managing agency companies (most of which were
based in Calcutta), 80 per cent had been in jute, coal and tea in 1911, 66 per cent in 1931
and 64 per cent in 1951. There was some expansion in other fields, 63 new companies
being established outside jute, coal, tea and cotton between 1911 and 1931, and a further
18 between 1931 and 1951. Companies in these peripheral fields represented 32 per cent
of the total managed in 1931 and 35 per cent in 1951, as against 17 per cent in 1911. Yet a
comparison with Indian managing agency houses seems to demonstrate a lack of
adventurousness among the expatriates. Of companies managed by the three leading
Indian managing agencies in 1911, none were in jute, coal or tea; only one company was
managed in these fields in 1931 and only three in 1951. The Indian houses had much
more extensive interests in cotton and, increasingly, in other sectors of the economy. In
contrast to the expatriates, the great period of expansion for the Indian houses was in
1931–51 rather than in 1911–31. In 1911 the Indian houses had managed six firms, four
in cotton and two other; in 1931 they managed 19 firms, one in jute, 10 in cotton and
eight other; by 1951 they managed 88 firms, 72 of which were outside the old staple
industries. Whereas the expatriates had expanded outside their core in the 1910s and
1920s, before the benefits of tariff protection had had much effect on the process of
import-substitution, the Indian managing agencies boomed in the 1930s and 1940s,
profiting from protection and the war economy, and establishing 63 firms outside the
traditional sectors, as against only 18 established by the expatriates.

[8] Ray, *Industrialization*, p. 356.

such as chemicals and machine tools. It is also possible that the fact that the expatriate firms were so heavily committed to the old staples, none of which were buoyant in the 1930s, meant that they were restrained from expanding elsewhere.[9] Without a closer study of the decision-making processes and capital resources of individual firms no clear conclusion can be reached on this point.

A more rigorous comparison with their successful rivals offers some further clues to the causes of the decline of expatriate business houses. For eastern India, the obvious comparison is with the Marwari entrepreneurs who rose to prominence in local and national industry in the 1930s and 1940s. These businessmen were able to convert substantial

[9] Estimates of the profitability of Indian industries in our period are very difficult. The only comprehensive series is the index numbers calculated by the Economic Advisor to the Government of India for 1928-42, with 1928 as base (see S. Subramanian and P. W. R. Homfrey, *Recent Social and Economic Trends in India* (Delhi, 1946), Table XVII; reproduced, with a number of major errors of transposition, in Ray, *Industrialization*, Table 15). This index shows that jute profits fell sharply between 1928 and 1930, reaching 9% of their 1928 level in 1931, and then did not recover to 40% of their 1928 level until 1940 (in 1938 there was an average loss). Profits in tea recovered faster, but on average losses were made in 1931 and 1932. Profits in coal were more buoyant than those in jute, but even so regularly exceeded their 1928 level only after 1938. By contrast, profits in sugar boomed from 1931 onwards, reaching 250% of their 1928 level in 1932 and 1933, while profits in paper were virtually unaffected by the slump and regularly passed their 1928 level from 1933. The shortcoming of these figures is that they do not provide comparisons of relative profitability for the base year. General evidence from the *Investors' India Yearbook* and the annual *Review of the Trade of India* suggests that in 1928 tea, coal and sugar were not particularly profitable compared to earlier years, while returns in jute and paper were relatively good. The detailed analyses of working of various companies available in the *Investors' India Yearbook* for 1928-29 indicate that average gross profits, as a percentage of paid-up capital, for 47 jute mills in 1928 was 43%; for coal the average figure for 68 mines was 13%, although 18 of the mines made a loss; for 3 paper mills the average profit was 7.6% of paid up capital, and for 4 sugar mills 7.5%.

Overall, the performance of coal mines in the 1920s was mixed. While large mines with good machinery paid good dividends for most of the decade, about half the coal companies at work paid no dividends at all in the 1920s (see D. H. Buchanan, *The Development of Capitalist Enterprise in India* (New York, 1934), pp. 266-7). There is evidence that the jute industry was strikingly profitable in the fifteen years after 1915, allegedly earning 90% p.a. on its capital between 1915 and 1924 according to two Dundee labour leaders—not, perhaps, the most dispassionate of analysts. Buchanan concluded that 'it is doubtful if any other group of factories in the world paid such handsome profits between 1915 and 1929', although he stressed that individual cases sometimes went against the trend (*ibid.*, pp. 252-3). It is only fair to say that the evidence available at present is so sketchy that it could equally well be used to argue that the expatriate firms refrained from expansion into new lines because their traditional activities were so very profitable in the 1920s, as that they failed to diversify because their traditional activities were so unprofitable in the 1930s.

Finally, it is worth noting that the three staple expatriate industries—coal, jute and tea—had been subject to periodic over-production since the late nineteenth century.

speculative and trading profits made during the first world war and in the 1920s into the basis for a move into industry during and after the depression of the early 1930s. By the second world war firms such as Birla Brothers, with interests in cotton, jute, sugar and paper were beginning to dominate the industrial scene in Calcutta, and to plan moves into a wide range of consumption and capital goods once the war was over. The take-over of expatriate interests in Bengal after 1945 was largely engineered by these Marwari rivals and the spectacular development of some of them—Birlas, Juggilal Kamalpat, Surajmull Nagarmull and Sarupchand Hukumchand for example —was partly based on the ingested corpse of the old expatriate structure. Largely through the efforts of one scholar—T. A. Timberg—the rise of the Marwaris has been much more fully studied than the decline of the expatriates. Timberg's explanation of this success covers a number of points:

They attained and retained their capital-accumulating position in the social structure for several reasons. They did not sink too much of their capital in land—but preferred more risky and perhaps more profitable pursuits (a psychological and ideological explanation). They had relatively easy access to credit, information and manpower because of their organization as a commercial community (an institutional-structural explanation). Their circumstances and connections enabled them to migrate throughout India and enter several profitable commercial lines opened up by the British (an historical circumstantial explanation). If any of the above statements had not been true, their success would have been foreclosed. The integrating element is that the psychological and ideological attitudes were developed by an institutional-structural specialization in trade and the presence of historical opportunities which traders from a declining area could search out.[10]

However, many of these statements about the Marwaris could equally well be applied to the expatriates, and yet one group rose while the other fell. Elsewhere Dr Timberg has stressed the economic integration of the Marwari community as a vital factor in their development:

The advantages which Marwari firms enjoyed were connected with their being parts of efficiently developed 'Resource Groups' for the exchange of information, the provision of credit and for the accommodation of fledgling businessmen.[11]

<hr/>

[10] T. A. Timberg, 'The Rise of Marwari Merchants as Industrial Entrepreneurs to 1930' (Ph.D. thesis, Harvard University, 1972), pp. 235–6, quoted in Ray, *Industrialization*, p. 286.
[11] T. A. Timberg, 'A Study of a "Great" Marwari Firm: 1860–1914' in *Indian Economic and Social History Review*, VIII (1971), p. 265.

Again, however, this does not seem conclusive; if one were to substitute the word 'Scots' for 'Marwari' in the above quotation, it could equally well apply to the expatriate community in Calcutta.[12]

One further point of comparison remains between the expatriate firms and their Marwari competitors—access to capital for investment in new projects. Dr Timberg has stressed that a major factor in the rise of the Marwaris in preference to other Indian would-be industrialists was their access to large accumulated capitals or its surrogate, credit. The fact that the Marwaris had a long history as a trading community is of great importance here:

The genius of a trading community lies in its manipulation of credit. With this genius for credit accumulation it is no wonder that trading communities managed to acquire the capital resources which have enabled them to play a dominant role in the industrial development of India.[13]

[12] Dr Timberg is strangely uninterested in making comparisons with the expatriates: the question which he is trying to answer is why Marwari entrepreneurs were so much more successful than other Indian groups, especially the Bengalis.

One wider comparison should also be discussed here. Some economic historians of Japan are fond of pointing to what is thought to be the unique structure of Japanese trade and industry—the *zaibatsu* firms—as a major factor in Japanese economic growth in the late nineteenth and early twentieth centuries. The major *zaibatsu* (Mitsui, Mitsubishi, Sumitomo and Yasuda) rose to prominence in the 1920s; their strength is thought to have been a well-integrated institutional structure capable of combining trade, industry and finance and able to branch out into several fields at once. As Prof. Rosovsky has stressed: 'They provided a low-income Japan with the possibility of exploiting scale economies, and their diversification permitted what Lockwood has called "combined investment"—i.e. the simultaneous development of complementary industries. Zaibatsu also economised what must have been a scarce factor, i.e. individuals capable of running modern businesses; and through the operation of their affiliated banks they were most adept at mobilising scarce capital resources. Given that the issue of that day—as now—was growth rather than economic democracy, there developed in Japan a certain kind of "bigness" which was unacceptable elsewhere but quite suitable in this setting'. H. Rosovsky, 'What are the "Lessons" of Japanese Economic History?' in A. J. Youngson (ed.), *Economic Development in the Long Run* (London, 1972), p. 241.

But it is worth asking just how unique the *zaibatsu* system was, at least in these respects. If one were looking around the world of 1914, or even of 1929, for comparisons with it, the expatriate firms of British India would seem to fill the bill exactly. They, too, had achieved vertical and horizontal integrations that allowed them to indulge in 'combined investment'; they, too, had linked trade and finance with industry; they, too, economized on management skills through the managing agency system. In fact, in 1914, the sector of the Indian economy that operated on modern business lines could be said to have been more *zaibatsu* dominated than was the Japanese one. And yet the expatriate firms of India declined, relatively and absolutely, at the same time as the Japanese *zaibatsu* that imitated their structure so closely were rising.

[13] T. A. Timberg, 'The Origins of Marwari Industrialists' in R. and M. J. Beech (eds), *Bengal: Change and Continuity* (Michigan State University, Asian Studies Center, South Asian Series Occasional Papers no. 16, mimeo.), p. 151.

The implication is that Marwari firms were able to use the profits of
trade and speculation, as well as contacts made in these fields, to
finance industrial ventures. Thus Birla Bros. increased their capital
base fourfold as a result of speculation during the first world war,
moved from that into jute trading in the 1920s and from that into
industry in the 1930s.[14] Other evidence also suggests that much of the
new industrial expansion by Indian entrepreneurs in the 1930s was
similarly based on speculative profits dating from 1914–18, combined
with access to bank credits and accumulated trading profits seeking
new outlets during the Great Depression.[15]

The obvious question to ask is whether the expatriate firms had less
access to venture capital of this kind during the inter-war period.
There is little evidence to suggest that they played much part in the
speculative markets of the first world war, but they certainly made
phenomenal profits out of some sectors of their business—notably
jute—in the later stages of the war. What we do not know is what
happened to these profits after 1918. Huge dividends were paid out by
jute mills in the immediate post-war years, totalling 141 per cent of
ordinary capital in 1918, 125 per cent in 1919 and 109 per cent in
1920.[16] There are no accurate estimates of the extent of reinvestment
or repatriation of either distributed or undistributed profits in the
post-war years, but there is some empirical evidence for both activities.[17] /Yet it certainly is possible to suggest that such profits as were

[14] Ray, *Industrialization*, pp. 278–9.
[15] See B. R. Tomlinson, *The Political Economy of the Raj: the Economics of Decolonization in India 1914–1947* (London, 1979), p. 43.
[16] See *The Gazetteer of India Volume III: Economic Structure and Activities* (New Delhi, 1975), p. 474. The three mills whose dividends were surveyed by Buchanan—Budge Budge, Fort Gloster and Gourepore—paid dividends amounting to 215%, 180% and 300% of capital stock in 1918; 110%, 150% and 220% in 1919 and 132.5%, 200% and 250% in 1920 (see Buchanan, *Capitalist Enterprise*, p. 252).
[17] For evidence of repatriation see the many accusations made by Indian businessmen and politicians about rupee exchange policy in 1919–20 being determined to aid the transfer of expatriate resources to Britain. For a case of reinvestment, see the case of Bird-Heilger's 'war baby' companies below.
The balance of payments data available do not enable an accurate estimate of actual repatriation in individual years to be made. Dr Banerji assumes that all dividends paid by Indian rupee and sterling companies were repatriated; this gives him, on the basis of a calculated dividend series, a total figure of Rs 299.6 crores for repatriated profits for 1921–38, which can then be set against the total of Rs 111 crores worth of new private foreign investment in the same period (see Banerji, *India's Balance of Payments*, pp. 86, 171 and 175: this figure for private foreign investment differs from that given in *ibid.*, Table XI, p. 183, because capital invested in corporations and Native State loans has been excluded). However, all these figures are based on so many untestable assumptions, and are at such a high level of generalization, that it would be unwise to make too much of them.

not repatriated were likely to have been invested inside the existing core of expatriate firms' activities, and thus eventually to get trapped inside declining sectors of the colonial economy.[18]

Dr Timberg has suggested that access to capital was the vital factor in determining the advance of the Marwaris over other Indian rivals in the early twentieth century, and that the move into industry was more a consequence than a cause of the availability of funds. The general question of whether there was a relative or absolute shortage of capital for industrial development in India in the inter-war period is still the subject of much debate;[19] what is more certain is that some groups in the Indian economy were better able to mobilize such capital than others. The bulk of new capital came from private sources—from within the family, within the firm, or from trade or speculation. Most Indian industrialists were wary of the somewhat rudimentary and unstable stock exchanges in Calcutta and Bombay. As late as the early 1950s only 9 per cent of the funds used by large companies in India came from share capital, while 65 per cent of the total funds used by Indian industry came from internal sources.[20] Through the managing agency system Indian industrialists supplied a good deal of the capital employed in firms that they controlled, either directly or, more often, from investment, insurance or banking companies within the groups of which the managing agency house was a part. Traditionally, the expatriate managing agencies had access to sources of capital denied to their Indian rivals—shares issued in sterling companies on the London stock exchange, for example. However, in practice, it seems that the expatriate firms were also largely dependent on internal sources of finance by the inter-war period,[21] and many of the

---

[18] According to Bagchi's figures, real investment in the jute industry (based on machinery imports at constant prices) averaged Rs 1.41 crores p.a. between 1920–21 and 1924–25 (Rs 3.89 crores p.a. at current prices), as against an average of Rs 1.2 crores p.a. (Rs 1.98 crores p.a. at current prices) in 1908–09 to 1913–14, and an average of Rs 0.84 crores p.a. (Rs 1.58 crores p.a. at current prices) in 1924–25 to 1928–29. Imports of jute machinery accounted for 11% of the total current value of all imports of machinery into India in 1920–21 to 1924–25, and 36% of the total value at 1904 prices (see Bagchi, *Private Investment*, pp. 80, 273).

[19] For the latest contribution see Ray, *Industrialization*, pp. 228–30.

[20] G. Rosen, *Some Aspects of Industrial Finance in India* (Glencoe, 1962), pp. 42, 53.

[21] Thus Buchanan remarks of coal companies in the 1920s that 'the principal source of capital has been the trading community of Calcutta, especially the firms of managing agents' (Buchanan, *Capitalist Enterprise* p. 267). Bagchi makes the same point about jute: 'Capital for most of the mills came from investors resident in India. . . . A large proportion of the initial capital probably came from the managing agents themselves. Some companies also found practically all the money needed for working capital in this way. . . .' (Bagchi, *Private Investment* p. 275.)

larger groups contained investment companies which could mobilize
funds indirectly for use in other firms managed by the group. Of the
Rs 5,88 lakhs of new funds raised by one major expatriate group,
Bird-Heilger, between 1951 and 1958, for example, only 2 per cent
came from shares; 36 per cent came from internal sources and 62 per
cent from loans.[22] With industrial expansion so dependent on internal
sources of capital it is clear that declining groups would find it hard to
invest their way out of difficulties, even without any predilection for
repatriating such profits as were made.

   To sum up, it is not possible to come to any firm conclusions from
the general evidence available as to why the expatriate business houses
of eastern India failed to match the expansion of some of their Indian
competitors in the years from 1914 to 1947. Both the standard hypoth-
eses—that these firms were undergoing a process of planned, or
enforced, retreat brought about by political changes and expectations
of a worsening relationship with a future nationalist government; or
that the expatriates suffered a natural process of decline brought
about by over-commitment to unprofitable sectors of the economy—
seem plausible, but neither appears conclusive. To take the analysis
further it is now necessary to switch from the general to the particular,
and to look in some detail at the fortunes of one expatriate firm,
Bird-Heilger.

*   *   *

To write the history of business enterprise it is necessary to use the
records of major firms and business institutions. For the expatriate
enterprises of Calcutta such records are hard to come by. The papers
of one major managing agency house—Shaw Wallace—are now available to scholars in the Guildhall Library, London, although they
have not yet been utilized. An alternative source, on which much of
what follows is based, is the collection of papers of Sir Edward Benthall, deposited in the Centre of South Asian Studies, Cambridge.[23]
Benthall was a major figure in the expatriate community of Calcutta
after 1919, the head of a large business group (Bird-Heilger), a
member of the board of the Imperial Bank of India and of the Reserve
Bank of India, a representative of European business interests in the
Council of State and in the Bengal legislature, a spokesman in the

[22] R. K. Hazari, *The Corporate Private Sector* (New Delhi, 1966), p. 117. One lakh is one
hundred thousand, usually written 1,00,000.
[23] I am grateful to Sir Paul Benthall for permission to consult his brother's papers.

constitutional discussions of the early 1930s, a frequent President of the Associated Chambers of Commerce and the Bengal Chamber of Commerce and a member of the Viceroy's Executive Council in the latter half of the second world war. His papers consist of a diary, material dealing with legislature politics and the Round Table Conferences, and correspondence on business matters with his partners. It is this last section of the collection that is most important for our purposes. Unfortunately, the business correspondence covers only the months in which Benthall was absent from India—in 1928–29, 1935, 1937 and 1941—and thus provides a series of glimpses at the period rather than a continuous narrative.

Bird and Co. was an old European managing agency which had originated as a firm supplying labour to the railways. The firm expanded rapidly so that by 1914 it controlled the largest block of investment in jute and coal in India. F. W. Heilger, a group with smaller interests in jute and coal, but with large funds sunk in the biggest paper manufacturing complex in India (the Titaghur Paper Mills), merged with Bird in 1917. At that date their combined organizations and associated concerns had a capital of over £20 million, a revenue of £3 million and over a hundred thousand employees. During the war the group expanded into silica brick manufacture, electricity supply, coke production, limestone quarrying, structural steel works and repairs and steel rolling. In the post-war boom Birds floated the United Steel Corporation of Asia, designed as the largest steel plant east of Suez, to be established with technical collaboration from Cammell Laird & Co. However, this plan never reached fruition and a number of other new ventures in tanning, graphite production and saw milling quickly ran into difficulties. The failure of these 'war baby' companies left its mark on Birds for the rest of the inter-war period. The firm had to write off Rs 90 lakhs in the 1921 accounts and the total cost of retrieving the situation was estimated at £1.25 million.[24] During the 1920s and 1930s Birds expanded in old lines but eschewed any major innovations. At the outbreak of the second world war the group was mainly based around jute exporting and manufacture, coal production and paper production. Birds then held managing agency contracts for 13 coal companies, 10 jute mills, 4 jute baling companies, 5 engineering companies, 3 quarrying companies, 7 invest-

---

[24] This account is drawn from Ray, *Industrialization*, pp. 268ff, which relies on the company history, G. Harrison, *Bird & Co. of Calcutta: A History Produced to Mark the Firm's Centenary 1864–1964* (Calcutta, 1964, privately printed). 'Birds' is used in this article as a convenient title for the whole group.

ment companies, a saw mill, a patent stone company, an oil distribution company and the Titaghur Paper Mills. In addition, the group
had important selling agencies in sugar and cement for Indian manufacturers and in other fields such as paint and adding machines for
foreign manufacturers.[25]

Of all the leaders of the expatriate business community Benthall was
one of the most willing to adapt to changing relations with Indian
businessmen. Although he fought hard in constitutional discussions to
ensure protection against commercial discrimination, he recognized
that such agreements would be a poor substitute for a genuine spirit of
co-operation.[26] G. B. Morton (a partner in Bird's Calcutta office)
echoed Benthall's own views when he wrote to him in July 1941: 'I
entirely agree with you that it will be better for us if we can collaborate with Indian capital and management. . .'.
Morton went on to comment on proposals for commercial safeguards:

Their actual value has always been doubtful but if they are not likely to be
required it would seem that India will not mind giving them. Like good
agreements . . . they can then be locked in the safe and never referred to
again.[27]

In the late 1920s Benthall was able to see that, if forced to retire from
India for health reasons, going into partnership with a major Indian
group was a viable plan for the future.[28] By the mid 1930s he was
planning to increase indianization in technical and supervisory staff in
the jute mills, although largely to save on salary costs,[29] while by 1939
his behaviour in building bridges with Indian entrepreneurs had
attracted the condemnation of the Finance Member of the Government of India, Sir James Grigg.[30]

[25] See unsigned note 'Re. Accounts and Finance Department' of 15.4.41 in Benthall
Papers (henceforth BP) XVI, and advertisement in *Investors' India Yearbook 1938–9*. In
terms of size of capital, jute trading and manufacturing overshadowed everything else,
next came the coal mines, with Titaghur Paper Mills coming not far behind the entire
coal group; other manufacturing interests were small by comparison (see Ray, *Industrialization*, pp. 270–1).

[26] See E. C. Benthall to Sir George Godfrey of 21.11.31 in BP VII and E. C. Benthall
to P. H. Browne of 12.11.31 in BP II. The internal correspondence of Birds' partners is
riddled with nicknames and initials; for the sake of convenience these have been replaced
in the references by surnames.

[27] G. B. Morton to E. C. Benthall of 22.7.41 in BP XV.

[28] Diary Entry 24.1.29 in BP VII. Benthall went on to note that in this case he would
keep the 'master hand' himself.

[29] E. C. Benthall to J. A. McKerrow of 29.6.37 in BP XI: a marginal note states that
this had been the policy at TPM for some time.

[30] See P. J. Grigg to H. V. Hodson of 24.1.39 in Grigg Papers file 2/11, quoted in
Tomlinson, *Political Economy*, p. 53.

Dr Ray uses the example of the history of Birds in the inter-war period to demonstrate the innate conservatism of expatriate enterprise. Certain remarks by Benthall, commenting on the collapse of the 'war baby' companies—a stress on 'sound business', on 'consolidating the business' and a resolution not to become involved again in ventures 'beyond the firm's normal experience'—are taken as indicative of a declining entrepreneurial attitude.[31] The experience of the war babies, and of other expansionary schemes after 1918, certainly stayed in Benthall's mind for the rest of his career. As he wrote to George Morton in February 1941 about a planned re-equipment of the Titaghur Paper Mills:

Renovations *must* slow up because we *must* also have a first class cash position to face the future keen struggle for markets. Do not. let the engineers run away with themselves in good times as we did in the last war boom (except at Titaghur).[32]

Yet the case needs more evidence than this. It is hardly surprising that a private partnership faced with considerable annual losses and a substantial bill for reorganization after failed expansion would see the need for 'sound business' immediately afterwards. But this is not to say that the position could not change thereafter or, if it did not do so, that new factors did not become important. The fact that Birds burnt their fingers in 1918–21 does not mean that the firm would necessarily refrain from expansion thereafter. We must now consider the day-to-day problems that Birds faced in more detail, and the best place to begin is to investigate their fortunes in their most important area of activity, the jute industry.

The jute trade and industry of Bengal is often regarded as the archetypal expatriate business sector. The control that the expatriate firms exercised over the marketing and even the production of raw jute has often been stressed.[33] So has the ability of the established firms, working through the Indian Jute Mills Association, the most powerful and effective manufacturers' association in India, to control the jute industry to their collective advantage.[34] The expatriate firms

---

[31] Ray, *Industrialization*, pp. 270–1.

[32] E. C. Benthall to G. B. Morton of 22.2.41 in BP XVI.

[33] See for example Bagchi, *Private Investment*, pp. 263–4, 267–9; R. K. Ray, 'The Crisis of Bengal Agriculture 1870–1920—the Dynamics of Immobility' in *Indian Economic and Social History Review*, x (1973), pp. 244–79; and S. Mukherji, 'Imperialism through a Mercantilist Function', in *Essays in Honour of Prof. S. C. Sarkar* (New Delhi, 1976), p. 731.

[34] Thus, as Bagchi notes of the period 1914–29, 'the mills on the Hooghly had practically a captive supply of jute, and they also were monopolists as far as jute manufactures were concerned' (*Private Investment*, pp. 275–6).

involved in the processing of jute also dominated the exports of the
raw material to manufacturing centres abroad.[35] Yet the history of
the jute industry is one of production constantly outstripping demand.
This problem had arisen as early as the 1870s, and the IJMA had
been founded in 1884 to regulate production by limiting the number
of hours worked in each mill and by discouraging extensions or new
mills except at times of boom.[36] It is usually argued that up to the late
1920s the members of the IJMA were able to determine the price paid
for raw jute in Bengal, and the overseas price of exported raw jute,
both directly and indirectly.[37]

Yet if the expatriate firms exercised hegemonic control over the jute
trade up to the 1920s, their position weakened considerably thereafter.
As early as 1928 Birds were becoming concerned about the difficulties
of extracting raw jute from the up-country centres. It was alleged that
cultivators were now willing and able to hold up the crop to ensure
better prices.[38] A more serious threat was the activities of Indian
merchants operating through the *futka* bazaar, or futures market. Indian merchants had always played a part in the marketing of jute,
providing advances to cultivators and arranging for shipment to Calcutta. Before 1914 it may be that they acted only as agents for, or
under the influence of, the expatriate firms,[39] but even before the first
world war the IJMA was becoming concerned about the way that
'speculative' activities by Marwari merchants were affecting jute
prices.[40] The operations of the *futka* market, from which the expatriate firms appear to have been effectively excluded,[41] had achieved
considerable importance by 1929. In that year G. D. Birla made a
determined, although ultimately unsuccessful, effort to corner the raw

[35] Exports of raw and manufactured jute represented on average over 50% of the
exports of Indian merchandise from Calcutta in the 1920s, and about 25% of India's
total merchandise exports.

[36] See *Investors' India Yearbook 1925–6*, pp. 183–4.

[37] See Ray, 'Bengal Agriculture', pp. 260–5. Timberg, on the other hand, notes that
'by 1915 we read: "A large share of the sea-borne and inland trade of Calcutta was in the
hands of Marwari merchants"' (*Origins*, p. 163).

[38] M. P. Thomas to E. C. Benthall of 4.12.28 in BP I. The *Investors' India Yearbook*
noted in 1926–27 that 'growers have realized that a crop of over 100 locs means poor
prices and are in consequence holding up jute which they are storing in the villages in
peels' (p. 182).

[39] 'In the internal trade in jute, the Europeans were the dominant element as soon as
one left the villages' according to Bagchi (*Private Investment*, p. 265).

[40] See *ibid.*, p. 278 and fn. 45.

[41] See E. C. Benthall to Sir George Godfrey of 15.5.29 in BP VII: 'Since I see no
possibility of stopping the existing phutka we might as well acknowledge the fact and try
to get one in which we can safely and openly deal'.

jute market by selling at Rs 6 below the packing cost, backed by his operations in futures.[42]

While the expatriates continued to deplore the existence of this important market that they could not control, and made frequent appeals for government to regulate it, their Marwari rivals developed futures trading to a fine art. Whereas Benthall argued that *futka* trading destabilized the jute market, and led to cut-price exports as unsuccessful speculators were forced to sell short on the spot market, Birla contended that futures trading helped the balers by enabling them to adapt pricing policy to expected demand.[43] By the mid 1930s the Marwari traders had certainly managed to capture a good deal of the jute export trade. In the busy season of 1934–35 Indian balers shipped 37 per cent of the total raw jute exports, and supplied 44 per cent of the jute shipped to Dundee. By this date the Indian exporters had replaced the expatriates as the main suppliers of American, Russian, German, French, Belgian and Dutch mills and had even captured a third of the Japanese market in which the expatriates had no share. Benthall suggested a number of reasons for this state of affairs— the habit of the London firms, even the London end of Birds, of buying in sterling rather than commissioning purchases through their expatriate partners in India; the ability of Indian shippers to trim prices by hedging in *futka*; the more generous credit facilities offered by continental mills; the superior information that Indian shippers had about market conditions; and the fact that the standard commissions and profit rates charged by the expatriate firms made them uncompetitive. As Benthall noted, 'the enterprise and efficiency of the modern Marwarri [*sic*] merchant cannot be expected to be fully appreciated abroad'.[44] By the mid 1930s, then, it is clear that Indian enterprise had destroyed the hegemony of expatriate firms over raw jute exports, largely because it had developed a new market institution that the expatriates could not control and because of better contacts both up-country and abroad.

Loss of control over the raw jute export market did not necessarily damage the expatriates' hold over jute manufacturing. However, the history of the jute mill industry in the 1920s and 1930s reveals much

[42] Diary Entries 10.2.29, 19.2.29, 7.3.29 and E. C. Benthall to Sir George Godfrey of 15.5.29 in BP VII.

[43] E. C. Benthall to Sir George Godfrey of 15.5.29 in BP VII.

[44] See 'Note as to a basis of discussion between Sir E. C. Benthall and Bird & Co. (London) Ltd.' of 25.6.35 and unsigned comment on this of 27.6.35 in BP X. The most successful Indian firms were Cotton Agents (Birla Bros.), Nagarmull, Tolaram, Lohia and Ramjeedas.

the same process at work. The old techniques of expatriate hegemony, developed at a time when they faced little effective competition, proved inadequate against a concerted attack from outside. In addition, the jute industry illustrates another important point about the economic history of modern India. The Calcutta jute mills never even tried to pretend that they were operating in a free market. By and large, the history of jute manufacture in India is the history of a cartel, although the course of that history was not always what the cartel wished it to be. Other industries, as they emerged in India in the first half of the twentieth century, also attempted to control their environment by combination, and the story of Indian industrialization ought not to be studied in isolation from this tendency. The jute industry illustrates the problems well, for the IJMA was the largest and most effective of the manufacturers' cartels. The existence of the IJMA affected the development of the jute industry profoundly, and also influenced the relationship between expatriate firms and their Indian rivals. Once Indian entrepreneurs started to set up jute mills in the late 1920s— often, it was alleged, as a way of diversifying risks taken in trading in raw jute futures[45]— then the expatriates had to try to reach some accommodation with them. Although numerically the expatriate firms dominated the IJMA throughout our period, the ability of Indian entrepreneurs to threaten to leave the Association, or simply to set up in competition with it, gave them a considerable amount of leverage in decision making. In addition, the development of the *futka* market had, by the 1930s, disturbed the arrangements by which expatriate-run mills bought up raw jute at satisfactory prices.[46]

This is not the place to write the long, complex and somewhat mournful history of the IJMA restriction schemes. For our purposes it is enough to note that, with a short break in 1920–21, the IJMA operated restriction fairly successfully until 1930. Then, however, the attempt to combat the effects of the depression put a great strain on the Association and in 1931 two major mills broke away from it. In 1932, after the intervention of the Governor of Bengal, a new restriction scheme was introduced, which lasted until the IJMA gave notice to terminate it in September 1935, a decision which came into effect in

[45] See G. B. Morton to E. C. Benthall of 23.8.35 in BP X.
[46] In 1932 the spokesman of the expatriate-dominated Calcutta Jute Dealers' Association complained that the growth of the *futka* market had meant that European mills could no longer obtain jute at an acceptable price. While Indian merchants took note of the futures market in offering rates for up-country jute, the expatriates did not, basing their rates solely on an estimate of expected demand and supply within the IJMA restriction scheme (see Bagchi, *Private Investment*, pp. 283–4).

April 1936. Attempts to organize a new scheme then failed, and the Government of India declined to intervene. In September 1938 the Government of Bengal limited by ordinance the number of hours that mills could work, and in January 1939 a new agreement was finally signed which, for the first time, included non-Association mills as well as IJMA members.[47]

A number of points are worth stressing here. Firstly, the Association always had difficulty in enforcing its agreements and, until 1939, the effectiveness of these agreements was compromised by the existence of a growing number of mills outside the Association. Thus the fundamental problem of over-capacity was never solved. As Benthall pointed out in 1935, over the period 1930–35 the jute mills of India had 90 per cent more looms than in 1920 (evidence of considerably increased investment), but produced only 20 per cent more goods. In addition, mills founded outside the Association, a process which had begun only in 1928, now produced 13 per cent of all jute manufactures.[48] The Government of India had an even more gloomy prognosis:

Even in 1912–14 the mills were working for about half the possible weekly hours, and the machinery then in existence was capable of meeting a substantially higher demand than India had known before or has known since. Today the disparity between actual and potential production is immense. The existing demands could possibly be supplied by a quarter of the machinery now available, and the highest demand ever reached could probably be satisfied by a third of the existing mills.[49]

By the mid 1930s the Government of India was concerned that restriction of production in India encouraged manufacturing centres elsewhere. Benthall, on the other hand, was more worried by the fact that restriction schemes prevented sound and efficient companies, such as those managed by Birds, from realizing their full potential, while sustaining inefficient producers and encouraging newcomers.[50] The existence of the restriction scheme in the early 1930s meant that a new manufacturer could either join the IJMA, and be allocated working

[47] This account is based on *ibid.*, pp. 280–3 and the excellent annual summaries in the *Investors' India Yearbook*.
[48] 'Government intervention in the jute trade', memorandum by E. C. Benthall of 29.6.35 in BP V.
[49] The Government of India estimated that in 1935 production of jute manufactures in India was somewhat below its pre-war level, while the number of mills had increased by 60%, the number of spindles by 60% and the number of looms by 90%. See 'Memorandum re the question of controlling the output of manufactured jute in Bengal' enclosed with Addl. Secy. Government of Bengal (Finance, Commerce and Marine Department) to Secretary Indian Jute Mills Association no. 8775 of 12.3.35 in BP V.
[50] 'Government intervention in the jute trade', *loc. cit.* BP V.

arrangements that allowed even the least efficient to make some profit, or else stay outside the Association and undercut its prices by working longer hours or double shifts. The problem of new mills founded by Indians had become serious by the mid 1930s and was the cause of the IJMA's decision to abandon the 1932 restriction scheme. The growth of new mills was of concern to established Indian manufacturers as well as to the expatriates. New mills were now very cheap to set up, and good returns were assured outside the Association. As B. M. Birla lamented in 1934 (Birla Bros. were members of the IJMA by this date):

In former years, in order to build a new mill one had to buy new machinery and spend a very large amount on buildings, power plants and coolie lines, etc. Nowadays those who erect new Jute Mills generally resort to second-hand looms and put them in rented sheds and take the required power from the Electricity Supply Corporation and thus complete their Mills with a very small capital. A factory of 100 looms of this kind can easily be put up with a capital of about 1½ lacs of rupees. A small mill of 100 looms working 120 hours per week is able to produce as much as an Associated Mill of 300 looms due to the restrictions on the latter.[51]

Benthall was anxious to return to free competition in 1935, for he saw this as the only way in which the industry could be rationalized. Birds' mills were thought to be sound and efficient and to have nothing to fear from the collapse of the IJMA agreement. But the other expatriate firms were not so happy. As the *Investor's India Yearbook* had noted in 1929, the frequent but unimplemented threat of the IJMA to resort to free competition if new mills were founded outside its control sounded like a bluff.[52] In 1935 Scott, the Secretary of the IJMA, told Morton of Birds that ending the restriction scheme would hit expatriate-controlled mills as they would not be able to compete with their Indian rivals. Morton, who disbelieved Scott's figures on competitiveness and supported Benthall's case for a free for all, surmised that ending control might well affect the short-term profits of managing agents, and that those directors of expatriate managing agency houses who were nearing retirement might object to this.[53] Benthall's arguments on this point, and to some

[51] Memorandum by B. M. Birla, enclosed with letter to E. C. Benthall of 14.3.34 in BP X. It is interesting to compare this estimate of initial capital required to found a jute mill in 1934 with Bagchi's estimate (see *Private Investment* pp. 264, 274) that the minimum investment needed for a viable jute mill in the period 1910–23 was over Rs 2 million. On Bagchi's figures for 1923 a mill of 100 looms would have cost Rs 16 lakhs for machinery alone, and Rs 27.5 lakhs overall. Thus the 300 loom Associated mill such as Birla refers to could represent an investment of almost 50 times the new one capable of equal output under the IJMA scheme.
[52] *Investors' India Yearbook 1928–9*, p. 183.
[53] Memorandum by G. B. Morton of 22.8.35 in BP X.

extent those of his opponents within the IJMA also, seem to have been based more on rational business calculations than on a sense of imminent retreat from the colonial economy.

The problems of the jute industry also illustrate well Benthall's views on seeking help from government. Casting around for a new basis for agreement in 1935, the majority of members of the IJMA wanted to ask the Government of India to help impose and run a restriction scheme. Although almost all the expatriate firms were in favour of this, Benthall was not. He saw the dangers of encouraging government intervention in industry to be increased by the possibility that that government might shortly be controlled by Indian politicians, partly because those politicians would have close connections with his business rivals.[54] But more important than this was the possibility of over-regulation and general political chicanery, and Benthall thought that the dangers of this to industry following closer government intervention were as real with the Conservative government in the United Kingdom as with a future nationalist government in Bengal.[55] In any case, as we have already seen, the majority of expatriate firms in the IJMA were quite happy to pay the price of government intervention if a new restriction scheme could be imposed. In the event, the Government of India rejected the IJMA's overtures, arguing that rationalization should take place by competition, that cartels were not in the best interests of the cultivator or the consumer, that maintaining Indian prices of manufactured jute artificially high encouraged competition from elsewhere, and that to intervene in favour of the IJMA would set a dangerous precedent for other industries.[56]

The essential problem which the expatriate firms faced in the jute trade and industry in the 1930s was that of controlling supply. Certain expatriate firms, such as Gillanders Arbuthnot and Begg, Dunlop & Co., had been happy to buck the IJMA's regulations while they saw a

[54] See *ibid.* and E. C. Benthall to Mr Campbell of 26.6.35 in BP X.

[55] 'Government intervention in the jute trade' *loc. cit.* BP V.

[56] On this last point, New Delhi commented, '. . . the Government of India cannot overlook the fact that if they agreed to restrict production for jute manufacturers those engaged in other industries could claim similar assistance. There are very few industries in which potential production is not greatly in excess of actual demand, and in which a measure of protection from internal competition would not result in temporary benefit to the capitalists concerned.' 'Memorandum re the question of controlling the output of manufactured jute in Bengal' *loc. cit.* BP V. In 1932 the Government of India had refused to become involved in imposing a restriction scheme for jute because of fears of being sucked into the position of regulating the internal economy too closely. The idea of using labour legislation to prevent non-Association mills working longer hours had been specifically ruled out of consideration. See Government of India Finance Department file 17(65)F of 1932 (NAI).

profit in it in the 1920s, but by the 1930s the vast majority of the expatriates—Benthall excluded—saw a continuation of control as their only hope. Benthall argued that the IJMA cartel had been following a mistaken policy for some time; as he wrote in 1935, 'by over-restrict-ing . . . we have maintained our profits but at the expense of weakening our position in the Trade vis-a-vis local and overseas mills'.[57] In reality, however, the problems of the expatriate firms in jute went deeper than this. In both the trade and the industry their old hegemonic power had been blown away by new, powerful rivals. This seems to have had more to do with the emergence of new economic forces and institutions from within the previously 'unorganized' sector of the Indian economy than with any conscious decision by the expatriate firms to cut their losses and depart.

For the expatriate firms of Calcutta jute was a declining industry in the 1930s, and one from which lessons are difficult to draw because of its complex and confusing structure. A different perspective on the limi-tations at work on Bird-Heilger's activities can be obtained by looking now at an industry in which the firm attempted to expand in the 1930s, planning a considerable diversification of its interests. This was steel, a field which Birds had failed to exploit in the post-war boom and to which they were to turn again in 1935.

In the mid 1930s the Tata Iron and Steel Company (TISCo) enjoyed a virtual monopoly of steel production in India. But Tatas did not produce their steel entirely from their own resources. Their Jamshedpur plant was an important market for coal, limestone and silica bricks produced by companies managed by Birds, and also for pig iron pro-duced by the Bengal Iron and Steel Company (BISCo) and the Indian Iron and Steel Company (IISCo), both of which were managed by Martin Burn, a Calcutta managing agency house jointly controlled by Indian and expatriate interests. Birds also supplied coal to these iron producers. In 1935 Tatas found their monopoly threatened by the plans of Charles Perin, an American technical expert who had previously been employed by TISCo, to establish a new steel plant in India using capital from London and the United States. Martin Burn were concerned about the future of their pig iron production should this new company become established and Birds were worried that falling demand for pig iron (in Japan as well as in India) would affect their sales of coal. In these circumstances the three India-based companies—Tatas, Martin Burn and Birds—began negotiations to collaborate in setting up a new steel company that would shut any foreign intruders out from the Indian

[57] 'Government intervention in the jute trade' *loc. cit.* BP V.

market.[58] Tatas, who took the lead in the negotiations, were to provide 50 per cent of the capital and to supply 50 per cent of the directors; Martin Burn and Birds were to supply 25 per cent of capital and directors each. The Tata board was anxious that any future developments in Indian steel production should remain under their control. As J. B. Sanklatvala explained to Benthall, although it would be possible for Tatas to expand production at Jamshedpur quickly and easily,

we have decided, however, that it is wiser in the interests of the country generally to take a longer view (and we hope that in the long run it will prove as good for ourselves) by giving practical effect to our realisation that there are other existing industries in India which have scope for developing sooner or later into steel-making. We think that in the long run it will be better if these interests, or as many of them as can be brought together on a reasonable basis, join forces for the purpose of new development.[59]

Despite these hopes, the negotiations quickly ran into difficulties. For Martin Burn the main problem was that of imposing a corporate strategy on the directors of the Bengal Iron and Steel Company. Under the terms of a merger agreement, BISCo was entitled to a share of the profits of any venture in steel production that involved the Indian Iron and Steel Company; its directors were also anxious to get the best value possible for its assets as the price of co-operating with the new company, and were prepared to bargain with Perin as well. The IISCo directors, on the other hand, led by Biren Mukherjee who was becoming the dominant partner in Martin Burn, were unhappy with Tatas' insistence on majority control over the new company.[60]

By November 1935 Martin Burn had abandoned the new project; they were to set up their own steel company, the Steel Corporation of Bengal, in 1937 following an amalgamation of BISCo and IISCo. Tatas were still prepared to go ahead in partnership with Birds alone, supplying 60 per cent of the capital and directors.[61] But Birds now had doubts as to whether they could raise the capital required—Rs 82.5 lakhs worth—and this scheme came to nothing also. However, Birds' plans to become involved in iron and steel production did not end here. In 1937 the firm was again involved in negotiations, this time with the Japanese firm of Kishimoto Shoten, to establish a pig iron foundry. The Japanese were anxious about future supplies of pig iron from IISCo and wanted to

[58] This account is based on papers in BP VI. Perin's plans came to nothing.
[59] J. B. Sanklatvala to E. C. Benthall of 1.9.35 in BP VI.
[60] See A. R. Dalal to H. P. Bennett of 16.10.35, E. C. Benthall to J. A. McKerrow of 19.10.35, Biren Mukherjee to J. B. Sanklatvala of 16.10.35 and 'Aide Memoire' by J. A. McKerrow of 23.8.35 in BP VI.
[61] Telegram Sanklatvala to Benthall 13.11.35 in BP VI.

set up an iron works of their own in India, using Birds coal and under Birds management. Kishimoto Shoten got as far as making arrangements to dodge the Japanese currency restrictions and export capital to Birds by over-paying them for pig iron exports and by selling shares they owned in Indian companies, but eventually the international complications of the period, in particular Japan's increasing involvement in China, put paid to the scheme.[62]

The story of Bird's attempt to enter the field of iron and steel production reveals a number of interesting features. The first is that the expatriate and Indian entrepreneurs involved were anxious to combine against the new threat from abroad to steel sales in India posed by Perin's scheme of 1935. While in London in that year, Benthall went to great lengths to ensure that Perin's plan would not be backed by British capital. He had extensive talks with Montagu Norman at the Bank of England and with Sir Andrew Duncan, of the British Iron and Steel Federation, who was Norman's chief adviser on the industry. Benthall was able to persuade both men that it would be a mistake to encourage British steel interests to move into India under Perin's wing. Norman offered his support on this,[63] while Duncan went further in stating that the future of the steel industry in the empire as a whole should be organized on the basis of agreed cartelization between ogiopolistic local producers. As Benthall noted:

He [Duncan] rated the advantage of competition below the advantage of rationalisation (though he avoided the use of that word). He considered that the form of competition that was most desirable was internal competition in an organised industry, and that the day was past when rival groups should be set up to try to do each other down.[64]

For their own part, the directors of Birds had no qualms about joining a company dominated by Indian interests. Indeed, they saw this as a positive advantage. As Benthall pointed out, a major benefit of going in with Tatas was that 'it is, I think, farsighted to consider having some of our Indian assets under Indian control':[65] McKerrow, another partner, was equally anxious to exclude foreign interests from any new company;

[62] See Note by E. C. Benthall 26.3.37; S. A. Roberts to H. P. Bennett 1.4.37; telegram Birds (Calcutta) to Birds (London) of 10.5.37 in BP XI; E. C. Benthall to S. A. Roberts of 19.9.37 in BP XIII and E. C. Benthall to S. A. Roberts of 8.11.37 in BP XIV.
[63] E. C. Benthall to J. A. McKerrow of 19.10.35 in BP VI. Norman was an important figure because the Bank of England was heavily involved in providing finance for the British iron and steel industry.
[64] 'Memorandum of Discussion with Sir Andrew Duncan 1.11.35' by E. C. Benthall in BP VI.
[65] E. C. Benthall to J. A. McKerrow of 28.11.35 in BP VI.

as he noted in August 1935—'we feel it would be much better to make the complexion of the new Company entirely Indian (though not quite black!)'.[66]

The second important point is that Birds were eventually prevented from diversifying into steel production because of a shortage of capital. Once Martin Burn had dropped out of the tripartite negotiations in late 1935, Benthall knew that there would be problems on this front. The Rs 75 lakhs that had to be raised under the original scheme were feasible, provided that generous allowances were made for the plant and equipment of the Bird companies to be brought in, but under the new plan for a joint venture with Tatas less was to be allowed for these assets. Of their total share of Rs 82.5 lakhs for the joint venture Birds would have to find around Rs 50 lakhs in cash. This was beyond their resources without extensive borrowing from a bank (which would be very expensive) or a public share issue in the new company (which would be unlikely to succeed since initial returns would be low). Benthall estimated that the firm could raise only about Rs 30 lakhs of venture capital, and even this would mean sacrificing the partners' profits for seven to ten years. He concluded that the risk was not worth taking, and it seems to have been for this reason that the negotiations with Tatas eventually collapsed.[67] The abortive discussions with Kishimoto Shoten two years later tell the same story—only if capital were available from elsewhere could Birds go ahead with pig iron production. The failure of the firm to expand into this important new field seems clearly to have been caused by a lack of capital, not a failure of will or an over-cautious entrepreneurial attitude. A shortage of liquid funds, rather than an obsession with sound business practice, or a concern not to become involved with enterprises outside the firm's normal experience, was the major constraint.

The problem of raising capital assumed an even greater significance for Birds in the late 1930s and early 1940s. The firm has the general reputation of being more concerned than most expatriate houses with maintaining direct control over the companies it managed by investment in them. The evidence of the Benthall papers suggests that this reputation is well founded. Benthall himself was intensely wary of placing the firm in a position in which share dealings could threaten the managing agent's control over the companies in their network. Since proxies could be employed in registering shares, and since transfers of shares to other holders were often not recorded, the threat to any public

[66] J. A. McKerrow to E. C. Benthall of 23.8.35 in BP VI.
[67] E. C. Benthall to J. A. McKerrow of 3.10.35 and 28.11.35 in BP VI.

company of a takeover by rival interests was often a real one.[68] The aim of such operations could be to disrupt the overall corporate strategy on behalf of another corporation, to seek a speculative profit from cornering shares, to buy a seat on the board and there demand increased dividends,[69] or termination of the managing agency agreement. There was considerable concern in Birds' Calcutta office in 1941, for example, when it was discovered that a Bombay solicitor named Chaiwala had bought up over 13 per cent of the shares in one Birds company, Kumardhari Engineering Works, as well as considerable blocks of shares in other companies. Frantic letters were exchanged between the partners until it was discovered that Chaiwala was simply being speculative and did not wish to convert his shareholding into influence over management.[70]

This sort of threat was always present for Birds' public companies. To combat it Benthall had ruled in 1929 that a holding of 25 per cent of the issued share capital of all public companies was essential to ensure control.[71] By 1941, concerned by the coming of self-government and the fact that the renewal of managing agency agreements was on the horizon, Benthall increased the requirement to a 33 per cent holding.[72] This he thought adequate as no more than two thirds of the shareholders had ever attended a company meeting. The problem was that securing this sort of control was expensive, and circumstances in the late 1930s and early 1940s made this expense a considerable strain on the partners' financial position.

Benthall and his partners never tried to control directly all the public companies which they managed. Only in one manufacturing company—Ondal Coal—did the partnership itself own more than 5 per cent of the shares issued. Major blocks were, however, held by investment companies within the group, by trustee companies and by outside shareholders who had given the managing agents proxy powers. Proxies were particularly important in the jute industry. Whereas the group itself held on average only 11 per cent of the shares of the jute mills it

[68] It was increased by the practice of rival groups of shareholders hiring attorneys to represent them at shareholders' meetings. In Bombay often the only people who attended such meetings were the rival advocates hired by each side (see E. C. Benthall to Sir George Godfrey of 15.5.29 in BP VII).

[69] As Benthall wrote to his brother Paul in 1941 of the Orissa Mineral Development Corporation, 'it has in the past been a great advantage that in this Company we have been able to avoid interference from the shareholders. We have in consequence been able to build it up into its strong financial position.' E. C. Benthall to A. P. Benthall of 5.10.41 in BP XV.

[70] See correspondence in BP XV.

[71] Diary entry 10.9.29 in BP VII.

[72] E. C. Benthall to A. P. Benthall of 24.8.41 in BP XV.

managed in 1937, proxies increased the average holding with control to 42 per cent, with only one company—Clive Mills Ltd.—below the magic 33 per cent mark.[73]

The investment companies within the group were a new departure of the 1930s, an attempt to secure Indian finance while retaining corporate control. Birds Investments Ltd, the largest of these public investment companies, was founded in 1936 'to invest the monies subscribed by the Shareholders in the shares and debentures of companies, particularly those connected with the business and industries in which the firm of Bird and Co. and F. H. Heilger and Co. are interested'. By 1938 the company had a paid-up capital of Rs 30 lakhs, and had made investments worth Rs 38 lakhs. Two smaller companies—General Investment and Trust Co. and Investment and Finance Co.—were much older, but were also expanded considerably in 1936. Both companies had the object of investing in 'carefully selected' companies as well as in public debt bonds.[74] The only breakdown of intercorporate share holdings that exists in the Benthall papers is for 1937; in that year neither General Investment nor Investment and Finance held any significant number of shares in Bird-Heilger companies. Bird Investments, on the other hand, certainly was an important investor within the group. However, only 24 per cent of the shares that it held, and none of the debentures, were in Birds companies: the only major holdings in individual public companies in the complex were a 40 per cent holding in the Churilia Coal Co. and a 17 per cent one in the General Investment and Finance Co.[75]

The establishment of public investment companies which could channel Indian funds into Birds companies gave the partners of Bird-Heilger some room in which to manoeuvre in combining new investment with

[73] 'Memorandum on shares held in Birds Companies by subsidiaries', enclosed with A. P. Benthall to E. C. Benthall of 28.10.37 in BP XIV. This meant, of course, that the companies had to be run in such a way as to please the shareholders who had given proxy powers to the managing agents.

[74] See listings for these companies in *Investors' India Yearbook 1938–9*. By 1938 General Investment had a capital of Rs 2.5 lakhs and investments worth Rs 3.4 lakhs, while Investment and Finance had a capital of Rs 4.5 lakhs with investments worth Rs 7.5 lakhs. Sir Edward Benthall, and his brother Paul, were also involved in several other investment companies, notably the New India Investment Corporation. This company, founded in 1936 with a capital of Rs 23 lakhs, had an Indian majority on the board and an Indian firm of company secretaries. The directors included E. C. Benthall, Sir Badridas Goenka (Chairman) and G. D. Birla. It was Benthall's 'firm friendship' with Goenka that had got him involved in this (see E. C. Benthall to A. P. Benthall of 15.12.37 in BP XIV).

[75] See Birds Investments Ltd balance sheet for 30.9.37 and 'Memorandum on shares held in Birds Companies by subsidiaries' in BP XIV. The balance sheet gives only the number of shares held, not their worth.

continued control. But the advantages that this innovation brought were smaller than might have been expected. Only one company—Birds Investments—had bought significant numbers of shares in the group's ventures before the second world war, although this state of affairs seems to have altered later.[76] In addition, the group had to retain control of the investment companies themselves. Figures for the group's holdings of the shares of these companies are not available for our period, but in 1958 these were remarkably high. Then the partners held 43 per cent of Birds Investments, 64 per cent of Investment and Finance and 70 per cent of General Investment and Trust.[77] To a considerable extent, then, these companies had become a way of recycling private investment by the partners, rather than a way of attracting in new capital from outside the firm.

In 1937 the most important source of inter-corporate investment was a private trust company, Eastern Investments Ltd. Of the total number of shares in managed companies owned within the group in 1937, Eastern Investments held 71 per cent, just under 300,000 in total. Eastern Investments was the major source of controlled finance for a number of companies, notably the Bandroochuck Coal Co. (99 per cent of issued shares), the Burrakur Coal Co. (26 per cent of issued shares), Titaghur Paper Mills (28 per cent of issued shares) and Clive Jute Mills (11 per cent of issued shares).[78]

Eastern Investments was run by the trustees of the estate of Lord Cable, who had been the dominant partner of Birds until 1927 (Benthall was Lord Cable's son-in-law). The company provided a source of strength for the rest of the group, but also a potential source of weakness. Eastern Investments was not controlled or run directly by the active partners of Birds[79] and when, in the late 1930s, the trustees wanted to sell out shares in managed companies major problems were created. This was especially so for control of Clive Jute Mills, the jute company for which the managing agency had the fewest share proxies and in which the group's control, even with the Eastern Investments block of 11 per cent, was weakest. When the Cable trustees began selling Clive

[76] By the 1950s all the investment companies had become a very important source of intercorporate investment and control (see Hazari, *Corporate Private Sector*, pp. 118–9, 131–2).

[77] *Ibid.*, p. 119.

[78] 'Memorandum on shares held in Birds Companies by subsidiaries' *loc. cit.* in BP XIV.

[79] H. P. Bennett of the London office was a trustee, but could be outvoted by the other executors. It is worth noting that the terms of Lord Cable's will laid an obligation on his successors to continue in business in India, and thus the alternative of repatriation or diversification was not open to them.

stock in late 1941 the partners were faced with the need to find extra cash to maintain their control. Overall the trustees were planning by December 1941 to sell Rs 90 lakhs worth of shares in Birds companies and the firm could not find more than between Rs 10 lakhs and Rs 30 lakhs to replace these holdings.[80] The prospect of setting up a public company to buy these shares was not attractive. As Morton argued: 'Once the public were concerned with the firms, we all believe that their disintegration would not be long delayed and we are all strongly opposed to any such step if it could be avoided by any practical means.'[81] Owing to a gap in the Benthall papers the end of this story is not known.[82] However, the problem of being second-generation entrepreneurs may well, in this respect, have held Benthall and his associates back from plans for major new capital investments to take advantage of the opportunities offered by the expansion of demand for Indian-made products during the second world war.

The need to spend money to secure control over the companies they managed may have inhibited the partners of Birds in considering expansionary schemes after 1939. Yet there were also other factors which held them back, in the early years of the war at least. In a discussion on whether to begin machine tool production at the Kumardhabi Engineering Works in late 1941, for example, the partners decided against expansion on business grounds. Although the government was offering to pay the costs of the machinery (but not of construction) for such an expansion by a loan to be redeemed in part by buying back the machinery with a reduction for wear and tear after hostilities, the partners saw this as a bad bargain. They envisaged that after the war much cheaper sources of machinery would be available, and that the equipment supplied by government would make too limited a range of product.[83] Both Benthall and his partners were anxious to expand the firm's activities once the war was over, but thought that a sound capital base was the first necessity. Only once this had been achieved would Birds be able to compete with larger rivals.[84] The partners saw difficulties ahead, but few insuperable ones. As Morton wrote to Benthall in July 1941:

[80] See E. C. Benthall to A. P. Benthall of 24.8.41 in BP XV: E. C. Benthall to G. B. Morton of 17.8.41 and G. B. Morton to E. C. Benthall of 8.12.41 in BP XVIII.

[81] G. B. Morton to E. C. Benthall of 8.12.41 in BP XVIII.

[82] In 1948 the managing agency of Clive Mills was transferred to Shree Krishna Investment Co. Ltd.

[83] Minutes of Partners' Meeting of 3.1.41. in BP XVIII.

[84] E. C. Benthall to A. P. Benthall of 25.1.41 and E. C. Benthall to G. B. Morton of 9.11.41 in BP XV.

I entirely agree with you that it will be better for us if we can collaborate with Indian capital and management, though we shall have to tread warily in regard to the question of industrial expansion. Most industries which are already established seem likely to be overproducing after the war and it will therefore be necessary to find fresh industries or in some way increase the internal demand for locally made commercial products. I think we shall have to avoid like the plague any industry which involves protection as it would seem likely that any peace must be based on closer international collaboration and freedom of trade.[85]

The partner's assessment of the future in 1941 reflects an innocence of the requirements of total war, and its social and economic effects, that was widespread in India before fighting began against the Japanese.[86] By the end of the war, however, after three years of frenetic attempts by government to control and direct the economy, and after his own experience as a member of the Viceroy's Executive Council, Benthall was less sanguine. He was now especially concerned about the way in which Indian industrial interests—represented by Sir Ardeshir Dalal as Member for Reconstruction on the Executive Council—seemed to be planning to turn the Government of India into the executive arm of the Federation of Indian Chambers of Commerce and Industry. Benthall was shocked that in all his time in office he had had no single discussion on the future of expatriate business, or about business in any form, with the Finance Member or the Viceroy; and he predicted that if Dalal had his way, licensing of industrial expansion and control of capital issues would be manipulated to drive all expatriate businessmen out of India in twenty to thirty years.[87] Yet Benthall's determination to stay on was not diminished. Although he now feared that the interests of expatriate businessmen were being ignored totally by the Government of India and the United Kingdom Government, and although he argued bitterly that 'whatever Churchill may have said, he is presiding at the liquidation of the British Empire which lives by its imperial trade position', his resolve was not weakened: 'We *will not* be eliminated. We must hang on to our position by our eyelids as the only hope of the British Empire's future existence.'[88] Even at the last and greatest crisis of expatriate businessmen's expectations about the political future, Benthall had no idea of retreat.

[85] G. B. Morton to E. C. Benthall of 22.7.41 in BP XV.
[86] In 1941 Benthall saw the worst future as being simply that 'we are . . . at the end of an era in capitalist organisation and as time goes on we shall be less and less able to build up our resources out of profits as in the past' (see E. C. Benthall to A. P. Benthall of 25.1.41 in BP XVI).
[87] Diary entry 3.6.45 in BP VII.
[88] Diary entry 30.4.44 in BP VII.

The Benthall papers do not give us any idea of how this crisis was resolved. Overall, in fact, the collection is remarkably sparse in material about the day-to-day relations between Birds and the colonial government. The only subjects referred to in the sections dealing with business matters are the granting of concessions for mineral extraction and timber felling, tariff policy and stores purchase rules, especially for paper.[89] In general, Birds had certainly realized some time before 1939 that they could expect no favours from government, and had come to terms with this fact. Benthal had pointed this out to no less a personage than Gandhi in 1931:

He [Gandhi] claimed that in the past we had access to a government which had automatically and perhaps in many cases without any wrong given us advantages. We must in future expect that to be reversed. I agreed, and said that we had no objection to that state of affairs, provided we were not deliberately discriminated against. We had, on the other hand, definitely suffered in the last ten years from the fact that Government officers had been so anxious not to be accused of favouring Europeans that they had repeatedly in our experience given concessions to Indians when in equity Europeans had a prior claim.[90]

What was of concern to Benthall in the mid 1940s was not so much that government might be inclined to favour indigenous enterprise as that it now had greatly enhanced powers with which to do so. It was the coming of the 'permit raj' of the late 1940s and 1950s that forged the really important links between government and business in India. The decline of expatriate businessmen after 1947 may have been accelerated

[89] In the 1920s Birds had been anxious to preserve an Indian shareholding in Titaghur Paper Mills (preferably a holding by G. D. Birla) to aid the case for a tariff. By the late 1930s, however, the firm wanted no extension of protection as this would encourage new units of production which would threaten TPM's established market (see Diary entry 29.6.30 in BP VII and J. A. McKerrow to E. C. Benthall of 23.11.37 in BP XIV). TPM relied heavily on government purchases of paper to give an assured market and the company operated a ring for tendering with the other established paper manufacturers, Indian Paper and Pulp Co. and Bengal Paper Mills. When, in 1928, a new Indian company, the Punjab Pulp and Paper Mills, received a contract from the Punjab Government before it had even started production, Birds considered an appeal to the Commerce Member of the Government of India (see E. S. Tarlton to E. C. Benthall of 15.12.28 in BP I). However this did not prove necessary as the Punjab mill closed down after nine months.
[90] 'Memorandum of conversation with Mr Gandhi on 29.9.31 at 4, Deanery Street' by E. C. Benthall in BP II. This, of course, was advocacy, but then much of the evidence on which the opposite case of collusion between bureaucrats and expatriates to inhibit the growth of Indian industry is based is also advocacy. It seems as unwise to try to write the history of Indian industry in the twentieth century on the basis of the evidence given by aspiring industrialists to the Banking Enquiry Commission and the Tariff Boards as it would be to try to write the political history of the same period on the basis of the evidence given by aspiring politicians to the Indian Statutory Commission. Yet such evidence forms the basis of existing analyses of Indian industrial (under)development.

by the fact that few expatriates now had good contacts with the bureaucracy, but this failure was much more than just the mirror image of their earlier success. Only once the government of India began to try to plan the economy did its preferences among the entrepreneurial groups become crucial to those groups' relative performance.

*   *   *

The evidence of the Benthall papers suggests that the decline of expatriate enterprise in eastern India in the first half of the twentieth century had more to do with problems of capital than with uncertainties of political expectation. Nor is there any real evidence of ossifying entrepreneurial attitudes; it was circumstances, general and particular, not a lack of enterprise that did the expatriates down. Yet our analysis cannot stop here. An incomplete set of papers covering one expatriate firm is not a good enough sample on which to base sound generalizations. Nor is it perhaps very fruitful for historians to attempt to measure the entrepreneurial skills of dead businessmen on some overall abstract scale of endeavour.[91] Future research must attempt rather to open up the study of business institutions in India more widely to allow for a more schematic interpretation of events than that which can be obtained by trying to look solely into the minds of the actors on the stage.

The evidence of the Benthall papers suggests that neither of the two general propositions about the decline of expatriate business hitherto suggested are very satisfactory. Simple racial stereotypes are rarely appropriate;[92] stressing a lack of venture capital for new enterprise does not explain why this shortage existed. Benthall's correspondence indicates that the structure of 'organized' industry and commerce, and the inter-meshing between major firms and major sectors of activity, need to be studied further. Attempts to control supply and demand lay close to the hearts of all entrepreneurs in India between the wars. It was this concern for control, rather than an obsession with expansion for its own sake, that was probably the dominant motive in business activity. Some groups were better able to achieve this than others and profited accord-

---

[91] Apart from more weighty considerations, it is doubtful how many business historians would themselves pass the 'whelk-stall' test.

[92] Thus there was a crisis in the running of TPM in 1928–29 when Indian directors wanted higher dividends while the expatriate managing agents wanted increased investment. Benthall advised that an attempt be made to coerce the directors, 'as we can then at a future date make it clear to the Tariff Board that we made repeated efforts to get our directors to raise fresh capital and tackle the job properly but that they refused' (E. C. Benthall to E. S. Tarlton of 1.11.29 in BP I).

ingly. The vital factor here was not an alliance with government; it was instead relations with the vast and potentially very powerful 'unorganized' sector of the Indian economy, especially the up-country merchants, bankers and credit suppliers who controlled so much of Indian economic activity. The nature and influence of these institutions cannot be assessed by studying Tariff Board reports, Joint Stock Company blue books, the *Calcutta Stock Exchange Official Yearbook* or the *Investors' India Yearbook*. Yet it was the emergence of business groups from out of this shadowy underworld into the full glare of 'modern' business activity that has been the major influence on the course of Indian industrialization in this century, and that dictated the fate of the expatriate firms. To take one small point, it is clear from the Benthall papers that many industrial undertakings depended on rations of credit from their distributors in the form of advances on orders to keep going at all in the 1920s and 1930s;[93] the sources of credit and capital that such distributors possessed were rooted deep in the indigenous economy. More importantly, as the example of the jute trade studied above has shown, the links between the rising Indian industrial and commercial groups and the 'unorganized' internal economy severely damaged the ability of the expatriates to control their environment. The history of the sugar industry in the 1930s might well show the same trends—the successful firms were those which could ally with those local moneylenders and landlords who could control raw material supply and price, and these tended to be the Indian ones which had risen out of credit supply in the indigenous economy rather than expatriate ones which had poorer local knowledge and up-country influence.[94]

Up to now scholars studying the development of Indian industry in the first half of the twentieth century have paid too much attention to analyses based on generalized concepts of supply and demand constraints, technological innovation and adaptation, and factor endowments. It would be best for future research to concentrate more on the individual circumstances of particular firms and to try to answer questions about the institutional foundations of their enterprise and about their attempts to control or manipulate the larger producing and con-

[93] See especially 'Note of conversation with F. P. Pudamjee 31.7.35' in BP X. In general it seems to be very important to find out a great deal more about the distribution and sales aspects of Indian industrialization.

[94] For another, although rather different, example of the relations between the 'organized' and 'unorganized' business sectors in India, see A. D. D. Gordon, *Businessmen and Politics: Rising Nationalism and a Modernising Economy in Bombay 1918–1933* (New Delhi, 1978), Ch. 3.

suming economy of which they represented only a small part.[95] It may be useful to look at firms as particular centres of economic power, although not always effective ones, rather than as agents of abstract economic forces. Such economic power as each firm possessed must then be considered in terms of networks in other sectors of the economy, rather than simply in terms of its rivals in the 'organized' sector, or of its political allies and opponents.[96] If this were done it might well emerge that the really important question to ask about the decline of expatriate enterprise is how strong it ever was in the first place. Certainly the expatriates dominated the 'organized' economy of eastern India in 1900, and in 1950 they did not, but the 'organized' economy—although attractive to scholars and relatively easy to analyse—may not have been the decisively important sector. Even with their close contacts with a would-be interventionist government since 1947 Indian entrepreneurs in the 'organized' sector have often found difficulty in forcing petty traders, producers and consumers to conform to their vision of economic progress. It may be that expatriate businessmen were never in reality more than fleas on the buttock of Mother India; they have been replaced by parasites that have been more persistent and elusive, but that have not yet become a great deal more firmly established.

[95] Links between manufacturers and distributors, and the development of selling networks, seem to be an especially important subject. There is evidence, for example, that one reason why Birds did not go into cement manufacture through the Bisra Limestone Co. in the late 1930s was because they were being paid generously by Indian manufacturers to remain a selling agency alone (see S. A. Roberts to R. E. Alexander of 20.7.37 in BP XIII).

[96] A useful recent summary of the literature on theories of entrepreneurship and the nature of the firm is provided in A. G. Hopkins, 'Innovation in a Colonial Context' in C. J. Dewey and A. G. Hopkins (eds), *The Imperial Impact: Studies in the Economic History of Africa and India* (London, 1978), p. 83–7. What seems to be necessary in these terms for the study of Indian entrepreneurship is to remain close to Gerschenkron's position of the importance of changes in the structure of economic opportunities in determining the emergence of entrepreneurs, but to analyse the nature of these opportunities in something other than neo-classical terms. This is, of course, what Bagchi has tried to do, but he has not taken the individual firm as the basic unit of analysis. Indeed, in his *Private Investment in India*, he seems to have virtually no interest in particular circumstances at all.

Modern Asian Studies, **15**, 3 (1981), pp. 487–526.

Indian Business and the Congress Provincial Governments 1937–39

CLAUDE MARKOVITS

Centre National de la Recherche Scientifique, Paris

THE late 1930s saw a definite turn in political developments in India. Following the abandonment of Civil Disobedience in 1934, a prolonged period of internal peace helped the Congress, until then a broadly-based movement with a general commitment to fight foreign rule, evolve into a more organized party capable of aspiring to political dominance. In the process, its relations with different social forces took a more definite shape. While in the past the Congress had clung to the myth of an Indian society free of internal conflicts and united in opposition to the British, the growth of social conflicts in town and countryside forced it to take into account the competing aspirations of various groups.

Assuming office in seven provinces in July 1937 under a régime of qualified provincial autonomy introduced by the 1935 constitution, the party found itself confronted with the difficult task of accommodating these competing interests within a framework in which only limited financial resources were available; financial control at the centre remained firmly in British hands,[1] and provinces had largely inelastic sources of revenue. Among the interest groups which were making demands on the Congress ministries the most powerful was the Indian business class, which had expanded at a relatively quick pace during the period 1932–37, and which found itself increasingly alienated from the conservative economic policies followed by the Government of India. By the 'Indian business class' we mean here Indian big business, that is the small élite of big traders, financiers and industrialists which was largely concentrated in a few centres like Bombay, Ahmedabad, Calcutta, Cawnpore and Coimbatore. Though far from constituting a homogeneous group, these businessmen displayed certain characteristics which set them clearly apart from the mass of small traders, money-

I am grateful to Dr Sumit Sarkar for his comments on an earlier draft of this paper. The remaining errors of judgement are of course mine.

[1] See B. R. Tomlinson, *The Political Economy of the Raj. The Economics of Decolonization in India 1914–1947* (London, 1979), p. 131.

0026-749X/81/0406-0904$02.00 © 1981 Cambridge University Press

lenders, brokers and petty entrepreneurs which formed the bulk of the Indian merchant classes. They differed from the lesser interests in the size of their financial resources, the range and scale of their activities (from foreign trade to big industry), and their organizational skill. They had captured the leadership of most of the regional trade associations and had established in 1927 the first all-India business association, the Federation of Indian Chambers of Commerce and Industry, which was the closest thing to a lobby in India. This group had been a major source of funds for the Congress campaigns since the 1920s, and it had acquired some influence on the Congress High Command. While the businessmen expected to derive some advantages from the advent of the Congress ministries, they were at the same time apprehensive of the policy the latter would follow in labour matters.

How could the Congress accommodate capitalist demands along with the growing populist pressures and postures which were in evidence both outside and inside the Party? Conversely, would businessmen, who had always been careful of keeping good relations with the British, and had used nationalist agitations mainly as a means of extracting concessions from them, adjust to a situation in which some power of patronage had passed from the hands of the British into those of the Congress? These were some of the questions raised by the advent of the Congress ministries. After 1937 the British, though they were less in evidence, had not altogether disappeared from the Indian scene and therefore the political attitudes of the Indian businessmen during the 1937–39 period were determined by a complex interplay of national and provincial factors. Though this study will focus on the relations between Indian business and the Congress in the major Congress-ruled provinces (thus leaving aside Bengal and its strong Marwari business community) the impact of all-India trends will not be ignored.

Relations between Congress and Business before the Advent of the Congress Ministries

Relations between Congress and business at the national level had grown closer during the 1920s and the first phase of the Civil Disobedience movement (1930–31), but were severely strained in 1932–34. During these years, business support for the movement remained limited, while the Indian business class split over the issue of imperial preference and the Ottawa agreement. Though the small and medium-scale traders in Bombay embarked upon an effective boycott of

British business and directly confronted the authorities in 1932–33, even the most pro-Congress faction in big business, represented by a section of the Calcutta Marwaris led by G. D. Birla and by the Ahmedabad millowners, favoured the end of the agitation. Bombay big business openly broke with the Congress, and tried to use the Ottawa agreement to its own advantage by forming alliances with groups of British capitalists to fight more dangerous competition from Japan (in cotton textiles) and Belgium (in the iron and steel industry) in the Indian market. The Lees–Mody pact concluded in 1933 between the representatives of the Bombay cotton mills and of Lancashire epitomized the new course of Bombay business politics. The divisions within the ranks of the Indian capitalists persisted even after the abandonment of Civil Disobedience by the Congress, but they became less pronounced as Bombay business grew aware of the new moderation of the Congress leadership and found it increasingly difficult to conciliate its interests with those of Lancashire.[2] In 1936 common opposition to the Congress left drew both factions of big business closer to the dominant group of the Congress leadership.[3]

The decision by the Congress High Command to contest the 1937 elections in the provinces under the new régime of provincial autonomy showed that the Congress was ready to accept at least partly the new constitution. It exposed the basic weakness of its left wing, which had been preaching boycott of the elections. Business circles generally welcomed the Congress decision and some financial aid was promised to the Party.[4]

However, since the elections were fought on a provincial basis, the attitudes of businessmen were largely dictated by their relations with the Congress organizations at the provincial level, and not only by the rapport they had established with the High Command. The situation, thus, varied considerably from province to province. Prior to 1937, under the so-called 'dyarchy' régime, non-Congress provincial governments had only limited powers, but industry and civil works were among the transferred subjects and had conveyed some powers of

[2] This brief account of the politics of Indian business in 1932–36 is based on my unpublished Ph.D. dissertation, 'Indian Business and Nationalist Politics from 1931 to 1939: The Political Attitude of the Indigenous Capitalist Class in Relation to the Crisis of the Colonial Economy and the Rise of the Congress Party', Cambridge, 1978.

[3] See ibid., pp. 166–71.

[4] In February 1936, G. D. Birla held a series of talks with the Congress Parliamentary Board. He estimated the needs of the Congress for the election campaign at Rs 5 lakhs, of which he proposed to raise a large amount from the business community. See Bhulabhai Desai diary, entries for 2 and 10 February, Bhulabhai Desai Papers, Nehru Memorial Museum and Library, New Delhi (NMML).

patronage. In some provinces, the non-Congress forces in power had strengthened their links with the business class by giving businessmen ministries and other favours. This was, for instance, the case in the Madras Presidency, where a large section of the local capitalist class had been integrated with the power structure of the Justice Party.[5] Similar trends, though less conspicuous, had emerged in other provinces, particularly in Bombay and in the United Provinces. As a result, relations between business and the Congress provincial organizations were often strained. Actually one must distinguish between two levels of politics. At the lower level, that of the locality, traders and merchants seem to have increased their influence within the Congress in the post-1934 period, mainly through their control of financial resources.[6] But larger capitalists, that is, both big traders and industrialists, whose operations affected the entire economy of a province, generally kept aloof from Congress provincial politics, though there were of course exceptions. This explains partly the difficulties which the provincial Congress organizations had in raising funds for the election campaign and their need to appeal to the High Command for help. Thus, in a letter to Rajendra Prasad, the Congress leader of the United Provinces complained of lack of funds in his province,[7] adding that he thought that other Congress provincial organizations were similarly handicapped. In Bombay city, not much money was raised either.[8] In Bihar, Seth Dalmia, the big Marwari industrialist, gave some help, but on a limited scale.[9]

In spite of these difficulties, the Congress scored impressive victories in most of the provinces and showed that, outside the Muslim-majority provinces, it was the dominant political force in India. It won an absolute majority in six of the eleven provinces (Bihar, Central Provinces, Madras, Northwest Frontier Province, Orissa and the United Provinces) was close to it in Bombay, emerged as the single largest party in Assam, and fared badly only in the three Muslim-major-

[5] David Arnold, *The Congress in Tamilnad. Nationalist Politics in South India, 1919–1937* (Delhi, 1977), p. 158.

[6] This trend is noticed for the United Provinces in G. Pandey, *The Ascendency of the Congress in Uttar Pradesh 1926–1934. A Study in Imperfect Mobilization* (Delhi, 1978), p. 57, and in Arnold, *The Congress in Tamilnad*, p. 168, for Madras.

[7] Pandit Pant to Rajendra Prasad, 11 May 1936, intercepted letter. Government of India, Home (Poll.), 14 May 1936, National Archives of India, New Delhi (NAI).

[8] Two of the most influential figures in Bombay big business, the cotton magnates and financiers Sir Purshottamdas Thakurdas and his cousin Sir Chunilal Mehta, pointedly refused to contribute. B. R. Tomlinson, *The Indian National Congress and the Raj, 1929–1942. The Penultimate Phase* (London, 1976), p. 82.

[9] *Ibid.*, p. 82.

ity provinces of Bengal, the Punjab and Sind, in which it nevertheless won most of the general (non-Muslim) seats. An analysis of the election results gives interesting indications about the political complexion of Indian businessmen.

A first set of conclusions can be drawn from a careful reading of the results of the elections to the seats reserved for Indian commerce. Under the new régime, a total of twenty-three seats in ten Provincial Assemblies[10] were reserved for Indian commercial, mining and industrial interests (including two seats reserved for Indian tea planters in the Assam legislature). Of these, the Congress Party contested only six and won three. Eight other seats went to businessmen known for their pro-Congress leanings, while a further seven seats were won by known anti-Congressites, three of whom were elected contesting against a Congress candidate. The remaining seats went to businessmen without known political leanings, though some of them might have been Congress sympathizers. Table I shows the results to the commercial seats in each province.

This table shows wide differences in the political behaviour of businessmen in various provinces. In Madras, where industry was still dominated by British capital (with the exception of Coimbatore, which was the largest centre of the textile industry in the province), the opposition to the Congress from large Indian trading and moneylending interests was demonstrated by the failure of the Congress Party to secure any of the reserved seats. In the Nattukottai Nagarathar Association constituency, the Congress candidate was defeated by Muttiah Chettiar, a merchant prince and a banker, the head of the Nattukottai Chettiar community, which dominated the financial scene in south India and had huge interests abroad. He had been a minister under the Justice Party régime, and became the leader of the Justicite opposition to the new Congress régime. The Congress also lost the seat for the Southern India Chamber of Commerce. If one keeps in mind that in the 1934 elections to the Central Legislative Assembly, the Congress had secured its only seat in a constituency reserved for Indian commerce in Madras, the 1937 results will undoubtedly appear as a setback. In the Central Provinces also, the anti-Congress feelings of one section of the traders and industrialists were shown by the defeat of the Congress candidate to the Berar commerce seat (which included Nagpur, the only big commercial and industrial centre in the province) at the hands of one of the biggest Marwari millowners of the province.

[10] There was no seat reserved for commerce in the Northwest Frontier Province Assembly.

TABLE I

Results of 1937 Provincial Elections. Seats Reserved for Indian Commerce

I	II	III	IV	V	VI	VII
Assam	3					3
Bengal	5			3	2	
Bihar	2			2		
Bombay	4	1	1	2	1	
Central Prov.	2	2	1		1	
Madras	2	2	0		2	
Orissa	1					1
Punjab	1					1
Sind	1	1	1			
United Prov.	2			1	1	

I name of the Province; II no. of seats reserved for Indian Commerce; III no. of seats contested by the Congress; IV no. of seats won by the Congress; V no. of seats won by pro-Congress businessmen; VI no. of seats won by anti-Congress businessmen; VII no. of seats won by others.

Sources: A Brief Analysis of the Election Results. Issued by the Political and Economic Information Department of the All-India Congress Committee (AICC). Reproduced by N. Mitra (comp.), *Indian Annual Register, 1937*, vol. I, pp. 168 ff (Calcutta, 1937), and *Indian Yearbook 1937–38* (Bombay, 1938).

The United Provinces results revealed the political division among Indian businessmen in this largely agricultural province in which Cawnpore was the only big industrial centre. Sir J. P. Srivastava, a Cawnpore industrialist who was a supporter of the Hindu Mahasabha and a determined adversary of the Congress (he had been a minister under dyarchy and contested the election on the ticket of the National Agriculturist Party, which represented the most reactionary faction of the United Provinces zamindars), was elected to one of the seats reserved for the Upper India Chamber of Commerce, a British-dominated commercial association. In the joint constituency formed by the United Provinces Chamber of Commerce and the Merchants' Chamber of the United Provinces, Lala Padampat Singhania, a pro-Congress business magnate of Cawnpore, defeated in a straight fight another magnate, Rameshwar Prasad Bagla, who was an opponent of the Congress.[11]

[11] Singhania defeated Bagla by 101 votes to 67. P. Reeves *et al.*, *A Handbook to Elections in Uttar Pradesh 1920–1951* (Delhi, 1975), p. 308.

In Bombay, the Congress contested only the seat reserved for the East India Cotton Association and won it. Pro-Congress businessmen were elected in the Ahmedabad Millowners' Association and Indian Merchants' Chamber constituencies. But in the Bombay Millowner's Association constituency, Sir S. D. Saklatvala, of the Tata group, was returned unopposed. Both the Millowners' Association and the Tata group had in the past followed an anti-Congress line, and though they had become more cautious lately, they could not be counted as supporters of the Party. In Bengal, there was a clear-cut division. Out of five members elected from the reserved constituencies, three could be considered pro-Congress. They were the two nominees of the Bengal National Chambers of Commerce and the one of the Indian Chamber of Commerce. Among them, was Nalini Ranjan Sarkar, who became Finance Minister in the non-Congress ministry formed after the elections, but who was known to be close to the B. C. Roy faction of the provincial Congress. The other two members elected for commerce, from the Muslim Chamber of Commerce and the Marwari Association, were opponents of the Congress. Finally, the Congress and its allies had their greatest victories in Bihar and Sind, where they won all the commercial seats.

The overall results thus reveal a fair amount of support for the Congress from the electorate in the reserved constituencies (which represented the upper strata of the Indian business community), despite the existence of strong pockets of opposition in two or three provinces.

Other indications about businessmen's participation in the political process are to be found in an analysis of the results of the elections to the non-commercial seats. It was customary for some big businessmen having an interest in politics to seek election from either urban or rural seats. In the 1934 elections to the Central Legislative Assembly, some businessmen were elected to such seats,[12] generally as independents. There is no precise data available on the number of businessmen who tried to get elected in the 1937 elections, but one must draw attention to the following facts. Two figures of local big business who contested on non-Congress tickets suffered crushing defeats at the hands of the Congress in two rural constituencies of the Cawnpore district.[13] The only representative of big business who was elected as an independent in

[12] Among them was Sir Cowasji Jehangir, a big Parsi financier and industrialist, who was elected from Bombay Central (Non-Muhammedan Urban).
[13] They were Vikramjit Singh, a big Cawnpore merchant and one of the leaders of the United Provinces Chamber of Commerce, who contested on a Hindu Sabha ticket; and Lady Kailash Srivastava, Sir J.P.'s wife, who stood as independent. Reeves *et al.*, *Elections in Uttar Pradesh*, p. 273.

the face of Congress opposition was Lalchand Hirachand who stood successfully from a rural constituency in Maharashtra. Being the son of Walchand Hirachand, one of the biggest Indian capitalists in Bombay, he could rely on the vast rural clientage provided by his father's sugar factory situated in the area.

Apart from the sugar magnates, few businessmen could draw upon a client network in the countryside, and this seriously limited their possibilities of getting elected in rural constituencies without the support of a party machinery. With the multiplication in the number of voters brought about by the enlargement of the franchise,[14] electioneering was no more only a question of resources, but necessitated organization, which only a political party and not an individual could muster. This is demonstrated *a contrario* by the electoral successes of some big Muslim merchants who contested on Muslim League tickets from Muslim rural seats.[15] The reasons why the Muslim League was more generous than the Congress in giving tickets to businessmen were twofold: firstly, the Muslim League had less resources and talent than the Congress; secondly, contesting on a League ticket did not expose a businessman to the active hostility of the British authorities, while siding too openly with the Congress might have had dangerous consequences.[16] Also, the growing communal alignment among Indian businessmen favoured the League more than the Congress.[17]

There was, thus, no perceptible increase in the direct participation of businessmen in electoral politics. Businessmen tended to work more behind the scenes and tried to use the financial weapon to influence the Congress.[18] But the overwhelming victories won by the Congress in most of the provinces did not leave them much room for manoeuvring.

[14] The total number of voters grew from 7 to 36 millions. The really poor remained excluded, but there was an extension of the franchise to the urban working class and lower middle classes, and to the middle peasantry. See Tomlinson, *Indian National Congress and the Raj*, p. 71.

[15] Among them A. H. Ispahani in Bengal and Ibrahim Rahimtoolla in Bombay.

[16] Many Indian businessmen were heavily dependent upon Government orders and contracts.

[17] Muslim businessmen, who faced increasing competition, even in their traditional fields, from Hindus, tended to close ranks in the 1930s and to support the Muslim League. Hindu businessmen on the other hand, especially those living in the Muslim-majority provinces of Bengal and the Punjab, found the Congress too soft with the Muslims, and many supported the Hindu Mahasabha.

[18] Thus businessmen pressurized the Congress into removing from their list of candidates some trade unionists whom they found too radical. In Bombay, the trade unionist Nimbkar lost the Congress ticket because of big business pressure. See *Times of India*, 11 November 1936. In Bihar, Seth Dalmia obtained the removal of a man who had organized a strike in his mills from the list of Congress candidates. Tomlinson, *Indian National Congress and the Raj*, p. 83.

The prevailing economic and social conditions under which the new Congress ministries, formed in July 1937, had to operate, caused them further anxieties.

The Environment of Provincial Autonomy: Major Constraints on Congress–Business Relations in the Provinces.

When the Congress ministries were formed in seven provinces, the Indian economy had just started to recover from the effects of the unprecedented depression of the early 1930s. The depression resulted in a fall in land revenue, which was the single largest source of revenue for the provincial governments,[19] and thus had a disastrous impact on provincial finances. While the Central Government had been able to overcome a financial crisis by 1932,[20] the provincial governments remained in a difficult situation throughout the thirties. Their inability to find new sources of revenue to supplement those in existence prevented them from making any significant contribution towards economic development. The share of civil works in the total expenditure of all the provincial governments actually fell during the first half of the 1930s, and the allocation for industries (a purely provincial subject since the 1919 reforms) remained at a measly one per cent.[21] In this context, the devolution to the provincial governments of increased responsibilities in matters of economic development and social welfare under the 1935 reforms, was bound to remain purely theoretical, unless accompanied by an increase in the financial resources of the provinces.

A small step in that direction had been made when the Government of India had accepted the recommendations of the Indian Financial Enquiry Committee of 1936,[22] headed by Sir Otto Niemeyer. The Niemeyer Award, as it came to be known, had allotted to the provinces 50 per cent of the revenue yielded by the income tax, the levy of which remained a prerogative of the Central Government. But it had been decided that during five years part of the transferable amount would be retained by the Centre for the consolidation of its own finances. The overall transfer of resources was therefore very limited. In the way the

[19] In 1929–30, land revenue accounted for 33.2% of the total revenue of all provincial governments, while the second largest single item, excise, accounted for 22.2%. Tomlinson, *Political Economy of the Raj*, Table 4.5, p. 156.
[20] See Markovits, 'Indian Business and Nationalist Politics', pp. 62–3.
[21] Between 1929–30 and 1934–35, the share of civil works in the total expenditure of the provincial governments fell from 10.9 to 8.6%. During the same period, industries dropped from 1 to 0.9%. Tomlinson, *Political Economy of the Raj*, p. 156.
[22] *Report of the Indian Financial Enquiry Committee* (London, 1936).

allocation had been made between the different provinces, the poorest ones, such as the newly-formed provinces of Orissa and Sind, had been favoured at the expense of the more developed ones, such as Bengal and Bombay, which were deemed to have sufficient resources. The business community in the latter provinces had reacted very unfavourably to the Niemeyer Award, protesting that lack of resources would hamper the work of the ministries.[23] Despite these hostile reactions the Niemeyer Award had the merit of offering some prospect of financial relief to the beleaguered governments of the poorest provinces.

Another innovation introduced by the 1935 reforms had been the freedom given to the provincial governments to borrow money directly from the market without having to go through the cumbrous financial machinery of the Central Government. Yet borrowing could be no more than an expedient; to attract investors, the provincial governments had to offer conditions at least as interesting as those given by the Centre, which meant that in the future the repayment of the debts incurred would necessitate a raising of the permanent revenue. All in all, existing conditions restricted considerably the possibilities of the provincial governments. Unless they managed to cut down notably administrative expenditure (which would necessarily mean a direct clash with a powerfully-entrenched bureaucracy) or to raise new revenue (which, given the inelasticity of land revenue, meant increased indirect taxation, never a popular measure), there was not much scope for a radical change in provincial policies. An added constraint was Gandhi's prohibitionist fad, which threatened to reduce one of the major sources of provincial revenue.

Financial constraints were not the only factor to influence business–Congress relations in the provinces. Labour problems also played an increasing role, due to the rapid growth of labour militancy in India from the mid-thirties and to the increased political weight of the trade unions.

India's labour movement, which had grown steadily throughout the 1920s, had suffered a setback at the end of the 1920s and during the early 1930s, because of repression, internal splits, and the unfavourable impact of the depression on worker's struggles. From 1935 onwards, the movement had started regaining strength. The number of registered unions and their membership showed an upward trend, strikes became more frequent, and the two largest federations of trade-unions initiated

[23] In an interview to the *Times of India*, 2 May 1936, Sir Purshottamdas Thakurdas had underlined that, during five years, there would be 'no elbow-room discernible for nation-building activities to Ministers in the provinces,' unless they raised new taxes.

a process of gradual rapprochement.[24] As the trade union movement grew in strength, it was able to make its weight felt in politics. The provincial elections in 1937 witnessed attempts at an adjustment between the Congress and the trade-unions over the sharing of the seats reserved for labour. While this was not possible everywhere, nevertheless the Congress was able to capture approximately half of the seats reserved for labour in the provincial assemblies.[25] To get workers' votes in the elections to the general urban seats, the Congress made big promises to them in its electoral manifesto. This attitude had paid off, as shown by the victories of the Congress candidates in most of the towns with a sizable working-class population.[26] The advent of Congress ministries in the majority of the provinces no doubt raised great expectations among workers and prompted them towards a greater militancy. During 1937, the labour scene in India was dominated by the great strike of the Calcutta jute workers, which affected an industry dominated by British capital, and received encouragement from the Congress. The Calcutta strike was a clear warning that labour unrest was growing, and there was not much likelihood that the Congress-ruled provinces of Bombay, Madras and the United Provinces, which had a sizable industrial labour force,[27] would be spared. As a matter of fact, the new Congress ministry in the United Provinces was immediately confronted with a general strike of the millworkers in Cawnpore.

Capitalists, particularly the large section which had manufacturing interests, were naturally disturbed at the growing incidence of strikes, and they were aware that Congress propaganda had helped nurture discontent among the workers. Despite handsome profits made in 1936–37,[28] they still entertained fears of a recession. Already the sugar industry, which had gone through an unprecedented boom in 1932–36, had been affected by an overproduction crisis, mainly due to unregulated competition among mills. Another distressing factor was the new

[24] C. Revri, *The Indian Trade Union Movement, A Historical Outline* (Delhi, 1972), pp. 204 ff.

[25] Out of thirty-eight labour seats, the Congress contested twenty and won eighteen. It won all the labour seats in Madras and the United Provinces, while in Bombay it contested and won only two of the seven reserved seats.

[26] The only exception was the Bombay Presidency, where Ambedkar's Independent Labour Party won some of the urban working-class seats.

[27] In 1937, out of 1,675,869 factory workers in India, the largest number was in Bengal, 566,458, followed by Bombay, 435,207, Madras, 186,630, and the United Provinces, 153,484. *Indian Yearbook, 1938–39* (Bombay, 1939), p. 538.

[28] According to the index of variable yield securities published in Statistical Research Branch, *Review of the Trade of India, 1938–39* (Calcutta, 1939), dividends paid by joint-stock companies reached a record index of 137 in March 1937 (1927–28 = 100).

depression which had started to affect the industrial countries. All this made Indian capitalists little inclined towards making concessions to workers, and suspicious of the efforts made by the Congress to woo labour.

The new Congress ministries therefore were faced with a difficult task: they had to try to conciliate the interests of two groups which had tended to support them in the elections and which both equally hoped that Congress rule would bring them benefits. The ministries were in danger of being subjected to contradictory pressures from above and from below. The Congress High Command, with which the capitalists wielded more influence than the trade unions, was likely to pressurize them towards taking a stand against labour; while local Congress organizations, more responsive to direct pressure from workers, would advocate support for their demands. The provincial governments would be hard put to find a middle way.

Apart from the problems posed by labour unrest, the Congress ministries would also have to arbitrate between the demands of urban and rural interests. Though conciliation was possible in many cases, as linkages were numerous between urban capitalists and big landlords in the countryside,[29] there was nevertheless the possibility that urban and rural interests would increasingly compete for scarce resources. Some capitalists were undoubtedly scared that, buttressed by Gandhi's well-known and increasingly radical rural bias, the Congress ministries would follow a course of hostility towards modern industry, and would restrict the opportunities for the urban interests to enlarge themselves.[30]

Given the difficult conditions in which the Congress ministries came to power, it is not surprising that business interests harboured some misgivings about their future course of policy. Generally speaking, no capitalists were offered ministerial posts by the Congress,[31] which preferred to rely on its own party workers, even if their technical qualifications were limited. This could only add to the diffidence of the capitalists. The only section which really showed enthusiasm at the advent of the Congress ministries was the Marwari group led by G. D. Birla. Birla and his friends had most of their interests in Bengal, a

[29] Many zamindars, besides Indian princes, held shares in Indian joint-stock companies. Some zamindars had themselves promoted sugar mills in Northern India in collaboration with merchants. Conversely, many Indian capitalists, especially in Northern and Eastern India were large-scale landholders.

[30] Such fears had been voiced in particular by Sir H. P. Mody, the spokesman of the Bombay textile industry and of the Tatas, as early as in 1935 in an interview to the *Times of India*, dated 14 August 1935.

[31] The only exception was in Madras where Yakub Hasan, a big Muslim merchant, was given the Public Works portfolio.

non-Congress province, and in the Indian States.[32] Therefore they could afford to take a long-term view of developments and see the new ministries as one more step towards a peaceful transfer of power at the Centre.[33] The capitalists who had the bulk of their interests in the Congress-ruled provinces, and particularly those in the Bombay Presidency, were more closely concerned with the policies of the Congress ministries.

Economic and Social Policies of the Congress Ministries in the Initial Phase (summer 1937–spring 1938)

The biggest single factor to influence the course of relations between Indian business and the newly-formed Congress ministries was labour unrest. The advent of popular ministries encouraged workers in the Congress-ruled provinces to press for the redress of grievances which had been accumulating for the last few years. Though most authors emphasize the economic aspects of labour demands in that period,[34] there is no doubt that political changes also played a role in the new upsurge in labour militancy. The election manifesto issued by the Congress in 1936 had promised to secure for workers 'a decent standard of living, hours of work and conditions of labour in conformity, as far as the economic conditions in the country permit, with international standards, suitable machinery for the settlement of disputes between employers and workers, protection against the economic consequences of old age, sickness and unemployment, and the right . . . to form unions and to strike for the protection of their interests.'[35] V. V. Giri, himself a trade-unionist and the Labour and Industries Minister of Madras, testified in his memoirs to the great expectations raised among workers by the advent of the Congress governments.[36] In most provinces the new ministries were soon confronted with an unprecedented wave of labour disputes; 1937 and 1938 were peak years in terms of incidence of labour trouble: one has to go back to 1928–29 to find comparable unrest. What is also significant is that while in 1937 Bengal was the province most

[32] Though Birla himself had sugar mills in the United Provinces.

[33] In a letter dated 25 May 1937 to Laithwaite, private secretary to the Viceroy, Birla expressed the hope that 'if once the Congress realises the potentiality of constitutionalism', it would 'stick to it to the end', Linlithgow Papers, India Office Library, London (IOL), Mss Eur F. 125, Vol. 118.

[34] See Revri, *Indian Trade Union Movement*, p. 222 and V. B. Karnik, *Indian Trade Unions. A Survey* (Bombay, 1966), pp. 110 ff.

[35] Quoted in Kanji Dwarkadas, *Forty-five Years with Labour* (Bombay, 1962), p. 50.

[36] V. V. Giri, *My Life and Times* (Madras, 1976), Vol. I, p. 130.

affected by disputes, due to the long strike in the jute mills, in 1938 the focus of the disturbances tended to shift to the Congress-ruled provinces, particularly Madras and the United Provinces. In 1937 Bengal accounted for more than two thirds of all man-days lost in India due to industrial disputes, but in 1938 its share had fallen to less than one third. Conversely, the share of the five Congress-ruled provinces of Bihar, Bombay, the Central Provinces, Madras and the United Provinces rose from less than one third to more than two thirds of the total.[37] Table 2 shows the changes in the location of disputes between 1937 and 1938.

TABLE 2

Industrial Disputes in Selected Provinces in 1937 and 1938

I	II	III	IV	V	VI	VII
Bengal	166	365,699	6,090,883	157	162,888	2,698,742
Bihar	14	14,946	222,509	21	27,471	1,103,130
Bombay	88	109,858	897,211	111	62,188	694,118
Central Prov.	5	9,701	222,094	14	18,260	307,043
Madras	61	60,980	656,404	52	65,290	2,226,049
United Prov.	15	63,350	704,940	14	53,851	2,046,868
All India	379	647,801	8.982,257	399	401,075	9,198,708

I Province; II no. of industrial disputes in 1937; III no. of workers involved in 1937; IV no. of man-days lost in 1937; V no. of disputes in 1938; VI no. of workers involved in 1938; VII no. of man-days lost in 1938.

Sources: C. Revri, *The Indian Trade Union Movement. An Historical Outline* (Delhi, 1970), pp. 217–19. *Labour Gazette*, Bombay, June 1939, p. 768.

In most Congress-ruled provinces, the number of disputes and of workers involved in them did not actually increase between 1937 and 1938, but the number of man-days lost multiplied spectacularly, an indication that strikes lasted longer. In 1938, half of the disputes ended in a settlement which was at least partly satisfactory for the workers.[38] Among causes of disputes, wage demands came first, but significantly, demands for the recognition of trade unions were on the increase.[39] This reflected the spectacular growth of the trade-union movement in 1937–38. The number of registered unions and their membership increased by fifty per cent in one year, an unprecedented fact in the

[37] Computed on the basis of Table 2.

[38] Out of 387 disputes in which settlements were arrived at during the year, in 181 or 46.77%, the workers were successful in gaining concessions. In 51 or 13.18%, they were completely successful and in 130 or 33.59% only partially successful. *Labour Gazette*, Bombay, June 1939, p. 770.

[39] Revri, *Indian Trade Union Movement*, p. 220.

history of the Indian labour movement.[40] Though the progress of unions was greatest in Madras, followed by the United Provinces, in other Congress-ruled provinces such as Bombay or Bihar, it was less than in Bengal.[41]

In the Congress-ruled provinces, Indian capital was generally dominant, and therefore bore the brunt of the labour unrest. In Madras and the United Provinces, where British-controlled mills employed approximately half of the workforce in the cotton textile industry,[42] the strikes tended to affect the Indian capitalists as much or even more than their British colleagues. In Madras, most of the strikes took place in or around Coimbatore where there were few British mills. In the United Provinces, the Cawnpore strikes hit both the Indian and British millowners. The nationality of the owners made visibly little difference to the striking workers.

Turning now to the policy of the Congress ministries in labour matters, their dilemma is nicely, though somewhat naively, summed up by a labour historian, who writes:

The [Congress] organization as a whole did not desire to alienate the vested interests. It was keen on retaining their friendship and cooperation. The Congress ministries were, therefore, faced with a difficult task; they had to do something to satisfy workers' demands but they had to see at the same time that employers did not get too angry or annoyed.[43]

Actually the Congress High Command was very conscious of the predicament in which the ministries found themselves, but it decided that, to avoid a bigger explosion on the labour front, concessions had to be made quickly to the workers. In October 1937 the Congress Labour Committee, after holding consultations with the labour ministers from the Congress-ruled provinces, passed a series of resolutions[44] aiming at the implementation of the programme of labour welfare chalked out in the Congress election manifesto. Yet the committee took care not to fix any time-limit for the implementation of these measures and left each

---

[40] The number of registered unions increased from 262 in 1937, of which 219 submitting returns had a membership of 257,308, to 420 in 1938, of which 343 submitting returns had a membership of 390,112. *Ibid.*, p. 234.

[41] *Ibid.*

[42] In 1939, 51.4% of workers in the textile mills of the United Provinces and 49.2% in those of Madras were employed in British-controlled mills. Computed on the basis of Annual Statement of Mills, included in *Bombay Millowners' Association. Annual Volume 1939* (Bombay, 1940).

[43] Karnik, *Indian Trade Unions*, p. 110.

[44] Resolutions of the Congress Labour Committee, Wardha, 25–26 October 1937, reproduced in *Indian Annual Register, 1937*, Vol. II, p. 378.

government free to choose the pace of the reforms. It limited itself to giving general guidelines.

The Congress provincial ministries responded by setting up enquiry committees to look into the question of wages in the textile industry. Such committees were formed in Bombay, the Central Provinces and the United Provinces. They were non-official bodies, in which representatives of capital and labour sat beside political workers and academics. These committees were subjected to contradictory pressures from the unions and from the employers' associations. They generally recommended wage increases which, though substantial, amounted to no more than a partial compensation for the wage cuts made during the depression. Their recommendations could be described as moderate, and in accepting them, the Congress governments showed that, though they were committed to trying to better the lot of the workers, they had no desire to hit capitalist interests too hard. In the case of Cawnpore, the enquiry committee appointed by the Congress government also recommended the recognition of the union, the Mazdoor Sabha, by the employers. The insistence in Cawnpore on the recognition of the union was no doubt due to the fact that it was controlled by Congress workers who were close to the ministry.[45] Elsewhere the question of recognition of the unions was left in abeyance, pending the establishment of a new legislation on trade disputes, which some governments were contemplating for the near future. On the whole, the Congress ministries showed commendable moderation in dealing with uncompromising capitalists. In spite of it, they could not avoid antagonizing capitalist interests.

Apart from the labour policy, the economic and fiscal policies followed by the Congress ministries during their first months of tenure of office had also a direct impact upon their relations with Indian capitalists. These policies were generally characterized by great caution bordering on conservatism. The new Congress ministries barely introduced any change in the budgets prepared by the caretaker governments which had assumed office during the few months of constitutional bickerings prior to the final acceptance of office by the Congress. The boldest step taken by some of the ministries was the issuing of provincial loans which were very successful with the public.[46]

The only exceptions to this cautious policy were the energetic

[45] On the labour movement in Cawnpore, see S. M. Pandey, *As Labour Organizes. A Study of Unionism in the Kanpur Textile Industry* (Delhi, 1970).

[46] In August 1937, five provincial governments, including the Punjab government but excluding Bombay, raised loans. See India Office Records (IOR), Financial collections, F/7/323, IOL.

measures taken by the Bihar and United Provinces governments to solve the overproduction crisis in the sugar industry of those two provinces. Firstly, a joint sugarcane conference, in which the representatives of the growers, manufacturers and traders took part, was convened by the two governments in Lucknow at the end of September.[47] Following it and after various consultations with the interests directly concerned, the Government of Bihar passed in the Assembly a sugar factories control bill, which was soon followed by a similar bill passed by the United Provinces Assembly. Those bills aimed at regulating the supply of cane to the mills, in a way which would ensure remunerative prices for the cultivators and check overproduction. The Congress governments of Bihar and the United Provinces wanted basically to satisfy their rural clientele, especially the middle peasantry which had taken to sugarcane cultivation on a big scale, but they also wanted to conciliate the manufacturers who were a powerful lobby, especially since they had formed in 1937 a combine called the sugar syndicate. Therefore they introduced in their bills a clause which forced all sugar mills to join the syndicate.[48] This particular clause was irksome to some sugar mill-owners who had stayed away from the syndicate[49] but it helped to ensure a high degree of coordination among the producers. The bills proved beneficial to the sugar industry of Bihar and the United Provinces as well as to the growers. The only victim was the consumer, who had to pay a higher price for his sugar. In the case of the sugar industry, the Congress governments acted as mediators between two groups, the growers and the manufacturers, whose interests were easy to conciliate, but who had found it difficult to come to a direct agreement.

In other provinces, initial measures in favour of Indian industry included a review of the purchasing policies of the various government departments, with the aim of increasing the purchase of swadeshi goods,[50] and the appointment of various committees on industrial policy.[51]

[47] See Proceedings of the joint sugarcane conference convened by the Governments of the United Provinces and Bihar and held at Lucknow on September 29 and 30 1937, in Rajendra Prasad Papers, NAI, File XIII/37, Collection I, sr 106.

[48] This brief account of sugar policy in Bihar and the United Provinces is based on a Memorandum submitted to the National Planning Committee by the United Provinces Government Industries Department, particularly on pp. 107–8. Copy in AICC Papers, NMML, 1939 File G-14.

[49] See G. D. Birla to Rajendra Prasad, 21 December 1937, Rajendra Prasad Papers, File XIII/37, Collection I, sr 127.

[50] See for instance *Two Years of Congress Rule in Madras*, published by the Madras Legislature Congress Party, undated, p. 38.

[51] In Bombay the government set up an industrial advisory board, the role of which

The intentions of the Congress ministries in matters of economic and fiscal policies were made clearer at the time of the preparation of the new budgets for 1938–39, which were the first genuine Congress budgets. By then the financial situation of the provincial governments had slightly improved, following the payment of the first instalment by the Centre from the income-tax receipts.[52] Yet this increase would have to be partly used to compensate for the expected loss in excise revenue due to the introduction of prohibition in some provinces.[53] Therefore there would not be much scope for a large increase in expenditure, unless a government was ready to resort to deficit budgetting. The United Provinces government was the only Congress government which presented a deficit budget for 1938–39.[54] Other provincial governments pursued a more orthodox policy.[55] Generally the bulk of the small increases in expenditure went to education and rural development, two very Gandhian subjects, and industry got very little.[56] The Premier of the United Provinces, Pandit Pant, did not hide his rural bias. In a talk to merchants at the end of 1937, he stressed that industrialization would not solve the problem of unemployment to any appreciable extent in his populous province, and pledged to give priority to agricultural development.[57] In most provincial budgets, the bulk of the projected increases in aid to industry was directed towards the cottage and small-scale industries, particularly to the production of khaddar.[58]

The policies followed by the Congress governments during their first months in office were generally not very different from those followed by the non-Congress ministries during the dyarchy régime, nor did they

was never very clear, and appointed in March 1938 an Economic and Industrial Survey Committee, to review the position of small industries in the province. See Government of Bombay to Sir Purshottamdas Thakurdas, 23 March 1938, Thakurdas Papers, NMML, File 212.

[52] While the Finance Minister in Bombay had predicted a deficit of Rs 10½ lakhs for the financial year 1937–38, there was a final surplus of Rs 18½ lakhs, due to the payment of Rs 27 lakhs by the Centre from the income tax. *Times of India*, 26 February 1938.

[53] Prohibition was first introduced in 1937 in the Salem district of the Madras Presidency on an experimental scale, then extended to other districts of the Presidency and other provinces, particularly Bombay.

[54] See details of provincial budgets in annual issues of the *Indian Yearbook*.

[55] In Madras the Congress ministry presented regularly surplus budgets. *Ibid.*

[56] In Bombay the budget presented in the Assembly for 1938–39 included supplementary expenditure of Rs 34 lakhs on education, Rs 39 lakhs on rural development and only Rs 7½ lakhs on industry. *Times of India*, 26 February 1938.

[57] *The Pioneer*, 13 November 1937.

[58] See *Two years of Congress Rule in Madras*, p. 33: 'With a view to encourage the production of handloom cloth, the Madras Sale of Cloth Act was enacted and the Khadi (Name Protection) Act was extended to the Province'. Rs 2 lakhs were set apart for khadi production in each budget, and grants were given to the All-India Spinners Association.

differ widely from those followed by the non-Congress governments in the few provinces where the Congress had not come to power. The Congress governments made some concessions to the workers, largely to defuse a tense situation on the labour front, increased to some extent expenditure on rural development and cottage industries to consolidate their power base in the countryside, and generally let the bureaucracy operate with a more or less free hand.[59] But this cautious policy failed to satisfy the capitalist interests which had hoped for a more active industrial policy. It also created fears that their interests would be endangered. We shall now turn to the response of the business class to Congress policy in the provinces.

The Initial Business Response

While analysing the responses of the Indian capitalists to the policies followed by the Congress provincial governments, one should not overlook the fact that they were not only dictated by provincial events, but also by the state of Indo-British economic relations, in particular by the trade negotiations which were being held between the two governments. The aim of these negotiations was to conclude a new agreement in place of the Ottawa agreement denounced by the Indian Central Legislative Assembly in 1936.[60] Indian businessmen were represented in those negotiations by Birla, Kasturbhai Lalbhai[61] and Thakurdas as unofficial advisers to the Government of India. As long as there seemed to be a reasonable chance of reaching a satisfactory agreement with Britain on this question, businessmen were keen to avoid antagonizing the British authorities by extending too open a support to the Congress ministries. The trade negotiations influenced the attitude of the Indian capitalists in another more direct way: any increases in the wages of textile workers, such as were recommended by the various enquiry committees in some of the Congress-ruled provinces, were bound to result in an increase in the production cost of Indian cotton textiles and therefore to render imported textiles more competitive on the Indian market. Indian cotton millowners, still the largest group among Indian capitalists, could not at the same time accept a reduction

[59] Thus Giri complains in his Memoirs that the Premier of Madras, Rajagopalachari, tended to favour the British ICS officers and to give them a free hand. Giri, *My Life and Times*, p. 118.

[60] For a detailed analysis of these negotiations, see Markovits, 'Indian Business and Nationalist Politics', pp. 191-7, and Chatterji's article in this volume.

[61] A big Ahmedabad millowner and a close friend of Gandhi.

in the duties on British textiles entering India (a concession which the British Board of Trade urged them to make, in exchange for more advantageous conditions to Indian goods in the UK) and bear increased internal costs of production. This extraneous factor explains largely why Indian capitalists opposed so stubbornly any concessions to workers in matters of wages and therefore came to an open clash with the Congress governments.

Relations between Congress and business became particularly strained in the United Provinces, because of continuous labour unrest among the textile workers in Cawnpore. In that town most of the mills were controlled by British capitalists, yet there was a lot of Indian capital invested in them. Besides, two of the biggest cotton magnates, Sir J. P. Srivastava and Lala Padampat Singhania, were Indian, the latter also one of the leaders of the Federation of Indian Chambers of Commerce and Industry (FICCI) and a well-known supporter of the Congress. When the Pant ministry was formed in July 1937, a general strike had been going on in Cawnpore for several weeks. After some initial hesitation, the new ministry decided to ask the millowners to make one major concession to the workers by recognizing the Mazdoor Sabha. The capitalists, both British and Indian, who had formed the Employers' Association of Northern India to defend their interests against labour,[62] were most reluctant to accord recognition as they alleged that the Mazdoor Sabha was not a genuine union, but a political organization preaching the overthrow of the capitalist system. Eventually they were forced to give in to Government pressure, but they resented it considerably.[63] In fact, they never forgave the United Provinces Congress government for having sided with the workers. A few years later in the course of a private conversation Sir J. P. Srivastava revealed that the Indian industrialists of Cawnpore, all Hindu, became thereafter such bitter opponents of the Congress ministry that they went to the length of subsidizing the Muslim League in the province.[64] Another result of the strike was the appointment of the Cawnpore

[62] See Pandey, *As Labour Organizes*, pp. 54 ff.

[63] In a communiqué, the employers said that they felt 'that they should not have been forced by government to recognize the Mazdoor Sabha as long as it remains constituted as at present'. *The Pioneer*, 12 August 1937.

[64] In *The Viceroy's Journal* (London, 1973), p. 102, entry for 30 November 1944, Lord Wavell writes: 'Srivastava [then a minister in Wavell's cabinet] . . . today told me that after the Congress success at the polls and assumption of office in the United Provinces in 1937, the leading industrialists—all, I think, Hindu—got together and decided to finance Jinnah and the Muslim League and also the Mahasabha, as the extreme communal parties, to oppose Congress who they feared might threaten their financial profits.'

Labour Enquiry Committee to look into the question of wages in the textile industry. While the committee was doing its work, the millowners under the pretext of an incident in a mill, withdrew their recognition of the Mazdoor Sabha.[65] Therefore, when the committee submitted its report in April 1938 recommending a twenty-one per cent increase in wages in the textile industry (it only amounted to a restoration of three-fifths of the wage cuts made during the depression), the situation was tense, and the rejection of the report by the Employers' Association triggered off a new general strike which lasted almost two months. Once again the question of the recognition of the Mazdoor Sabha became the main issue of contention between the two parties. During this second strike, the Government, under pressure from the local Congress organization, gave some support, though half-hearted, to the strikers,[66] and eventually the millowners had to give in again, though in the course of their negotiations with the ministry they managed to make their recognition of the Sabha conditional upon changes in its internal constitution. The attitude of the Government came in for strong criticism even from Singhania, a Congress supporter,[67] and in the United Provinces relations between Indian business and the Congress remained tense.

In the United Provinces, the Indian capitalists took a very uncompromising line in their dealings with the industrial workers and resented the attempts at arbitration made by the Congress ministry, because they thought that the government's mind was biased in favour of labour. There are specific reasons for the failure of the Congress and the capitalists to find an adjustment. One of the reasons was the weight of the British in the capitalist class of the United Provinces, and the close links between them and Indian capitalists. British capitalists had no reason to be particularly friendly to a Congress ministry, and their stand influenced their Indian colleagues. Another factor leading to confrontation was the strong position enjoyed by the Congress socialists and other leftist elements in the Congress provincial organization. These forces were able to pressurize the ministry into taking a stand in favour of the workers, thus further antagonizing the capitalists.

[65] *The Pioneer*, 30 November 1937.
[66] On 19 May 1938 Pandit Pant, receiving a workers' delegation, chided them for their lack of discipline. *The Leader*, 21 May 1938. But on 23 May, the United Provinces Congress Committee passed a resolution supporting the strikers and thereafter the attitude of the ministry to the strike changed. *Ibid.*, 25 May 1938. On 12 June the Government asked for the implementation of the recommendations of the report. *Ibid.*, 14 June 1938.
[67] *The Leader*, 29 June 1938.

In other Congress-ruled provinces Indian businessmen generally followed a less uncompromising line, but this did not prevent limited clashes with the provincial governments. In the Bombay Presidency, where the bulk of the cotton textile industry was concentrated, the Congress ministry immediately set up a Textile Enquiry Committee to review the wage situation in the textile centres of the province. Businessmen complained that they were not sufficiently represented on the committee, and they opposed the demands of the unions for a sizable increase in wages, under the pretext that the financial situation of the mills was precarious.[68] The proposals of the committee, embodied in the interim report released in February 1938,[69] were a compromise between the extreme demands of labour and the negative stand taken by the millowners. The immediate increases granted were not negligible[70] and they seemed to satisfy most workers, if not the most militant section of the working class. The millowners, according to the Governor of Bombay, Sir Roger Lumley, 'took some time in making up their minds',[71] but faced with the possibility of a general strike, they had no choice but to accept the recommendations of the committee. Yet the *Indian Textile Journal*, the mouthpiece of the Bombay millowners, did not hesitate to accuse the Bombay government of having played upon the threat of a strike to force them into accepting those recommendations.[72]

According to Lumley, the millowners, in exchange for their acceptance of the report, were able to extract from the ministry the promise that it would not introduce any new labour welfare measures for at least one year.[73] The Bombay government also committed itself to seeking an agreement with the Centre and other provincial governments for the standardization of wages in the textile industry on an all-India scale, so

---

[68] See Evidence of the Bombay Millowners' Association before the Textile Enquiry Committee, *Indian Textile Journal*, 15 December 1937, p. 84.

[69] See *Textile Labour Enquiry Committee*, Vol. I, Preliminary Report (Bombay, 1938).

[70] They were fixed at 9% in Ahmedabad, where wages were the highest in India, at 11.9% in Bombay and at 14.3% in Sholapur, the third big textile centre in the province, where wages were particularly low.

[71] Lumley to Linlithgow, report no. 12, 15 March 1938, Linlithgow Papers, Vol. 51.

[72] *Indian Textile Journal*, 15 March 1938, p. 192.

[73] Lumley wrote to Linlithgow: 'My information is that the decision of the millowners was not reached without some very plain speaking by the Congress Ahmedabad millowners to the ministers. I understand that these millowners, in heated interviews, pointed out that they had supplied in the past a large part of the Congress funds and that they were now receiving in return from the Congress governments very heavy burdens to bear. They extracted from the Ministers and from Sardar Vallabhbhai Patel a promise that further legislation providing sickness benefit and old-age pensions for the workers, the cost of which would be mainly borne by the millowners, should not be put into operation for at least a year.' Report no 12, 15 March 1938, Linlithgow Papers, Vol. 51.

that the millowners in the Bombay Presidency would not find themselves handicapped *vis-à-vis* their upcountry competitors, the millowners of other provinces and of the Indian States, who did not have to contend with similar burdens.

Though in March 1938 Lumley could write about the new outlook in Bombay that 'the prospect of serious labour trouble in the mills' had 'faded away',[74] and could rightly ascribe the change in the labour situation to the advent of a Congress ministry, the price paid by the millowners for industrial peace was indeed heavy. The foreseeable increase in the production costs of Indian textiles reduced the chances of reaching an agreement with Lancashire over the question of the duties on British textiles, and thus the Indo-British trade negotiations, the final success of which had become dependent on a direct agreement between Indian and British textile manufacturers,[75] were more or less doomed to failure.

In other Congress-ruled provinces, capitalists faced with similar labour unrest also made concessions on wages. This was the case in Coimbatore where, following a strike in the mills, the Madras government referred the problem to a court of enquiry whose rulings were accepted by both parties, and in the Central Provinces where an enquiry committee was set up on the Bombay model.

Thus in those Congress-ruled provinces which had a textile industry, the millowners were forced to make some concessions to labour in order to avoid more widespread trouble. Generally the Congress ministries took an attitude which, though only mildly sympathetic to labour, was enough to create suspicions among the capitalists that the Congress was becoming hostile to them. Actually it could be argued that by pressurizing the industrialists into giving in to moderate labour demands, the Congress saved them from a more dangerous confrontation. But most Indian capitalists were not farsighted enough to perceive this, and they tended to see only the immediate cost incurred by them from the policies of the Congress governments.

There were also differences in the responses of the capitalists, which were directly linked to the state of their relations with the Congress organizations in their respective provinces. In that respect, the United Provinces and Bombay represented two extreme cases. In the United Provinces, relations between local big business and the Congress had been strained for a long time, and among Congress national leaders it

[74] Lumley to Linlithgow, *ibid.*
[75] For a detailed account, see Markovits, 'Indian Business and Nationalist Politics', pp. 191–7.

was Nehru, not a great friend of the capitalists,[76] who wielded the greatest influence. The labour trouble in Cawnpore brought these already strained relations to a breaking point. In Bombay, big business, particularly the Ahmedabad millowners, had played a great part in Congress politics for many years, and benefited from close links with Patel, who kept a close watch on the activities of the Bombay ministry. Ready access to the ministry allowed local capitalists to negotiate when problems arose and often reach some kind of compromise.

Indian capitalists, generally dissatisfied with the labour policies of the Congress ministries, could not find great compensations in their economic policies. It is not that they had exaggerated expectations in that matter. They were very conscious of the many limitations under which the Congress ministries had to function, but they pointed out that even within such a restricted framework as that of provincial autonomy the ministries had powers 'which they could exercise for the development and progress of trade and industry'.[77] Speaking in March 1937 at the annual conference of Indian insurance companies, the Bombay business magnate Walchand Hirachand had expressed the hope that in the future Congress governments would be able 'to act in such a way . . . as to directly benefit Swadeshi enterprises'.[78] Yet, the actual policies of the Congress ministries during their first months in office disappointed even their supporters in the business class. In March 1938, the *Indian Textile Journal* came out with a severe condemnation of the industrial policy of the Congress governments and asked: 'Would the Congress play into the hands of the enemies of the industrial advancement of the country?'[79]

The discontent in business circles with the policy of the Congress in the provinces manifested itself in the tendency by big business groups to step up investment in the non-Congress provinces and even more in the Indian States. The exact extent of this movement is difficult to gauge but a few striking examples suggest that it was not altogether negligible.[80] Even pro-Congress businessmen, like Lala Padampat Singhania of Cawnpore, increasingly preferred to set up new factories in the Indian

[76] In 1936 many Bombay capitalists had condemned his socialist views, and though in the following period he had become more moderate, he was nevertheless still suspect in the eyes of many businessmen.

[77] M. C. Ghia, Vice-President of the Indian Merchants Chamber in a speech at a function in Bombay in honour of B. G. Kher, *Times of India*, 26 July 1937.

[78] *Times of India*, 8 March 1937.

[79] *Indian Textile Journal*, 15 March 1938, p. 200, 'The State and Industries'.

[80] Business groups which invested in the Indian States in 1937–39 included: Singhania (in Bhopal), Srivastava (in Rampur), Tata (in Baroda), Sassoon (in Travancore). This list is not exhaustive.

States where wages were lower, labour legislation almost non-existent, and taxation practically nil. Apart from the immediate profit motivation, such investments were also a clear, though discreet, way of conveying to the Congress leadership that the policies followed by the Congress ministries were antagonizing Indian capitalist interests.

What was also significant of the mood in Indian business was that in the face of the growing challenge from labour and the ambiguous attitude of the Congress, capitalists tended to close their ranks and to forget old enmities and feuds. In Cawnpore, the millowners, British and Indian, pro-Congress and anti-Congress, displayed remarkable unity in their fight against the Mazdoor Sabha and in their difficult negotiations with the Congress ministry. In the Bombay Presidency, the old rivalry between the textile manufacturers of Ahmedabad and Bombay City became less apparent. The Ahmedabad millowners used their own good relations with the ministry and Patel to negotiate on behalf of the entire textile industry of the province. Sectional differences among capitalists were becoming less acute and all-India organizations such as the FICCI were strengthening themselves. In what amounted to a spectacular break with a ten-year-old policy, the Tatas, the biggest Indian business group joined the FICCI in 1937. Their move was directly related to the advent of the Congress ministries: the Tatas, who had the bulk of their interests in the Congress-ruled provinces of Bombay, Bihar and the Central Provinces, wanted to benefit from the privileged relationship existing between the FICCI and the Congress. But at the same time it testified to the growing trend of unity among Indian capitalists in a threatening environment.

It seems that by the spring of 1938 the Congress High Command became aware of the danger of letting its good relations with the Indian business class be threatened by the policies of the provincial ministries. Pressure from the top leadership probably explains in part the shift which became noticeable in the labour and economic policies of the Congress ministries at that time.

The Shift in the Policies of the Congress Governments and the Improvement in Relations between Congress and Business

In the spring of 1938, the Congress governments started making efforts at placating capitalist interests and at improving their relations with the business world. The persistence of labour unrest in the Congress-ruled provinces even after substantial wage increases had been granted to the workers was a decisive factor. Congress politicians became increasingly suspicious of the motivations of the labour leaders in launching agitations, and they started to view communist infiltration as the root-cause of all the trouble. This led to a new policy in the matter of trade unions. Previously, the Congress leadership had sought adjust- ments with the existing organizations, particularly the All India Trade Union Congress (AITUC) and the National Trade Union Federation (NTUF), the two biggest federations, which had set up a joint council in 1938 to coordinate their activities. But none of these organizations was controlled by elements close to the Congress leadership: the AITUC was led by a coalition of Congress socialists and communists while the NTUF was the preserve of moderate politicians linked to the Servants of India Society. They were therefore not amenable to direct pressure from the Congress High Command and the latter had thus no way of directly controlling the labour movement. In the spring of 1938 the Congress leadership decided to set up a new movement which would be under their control, and would be organized on the model of the Ahmedabad Mazdoor Mahajan, a Gandhian union which had established amicable relations with the employers in that big textile centre. In an interview to the *Bombay Chronicle* Patel stressed the necessity of having workers' organizations which did not believe in the policy of class struggle, and he chided the existing unions.[81] Congress leaders made use of the Gandhi Sevak Sangh to create the nucleus of the future Hind Mazdoor Sabha (HMS) which became for a few years the labour branch of the Congress, prior to the creation of the Indian National Trade Union Congress (INTUC). Not surprisingly the Bombay government was in the forefront of the attempts at setting up new, more docile unions. The Minister for Local Government, L. M. Patil, proclaimed the intention of the Bombay Provincial Congress Committee to start their own working class organizations.[82] The Bombay Chief Minister, B. G. Kher, came under attack from trade unionists for using government money in order to help form pro-Congress unions.[83] But the main thrust in the new labour policy of the Congress governments was towards the introduction of a new legislation on labour relations, which would help to establish durable industrial peace in the provinces, and thus check the flow of capital towards the Indian States.

[81] *Bombay Chronicle*, 29 March 1938.
[82] Quoted in Revri, *Indian Trade Union Movement*, p. 232.
[83] Patel wrote to Kher in a letter dated 9 July 1938: 'the trade-union people have already begun to howl at you for employing men at government expense to organize labour unions rival to the trade-unions organized by non-officials.' Kher Papers, NMML, File 6.

The existing legislation, both central and provincial, had been effective in checking the growth of the trade union movement but it had no proper machinery for the settlement of industrial disputes. New legislation was mainly aimed at remedying this defect. The Madras government, dismayed by the spate of labour conflicts in this tradi- tionally peaceful province, was the first one to move in that direction. On 22 April 1938 the Labour Minister, V. V. Giri, presented the draft of a bill under the name of Madras Industrial Disputes Investigation and Settlement Act.[84] In Madras it never reached the statute book, but it served as the basis of similar attempts in other provinces. In Bombay, the Congress ministry took up the matter seriously and 'improved' considerably Giri's initial draft. In September 1938 they submitted to the Provincial Legislature the Bombay Trade Disputes Act, which was the most complex and effective piece of legislation ever devised in India for the settlement of industrial disputes. Though a provision for compulsory arbitration initially introduced by the framers of the bill was deleted from the final version,[85] the bill included a provision for a compulsory delay which could extend to several months before a strike or a lock-out could begin, a measure which drew applauses from the Governor of Bombay himself.[86] Introducing the bill in the Bombay Legislative Assembly, Kher made clear the intention of his government 'to promote legislation aiming at the prevention of strikes and lock-outs as far as possible'.[87] Though the bill was theoretically aimed as much at lock-outs as at strikes, it was nevertheless obvious that its framers were above all interested in stopping strikes. In any case, as lock-outs were generally declared in retaliation for strikes, it could be assumed that if there were no more strikes the incidence of lock-outs would tend to be less. The intention of curbing strikes was openly avowed by the Chief Minister who, in his Assembly speech, condemned labour unrest in the strongest terms and proclaimed that 'his government stood for class collaboration and not for class conflict'.[88]

Though the framers of the bill pretended to keep a balance between capital and labour, a detailed examination of its many clauses brings out the fact that it was heavily weighted in favour of the capitalist side. For

[84] Copy enclosed in Giri to Kripalani, 14 July 1938, AICC Papers, NMML, File PL 3(I), 1937.

[85] Dwarkadas, *Forty-five Years with Labour*, p. 79.

[86] Lumley to Linlithgow, Report dated 15 September 1938, Linlithgow Papers, Vol. 51.

[87] Bombay Legislative Assembly debates, 2 September 1938, quoted in *Indian Annual Register, 1938*, Vol. II, p. 149.

[88] *Ibid.*, 4 September 1938, *ibid.*, p. 157.

instance, though strikes and lock-outs were apparently put on the same footing, only strikes were penalized and not lock-outs.[89] The penalty for illegal strikes, which was six months imprisonment, was extremely high. There was also a complex clause regarding the registration of trade unions about which Nehru who, surprisingly enough, stated in a confidential note that 'on the whole the Act seemed a good one',[90] remarked that 'company unions' were 'definitely encouraged and given very great advantages over independent unions'. He also criticized the encouragement given in the bill to occupational unions, underlining that it would 'lead to the formation of numerous petty unions, usually on caste and community lines'.

The bill met with strong opposition in the Legislative Assembly from trade unionists, Ambedkar's independent labourites and the Muslim League, but the government was in such a hurry to have it passed that it did not even allow the formation of a Select Committee to look more closely into its merits. Eventually the Bill was passed on 5 November 1938 amidst angry scenes.[91] The haste with which the government acted showed that they wanted to put the bill into effect as soon as possible in order to establish their control over the labour movement in Bombay.

Yet the immediate effect of the passing of the bill was to provoke a general strike in the Bombay Presidency in protest against the 'Black Act', as well as demonstrations of solidarity in the other provinces. In Bombay city, the strike was joined by approximately half of the millhands, but it failed to gain much support in Ahmedabad and Sholapur.[92] The determined way in which the police under the Congress Raj dealt with the strikers[93] shocked the public,[94] but it showed that the ministry was determined to curb labour unrest at any cost.

The firm stand taken by the government against the general strike earned for it the approval of the Bombay capitalists, who had their own

[89] For a detailed analysis of the main provisions of the bill, see Revri, *Indian Trade Union Movement*, p. 226 ff.

[90] 'Confidential note on Bombay Trade Disputes Act,' 14 December 1938, Nehru Papers, NMML, File 150.

[91] *Times of India*, 6 November 1938.

[92] Lumley to Linlithgow, report dated 15 November 1938, Linlithgow papers, Vol. 51.

[93] The police opened fire upon demonstrators in different places in town, resulting in several dead and many injured. *Times of India*, 8 November 1938.

[94] The government had to agree to the setting up of a committee to enquire into the disturbances.

initial reservations regarding some of the clauses of the bill.[95] They could now forget them and look forward to an improvement in the labour situation in the province. The turn in government labour policy was soon epitomized by its attitude to the Bombay seamen's strike of December 1938. Not only did it refuse any kind of support to the strikers, but it even adopted harsh repressive measures against them.[96] The fact that many seamen in Bombay were employed by Scindia, the big navigation company led by Walchand Hirachand who had links with the ministry, might also partly account for the special callousness displayed by the Congress ministry.

The new attitude of the Congress governments *vis-à-vis* labour, much in evidence in Bombay, manifested itself also in other Congress-ruled provinces. In the United Provinces, after the conditional recognition of the Mazdoor Sabha by the employers and its capture by communist elements, labour trouble remained endemic in Cawnpore, but the Congress ministry ceased to show sympathy to the workers.[97] In Bihar, where conflict erupted in the Dalmia and Tata factories, which employed the bulk of industrial labour in the province, the government tried to reassure capitalists and contemplated the introduction of a trade disputes act on the Bombay model.[98]

During 1939, as compared to 1938, although there was a slight increase in the number of industrial disputes in India, the number of workers involved and days lost showed a downward trend, and strikes tended to be shorter in duration.[99] It is difficult to know if the new legislation in Bombay had an impact, since it came into operation only at the end of the year. What is clear is that the rapid pace of growth of the trade union movement in 1937-38 did not continue.[100]

If there were no spectacular strikes comparable to the Cawnpore strike of 1938, a disturbing trend from the capitalists' point of view was the appearance of a new phenomenon, the stay-in-strike. The first one

[95] Lumley wrote to Linlithgow in his report dated 15 September 1938 that the millowners feared that the 'cumbrous machinery' set up by the Act would make it difficult for them to introduce changes in their way of operating their factories. Linlithgow Papers, Vol. 51.

[96] See Karnik, *Indian Trade Unions*, pp. 114–15.

[97] In July 1939, the relations between the provincial trade union Congress and the provincial government reached the breaking-point, following a letter sent by the government to the Mazdoor Sabha, in which they had objected strongly to the preaching of class hatred by trade unions. *The Leader*, 14 July 1939.

[98] *The Leader*, 8 December 1938.

[99] In 1939, there were 406 disputes, involving 409,075 workers and resulting in the loss of 4,992,795 man-days. Revri, *Indian Trade Union Movement*, p. 260.

[100] Membership of registered trade unions showed little change between 1938 and 1939. *Ibid.*, p. 234.

took place in a Bombay textile mill in April 1939, and was strongly condemned by the provincial government.[101] It then spread to Madras and the Chief Minister, Rajagopalachari, indicted it in the severest terms in the Legislative Assembly.[102] Both ministries insisted upon the illegal character of such actions, but the existing legislation was not equipped to deal specifically with stay-in strikes. Therefore, in 1939, though there was some improvement on the labour front, industrial peace remained an elusive goal.

While the new labour policy adopted by the Congress ministries did not succeed in radically curbing labour unrest, it was nevertheless a welcome development for Indian capitalists. It showed that their fears of seeing the Congress adopt a line of hostility to capitalist interests were unfounded. The Congress was in fact striving for conciliation of different class interests: once it had given some satisfaction to the workers, it naturally tended to conciliate business interests. The Congress left was not strong enough to oppose that policy, although in one or two provinces it could influence government policy to a certain extent and make more difficult an adjustment with the capitalists.

There were also encouraging signs in the economic policies of the provincial governments, although concrete advantages gained by businessmen from such policies remained necessarily limited. The High Command increasingly tended to intervene on behalf of capitalist interests with the various provincial governments. Thus in July 1938 Patel, in a circular addressed to all the Congress chief ministers,[103] urged them to insure all government business with genuine swadeshi companies. He also asked them to put pressure on the textile industry and other protected industries to do the same. In February 1939, the AICC assured a big Indian chemicals firm that their instructions to the Provincial Governments were 'to patronise Indian industries in preference to foreign industries'.[104] In August 1939, Patel intervened personally with the Bombay Chief Minister to prevent the granting of a license for the electrification of Gujerat to a big British firm.[105] In Bombay the provincial government gave its guarantee to a few industrial projects, and thus helped their promoters to raise capital for

[101] Dwarkadas, *Forty-five Years with Labour*, p. 56.
[102] *Ibid.*
[103] Patel to Kher, 1 July 1939, Kher Papers, File 6.
[104] AICC to Alembic Chemical Works, 4 February 1939, AICC Papers, File G-72, 1938.
[105] In a letter to Kher, dated 3 August 1939, Patel urged the Chief Minister to refuse the license to the British firm of Killick Nixon which already held the license for Ahmedabad. Kher Papers, File 6. Yet such interventions directed specifically against British firms were very rare.

them.[106] The Madras Cabinet, urged by Patel, helped a big cement combine to get a license for the exploitation of a mineral quarry.[107] During the last phase of the Congress rule in the provinces, closer links were established between capitalist interests and Congress politicians, particularly in Bombay, but naturally there is little factual evidence available on such matters.

The improvement in the relations between Indian business and the Congress provincial governments facilitated the work of the National Planning Committee set up by the Congress at the end of 1938. Actually the decision of setting up such a committee was taken at a conference of industries ministers of the provincial governments. Business observers also took part, and Indian big business was fully associated with the work of the committee, which benefited from the active collaboration of the Congress ministries.[108] The conference also considered the possibilities of taking some immediate measures for the development of medium-scale industries in some of the provinces. An All-India Planning Commission was entrusted with the task of drafting a programme of immediate action,[109] but its work was cut short by the war and the resignation of the Congress ministries.

The rapprochement between Indian business and the Congress was facilitated by the breach which took place between the unofficial advisers and the Government of India in the Indo-British trade negotiations. It started with the failure of the direct talks held in Simla in May 1938 between a Lancashire delegation and the representatives of the Indian textile industry.[110] Then after a few more months of protracted negotiations, in September 1938 the unofficial advisers advocated rejection of the last offer of the British Board of Trade; and the final negotiation resulting in the March 1939 agreement took place

[106] In a letter to Kher dated 5 July 1939, Manu Subedar, of the Indian Merchants' Chamber, protested against the stand of the Bombay government in giving its guarantee to the capital sunk in 'one or more industrial venture'. Kher Papers, File 6.

[107] C. M. Kothari, a Gujerati businessman of Madras, wrote to his friend Thakurdas in a letter dated 17 March 1938: 'there was a regular tussle in the Cabinet meeting to give the lease [of Trichinopoly] to Narayandas Girdhardas [a Madras businessman] and not to C. P. company [part of the Associated Cement Companies combine] and everyone of the ministers was in favour of giving the same to him, except Rajaji and Dr. Subborayan. In that meeting Rajaji read a letter from Vallabhbhai mentioning amongst other things that the lease may be given to C. P. Cement Co. as the company has necessary capital.' Thakurdas Papers, File 206.

[108] The Madras ministry was the only one to show a reluctance to collaborate. Giri, *My Life and Times*, p. 161.

[109] There is a detailed account of the conference in *Indian Annual Register*, 1938, Vol. II, pp. 288–292.

[110] Markovits, 'Indian Business and Nationalist Politics', p. 197.

only between officials, the business community not being associated any more in the process.[111] The policies of the Congress ministries had a direct effect on the negotiations, insofar as they refused to give the advisers any guarantee that they would not impose any more burdens upon the textile industry, thus preventing the latter from making concessions to Lancashire which would have permitted a settlement with the Board of Trade.[112]

The March 1939 agreement drew unanimous condemnation in India from political as well as from business circles. It helped to consolidate further the rapprochement between business and the Congress at the national level; but from the end of 1938 onwards financial difficulties in the provinces had put the relations between Indian business and the Congress governments under fresh strain and threatened to cancel all the gains made during the previous period.

The Final Phase of the Congress Ministries: New Strains in Congress–Business Relations

Towards the end of 1938, the Congress provincial ministries faced an impending financial crisis, and they resorted to measures which alienated capitalist interests to a certain extent. The framing of the new budgets for 1939–40 forced the ministries to take a closer look at the precarious condition of their finances, due on the one hand to the loss of revenue caused by the introduction of prohibition, and on the other hand to the necessity of increasing expenditure if projected measures for rural upliftment were to be effectively implemented. During the debate on the budget in the United Provinces Legislative Assembly in March 1939, Sir J. P. Srivastava pointed out that in the last twenty months the provincial government had incurred supplementary expenditure up to Rs 1.6 crores, while the loss in its excise revenue due to prohibition

[111] *Ibid.*, pp. 229–32.

[112] See the correspondence between Thakurdas, one of the unofficial advisers and Iyengar, Secretary to the Government of Bombay, Finance Department, in August 1938. In a letter dated 18 August Thakurdas wrote: 'if the textile industry is to make the sacrifice indicated in the proposals [of the Board of Trade] under piece goods and prints, obviously they will not be able to stand any more burden which provincial governments in India may have in mind to put on them'. Copy in Kher Papers, II, File 3. In a letter dated 25 August, Iyengar replied that it was impossible for the ministers to commit themselves in advance on the final outcome of the labour enquiry committee and that they considered 'that the terms of the Indo-British pact must be judged on the basis of the facts as they are today'. Copy enclosed in Irwin, Secretary to the Governor of Bombay, to Puckle, Secretary to the Viceroy, Linlithgow Papers, Vol. 52.

amounted to Rs 0.4 crores. Therefore supplementary resources of 2 crores had to be found, of which approximately 1.3 crores were already provided by the levy of various small taxes and duties, but there remained a balance of Rs 0.7 crores.[113] Though the United Provinces were a special case even a financially sound province like Bombay was also looking for new sources of revenue.[114] The Congress ministries had therefore no alternative but to increase taxation, however unpopular such a move was bound to be. The only choice which they could exercise was, which categories of the population would have to bear the burden of the increase. Though Bihar and Assam, two almost exclusively agricultural provinces, tried to introduce an agricultural income tax, Congress ministries in other provinces sought to avoid taking such a step which would create opposition to the Party in the countryside, especially among the landholding classes which were the main power base of the Congress régimes. Therefore they decided to shift the main burden towards the less inflammable and less strategic urban areas.

The possibilities of levying new taxes were severely limited by the constitution, which reserved the levy of income tax of any kind to the Central Government. The United Provinces government tried to get around the difficulty by introducing an employments tax, which was an indirect way of taxing the incomes of merchants and employers of labour. Not surprisingly their proposal met with determined opposition from the trading and industrial interests of the province. After the employments tax bill had been passed by the Assembly on 16 April 1939, a protest conference was convened, in which prominent businessmen participated.[115] A few days later a memorandum was sent to the Viceroy by seven associations representing the bulk of commercial and industrial capital in the province, underlining that the tax was *ultra vires* of a provincial government, and asking the Viceroy to refer the case to the newly-established Federal Court.[116] The last months of Congress rule in the United provinces saw the local business class put up a stiff fight against the financial policy of the Congress ministry.

In other Congress-ruled provinces the ministries generally followed a

[113] United Provinces Legislative Assembly debates, 13 March 1939, quoted in *Indian Annual Register, 1939*, Vol. I, p. 220. The budget presented for 1939–40 made for a deficit of Rs 38 lakhs, of which Rs 30 lakhs were to be covered by the employments tax.

[114] Lumley to Linlithgow, 26 December 1938, Linlithgow Papers, Vol. 52.

[115] *The Leader*, 19 April 1939.

[116] Memorandum submitted by the Upper India Chamber of Commerce, the United Provinces Chamber of Commerce, the Merchants' Chamber of the United Provinces, the Indian Sugar Producers' Association, the Employers' Association of Northern India, the Cawnpore Sugar Merchants' Association, the Cawnpore Sugar Brokers' Association. *The Leader*, 20 April 1939.

more cautious policy, and the projected increases in taxation were less, but even the modest proposals regarding taxation of urban incomes were strongly resented by the business class. In Bombay the ministry sought to increase the electricity duty, and to introduce an urban immovable property tax, as well as a sales tax on petrol and cloth.[117] In Madras the Rajagopalachari ministry moved a bill for the imposition of a general sales tax, which the Chief Minister defended openly on the ground that part of the burden of taxation had to be shifted from the cultivator to the urban trader.[118]

In Bombay, business opposition to the financial policy of the ministry centred around the urban property tax and the sales tax on cloth. Opposition to the former ran high, because of the speculative boom which had been taking place in Bombay for many years and had incited many traders to invest heavily in urban properties. A renowned economist defended the proposal on the ground that it would help to curb unhealthy speculation, and would act as an incentive to investment in industry, thus ultimately proving a boon to capitalist interests;[119] but these sophisticated arguments cut no ice with the merchant classes which continued to agitate against the bill until the resignation of the ministry.[120]

The sales tax on cloth raised an even stronger storm in the textile industry, although in that case also it was argued by a pro-Congress economist that since the tax would be levied on imported cloth as well, it would not have an adverse effect on the local mills.[121] The unexpectedly violent reaction of the millowners to this relatively minor issue could be explained by the difficult situation in which the textile industry in the Bombay Presidency found itself in 1939, after a few years of continuous prosperity. The major causes of the new difficulties seem to have been the bad crops which reduced the purchasing power of the peasantry, the renewed vigour of the Japanese offensive on the Indian market,[122] and the increased competition from upcountry mills in India where the cost

[117] See Lumley to Linlithgow, report dated 15 February 1939, Linlithgow Papers, Vol. 52.
[118] In a speech in the Madras Legislative Assembly on 16 March 1939, quoted in *Indian Annual Register, 1939*, vol. I, p. 182. On this occasion Rajagopalachari castigated merchants and traders for their refusal 'to pay even one pie out of one rupee'.
[119] C. N. Vakil in *Times of India*, 21 February 1939.
[120] An added factor was that many property-holders were Muslims, which gave the agitation a communal turn.
[121] V. K. R. V. Rao, in *Bombay Chronicle*, 21 February 1939.
[122] In 1938–39, sales of Japanese piecegoods showed an increase of 40% over the figures for the previous year. Computed on the basis of data in A. K. Bagchi, *Private Investment in India, 1900–1939* (Cambridge, 1972), p. 238.

of labour was lower than in the Bombay Presidency. In July 1939, in Bombay city alone four mills had been forced to close down, making 18,000 workers idle, while most of the mills had ceased to work a full double-shift.[123] This difficult situation led the millowners to oppose fiercely all attempts at imposing supplementary burdens on them. In March 1939, Kasturbhai Lalbhai a friend of the Congress, delivered a scathing attack on the policies of the Congress governments towards the textile industry.[124] From April 1939 onwards, Lumley saw evidence of a 'widening breach between Congress and the millowners'.[125] The latter tried to avoid giving their workers the supplementary wage increase to which they had committed themselves in accepting the recommendations of the Textile Labour Enquiry Committee, but they could not bring the government to support them, and eventually had to pay up.[126] Failure to avoid an increase in their labour costs prompted the Bombay and Ahmedabad millowners to try to obtain the agreement of the entire textile industry to a scheme of reduction of output.[127] But millowners in other regions, less hit by the crisis, refused to countenance the scheme and the industrialists of Western India were left in the lurch.[128]

They were more successful in their fight against the proposal for the fixation of a minimum wage, which the Textile Labour Enquiry Committee, still working on its final report, was known to be contemplating. In August 1939, Gulzarilal Nanda, Parliamentary Secretary to the Government of Bombay, and the real power in matters of labour policy, hinted, while the committee were still sitting, that in view of the difficult situation in the textile industry, the government would oppose any move tending to put up wages.[129]

With the worsening of the situation in September 1939, the millowners sought more radical measures. Thus the Ahmedabad millowners obtained the agreement from Patel to a twenty per cent cut in wages, to be implemented after discussions with the unions.[130] Yet

[123] 'Indian Textile Industry in the Doldrums', Indian Textile Journal, 15 July 1939, p. 392.
[124] In an interview to the Times of India, 3 March 1939, he complained that the provincial governments were 'out to crush' the cotton textile industry.
[125] Lumley to Linlithgow, report dated 15 April 1939, Linlithgow Papers, Vol. 52.
[126] Lumley to Linlithgow, report dated 15 May 1939, ibid.
[127] Indian Textile Journal, 15 July 1939, p. 392.
[128] Ibid., 15 August 1939, p. 431.
[129] Gulzarilal Nanda to Bombay Provincial Congress Committee, quoted in Indian Textile Journal, 15 August 1939, p. 430.
[130] Ibid., p. 431. One wing in the Ahmedabad Millowners' Association led by Kasturbhai Lalbhai agreed with Patel's proposal to hold discussions with the unions, while another section, headed by Sakarlal Balabhai, advocated unilateral measures.

the same Patel restrained the Bombay Government from sanctioning a twenty per cent increase in the price of cloth, as demanded by the industry.[131] Therefore just on the eve of the war, which suddenly ended the crisis, the situation in the textile industry of the Bombay Presidency was so chaotic that it tended to affect adversely the relations between the largest group of capitalists in the province and the Congress ministry.

Apart from the United Provinces and Bombay, other provinces also witnessed a deterioration in the relations between Indian business and the Congress. In Madras, where there was tremendous opposition to the sales tax proposal from the merchant community, a new provincial loan met with little success, a fact which the Governor of the province attributed to the hostility of capitalist interests to the Congress ministry.[132] In Bihar, renewed trouble in the Tata factories created a tense atmosphere.[133]

The financial difficulties which the Congress ministries had to face made an adjustment between the overall compulsions of governmental action in the provinces and the sectional interests of Indian business more and more difficult. Even in Bombay, which of all the provinces had the government best disposed towards capitalist interests, tension was mounting. When its immediate interests were at stake, as was the case in the textile industry crisis of mid-1939, even the most pro-Congress section of the capitalist class, the Ahmedabad textile manufacturers, did not hesitate to attack violently the ministry and tried to pressurize it into taking unpopular measures. On the other hand even the most pro-capitalist among the Congress politicians, such as Patel, could not find any way of avoiding a clash with capitalist interests, without at the same time renouncing the basic tenets of their political faith, including prohibition, which was partly responsible for the aggravation of the financial crisis in the provinces. Patel must have been aware of all this when in July 1939 he mentioned for the first time the possibility of the Congress ministries resigning, if military expenditure was not drastically reduced and if the provinces were not granted a greater share of the income-tax receipts.[134] Undue prolongation of the experiment of autonomous provinces without adequate financial resources would have

[131] Patel to Kher, 17 September 1939, Kher Papers, File 6.
[132] Erskine to Linlithgow, 6 July 1939, Erskine Papers, IOL, London, Mss Eur. D 596. In a reply dated 12 July, *ibid.*, Linlithgow expresses his surprise at Erskine's views and points out that most likely the international situation is the main cause of the shyness of the investing public in Madras.
[133] See A. R. Dalal's call to the Bihar government to intervene to restore peace in Jamshedpur. *The Leader*, 14 August 1939.
[134] *The Leader*, 23 July 1939.

led to a further deterioration in relations between Congress and business in the provinces, which in its turn would have endangered the emerging alliance between Congress and Indian big business, as symbolized by their collaboration in the National Planning Committee. The interests of both the capitalists and the Congress, therefore, required an end to this uneasy situation. This explains why the capitalists took with equanimity the news of the resignation of the Congress ministries under the pretext of Linlithgow's rash move in committing India to the war without prior consultation with the Assembly. While they had nothing to gain from a continuation of Congress rule in the provinces, the prospect of easy war profits became alluring. It was once again important to establish good relations with the British authorities, and a large section of the Indian business class set to the task. The Congress ministries went down unsung and unregretted. Yet with the benefit of hindsight, we can see that the 1937-39 period was decisive in placing the relations between the Congress and business on a more assured footing. It is worthwhile attempting a detailed assessment of it.

Conclusion

The advent of the Congress governments in most of the provinces of India did not result in major changes in economic and fiscal policies, which were basic to the prosperity of Indian capitalists, since control of finances and customs remained in British hands. The impact of the new governments was felt mainly in the realm of labour and agrarian relations, two domains in which provincial governments had powers to legislate. It was also felt, though to a lesser extent, in the field of industrial policy. Large sections of the Indian capitalist class remained unaffected by the direct impact of the Congress ministries. Those businessmen who were engaged mainly in foreign trade, also those who had the bulk of their interests in the non-Congress provinces and in the Indian States (including a large section of the Marwari community, the largest of the Indian business communities) did not suffer or gain as a result of the policies of the Congress. Given those limitations, the period under review saw significant developments which had a lasting influence on the relations between Indian business and the Congress.

The most important result of the period of provincial autonomy was a definite shift in the labour policies and ideology of the Congress. While in the previous period, starting with the Karachi declaration on fundamental rights, Congress had tended to be vaguely sympathetic to workers' demands but had not been deeply involved in the labour movement (with the exception of Ahmedabad), it now found itself suddenly confronted with an unprecedented wave of labour unrest sweeping the entire country. Congress response to labour unrest was largely shaped by the fact that it had already established a relationship with the capitalists and could ill afford to upset it, since in the event of a new struggle with the British, it would again need financial help from the businessmen. Though the Congress governments made some concessions to the workers, they mainly aimed at keeping the labour movement within definite bounds. To achieve this, Congressmen were drawn into intervening more actively in the affairs of the labour movement. There they clashed with other organized groups, particularly with the communists, who were not very strong but had pockets of influence mainly in Bombay and Cawnpore. As a result of this confrontation, the Congress labour policy became dominated by a fear of communist infiltration, which drove them towards following a policy of greater moderation. For the Congress, labour policy became largely synonymous with labour administration; struggles were seen as unnecessary and dangerous and direct peaceful dialogue between employers and workers was favoured as the only solution to all problems. The Bombay Trades Disputes Act expressed the essence of the Congress philosophy of labour relations: conciliation was to be favoured at all costs. Though this approach tended to work to the advantage of the capitalists, it could also clash with their interests, since in some cases they themselves sought confrontation and were prevented from achieving it. Yet the Congress blueprint for industrial relations was clearly designed to favour capitalist interests, and the Indian business class, which prior to 1937 had harboured fears that the Congress would not be able to control labour, could feel reassured that a Congress Raj would be as effective as the British Raj, if not more so, in dealing with the working class.

In other fields also the policies pursued by the Congress ministries helped to dispel fears entertained by the capitalists. For instance, widespread apprehensions about nationalization of public services and key industries were set at rest by the policy of collaboration with private enterprises pursued in the Congress-ruled provinces.

The question of capitalist attitudes to the policy of rural upliftment followed by the Congress ministries is, however, more complex. Rajat Ray has argued that this policy was basically in the interest of the capitalists, since it ultimately aimed, by raising the standard of living in the countryside, at enlarging the internal market for industrial goods.[135] Yet, apart from the fact that it could be seen as a diversion of scarce resources which could have been utilized more efficiently in giving direct aid to industrial development, another inherent danger in this policy was underlined by the President of the United Provinces Merchants' Chamber. He expressed fears that, if not supported by appropriate measures to relieve indebtedness, the rural upliftment drive of the Congress governments might result only in an increase of social tension by raising expectations without being able to satisfy them.[136] Basically capitalists, though they might be interested in agricultural development, had a stake in the preservation of the social status quo in the countryside, and any attempt at disturbing it even mildly, as in the United Provinces with the 1939 Tenancy Bill, was looked upon with suspicion. The enlargement of the internal market was a secondary consideration compared to social peace. Yet the emergence of a wealthy tenantry in some regions like Gujerat was a welcome development, provided this group did not compete too directly with urban capitalists for governmental resources. In any case further research into the problem of rural–urban linkages, a neglected field, is needed before we can form a clearer picture of the situation.

As far as the related question of large versus small-scale and cottage industries is concerned, things are not very clear either. Though it can be rightly argued that there was no fundamental opposition of interests between the cotton mills and the handlooms (since the latter were largely fed with yarn from the mills), it should yet be noticed that in Bombay, the millowners resisted attempts by the provincial ministry to allot production quotas to the mills and the handlooms, and to reserve a share of the market to cottage production.[137]

By the end of the 1930s despite the setting up of the National Planning Committee, the options of the Congress in matters of economic policy were far from clear and priorities had not been sorted out. Questions of relations between agriculture and industry, large and small-scale industries, the place of foreign capital, were still unresolved. Congress economic thought was still in a state of flux, with 'Gandhians' and socialists battling about modern industrialization, and it took a few more years before a clearer picture started to emerge.

Within a general framework marked by a growing trend of modera-

[135] Rajat Ray, *Industrialization in India, 1914–1947, Growth and Conflict in the Private Corporate Sector* (Delhi, 1979), p. 70.
[136] *The Leader*, 5 March 1938.
[137] See Evidence of Bombay Millowners' Association before Bombay Economic and Industrial Survey Committee, 35th meeting, 7 August 1939, in Thakurdas Papers, File 212.

tion in social matters, there were nevertheless significant nuances, in the way different Congress ministries tried to grapple with the problems. In that respect, Bombay and the United Provinces represented two opposite poles. In the United Provinces a trend of mildly radical populism was noticeable in some of the policies of the Congress government and it led to a permanent estrangement of vested interests from the ministry. In Bombay, by contrast, the Congress Government displayed a strong anti-labour, pro-capitalist and pro-rich peasant bias. Madras was a slightly special case, for the 'radical conservatism'[138] of the Chief Minister, Rajagopalachari, strongly influenced the policy of the provincial ministry and gave it a pro-rich peasant tinge more pronounced than elsewhere, while urban interests felt neglected.

Business responses, therefore, varied from one province to another. In Bombay a close relationship developed between big business and the ministry, though it was endangered towards the end of the period by financial difficulties. Even British business expressed its satisfaction at the course of policy followed by the Congress ministry.[139] On the contrary in the United Provinces big business was in the forefront of the opposition to the Congress government. In Madras also a trend of opposition was clearly noticeable. Everywhere Muslim businessmen tended to oppose the ministries and to align with the Muslim League.

Though Congress provincial governments were not always successful in accommodating Indian capitalist interests and could not prevent conflicts from arising between them and sections of the business class, an overall view of the two years of Congress rule in the provinces reveals that a certain amount of stabilization did occur in relations between business and Congress. While during the war many businessmen reverted to a policy of close collaboration with the British authorities in order to benefit from the war orders, the business class as a whole did not break with the Congress during the war period, and when the Party made its final bid for power, businessmen found themselves in a position to influence developments to a certain extent. The first years of Congress rule after 1947 witnessed a pattern in the relations between Congress and business which bore some similarity to the one which had emerged during the period of provincial autonomy.

[138] See A. H. R. Copley, *The Political Career of Rajagopalachari, 1937–1954. A Moralist in Politics* (Delhi, 1978), for an analysis of Rajaji's views.
[139] See the speech of the Chairman of the Bombay Chamber of Commerce, A. MacIntosh, in *Bombay Chamber of Commerce, Annual Volume 1938* (Bombay, 1939), p. xxvii.

Modern Asian Studies, **15**, 3 (1981), pp. 527–573.

Business and Politics in the 1930s

Lancashire and the Making of the Indo-British Trade Agreement, 1939

B. CHATTERJI

University of Hyderabad

DURING the inter-war years there were significant developments in Indo-British economic and political relations. It is in the context of these developments that this paper will seek to study the complex relationships between the different fractions of businessmen, British and Indian, the Government of India, the Home Government and the Indian National Congress. The major theme of this paper is the attempts made in the 1930s by governments and businessmen to reorganize the economic relations between Britain and India to take account of changes wrought by the first world war, the world depression, and the ascent of Indian nationalism. One question which dominated these negotiations was the long-standing issue of duties on cotton goods imported into India. This issue served to bring into sharp focus the different views of the imperial rulers, British businessmen in India, Indian businessmen of different sorts, and nationalist politicians, on the immediate future of the economic link between Britain and India. The question of cotton duties dogged the talks on economic cooperation from the tariff negotiations of the early 1930s, through the period of the Ottawa agreement and Lees–Mody pact, to the Indo-British Trade Agreement of 1939.

General Background: Britain's Economic Stake in India[1]

India's importance to Britain up to the first world war is well known and extensively documented. Even in the postwar years her commercial and financial value to Britain continued to be immense.

I am grateful to Chris Baker, Chris Bayly, Sabyasachi Bhattacharya, Jayati Ghosh, and Ruchira Chatterji whose comments and editorial help greatly assisted me in preparing this article for publication.

[1] This section is based on material in B. Chatterji, 'Lancashire Cotton Trade and British Policy in India 1919–39', Unpublished Ph.D thesis Cambridge 1978, Introduction.

0027-749X/81/0406-0904$02.00 © 1981 Cambridge University Press

During the inter-war period world trade as a whole was stagnant, but there was a marked change in the commodity pattern. There were increases in the shares of engineering and chemical industries and a sharp fall in textiles.[2] Britain's share in world trade fell in all commodities (both in the growing and declining groups) between 1913 and 1929, and then stabilized in most commodity groups between 1929 and 1937.[3] Part of the reason for this disappointing export performance is to be sought in the growing cost of British exports, mainly due to high relative wage costs.[4] Significantly, however, while the loss of competitiveness continued in the period 1929–37, there was little further shrinkage in her *share* of world markets, perhaps because Britain's empire provided a cushion with its system of preferential tariffs.[5]

Britain's export losses had important policy implications. Even in the late 1920s exports accounted for 37 per cent of total manufacturing output. Even as late as 1938, exports were 10 per cent of national income. During the inter-war period as a whole, the rate of growth of British exports was not only less than the rate of growth of world trade, but also less than the overall rate of growth of the British economy. Although by the late 1930s exports as a source of growth were much less important to the British economy, they had become vital in the context of Britain's growing balance of payments difficulties.[6] In the 1930s the invisible earnings which had met her growing trade deficit themselves came under strain and this underlined the need to preserve and if possible expand British merchandise exports.[7]

Throughout the inter-war period, India continued to be one of Britain's most important markets. Up to 1935, India was the single largest market; after 1935 she was among the top three.[8] But whereas in 1913 India was chiefly important for cotton goods and for iron and steel, the commodity pattern was transformed thereafter. The changing composition of Indian imports reflected the trends in world trade. However, India's importance for British trade continued to be viewed in terms of both the declining and growing sectors, in both of which Britain was non-competitive. India was a major buyer, indeed often the largest

---

[2] *Ibid.*, Table A, p. 13.

[3] *Ibid.*, Table B, p. 15.

[4] *Ibid.*, Table C, p. 16; and Alfred Maizels, *Industrial Growth and World Trade* (Cambridge, 1963), p. 226. Maizels' study shows that Britain's loss due to import substitution was small compared to those of France and Germany.

[5] Chatterji 'Lancashire Cotton Trade', Table D, p. 18. Cf. Aldcroft and Richardson, *The British Economy* (1969), p. 267.

[6] B. Chatterji, 'Lancashire Cotton Trade', pp. 12–18.

[7] See Moggridge, *British Monetary Policy* (1972), pp. 126–9.

[8] See *Statistical Abstracts of the British Empire*.

buyer, of many of the products of Britain's 'new' industries.[9] In the face of increasing foreign competition British exporters wished to gain better access to this potentially lucrative market. Besides, India was enormously valuable for Britain's income from overseas investments and other invisibles. The shrinking of this surplus on capital account, in the context of a widening trade deficit, made it all the more important that existing sources of income should be maintained.

During the 1920s Britain continued to invest overseas, but on a lesser scale than before the war. But not only the volume but also the geographical distribution of British overseas investment was changing. By 1930, the empire's share of these investments had risen to almost 59 per cent; India (excluding Ceylon) had become the second largest area of British investment within the empire. India contributed substantially (around 15 per cent every year) to Britain's net balance of invisibles during the 1920s and the 1930s.[10]

During the inter-war period, then, India continued to be vital to Britain and British officials and businessmen looked to the maintenance of India's place in the imperial system. The period as a whole did see the weakening of the links between the imperial and Indian economies as a result of a complex interaction of events—the rise of powerful competitors in staple export markets, the development of the forces of nationalism in India, and changes in the structure of the international economy and Britain's place therein. But the changes did not take place overnight or in any clear-cut manner. Thus policy makers and businessmen tried both to preserve (or to recreate, after the ravages of the first world war) the old system, and to come to terms with the new circumstances. British policy in India throughout this period reflected these conflicting strands; but the purpose remained the same, namely, to preserve India's place in the imperial system.

The Importance of Lancashire

Lancashire's weight in the British economy up to 1913 is undisputed. It has been argued that thereafter the growth of the British economy was based on important structural changes, especially shift of resources to the 'newer' industrial sectors.[11] It is true that Britain had her share of

[9] Chatterji 'Lancashire Cotton Trade, Tables G and H, pp 23–4.
[10] Ibid., Table J, p. 27.
[11] See, for example, Aldcroft 'Economic Growth in Britain in the inter-war years—a reassessment', Economic History Review, XX (1967); Aldcroft and Richardson, The British Economy, Chs 6 and 7.

the new high growth industries based around goods like chemicals and automobile manufacture, but even in the late 1930s they were a rather small sector of the overall national economy in terms of employment, net output per man and capital stock.[12] Furthermore, the annual growth rate of the economy was only a little more than 1.5 per cent between 1924 and 1937. The structure of the economy was slow to change. The old industries, especially textiles, remained significant in the economy and their share in Britain's exports continued to be dominant for most of the inter-war period. Even in 1935 textiles and clothing accounted for 5.6 per cent of total national income, and were the second largest manufacturing industry. Textiles were still Britain's largest export (18.8 per cent) of which cotton manufactures alone accounted for 10.6 per cent, second only to machinery (12.9 per cent).[13] So, although from around 1930 it became abundantly clear to all concerned that the future of the British economy lay in other fields, the relative size of the declining industries like textiles, as well as the existence of massive unemployment concentrated in them, obliged the government to preserve their export markets while at the same time seeking to encourage the development of new industries to absorb the surplus population and to aid the process of 'rationalization'.

The political dangers of continued depression in an important area like Lancashire bedevilled successive governments. Although by 1936 the aggregate of other industries in Lancashire employed more people than the cotton industry, the latter remained the largest industry in the region and despite some progress of 'rationalization' remained depressed even in 1939. In this context official concern for Lancashire was clearly evident. Inevitably this concern had implications for British policy in Lancashire's most important market, India; the cotton lobby of 60 M.P.s in the House of Commons made sure that officials accommodated the interests of Lancashire within the growing constraints of the situation in India and consistent with overall British commercial, financial and political interests there.[14]

[12] See B. W. E. Alford, *Depression and Recovery ? British Economic Growth, 1918–1939* (1972).
[13] See C. H. Feinstein, 'Production and Productivity 1920–63', *London and Cambridge Economic Bulletin* (1963), Table I; P. Deane and W. Cole, *British Economic Growth* (1967), Table 40, p. 175, Table 79, p. 299; R. Robson, *The Cotton Industry in Britain* (1957), Table p. 355; B. R. Mitchell and P. Deane, *Abstract of British Historical Statistics* (1962), pp. 304–6.
[14] See Chatterji, 'Lancashire Cotton Trade'; cf. Ian Drummond, *British Economic Policy and the Empire 1919–1939* (1972), Ch. IV; Clive Dewey, 'The eclipse of the Lancashire Lobby and the concession of fiscal autonomy to India', in Dewey and Hopkins (ed.) *The Imperial Impact* (1978).

Despite the succession of economic and fiscal crises during the 1920s, the governments in London and Delhi strove to find a way to accommodate British commercial interests—specifically Lancashire's trade in cotton piecegoods—within the framework of fiscal autonomy and 'discriminating protection' in India.[15] At the same time, they aimed to secure British financial interests in India by stabilizing the exchange value of the rupee at 1s. 6d. But from the end of the decade onwards, new circumstances disturbed the calculations of government, businessmen and rentiers (British and Indian) about their short-term and long-term interests and about the options available to them. For the imperial policy-makers the main problem was to reconcile British imperial interests as a whole in India with the specific British interest represented by Lancashire. Lancashire and its exports remained a substantial feature of the British economy, and Lancashire millowners still carried substantial political weight. But in the early 1930s, several different problems converged—the overall maintenance of the Raj in the face of political attack, the need to safeguard Britain's financial stake in India, the collapse of the international economy, the prospect of developing India as a market for the more dynamic sectors of British industry, the objective conditions in India making for cooperation and compromise between expatriate and indigenous businessmen, and the diplomacy required to achieve constitutional reforms. Government policies and private interests had to adjust constantly to this shifting bed of political and economic concerns.

Government, Businessmen and Nationalists in the early 1930s

The Great Depression created grave new problems for India. In 1930 prices of Indian exports fell by 31.5 per cent and until 1932 remained very low.[16] All sectors of the economy did not suffer equally during the depression. The industrial sector remained relatively stable and even recorded some growth,[17] but the depression hit the countryside hard, heightening turbulence and perhaps adding to the tensions in rural society.

[15] See Chatterji 'Lancashire Cotton Trade'; Chs 2, 3 and 4.

[16] Although in the mid-1920s India's exports boomed and there was some expansion of industries, the 1920s cannot be regarded as a period of unqualified stability and growth. Agricultural prices, internal and external, began to fall from 1926. In the inter-war period as a whole, there was a considerable growth of population, while agricultural production seems to have been relatively stagnant. The rural economy was therefore highly vulnerable.

[17] The position of particular industries, for example the Bombay cotton industry, varied.

Throughout the 1930s, the spectre of rural violence continued to haunt both the government and the Indian establishment, a nightmare made more frightening by the possibilities of an alliance between nationalism and rural jacquerie. In the first half of 1930 Government focused on three ways of solving the problem. They turned to force, they tried to strengthen the position of the more 'moderate' political leaders (constitutional advance), and they attempted to offset the effects of the depression by seeking the best terms for India at Ottawa.

The growing tide of agrarian and urban unrest had worried Delhi and London since 1928. They had cracked down on the communists but also decided to see what could be done to allay the bases of discontent.[18] Inevitably these preoccupations had a bearing on constitutional reform. The appointment of the Statutory Commission in 1928 stimulated political reactions rather than lulled them to sleep. By the end of 1928 the Viceroy, Lord Irwin, was alarmed at the unity of Indian political opinion against the Simon Commission, and once again decided that the 'moderates' must be rallied. Anticipating a boycott of the Statutory Commission's Report, Irwin made his famous declaration that Dominion Status was the goal of British policy in India. The announcement of the date of the Round Table Conference was held back as a trump card.

The Government's initiative was hampered by Gandhi's equivocal response. On 2 November 1929, the Congress had issued its 'Delhi Manifesto' and in December 1929 the Lahore Congress, with its left-wing in control, passed resolutions that the ultimate objective of the Congress was severance of the British connection. Gandhi now had a double purpose: to unify the Congress movement and at the same time to discipline the rising militancy of the left wing. Paradoxically his solution to control the growing tension in the country and to get the movement to speak with one voice, was to launch Civil Disobedience.[19]

[18] 'Mark my words', Linlithgow as chairman of the Royal Commission of Agriculture had written to Baldwin in 1927, 'our troubles in India are due at root far more to economic causes than many of the clever ones suppose. Unless by good administration we secure to the cultivator "a fair share of the good things of life" (probably you remember your own words), we shall lose our jobs and we shall deserve to'. Linlithgow to Baldwin, 4 November 1927. Baldwin MSS 102. Regarding the labour situation the Viceroy wrote to the S/S '... the most effective way to remove industrial unrest is improvement of labour conditions. The nettle has to be grasped some time and what better time is there likely to be than now when ... it is important to show that measures for maintenance of order do not mean want of sympathy with labour'. S/S to Viceroy, Pvt. Tel. 13 September 1928, Halifax MSS 9.

[19] Indeed, Gandhi regarded the outbursts of violence to be the 'froth coming to the surface in an agitated liquid'. 'The Cult of the Bomb', Young India, 2 January 1930, Collected Works [C.W.] 42, p. 361. Constitution making, he regarded 'a good pastime

But whatever Gandhi's thinking, from the Government's point of view Civil Disobedience simply increased their worries about the state of India.[20] Initially, many businessmen viewed Civil Disobedience as an excellent means of wringing concessions out of Government. But as the movement developed and tended to get out of hand, they increasingly desired a compromise with the Government and brought pressure on Gandhi to come to terms.

Even if the overall parameters of the nationalist movement were 'bourgeois' there were tactical differences, often acute, between Indian business groups both about short-term objectives and long-term perspectives. Most Indian industrialists preferred the path of constitutionalism, and most of them kept aloof from active politics. Naturally, they feared any mobilization of the masses in politics which might turn into a general movement of violence and disruption.[21]

under healthy conditions. But it is deceptive and ruinous when the patient for whom a new constitution is prescribed is about to die'. 'Borderland of Insolvency', *Young India*, 27 February 1930. *Ibid.*, p. 422. When the Congress refused to participate in the First Round Table Conference, Gandhi's strategy was to make Congress abstention a source of pressure on the British Government to make generous concessions. At the same time Gandhi disassociated himself completely from those who took to violence. He summed up his dislike for violence as follows: 'From violence done to the foreign ruler violence to our own people whom we may consider to be obstructing the country's progress is an easy natural step'. 'The Cult of the Bomb', *ibid.*, p. 362. Civil disobedience alone in his opinion could save the country from 'impending lawlessness and secret crime'. As he explained to C. F. Andrews 'To sit still at this juncture is stupid . . . I have made up my mind to run the boldest risks. I have arrived at this definite conclusion as a result of deep and powerful thinking. Lahore revealed it all to me. The nature of the action is not yet clear to me. It has to be Civil Disobedience.' Gandhi to C. F. Andrews, 9 February 1930, *ibid.*, p. 444.

[20] 'If it is true', Benn wrote to Irwin, 'that the Youth leagues and Terrorist organisations have really got control of the situation . . . it might be that even Gandhi's support, with his doctrine of, and possible belief in, non-violence might be worth having, and even necessary, to rally those who are yet untouched by what is becoming an ordinary, violent nationalist insurrection'. He hoped that Hindu aversion to violence and the coming of the rains would ease the situation and wanted steps to be taken to get to the Conference Table 'somebody whose name and influence will win the support of millions'. Benn to Irwin, Pvt. letter, 20 June 1930, Halifax MSS 6. See also Benn to Irwin, Pvt. Letter, 29 May 1930, *ibid.* See also CAB 24/213 C.P. 214(30), Memo by S/S C.P. 274(30), C.P. 289(30), CAB 24/213, C.P. 242(30) and CAB 27/470 BDG(30) *passim*. Meanwhile, concerned over the spread of indiscipline among platoons of Indian infantry, military bosses in London prepared to order a general mobilization. See CAB 27/422 I.U. (Committee on Indian Unrest), especially 1st Meeting, 30 April 1930.

[21] Witness the attitude of the Bombay millowners and the Marwari piece goods importers of Calcutta during the Swadeshi movement in 1905. See S. Sarkar, *The Swadeshi Movement in Bengal 1903–1908* (1973), pp. 142–3; A. P. Kannangara, 'Indian Millowners and Indian Nationalism', *Past and Present*, No. 40 (July 1968). During the first non-cooperation movement most big industrialists held themselves aloof and some of them set up the Anti-Non-Cooperation Society. See Purshottamdas Thakurdas [P.T.]

Certainly during the 1920s most sections of Indian business had reacted sharply against the Government's economic policies.[22] So they had tended to gravitate towards the Congress since the movement looked as if it might prove a useful platform for their economic grievances. Provided Congress did not stray from the safe paths of constitutionalism and moderation, they could see advantages in backing it in their dialogue with the Raj. At the same time, labour unrest tended to make them more conscious than ever of the need to bring state power behind them. The businessmen needed the Government; they also needed the nationalists. Meanwhile businessmen's need of Government was matched by a growing realization by the Government that they needed the men of wealth.

During the early 1930s there was a swing among the Indian businessmen towards a policy of more substantial compromise with the Raj, and they found Irwin anxious to meet them half way.[23] The 'liberal' and 'moderate' leaders, including the prominent Bombay businessman Purshottamdas Thakurdas, issued a statement from Bombay welcoming Irwin's declaration. A more demanding (though still compromising) Delhi Manifesto[24] was issued by the Congress supported by the less moderate business elements. The leading Calcutta businessman and nationalist, G. D. Birla, preferred the Delhi Manifesto to the over-eager welcome accorded by the Liberals. He had always pleaded for caution in expressions of public support for the Viceroy, and he rebuked Thakurdas for his clumsy haste.[25] The Congress eventually

MSS 24 (1–3). In Thakurdas' view 'the classes that have no stake in the country are mustering strong about Gandhi. The commercial classes are naturally more thoughtful and more anxious about the wisdom of such action'. Many businessmen wanted non-cooperation to be eradicated 'root and branch and bring around the people to sanity and sober common sense'. Thakurdas to T. Holland, 16 October 1920; Adarji Dalal to Thakurdas, 19 October 1920, P.T. MSS 24/II.

[22] The greatest battle that businessmen fought with the Government was over the rupee ratio question. It was around this issue that businessmen built up a comprehensive argument against British economic policies in India and their disastrous consequences for the Indian economy. There were other issues which engaged the business classes in bitter conflict with the Government, among them protection to the cotton textile industry, the struggle for mastery between Indian and British jute interests in eastern India, Scindia Steam Navigation's efforts to oust Lord Inchcape's BISCO. To fight their battle with the Government the businessmen had increasingly to seek the support of the nationalist movement.

[23] See Irwin to Thakurdas, 26 October 1929, P.T. MSS 91.

[24] The Congress expected a Round Table Conference 'not to discuss when Dominion Status was to be established, but to frame a Dominion Constitution for India'. It expected that political prisoners would be released and that it would send the majority of the Indian delegates to the Conference.

[25] Birla was surprised at the Bombay leaders issuing their own statement and even more surprised 'how a cautious and shrewd man like you [Thakurdas] could have

decided that even the Delhi Manifesto was too mild. Towards the end of December the Congress Conference at Lahore rejected it, called for debt repudiation and a movement for complete independence, and Gandhi prepared to launch Civil Disobedience. Seeing these developments in nationalist politics Thakurdas felt extremely perturbed. He urged liberal and moderate leaders like Sapru and Malaviya to unite the rest of political India 'to make up for this lapse by the Congress'.[26] At the same time he wished to press home to the British authorities that the best way of strengthening the hands of the Liberals and the moderates was by granting generous concessions to India.[27]

But Thakurdas' attitude was not shared by other spokesmen of the business community. The deepening depression and the Government of India's stringent monetary policy combined to stiffen the attitude of many businessmen.[28] In March 1930 the Government hustled through the Cotton Protection Act, with a preferential treatment for Lancashire, and this made matters worse. A large group of nationalists led by Malaviya resigned from the Legislative Assembly. Many spokesmen of business interests urged support for Gandhi's movement as a means of

committed such a haste . . .'. Birla himself was in favour of accepting the government's offer of a Round Table Conference especially since 'the Viceroy seems to be sincere and . . . I think his hands ought to be strengthened', but on conditions implied by the Delhi Manifesto. Birla to Thakurdas, 30 October 1929, P.T. MSS 91. But he warned that 'the Viceroy alone is not the deciding factor; there are others more powerful than the Viceroy, and what guarantee is there that a different . . . interpretation [of the purpose of the Round Table Conference] may not be put . . .'. Indeed his discussions with the Viceroy had confirmed his misgivings. 'In Englishmen we are dealing with the best . . . diplomats of the world. The Viceroy and Cabinet are bent upon placating us, not because they have got a soft corner in their hearts for India but because they realise the gravity of the situation, and I am sure that we should not make ourselves unduly cheap because we don't gain anything by that'. So Birla along with Ambalal Sarabhai underlined the dangers of not keeping in step with the Congress on the question of constitutional reforms. The Delhi Manifesto was a 'good one' with the invaluable advantage of carrying 'with us extremists like Jawaharlal Nehru and others'. Birla to Thakurdas, undated, early November 1929; 3 November 1929; Thakurdas to Birla, 5 November 1929; Sarabhai to Thakurdas, 5 November 1929, P.T. MSS 91.

[26] Thakurdas to Sapru, 27 December 1929; Thakurdas to Malaviya 14 January 1930, P.T. MSS 91.

[27] If concessions were made he assured Campbell Rhodes that 'British interests in India would be treated . . . with a certain sanctity . . .'. Thakurdas to C. Rhodes, 6 February 1930. See also Thakurdas to Sapru, 8 January 1930, where he argued that Sapru's efforts to rally people in favour of the Round Table Conference would not stand any chance of success if he insisted on demanding that Indians be made masters in their own home. P.T. MSS 91.

[28] 'The present form of Government and its sins of commission and omission are greatly responsible for the present state of affairs and particularly for Gandhiji's movement. Unless there is a general improvement in the economic condition of the people and the cultivators have a stake in the country, Bolshevik propaganda will find fertile soil in India'. Ambalal Sarabhai to Thakurdas, 28 March 1930, P.T. MSS 91.

strengthening Gandhi's hand in negotiating with the Government.[29] Even these businessmen, however, shared Thakurdas' concern over the potential dangers in the situation. As Lalji Naranji put it: 'Mahatma Gandhi's movement has diverted the people from violent methods . . .'. Fiscal autonomy he considered a 'total myth'. He insisted that it was

very necessary that the mercantile community should express very clearly the situation created by the British Government in withholding from India the constitution acceptable to them, which will give real control of the purse of the country, is very serious [*sic*] and that it will be the only solution that will save India from going into further trouble. Political and economic matters are so much intermingled that you cannot get one without the other. It is the duty of economists to point out to the Government that it is undesirable for them to continue the economic policies that they are now pursuing at the dictates of the Cabinet in Great Britain. We can also tell politicians, *including Mahatma Gandhi* [emphasis added] that it is undesirable to create a feeling of disregard for any authority of the Government. I notice that this disregard for authority will have very disastrous after effects, which no Government of Swaraj will be able to recover and bring the country back to normal conditions.[30]

Gandhi's Civil Disobedience movement started in April 1930. By mid-1930 his business allies had moved closer to the attitude adopted by their 'moderate' colleagues. To keep the agitation alive, Nehru and others urged a more active rural campaign. But 'uncontrolled' unrest grew in the countryside. Despite the hesitations and limitations of Congress involvement in rural movements, no-revenue campaigns showed strong tendencies to turn into no-rent movements. Economic distress, police brutality and hopes of 'Ram-Raj' aroused by Gandhi, combined to create a troublesome situation.[31] There were signs that the rural movement might gain its own momentum and go beyond the desire of the Congress leadership. As the Government imprisoned the established Congress leaders, the direction of the movement at the lower

[29] Gandhi's 'Eleven Point Programme' was an attempt to incorporate the basic economic demands of the capitalists and was to represent the 'body' of independence. As Lalji Naranji put it: 'I in my commercial way of thinking, believe more in Gandhiji's policy . . . Gandhiji's 11 points or demands are more of economic nature than of mere political nature. It is therefore that commercial community have put more explicit faith in Gandhiji or his organizations.' Quoted in S. Sarkar, 'The Logic of Gandhian Nationalism: Civil Disobedience and the Gandhi-Irwin Pact (1930–1931)', *Indian Historical Review* Vol. III, No. 1 (1976), p. 123.

[30] Naranji to Thakurdas, 28 March 1930. See also Sarabhai to Thakurdas, 28 March 1930, P.T. MSS 91.

[31] For Government's concern about the situation, see Halifax MSS 1 6 *passim*, especially Viceroy to S/S, 30 July, 2, 13 August, 12, 29 September, 18, 31 December 1930. For the officials' view of rural trouble in Madras, Bihar, Punjab, U.P., N.W.P., and Bengal see Halifax MSS 24, 25 *passim*.

reaches of Indian society fell more and more into the hands of 'less inhibited elements' both in town and country.[32]

All this tended to prove that Thakurdas' misgivings about Civil Disobedience were well founded. So Gandhi's business friends were now determined to bring pressure on him to call off an increasingly dangerous campaign. They also wished to see the Government come to terms with the Congress. Thakurdas who had now thrown in his lot with his more nationalist colleagues, Birla, Ambalal Sarabhai and Lalji Naranji, now commented on the fears and desires of the class as a whole: 'I myself believe', he wrote to the Finance Minister of the Government of India, George Schuster, 'that if Government delay things too long even Mr. Gandhi may be disowned by the Congress people, and the real mischiefmongers may get the upper hand in the Congress ... Mr. Gandhi's agitation is bad, but it may prove to be better than some other more vicious agitation to follow should Government hold out unduly.'[33] From early 1931 this pressure increased and on 5th March 1931, Gandhi signed the pact with Irwin in search of 'truth'.[34] Congress was to participate in the Round Table Conference and negotiate for a constitution with 'safeguards' for British interests.

Indian businessmen wanted a quick and hygienic solution of the problem of constitutional reforms, not only so that India might gain more mastery over her own economic fate, but also so that agitation might be curtailed and social order preserved. Yet one stumbling block in the way of a rapid settlement of the constitutional reforms was the Lancashire lobby in British politics which threatened to veto the reforms unless it felt that Lancashire's interests were being properly safeguarded. Political realities, and later mutual hostility to the commercial assault from Japan, dictated that the Indian millowners reach some form of compromise with their old antagonists in Lancashire.

In this search for compromise, the Bombay millowners were much more eager than those of Ahmedabad. In the years between the wars Bombay millowners faced severe problems. During the war and in the

---

[32] See Sarkar, 'The Logic of Gandhian Nationalism'.

[33] Thakurdas to Schuster, 30 May 1930, P.T. MSS 91. Thakurdas expressed the dilemma of the businessman thus: 'The position in the country, and especially amongst the Commercial classes is getting more and more entangled, and there is not the slightest hope of this state of affairs improving without the political situation settling down. I am getting more nervous about a crop of insolvencies and consequent disaster'. But at the same time, 'I have never overlooked the fact that the Viceroy must come to an understanding with the Mahatma before we can have peace'. Thakurdas to Rangaswamy, Editor of *The Hindu*, 4 June 1930. See also Thakurdas to Motilal Nehru, 4 June 1930, *ibid*.

[34] Interview to the Press, 16 March 1931. *C.W.* 45, pp. 261–2.

immediate post-war boom, widespread financial speculation had led to the capital values of the Bombay mills becoming unduly inflated. When the boom broke in 1922, Bombay mills found it difficult to adjust to the new conditions. Owing to their overcommitment to coarse varieties of piecegoods and higher costs, millowners in Bombay were more directly affected by the growing Japanese competition than Ahmedabad and they faced increasing competition from up-country mills. In the 1920s the Bombay millowners' demand—not very successful—for protection was directed more against Japan, and in order to overcome Lancashire's opposition they had even approached Lancashire privately with schemes of market sharing in India. Meanwhile their efforts to cut costs were inhibited by the volatility of their labour force. The dangers posed by the strikes of the 1920s were augmented by the fact that they were organized by Communists rather than by Gandhi, as in Ahmedabad.[35] These factors determined the specific attitude of the 'liberal', 'moderate' Bombay millowners towards Government, Congress and Lancashire.

From the start Bombay millowners had no time for Civil Disobedience, which was particularly strong in Bombay city. As in 1921–22, it received its greatest support from merchants and petty traders.[36] It began to reach groups whose participation was ominous for the millowners,[37] since millowners feared that the workers would lose sight of non-violence and were nervous that a Congress and Communist alliance might join in promoting strikes among the workers. Although the communist-led labour movement in Bombay had been brutally crushed in 1928–29, the left wing was still powerful in the Royist Workers and Peasants Party. Constant 'hartals' had brought business to a standstill in 1930–31. Owing to general trade conditions, business and the unemployment situation were in any case bad; the political tension made the situation explosive.[38] Even those few millowners who had supported

[35] The happier state of affairs in Ahmedabad had as much to do with the millowners' prosperity as with Gandhi's influence over the working class. For the affairs of Bombay industry in this period, see Chatterji 'Lancashire Cotton Trades, Chs 3 and 4.

[36] Bombay proved to be the stronghold of the boycott movement. The merchants dealing in foreign piece-goods joined the movement in large numbers for the same reasons as in 1921–22. So strong was their support for Gandhi's movement that the rank and file of the Indian Merchant's Chamber forced Thakurdas to resign from the Legislative Assembly. See S. Kochanek, *Business and Politics in India* (1974), pp. 145–9.

[37] See Benn to Irwin, Pvt. letter 17 November 1930, enclosing letter from H. N. Brailsford, Halifax MSS 6. See also Sarkar, 'The Logic of Gandhian Nationalism'.

[38] Governor Sykes also sounded worried: 'Here we have the focus of the movement, and whatever may be true of the rest of India it cannot be tackled here on the theory that we are dealing with a limited political clique supported by only a section of the public. In Bombay city and most of Gujerat we have practically a mass movement'. Sykes to Irwin, 20 June 1930, Sykes MSS 2.

Civil Disobedience were now backing away from it and blaming it for their troubles.[39]

As the millowners turned against the Congress, so the Congress turned against them, and a relationship, strained at the best of times, now took a turn for the worse.[40] The boycott movement may have helped some Bombay mills to get rid of surplus stocks, but it prevented the millowners from using necessary imported yarn. By August 1930 the Congress Working Committee had drawn up a list of 24 mills in Bombay which were to be boycotted. Protracted negotiations between mill-owners and Congress leaders did not settle the issue.[41] By the early 1930s it was clear that the millowners would not look to Gandhi as their saviour.

After the short relief provided by the Gandhi–Irwin Pact, Civil Disobedience was again launched in 1932 and it came at a time of growing Japanese competition to the Bombay mills, as well as another round of rural disturbance and renewed left-wing activity, all of which was bad for the millowners.[42] With the renewal of boycott, the Bombay piece-goods market was closed for almost three months in 1932. Already, depressed prices had made Bombay's goods unsaleable; the closure of the market for such lengths of time devastated the position of the millowners. In early 1932, the boycott movement affected the raw

[39] See *Bombay Chronicle* [*B.C.*] 2 September 1930. 'The economic distress is increasing', wrote a perturbed Sarabhai, ' . . . the purchasing power of the people has gone down . . . Hungry masses will do anything. It is for those who have a stake in the country to come to the rescue of the poor, if not in the interests of the poor but to save themselves'. Sarabhai to Thakurdas, 17 November 1930, P.T. MSS 42 (VII). Many alleged that Ahmedabad was feeding the movement to take business away from Bombay. See *India Textile Journal*, September 1930, p. 541. The Indian Industries Association formed in mid-1930 and organized by Ness Wadia and Cowasjee Jahangir issued pamphlets telling the workers that unemployment was due to the Civil Disobedience Movement and Boycott. See *B.C.* October 1930. This kind of propaganda found active support from the Bombay Government and the pro-British press in India. See, for example, *Times of India*, April–October 1930, *passim*. Cf. *B.C.* particularly 17 March 1930, 5 July 1930, 12 August 1930. See also Sykes to Irwin, 8 September 1930. Sykes held confidential discussion with various professional people and was informed that commercial opinion was growing anti-Congress: ' . . . I am doing what I can to foster such a spirit'. Sykes MSS 2.

[40] See Chatterji, 'Lancashire Cotton Trade', Ch. 4.

[41] The Congress re-export scheme, formulated in 1931, whereby it was decided to set up a syndicate of millowners under Ness Wadia to buy up foreign cloth stocks in Bombay and re-export them, despite the horror it created in Lancashire, failed. Governor Bombay to S/S, 20 March 1931, L/PO/52.

[42] Sykes reported to Willingdon that communist influence was at work, 'and that the pressure brought to bear upon cotton merchants has in addition to the usual expression of anti-British and racial feeling, an anti-capitalist aspect'. Sykes to Willingdon, 13 May 1932, L/PO/50.

cotton market as well; and the Government's efforts to reopen the market did not succeed until the end of the year.

Throughout these trying times, the millowners' strategy was to work for a quick constitutional settlement. This meant coming to terms with Lancashire in order to remove its veto. This strategy was consistent with both their political desire for peace and their economic demand for protection against Japan.

The Response of British Businessmen

The political circumstances of the early 1930s also led British businessmen to reassess their prospects in India. Business leaders such as E. C. Benthall now helped formulate a strategy of compromise and cooperation with Indian businessmen.

The British mercantile community in India had been unhappy about the reforms of 1919 and had opposed them from the start.[43] In the 1920s many British businessmen had withdrawn capital from India and taken a gloomy view of future prospects.[44] To combat the growing challenge of Indian business, the expatriates set up ASSOCHAM and the Indian side responded with the foundation of FICCI. By the latter part of the decade the more far-sighted businessmen had decided that the sort of large-scale political conflict implied by the foundation of these political associations of Indian and British businessmen respectively was not likely to produce the best results. Benthall and others advocated direct commercial deals between Britons and Indians, Indianization of European firms,[45] and support for constitutional advance, as the best way of preserving British commercial interests and also of keeping intact Britain's invaluable connection with India.[46] Benthall welcomed

[43] See, for example, 'Bombay and the Political Situation in India', Full Report of the proceedings of an Extraordinary General Meeting of the European Association and its sympathizers held in Bombay, 2 October 1917; Addresses presented to the Viceroy and the Secretary of State, 1918 Cd. 9178 *Parliamentary Papers* [*P.P.*] XVIII.

[44] See B. R. Tomlinson in this volume.

[45] Some leading European businessmen contemplated going into partnership with Indians. Reflecting on his long-term business alternatives in India, Benthall noted in his diary that 'three courses seem possible: either to go into partnership with some rich Indian group (politics may make this desirable), always keeping the master hand myself or to go in with some other British firm in India (e.g. Andrew Yule), enhancing the position of both and remaining in active management, or to sell out the whole or part of the Indian interest—last course only as a "last resort".' Diary, 24 January 1928, Benthall MSS XII.

[46] Even if a constitutional solution proved impossible 'we have sufficient wit' Benthall felt, 'to look after our interests by force of arms if the worst came to the worst. We may

Irwin's declaration. It could, he felt, rally moderate businessmen like
Thakurdas who were willing to 'live and let live', and wean them away
from the actively intransigent characters like Birla.[47]

Yet against the background of political agitation and public disorder,
men like Benthall and Birla were moving towards one another with
astounding speed.[48] In the next few months, Benthall changed his mind
about Birla whom he found was now willing to 'concede our [commer-
cial] claims in return for responsibility at the centre', and to understand
the benefits of collaboration and 'small confidential meetings' among
businessmen.[49] Benthall's strategy was to concede the need for
Dominion Status in India. He believed that this concession could be
used to bargain for formal safeguards for British commerce, and would
also prevent more informal types of discrimination against British interests which might arise from a climate of political antagonism. At the
second Round Table Conference, he 'struck up almost a friendship with
Gandhi' on this basis, and found him 'well disposed towards the British
individually and collectively', though he added, 'being born a Bania, he
was as hard as nails in bargaining'. Through these troubled years
Benthall energetically preached his relatively conciliatory stand on
constitutional reforms. He was attacked by some of his business colleagues in the Royalist Group as a 'Bengali Sahib'.[50] But he was able to
have a gigantic Hindu bloc against us but we have potential allies in the Mussalmans
and the States and even with a Labour government and with a further swing of opinion
against imperialism and towards nationalism, I am confident that India will remain
within the Empire, and the greatest of Great Britain's customers, and the cornerstone of
our Empire. Granted a period of peace and granted this solidity of India, nothing can
prevent the country going steadily ahead as a field for merchant adventure . . .'. Diary,
25 December 1928, Benthall MSS XII.

[47] In his discussion with Birla in May 1930, Benthall formed the opinion that Birla
was definitely not out for any settlement of the political problem, 'but intended to go on
obstructing until the last . . . he seems to forget there is anyone else in India except the
Birla party'. Diary, 9 May 1930, Benthall MSS XII. Benthall with his multiple points of
contact with the official world schemed to split 'the Birla party's' influence among
Indian businessmen. 8 June 1930, 7 June 1930, discussion with Schuster. Diary, ibid.

[48] 'There appears to me', Benthall noted, 'to be real danger of a serious agrarian
upheaval in spite of his [sic] pathetic contentment. The Ryot must turn some time and it
is difficult to see how he can bear the burden of his loss with prices as they are'. Diary, 17
December 1930, Benthall MSS XII.

[49] Benthall recorded his conversations with Birla: 'He [Birla] explained that for the
last ten years of his life he had been taking up an attitude of opposition which was more
often than not of a bitter nature, because it was the only way in which he could bring
pressure to bear upon the subjects he had in mind. But that henceforward he desired to
work in collaboration and to drop all this hostility', Memo to ASSOCHAM, 4 October
1931, Benthall MSS XI.

[50] Many younger British businessmen in India felt 'that the senior businessmen were
content to buy appeasement in their time at any price which would afford peace in their
time of service'. Benthall MSS XII.

carry the ASSOCHAM with him.[51] Benthall insisted that India could be ruled by force, but that it was wiser to do so 'with the consent of the people'.[52]

Benthall was by no means a lonely prophet. As Earl Winterton aptly observed: 'All the more progressive and intelligent British Directors of . . . enterprises asserted, both in public and private, that support for eventual Indian self-government was necessary for British financial and economic interests in India'.[53] But if this was so, it was also true that there were traditional hostilities and suspicions between Indian and British interests. The next few years witnessed intricate wrangling and behind-the-scenes manoeuvring by Indian and British business to reach a settlement while securing their particular interests. Thus Benthall, while urging constitutional advance and condemning the obstructions of diehard ICS, military men and the 'reactionaries' among British businessmen, also used his influence to ensure that terrorism and violence were firmly dealt with[54] and that constitutional advance was combined with 'adequate safeguards' for British interests; 'Muslims, princes, and provincial autonomy' he saw as even better safeguards than specific clauses in the new constitution.[55]

[51] Writing about his role in these uncertain times he noted with satisfaction ' . . . Looking back, I have no doubt that the policy followed by the leaders of British business throughout this anxious time was right, for the responsible line we took over the twenty years leading up to the Independence capped of course by HMG to grant that Independence, prepared the way for the fair manner in which the Congress dealt with us when they came into power'. Undated note by Benthall, Benthall MSS XI, 'File on Gandhi'.

[52] 'The basis of business and of rule among Eastern peoples', he told the Conservatives in England in March 1931, 'is to keep your word . . . '. He repeatedly reiterated his belief in 'association of Indian capital and management together in business . . . '. Benthall MSS XIV.

[53] 'Order of the Day' (1953) p. 191. See also Halifax, Fullness of Days (1957), p. 151.

[54] See notes on his conversations with Teggart, Willingdon and Schuster in Benthall MSS XII.

[55] See Memo for ASSOCHAM, Benthall MSS XIV. 'I would ask you never to forget that it is Mohammedans who have stood by the Government of India in these last months of crisis, which, but for them, might have been as bad or worse than the crisis of 1919–21'. His colleague, Hubert Carr, had 'regular conversations with Aga Khan'. He regarded Wedgwood Benn as a 'criminal' for being 'Hinduised'. Diary 19 and 21 January 1931, Benthall MSS XII. The Muslims not being prominent in business in Bengal could be easy and useful allies. Benthall to Godfrey, 21 January 1931, ibid. T. Benthall to Godfrey, ibid. 'Aga Khan has impressed upon the Bengal Muslims that they must organise and get together with the Europeans'. 'The Aga Khan says that the Princes paid £100,000 into the Labour party funds—I wonder!!'. In provincial Autonomy he saw the possibility of preoccupying nationalist politicians with administrative affairs and providing 'time to estimate the truly selfish aims of those who have been guiding Indian politics hitherto'. Provincial Autonomy would develop provincial interests and this would help British interests, especially in Bengal where they were most

Similarly, Birla kept open his lines of communication with British business interests. Birla and Benthall met each other frequently. Both saw there was room for compromise; both feared the Congress being taken over by the 'left-wingers' and the nationalist movement moving into areas where industrial labour and rural India could threaten the Raj, its 'bandobast' and the existing social fabric. He appreciated all along the apprehensions of his class about the growing 'Bolshevik' tendencies of Indian politics and was anxious to find a road back to the safer pastures of constitutionalism. He, however, would still try for the best possible terms from the new constitution in the interests of his class. He believed that Gandhi was a live force capable of controlling the nationalist movement; Congress could still be manoeuvred as a legitimate spokesman of the Indian people in favour of constitutional change. Of course, there were others like the Bombay millowners whose ties with Congress were weaker and who were willing to bypass it in their search for political peace.

The crux of the problem for all businessmen was the question of the financial and commercial safeguards to be inserted in the new constitution. British interests (metropolitan and expatriate) sought, with the entire officialdom ranged on their side, to protect their interests. Numerous proposals for 'safeguards' were put forward—a 'convention of reciprocity' as a condition for constitutional advance; statutory protection applicable to all minorities or applicable to the British commercial community only, empowering the Governor General with instruments of instruction. Indian interests fought hard to limit the scope of these safeguards.

Imperial Economic Cooperation: the Ottawa Conference

Meanwhile the economic and political consequences of the depression led the imperial government to seek ways to revive trade and incomes through a system of mutual preferences within the Empire.[56] In Eng-

numerous. Speech to Conservative Committee, 16 March 1931, 'British Business and Indian Reforms', Benthall MSS XIV.

[56] In November 1930 the Labour government had set up a committee to prepare for the economic conference to be held at Ottawa. For the minutes and memoranda of this Committee see CAB 27/441. The Committee was reconstituted by the new government in 1931. In its first report, the Committee recorded that 'the failure of the Ottawa Conference to reach agreement on the large questions of policy remitted to it would be a fatal blow to Imperial interests, and that it is accordingly imperative that every effort should be made beforehand to ensure the success of the Conference'. Proceedings of the Committee, 1st Conclusion O.C. (31) 11 November 1931 and C.P. 288 (31) CAB

land spokesmen for British industry (such as the Federation of British Industries, hereafter FBI) supported the idea. They pointed to the increased importance of Empire for the British economy and prescribed imperial economic cooperation as the only possible way out for the crisis ridden and increasingly non-competitive British economy. The fact that Britain's rivals were already constructing their own economic blocs made such cooperation a 'vital and immediate . . . necessity'. The FBI looked to the Empire 'not from sentimental or altruistic reasons but from the point of view of practical self interest'.[57] Imperial economic cooperation was another name for complementary production, or the division of production between the more and the less industrialized parts of the empire. But the FBI clearly recognized that some parts of the empire had by this time developed varying levels of capitalist enterprise and the political complexities which went with them. Thus the purpose of imperial economic cooperation was not 'to arrest change, but wisely to direct and facilitate its course'.[58] The aim was to grant each country in the empire 'unfettered freedom' to develop 'economic' and 'sound' production—in other words to establish a *new* specialization of production between and within different industries in the empire. The success of this strategy depended upon bringing businessmen to the conference table in a spirit of 'cooperation' and 'goodwill', and managing to isolate issues of economics from politics, particularly in such troubled parts of the empire as India. Such negotiations, it was hoped, would lead to a mutually beneficial settlement of interests 'based upon sound conceptions of law, order and civilisation'.[59]

*   *   *

In 1931, free trade finally flew out of the window in the slipstream of the gold standard. Not only British industrialists but financiers also, hoped to strengthen sterling by encouraging a surplus of imports from the

27/473. See also Memo by S/S Dominions, 'Questions for the Conference', 13 November 1931 O.C. (31)2, *ibid.*

[57] FBI, *Industry and the Empire* (1932) ' . . . Great Britain has the possibility of creating (with her empire) an economic group of unlimited possibilities'; without it her competitive position would be 'extremely disadvantageous'. FBI, *Industry and the Nation* (1931), circulated to the Cabinet as O.C.(31) 72 CAB 27/475.

[58] See FBI, Report to the British Preparatory Committee to the Imperial Conference, 'British Economic Policy with Regard to the Dominions', CAB 58/6; The EAC Committee Report on Empire Trade, 12 June 1930, CAB 58/5 and 3 July 1930 CAB 24/213 C.P. 228(30). For the TUC's support for a scheme of inter-imperial economic cooperation see CAB 24/215 C.P. 317(30). See also Inter-Departmental Committee on Inter-Imperial trade, O.C. (30)28 CAB 27/473; Federation of Chambers of Commerce of British Empire, Report of the 12th Congress 1930, Copy in Benthall MSS XVI.

[59] FBI, *Industry and the Empire.*

Empire. Such imports would adversely affect the balance of Britain's commodity trade, yet they would strengthen the sterling balances held in London by the empire countries and make it easier for their governments to meet their sterling obligations without recourse to new loans. This would reduce the fear that in the difficult circumstances of the 1930s some empire country might default on its financial obligations, and thus increase confidence in sterling.[60]

These issues were to be thrashed out at the imperial economic conference at Ottawa in 1933. The aims of the conference were especially appropriate for Britain's relations with India. Optimists believed the conference could provide a palliative to India's immediate economic troubles, ensure Britain's long-term commercial prospects, and also lay the groundwork for rapprochements between recalcitrant interests like Lancashire and its Indian counterpart. Moreover, India was still the largest single market for British goods, and was a debtor country whose ability to service her debts had been severely hit by the collapse of her export trade in the worldwide slump. Only the massive export of gold from India in 1931–32 had enabled her to meet her obligations in London, but this could only be a temporary measure and could not disguise the fact that India's commercial weakness presented a threat to the stability of sterling. It was vital to draw India into the business of 'imperial economic cooperation' and to re-establish India's favourable balance of trade so as to prevent the drying up of remittances, depletion of reserves and excessive borrowing.[61] World markets were depressed already; India could encourage her exports through devaluation but this was unacceptable to Britain. In any case, in the conditions of the 1930s it was doubtful if Indian goods could have found buyers outside the U.K. Moreover, if India could sell elsewhere, at a time of growing bilateralism this would have destroyed the foundations of inter-imperial economic cooperation that British industrialists were trying so hard to lay at Ottawa.

[60] This point is of vital importance for the understanding of the Ottawa Agreements. See in this connection Memorandum by H. D. Henderson, as Secretary of the Cabinet's Economic Advisory Council, 'Sterling and the Balance of Trade', 28 January 1932, reprinted in Henry Clay (ed.), *The Inter-War Years and Other Papers—A Selection from the Writings of Hubert Douglas Henderson* (1955). See also L. S. Amery, *My Political Life*, Vol. III (1955), p. 31. Undoubtedly by giving preference to the products of the Empire countries in the U.K. market, the Ottawa Agreements helped to reduce the impact of the depression on those countries.

[61] See 'India and the Management of the Pound Sterling' Memo. for the use of the Delegates of India at Ottawa, undated 1932, Templewood MSS 59. See also Statement made by Sir George Schuster at a Meeting of the Committee on Monetary and Financial Questions, 28 July 1932, L/PO/271.

But combating India's economic problems was not a simple matter. India's political and economic problems were hopelessly interlocked. The depression and Whitehall's stringent monetary policy for India in 1930–31 had led to a sharp fall in rural incomes and a consequent rise in rural disorder. Businessmen and officials in both India and Britain were convinced that unless India's economic position could be improved the whole social fabric and the Raj itself were at risk.[62] Men like Schuster urged monetary solutions, but these were ruled out and the politicians instead sought means to revive India's foreign trade.[63] Furthermore the officials were convinced that a satisfactory solution of India's economic problems within the framework of imperial economic cooperation would smooth the path of constitutional negotiation. A reciprocal trade agreement based on principles of 'cooperation' could secure British commercial interests under a system of Fiscal Autonomy in India and so could help avoid wrangle over the 'commercial discrimination' clauses in the constitution; it stood a good chance of placating both the Lancashire lobby and the Churchillian diehards who threatened to hinder the passage of the reforms.[64] A lot hung on the Ottawa conference.

All the major sections of Indian businessmen found the economic and political purposes of the conference appealing. But there were delicate questions involved in selecting which businessmen should be involved in the Ottawa negotiations.[65] The Secretary of State for India, Hoare, appreciated that it was necessary to include businessmen who carried

[62] 'Unless we can restore the agricultural position', Willingdon warned, 'revolutionary action stands a real chance of success'. Willingdon to Hoare, Pvt Letter 28 September 1931, Templewood MSS 5. See also 'India and the Management of Pound Sterling' undated 1932. By 1932, the situation in U.P., Bengal, Bihar and Gujerat was critical. See Hailey to Hoare, 28 February 1932, Templewood MSS 15; Hoare to Willingdon stating views of Anderson, Governor of Bengal, 27 October 1932, Templewood MSS 2. The possible spread of discontent to the Punjab was viewed with the greatest concern, even by the financial wizards of London. The Punjab peasantry provided the bulk of the Indian army and if present conditions prevailed 'that way lay disaster'. See Note by R. A. Mant and H. Strakosch, 8 February 1932, 'The Effect on India of the Fall in Prices and British Monetary Policy', Enclosed with Hoare to Willingdon, Pvt letter 26 February 1932, Templewood MSS 1.

[63] See Hoare to Willingdon, Pvt letter 29 September 1932, enclosing a confidential report on discussions of monetary and financial questions at Ottawa between Henry Schuster and Henry Strakosch and the British delegation at Ottawa, Templewood MSS 1. Statement by Strakosch to the 'Committee on Monetary and Financial Questions' 28 July 1932 and Statement by Chamberlain, 29 July 1932. L/PO/271.

[64] See CAB 27/520 C.I. (32) 15th Meeting, 15 October 1932, 29th meeting, 1 December 1932; CAB 27/521 C.I. (32)51; L/PO/270, L/PO/282 passim; Hoare to Willingdon, Pvt Tel. 19 February 1932, Templewood MSS 11.

[65] For the official discussion about how to ensure the political success of Ottawa, see CAB 27/473, Proceedings of the Committee on Proposed Imperial Conference, 5th conclusion, O.C.(31) 28 March 1932. L/PO/271 passim; Hoare to Willingdon correspondence February-March 1932, Templewood MSS 11.

weight with India's political leaders and thus advocated the selection of
Birla or Thakurdas.[66] Indeed, Birla approached Hoare privately and
gave assurances that he and Thakurdas would persuade FICCI to
cooperate with the Ottawa conference 'in the interests of India'.[67] After
the break-up of the second Round Table Conference on constitutional
reforms, Gandhi resumed Civil Disobedience in early 1932 and the
FICCI was torn between its faith in Gandhi as the most reliable of the
Indian nationalist leaders and its concern over economic distress and
political turmoil. By the middle of March, Birla had persuaded FICCI
to offer cooperation in order to forestall the 'serious upheaval in the
construction of society' which might follow if India's trade did not
quickly revive.[68] 'We realise the importance of the Conference', he
assured Hoare, 'and you may rely on our support in the right direction . . . we are all in favour of reciprocal arrangements on economic
grounds.' He wanted 'permanent peace between the two countries' and
pleaded to be given 'a chance to work for peace'. He stressed that the
cooperation of FICCI in both political and economic matters provided a
good guarantee of the successful operation of any agreements devised in
view of their good relationship with Gandhi. Birla drew a distinction
between Gandhi on the one side and the Congress on the other and
pointed out that it was Gandhi's acceptance of any agreement that
would promise lasting success.[69]

Birla's overtures and confidences impressed the Secretary of State.
The new Viceroy was less convinced. Lord Willingdon rebuked Hoare
for corresponding so frequently with 'that basically non-cooperating
fellow, motivated by selfish interests'[70] and advocated selecting for

[66] Hoare to Willingdon, Pvt tel. 5 March 1932. Templewood MSS 11.

[67] Birla also informed Hoare that he would continue his efforts to arrive at closer
cooperation with European businessmen. See Hoare to Birla, 27 January 1932, Birla to
Hoare 14 February 1932, L/PO/271, reproduced in Birla, *In the Shadow of the Mahatma*
(1953), pp. 45–6.

[68] Birla to Lothian, 14 May 1932, *ibid*, p. 55.

[69] Birla told Hoare in no uncertain terms why he stood by Gandhi. 'I need hardly say
that I am a great admirer of Gandhiji. In fact, if I may say so, I am one of his pet
children. I have liberally financed his khaddar producing and untouchability activities.
I have never taken any part in the Civil Disobedience Movement . . . I wish I could
convert the authorities to the view that Gandhiji and men of his type are not only friends
of India, but also of Great Britain, and that Gandhiji is the greatest force on the side of
peace and order. He alone is responsible for keeping the left wing in check. To strengthen
his hands is, in my opinion, therefore, to strengthen the bond of friendship between the
two countries . . . Probably the best way to success in this discussion is to give you our
cooperation as far as possible . . . If you think I can be of any use in bringing about
happy relations between the two countries you can always rely on my humble services'.
Birla to Hoare, 14 March 1932. *In the Shadow of the Mahatma*, pp. 46–9.

[70] Willingdon to Hoare, Pvt letter 21 March 1932. Templewood MSS 5. Willingdon's
view found support from L. J. Kershaw. See Tel. Federal Finance Committee to S/S, 27
March 1932. (From Kershaw for S. F. Stewart) L/PO/271.

Ottawa, business representatives who were known for their moderation in politics.[71] He believed there was 'little chance of any of that school of thought [i.e. FICCI] approaching the question in a broad-minded spirit', and pointed out that the involvement of FICCI members in the boycott movement in Bombay had already led the provincial government to consider taking 'drastic measures', against some of them. To include such bad characters in an Indian delegation to Ottawa would, in Willingdon's Manichean view, 'create a bad impression among government supporters and cannot be contemplated'.[72] Hoare dissented: 'It seems to me of great importance that we should get back on terms of cooperation with these people [like Birla] . . . Quite apart from the importance which I attach to their being represented at Ottawa from the point of view of Tariff negotiations, I think that their cooperation in that field might serve as a bridge to cooperation elsewhere'.[73] But Willingdon's continued intransigence succeeded in alienating FICCI and inducing Birla to bemoan the impossibility 'to do useful work when there is no response from the other side'.[74] He forecast that 'the Ottawa Conference has more or less been given a burial from its very inception', and that in this atmosphere there was 'no chance of a calm consideration of the issues involved on their own merits'.[75]

The Ottawa negotiations went ahead without the cooperation of FICCI and the Ottawa Agreement was signed in August 1932.[76] In some respects India did well out of it. Her position as a primary producer made her highly vulnerable to the depression and so preferences guaranteed by the U.K. benefited her economy. The U.K. remained the most stable importer of primary goods during the depression. The years 1930 and 1931 had amply demonstrated this when Britain's share of Indian exports was larger than during the immediately preceding years. The Ottawa Agreement increased this share even further. To the extent this

[71] Willingdon suggested the names of A. Chatterji (leader), G. Rainy, P. Ginwala, Shanmukham Chetty and Haji Abdullah Haroon. Willingdon to Hoare, Pvt tel. 2 March 1932, Templewood MSS 11.
[72] Willingdon to Hoare, Pvt tel. 17 March 1932, Templewood MSS 11.
[73] Hoare to Willingdon, Pvt tel. 22 March 1932, Templewood MSS 11.
[74] Birla to Hoare, 2 November 1932, *In the Shadow of the Mahatma*.
[75] Birla to Lothian, 14 May 1932, *ibid*, p. 55.
[76] Britain received preferences on about £55 million worth of her exports to India and granted preferences on about £47 million worth of imports from India (both figures at 1929–30 values). For details and analysis, see B. N. Adarkar 'The Ottawa Pact', in R. Mukherjee (ed.), *Economic Problems of Modern India*, Vol. I (1939). For the gains to Britain on particular goods see T. M. Ainscough, *Conditions and Prospects of U.K. Trade in India* (1933). See also H. A. F. Lindsay, 'Recent Tendencies in Indian Trade', *Journal of the Royal Society of Arts* [*J.R.S.A.*], LXXXI (1933); P. Ginwala, 'India and the Ottawa Conference' *J.R.S.A.*, LXXXI (November 1932).

helped to maintain incomes in India, it took the edge off economic discontent and also aided Indian industrialists. Britain welcomed the political significance of the Agreement which, it hoped, would ease 'difficulties with the constitutional changes in Parliament'.[77] Yet there was the danger that the Indian Legislative Assembly would reject the Agreement and thereby give ammunition to 'Winston and his army' to sabotage the reforms.[78] Willingdon believed that the opposition in the Assembly was 'engineered and influenced by . . . Indian commercial bodies led and paid for by Birla'[79] and was urged by Hoare to 'bring to bear the whole resources of the Government' to secure its passage.[80] The Assembly formally approved the Agreement[81] but the continuing dissatisfaction of the businessmen jilted by the unresponsive Willingdon made its future most uncertain. Meanwhile Indian acceptance was only one hurdle. Complications surrounding Lancashire's cotton interests ensured the Agreement's eventual demise.

*   *   *

In the crises of the early 1930s, the political and economic difficulties of the Home and Imperial Governments were aggravated by the persistent need to accommodate a recalcitrant Lancashire. In England, Churchill took the lead in organizing the cotton interests against the policy of conciliation, compromise and constitutional reform in India. Churchill was as much interested in the leadership of the Conservative Party as in diehard imperialism, and found India a useful stick with which to beat the Baldwin interest. Lancashire, with its sixty votes and its determination to counteract the worst depression in its history, was an asset which no opportunist could ignore.[82]

[77] Hoare to Willingdon, Pvt tel. 5 August 1932, Templewood MSS 11.

[78] Hoare to Willingdon, Pvt letter 10 November 1932, Templewood MSS 2. Its rejection by the Indian Assembly could 'damage the whole reputation of the Conference. The Chancellor of Exchequer in particular takes a most serious view upon this point'. Hoare to Willingdon, Pvt tel. 11 October 1932, L/PO/270.

[79] Willingdon to Hoare, Pvt letter 13 November 1932. See also Willingdon to Hoare, Pvt letter 6 November 1932, Templewood MSS 6.

[80] Hoare to Willingdon, Pvt tel. 11 October 1932 L/PO/270.

[81] Schuster reported that it was Shanmukham Chetty who was chiefly responsible for the Government's success. Chetty's eloquence had 'split . . . the ranks of the Nationalists . . . there are signs now of a cleavage in the commercial ranks and there is a chance of making a real split and detaching an important section to the side of cooperation and constructive work'. Schuster to Hoare, 12 December 1932, L/PO/271.

[82] Churchill had chosen 'wisely and well'. 'To surrender our Empire in India! To give way to sedition! How many true Conservatives breathe with soul so dead as to be deaf to such an appeal such as this'. *Economist*, 1 July 1933, quoted in G. Peele, 'Revolt Over India', in G. Peele and C. Cook, *The Politics of Reappraisal* (1975), p. 123. See also S. C. Ghosh, 'Decision-making and Power in the British Conservative Party: A Case Study of

In the complicated balance of interests—financial, fiscal, commercial, political—which the British had to achieve in India in the crisis of 1930–31, metropolitan finance was given top priority. Indeed these years saw, in the words of one historian, 'the last naked act of aggression against India' by British financial interests.[83] In essence this meant maintaining the level of the rupee at 1s.6d. and pulling out all the stops to ensure the flow of remittances from India to England.[84] It also required the Government of India to balance its own budget in order to assist the public image of sterling. The maintenance of these overriding interests of imperial finance required some diminution of other, more specific, imperial concerns. In order to balance the budget amid the storms of the depression, the governments in Delhi and London forced Lancashire to accept a rise in the duties on cotton in 1930 and 1931. Government did so reluctantly and softened the blow to some extent by creating a margin of preference for Lancashire goods in the Indian market.[85] The officials impressed on Lancashire the priority of the

the Indian Problem 1929–1934', *Political Studies*, XII (1965). It would be simplistic to view the Conservative diehard opposition to the Indian reforms as merely reflecting inter-party strife. Although nobody in the Conservative Party wished to lose India, there were fundamental ideological conflicts regarding the most effective means of maintaining this control. There was a consistency in Churchill's attitude towards imperial affairs. For an account of diehard opposition within the Conservative Party, see G. Peele 'Revolt over India'; S. Haxey, *The Tory M.P.* (1939); R. R. James, *Memoirs of a Conservative: J. C. C. Davidson's Memoirs and Papers 1910–1937* (1967). For Churchill's attitude and for examples of his sonorous prose about Britain's imperial mission, see H. Pelling, *Winston Churchill* (1974), pp. 345–65. See also Dennis Bardens, *Churchill in Parliament* (1967), pp. 173ff. The furore in Lancashire over the question of Indian reforms was more the result of a general nervousness felt by an acutely depressed industry straining to rationalize rather than a result of neglect of her interests in India. In the discussions over commercial safeguards Lancashire's interests were being specifically looked after by Lord Derby and J. Nall. See Templewood MSS 61, L/PO/270 and L/E/9/1150 *passim*; see also Baldwin MSS 105 *passim*. For a study of the problems of 'rationalization' of the Lancashire cotton industry, see Chatterji, 'Lancashire Cotton Trade', Ch. 1.

[83] B. R. Tomlinson, 'Britain and the Indian Currency Crisis 1930–32', *Economic History Review*, Vol. XXXII, No. 1 (February 1979), pp. 88–99.

[84] For the Bank of England's and Treasury's concern with maintaining overseas remittances necessitated by the deteriorating balance of payments and the consequent pressure on sterling from early 1930 see D. E. Moggridge 'The Financial Crisis—A new View', *The Banker* (1970); British Monetary Policy (1972); S/S to Viceroy, 24 January 1930, Halifax MSS 11.

[85] In 1930 cotton duties were raised from 11% to 15% along with a 5% protective duty with a minimum of 3½ annas per lb on 'plain grey' goods and on all cotton goods from outside the U.K. Under the Finance Act of 1931, cotton duties became 20% on British and 25% on 'foreign' goods. Later in the year an emergency surcharge was imposed making the rates on British goods 25% and 31.25% on foreign goods. For a detailed analysis of the events of 1930–31 concerning cotton duties, see Chatterji, 'Lancashire Cotton Trade', ch. 5, sec. 3.

larger imperial interest in India over the specific interest in the Indian textile market, but Lancashire still responded with some fervour. From Lancashire's standpoint, the tariff preferences of 1930 did little to prevent declining exports and much to create further uncertainty. The tariff measures had alienated nationalist opinion and the boycott and 'intimidation' by Congress volunteers caused concern. The boycott movement found ready support among importers faced with the impact of the depression and falling demand. Indian importers cancelled standing orders and pious reiterations of the 'sanctity of contracts' was no solution.[86] The millowners and politicians raised an agitation and threatened to move their considerable political weight into the camp of Churchill and diehards over the question of India's constitutional reforms. The millowners told the M.P.s that Gandhi was playing a confidence trick by saying: 'Help me to obtain complete independence and then we will see what crumbs of trade we will graciously allow to fall off our table for you'. Lancashire, they said, would hold out 'for our rights' in India.[87]

Irwin, Benthall and N. N. Wadia of Bombay attempted to soothe Lancashire by explaining that these concessions were necessary to avert 'big and bad agrarian trouble' which might undermine the Raj, but the millowners were not convinced. Prominent Lancashire men expressed their disgust at 'those Indians, and there were many, who were out of sympathy with the boycott, but suffered from the racial weakness of not having the "guts" to act on their convictions', and demanded that government place strict limits on any concessions envisaged in the forthcoming constitutional reforms. 'It is bad psychology', J. H. Rodier of the Manchester Chamber instructed Irwin, 'to waver when dealing with the peoples of the East.'[88]

At this juncture C. F. Andrews arranged a 'frank talk' between Gandhi and representatives of Lancashire.[89] The idea appealed to many in government and in industry.[90] One M.P. felt certain that if

[86] See Proceedings of the Manchester Chamber of Commerce, India Section, 29 April 1930, pp. 242–4. 9, 15, 22, 26 May and 5 June 1930, pp. 250–70, L/PO/289 *passim*. For the nature and extent of the agitation in Lancashire and official response see Chatterji, 'Lancashire Cotton Trade', Chs 1 and 5.

[87] Proceedings, India Section, 10 April 1931, pp. 167–8; 20 April 1931 and 1 May 1931, pp. 170–9; B.T. 56/35, CIA 1768/61 *passim*.

[88] Proceedings, India Section, 13 May 1931, pp. 201–16 and 2 June 1931, pp. 217–21.

[89] C. F. Andrews to Benn, 20 June 1931, L/PO/50.

[90] Officials felt that if Lancashire treated 'Indian representatives as representatives of a civilised power, good might ensue'. Board of Trade Note, 'Cotton Industry: Visit to Lancashire of Indian Representatives', undated July 1931; W. Graham to Benn 31 July 1931, B.T. 56/36 CIA 1768/82.

Gandhi saw the misery of the depression in Lancashire, his 'religiosity would be moved against the large profits that Indian millowners were making under a system of sweated labour'.[91] Of course there was the danger that Gandhi might fall into the hands of the 'wrong types' in Lancashire who would 'say the wrong things'. So officials arranged a meeting with 'responsible' and 'moderate' millowners and workers.[92] But Gandhi's chats with them were characteristically vague and different people made different sense of them. Gandhi himself had a 'lovely time'. George Barnes, once commerce member in India, was pleasantly surprised to find that 'his ideal was a partnership between India and England in industrial matters'. He quoted Gandhi as saying, 'If I could get a partnership on equal terms, I would endeavour to secure that all the imports needed by India were supplied by England alone, to the exclusion of all competitors'. Barnes felt, along with Hughes of the JCCTO, that the visit was very useful.[93] But J. H. Rodier who met Gandhi privately on the same day was startled by Gandhi's long lecture to him on the virtues of the Charkha and his statement that when a National government was formed 'if for a given period of time hand made and home mill-cloth did not suffice then the Government would place order for a definite amount of foreign cloth'. When this was repeated to the Manchester Chamber's recently formed sub-Committee on Indian Fiscal Matters, an angered E. Rhodes suggested that it was the duty of the sub-Committee to regard 'Gandhi as a deadly enemy' and that HMG should be pressed to put a stop to 'Gandhi's nonsense'.[94]

Everyone realized the gravity of the situation; the problems of Lancashire were supplying ammunition to the diehard elements within the Conservative party. The larger imperial interest again seemed to be in peril. Efforts were made by men like Sir Campbell Rhodes to bring the 'more sensible' cotton men in direct contact with politicians who could impress upon them the importance of not obstructing the constitution as the safest way to preserve British interests in India. Rhodes also hoped the Government would do something to bring about some tariff arrangements in India whereby Indian industry could concentrate on requirements of coarser goods and leave the superior stuff to Lancashire, eliminating Japan altogether from the Indian market. Rhodes appre-

[91] See W. D. Croft of the India Office to Director, Joint Committee of Cotton Trade Organization (JCCTO) 7 August 1931, L/PO/50.
[92] See H. G. Hughes (of the JCCTO), G. L. Watkinson (of the B.T.) correspondence, 26, 28 August and 10 September 1931, Note by Watkinson 15 September 1931, B.T. 56/36 CIA 1768/82.
[93] Barnes to Horace Hamilton B.T. 29 September 1931, *ibid.*
[94] Proceedings, India Section, 29 September 1931, pp. 241–2.

ciated the complications of the situation. Lancashire's demand that
Britain withhold a measure of fiscal autonomy from India was unreason-
able; constitutional advance was in fact the most useful option; big
business in India was 'sick of anarchy' and 'for their prosperity in the
future they will require a stable government and sound finance . . . I
believe that any new constitution can only function if the English and
Indian merchants and industrialists get together . . . and what is more
important, I believe that some of our Indian opposites are slowly coming
to the same conclusions '.[95]
One of the main objectives of the Ottawa conference, as we have seen,
had been precisely to aid this coming together. Although Lancashire
had no representative of her own in the British delegation, the Government had kept in close touch with the British Empire Trade Committee
in which cotton interests were represented as members of the FBI and
which pressed that 'no other single problem involved in Imperial economic policy . . . is of greater importance than a satisfactory settlement of
the treatment of the Lancashire export trade to India '.[96] The Manchester Chamber had also sent a private delegation to watch over the
negotiations and possibly to get close to 'Indian captains of industry'.[97]
Yet cotton was in fact taken off the agenda of the Ottawa Conference
because the Government of India had promised a Tariff Board enquiry
before the termination of the Textile Protection Act of 1930. It also
reckoned that such an enquiry would provide a more elegant and more
assured method of securing Lancashire's interests. Officials feared a
discussion at Ottawa of the question of a 'preference' for Lancashire in
India since it might bring the whole scheme of 'discriminating protection' in India under too close a scrutiny. In two very important cases
(steel and cotton) the policy of 'discriminating protection' had led
directly to a preference for Britain, though the Indian Government
insisted on labelling them 'differential duties', imposed in the interests of
industrial efficiency and the consumer. Such scrutiny might put at risk
the logic of schemes that claimed a protective tariff against *foreign*
imports was necessary for Indian industry, while at the same time a
discrimination in favour of *British* importers was necessary for the Indian
consumer. Lancashire's hopes thus lay in a 'differential duty' (made
possible under a system of 'discriminating protection') recommended by
a Tariff Board. The result attained was much the same; 'The choice of

[95] See Campbell Rhodes–Sam Hoare correspondence and Note by W. D. Croft, I. O.
18 November 1931, L/PO/50; Note by Campbell Rhodes, 27 December 1931, L/PO/52.
[96] CAB 21/367.
[97] See Proceedings, India Section, 12 April 1932, pp. 221–2; Hoare to Willingdon Pvt
letter 20 February 1932, Templewood MSS 1; Memo to HMG 'Lancashire Cotton
Trade with India and the Ottawa Policy', CAB 21/367.

the road by which it is sought' the Government of India reminded the
Cabinet, 'is all important, for while much Indian support may be
enlisted in favour of the differential system, Indian opinion would be
unanimously against it if it were proposed to grant preferences in respect
of a protective duty merely in order to benefit the U.K.'[98]

However, to everyone's horror, soon after the Ottawa conference had
concluded, the Tariff Board produced a complete lemon. The Government of India had assumed that the Board would recommend a differential duty which would favour Lancashire and had given appropriate
assurances to the Board of Trade. But in fact the Tariff Board recommended an all-round rise in tariffs on cotton goods. The Board of Trade
howled that this was a 'breach of faith' because the Government of India
was 'under positive obligation to us by article 11 of the Ottawa Agreement to consider the matter on a different basis and, by the secret
undertaking to give effect to any differential which may be found
justifiable'.[99] While the Board of Trade and the Government of India
began discussing suitable ways to dispose of this embarrassing report,
the flooding of the Indian market with Japanese textiles cheapened by
the devaluation of the yen provided a basis for new negotiations between
the various conflicting parties. The Government of India appointed a
new Tariff Board to look specifically into the question of imports of
non-British goods. This strategy seemed to be a copper-bottomed way to
gain benefits for Lancashire, yet at the same time the Government of
India could be seen to be working to protect the Indian market against
foreign (namely Japanese) intrusion.

The new Tariff Board delivered its report quickly and duties on
Japanese imports were accordingly raised first to 50 per cent and later to
75 per cent. The existing Indo-Japanese trade agreement was torn up,
and the embarrassing Tariff Board report was locked away in a bottom
drawer.[100]

Lancashire was not completely mollified by this deft bit of footwork,
and still threatened to disturb the progress of the constitutional reforms.
The Manchester Chamber prepared a batch of evidence to the Joint
Select Committee on the reforms and did not stint on including demands

[98] CAB 27/475 O.C. (31)88, Memo by the Indian delegation, 6 July 1932.
[99] Draft note by the President B.T. undated, January 1931; B.T. Note on the Report,
14 January 1931, B.T. 11/163 CRT 413.
[100] Willingdon wanted his 'Manchester friends to keep their mouths shut' to save his
government's reputation. Willingdon to Hoare, Pvt letter 12 June 1933, Templewood
MSS 3. These movements dovetailed with Britain's commercial and diplomatic relations with Japan. See Ann Trotter, *Britain and East Asia 1933–1937* (1975). For a study of
Indo-Japanese negotiations concerning cotton, see Chatterji, 'Lancashire Cotton
Trade', Ch. 6.

which would clearly enrage liberal opinion in Britain and about every shade of opinion in India. The evidence was not immediately submitted, but it was clearly a political time-bomb which the Government had only a short time in which to defuse.[101] Board of Trade officials attempted to reassure Lancashire that her interests were being cared for, but realized at the same time that the most promising tactic was still to arrange that Bombay and Lancashire should meet together and privately negotiate over their differences. Government authorities in London and Delhi and British businessmen concerned about 'peace', 'order' and economic cooperation within the Empire could all see good political arguments in a rapprochement and possibly a trade agreement concluded between Bombay and Lancashire.

There was a long list of candidates anxious to play the role of village barber in this prospective liaison. Officials in London and Delhi wished to prevent Lancashire's attempts to sabotage the constitutional reforms. Those far-sighted businessmen who had for a long time recognized the virtues of cooperation between British and Indian interests now felt, in Benthall's words, that the 'time is ripe . . . because there is at the present moment a bond of unity between the two in their joint opposition to Japan'.[102] Thakurdas, who represented the interest of India's cotton growers and merchants and who had some influence in the business community as a whole, was already campaigning for Lancashire to take more Indian raw cotton and was easily persuaded that such a concession might form part of a larger commercial deal. Clare-Lees of the Manchester Chamber and Homy Mody of the Bombay millowning fraternity were eventually brought to an assignation in August 1933.[103] After some elaborate courtship ritual, watched by a nervous array of officials and businessmen, the match was arranged. The Lees–Mody Pact was signed on 28 October 1933.[104] Bombay millowners conceded that

[101] For details see *ibid.*

[102] Benthall to Mothersill, 10 July 1933; Benthall to Cleminson, 10 July 1933, Benthall MSS XV. The Association of British Chambers of Commerce offered its offices for bringing millowners from Bombay and Manchester together. See Proceedings, India Section, 4 July 1933, p. 65.

[103] Lord Derby of Lancashire along with Hoare and Benthall played a very prominent role in the entire episode. Their task was difficult. The diehard wing of the Manchester Chamber of Commerce continued to bark and even Derby found the Chamber a 'difficult horse to ride', while Benthall lamented the 'incredible stupidity of its members'. See Derby to Hoare, 19 July 1933; Derby to Raymond Streat, 19 July 1933, Hoare to Derby, 21 July 1933; Derby to Hoare, 26 July 1933 L/PO/51; Benthall to J. S. Henderson, 25 July 1933, Benthall MSS XV.

[104] The Indian delegation was composed of eight millowners from Bombay, four from Ahmedabad and one each from Bengal, Kanpur, Baroda and Madurai. Millowners from outside Bombay could not bring themselves to agree to Lancashire's terms.

Lancashire could enjoy some benefit from differential rates, and agreed to reduce the emergency duties on cotton imports imposed during 1930–31 as soon as government's finances permitted. Lancashire agreed to recommend 'effective action' to increase the offtake of Indian raw cotton. In the wake of this agreement, the Manchester Chamber began using the blue pencil on its batch of evidence to the Joint Select Committee, the 1932 Tariff Board Report was finally killed, and the Government of India and HMG set down to driving a hard bargain in new negotiations with the Japanese. In 1934 the Lees–Mody Pact was incorporated as a Supplementary Agreement to the Ottawa Pact.[105]

Yet the match was never properly consummated. The stipulation that reductions in the tariffs would have to await improvements in India's revenue position caused such delay that Lancashire became impatient and distrustful. Meanwhile it soon became clear that Clare-Lees had made his match with the completely wrong partner. Birla and the nationalist group of businessmen, who had been standing rather frostily to one side ever since their exclusion from the Ottawa negotiations, did not object to the principle of negotiation and cooperation with British business but were not friends of Mody and the Bombay millowning fraternity. As the depression lifted and trade improved, and as the Indian National Congress returned to constitutional politics with some force in the mid 1930s, this nationalist group of businessmen became more confident and assertive. They were not pleased by the evidence of Lancashire's impatience to get its hands on the benefits of the Lees–Mody Pact,[106] and Mody was soon pilloried as a 'self-seeker' and a

Ahmedabad millowners in particular made it clear that the immediate objective of Indian industry was to supply the full requirements of the home market. Soon Mody came into open conflict with Kasturbhai Lalbhai and Mody managed to get the Bombay millowners to conclude an agreement with Lancashire. The 'pact' agreed that under the existing conditions, the Indian industry required a higher level of protection against foreign countries than against the U.K. Secondly, it laid down that when the revenue position of the GOI made it possible to remove the revenue surcharge of 5%, Bombay would not oppose the action. Finally it promised Indian support for tariff concessions on U.K. cotton yarns and artificial silk goods and established the principle of dealing in future with common problems affecting the two industries by direct discussions. Indian piece goods were to share any tariff advantages that Britain secured in Empire and overseas markets and the mission agreed to recommend 'effective action' to increase Lancashire's offtake of Indian cotton. The 'pact' was to remain in force until 31 December 1935.

[105] For the making of the Lees–Mody Pact and subsequent developments, see Chatterji, 'Lancashire Cotton Trade', Ch. 6.

[106] When Lancashire pressed the Government of India to incorporate the Lees–Mody Pact within the scope of the Ottawa Agreement, Birla felt perturbed. '... Unless the matter is taken up seriously I fear a great mischief would be done'. Birla to Kasturbhai Lalbhai, 14 November 1934. See also Birla to Thakurdas: 'The Mody–Lees

'lackey of Lancashire'.[107] Meanwhile Government instituted yet another Tariff Board enquiry with the intention that it would recommend implementing the provisions of the Lees–Mody Pact without the provisions which caused delay. But by the time the Board reported in March 1936, the business and other nationalist interests in the Indian Legislative Assembly had contrived a denunciation of the whole package of the Ottawa and Supplementary Agreements. Once again it looked as if the political legacy of Lancashire's interests in India had thrown a shadow across the attempts to find a path out of economic depression and political stalemate.[108]

But denunciation did not mean the end of the principle of economic cooperation. Among the Indian commercial classes, as the Viceroy gloomily observed, there was 'a conviction that if India denounced the agreement, the U.K. would, for political as well as economic reasons, hurry forward with offers of an agreement much more favourable to India'.[109] They knew that the Government of India was vitally concerned to get maximum advantage from the U.K. for India's trade both in order to mitigate social distress and disorder, and in order to provide the sterling balances to meet India's financial obligations in London. Moreover, since the world was slipping towards an era of bilateralism, securing markets for Indian products in the U.K. was the best way to guarantee India's market for goods imported from Britain. Expert official opinion in Britain also attached great importance to the maintenance and extension of what was now known as the 'Ottawa prin-

Pact, though concluded with good intentions, was a great blunder, but I think Lancashire has now tasted the human blood and they are no longer satisfied with the pact'. 10 November 1934, P.T. MSS 126. Labour leaders like N. M. Joshi complained that it was wrong in principle for the Government to accept an agreement entered into by private organizations while many others questioned the right of the Bombay millowners to speak for the whole textile industry of India. See *Annual Register* (ed. N. Mitra), I, 1934, pp. 60–1, 116, 127–30, 148–52.

[107] He was knighted soon afterwards.

[108] In bitterly attacking the Ottawa Agreement, the FICCI did not oppose its principle. But it wanted India's foreign trade to be diversified in terms of trading partners and wanted India to enter into a network of economic understanding with non-empire countries, as indeed the U.K. herself had done. See President's speech, Annual Conference of the FICCI, 1934. *Annual Register*, I, 1934, p. 41. The FICCI's arguments were elegant. However, given the conditions of world markets for India's exports and their fears of the disastrous potentialities of continued depression, one might have expected them to be thankful for what had been achieved at Ottawa. Their attitude may be explained by their calculation that if the Agreement was rejected by the Assembly, the Government would probably be forced to negotiate a new, more favourable agreement and might even be tempted to make greater concessions in the political field.

[109] Viceroy to S/S, Pvt. tel. 11 April 1936, L/E/9/1123.

ciple'—that is, imperial economic cooperation. More specifically they argued that while it was obviously desirable to attempt to preserve the market for British products which were in decline (like textiles), they should equally think about getting preferences for British products that were showing encouraging signs of growth (like chemicals, electrical goods, machinery, rubber manufactures, motor cars). Cotton textiles had clearly become an industrial speciality in India and 'nothing can stop India in the main from supplying her needs under these heads . . . British industries must seek new openings in other directions, and the trade figures show that the prospect is not at all a hopeless one'.[110] In these circumstances the Government of India had begun making preparations for a new trade agreement long before the Ottawa and Supplementary Agreements were finally denounced.

The Indian Capitalists, the Congress and the New Agreement

Any new agreement would have to be protected from the forces which had brought about the denunciation of 'Ottawa'. The spokesmen of British industry (the FBI) were consistently pragmatic. In their crusade for imperial economic cooperation they could not allow politics to disturb economic collaboration. They had all along insisted that governments must encourage industrialists to get together to talk shop devoid of politics, and that representatives of the economic interests must find their legitimate place in government delegations. Such a course was particularly appropriate given the political situation in India and had been applied to the negotiations over shipping, cement and cotton. The cotton arrangement, however, was the test case in this strategy because of its political significance both in India and the U.K. and the failure of the Lees–Mody Pact and the Supplementary Agreement in this field made the matter especially delicate. Raymond Streat of the Manchester Chamber of Commerce was aware of the responsibility of the Indian Government to get hold of the 'right' kind of Indian businessman to see that the new agreement was made on the right lines. Mody and the other 'moderates' had lost their usefulness; the power of the FICCI and its representatives clearly had to be taken into account. Although the FICCI was 'a highly nationalistic body' and its moving

[110] Note by G. Schuster, 'Economic Relations between the U.K. and India', 27 June 1934; Note by H. A. F. Lindsay of the B.T., 'Indo-U.K. Trade in the light of the Ottawa Agreement', July 1934; Note by Hoare, 30 June 1934, L/E/9/1147. See also Lindsay, 'Recent Tendencies of Indian Trade' *J.R.S.A.* LXXI (1933); D. B. Meek 'India's External Trade' *J.R.S.A.*, LXXXIV (1936).

force, Birla, was 'a rigid nationalist', the Lancashire men thought they could see signs of a change of heart. Streat cited as evidence Birla's talks with Lord Derby in the summer of 1934 when he had made 'vague suggestions' of a more cooperative attitude. 'More than one shrewd observer in Bombay', wrote Streat, 'stated that the capitalist supporters of the Congress Party were beginning to be a trifle nervous of the possibility that the Congress might turn definitely to highly socialistic policies . . . Even Kasturbhai Lalbhai [a wealthy Ahmedabad mill-owner and Gandhian] . . . self-confessed admirer of the communist ideal and most determined opponent of cooperation two years ago, spoke of the desirability of a period of "soft pedalling" so far as political agitation was concerned, and went out of his way to indicate that . . . he and his group were prepared to consider economic cooperation with the U.K. in general, provided they should be admitted into the councils at which policy should be hammered out'.[111]

In August 1936 the GOI invited Thakurdas, Birla and Kasturbhai Lalbhai to act as 'unofficial advisers' in the negotiations over a new Indo-British Trade agreement, and the invitation was accepted.[112] Grigg, the finance member, was probably alone in questioning the wisdom of the official choice. He totally distrusted the 'nationalist' businessmen, especially Birla, who, he believed, was aligned with Gandhi and the right wing of the Congress ('jackals of big business') in total hostility to the British connection. Gandhi was, Grigg thought, interested in 'sucking big business for his funds'; the businessmen needed Gandhi to keep Nehru ('honest but fanatical communist') under check and also to pay them back by leading another boycott movement[113] and Grigg thus saw 'no hope for a lasting settlement with India except in fighting and defeating our enemies [Congress and big business] now . . .'.[114] Although Grigg had understood an essential aspect of the situation he failed to grasp some of the extenuating factors. The politics of Indian businessmen was a complex phenomenon. Birla was too difficult for Grigg.

The Indian capitalist class suffered from a number of weaknesses. Reared in a colonial economy and subject to the backward pulls of an

[111] Raymond Streat, 'Cooperation between the U.K. and India: Indian Businessmen and Congress Party: The Future of Ottawa: Reactions of Economic Cooperation on Political Outlook . . . Possibilities and Probabilities', 16 January 1936. L/E/9/1038.

[112] E. C. Benthall of ASSOCHAM and Dr Subbarayan were the other members of the Panel of 'unofficial advisers'.

[113] '. . . If Gandhi is leading a disturbance they will do very well from a business point of view and . . . Nehru will be content to go at Gandhi's pace . . . so that they will kill two birds with one stone'. Grigg to Chamberlain, 30 March 1936, Grigg Papers (2/2/1a).

[114] *Ibid.* During the course of the negotiations, Grigg was to reiterate these objections.

inferior technology, its potentialities were further curtailed by a complex of interdependent factors during the inter-war period. Despite some industrialization India remained an agricultural economy. The stagnant nature of the agricultural sector was a long-term constraint on the growth of industry. From 1926 onwards the world agricultural depression revealed India's vulnerability as an exporter of primary goods. The Government's policy of 'discriminating protection' with its emphasis on 'discrimination' had little favourable effect on private investment. It was only from 1929–30 onwards that Indian industries enjoyed protection. The depression itself helped by cutting off imports, while the Government's revenue requirements and the precarious position of many Indian industries led to increases in import duties (with preference in favour of British goods). However, in 1930 and 1931 the positive effects of protection were somewhat offset by the deflationary fiscal and monetary policies of the Government. The industrial base remained more or less confined to consumer goods; the capital goods sector was largely undeveloped. There was no technological breakthrough worth the name in this period. These structural weaknesses of Indian industry entailed a long-term dependence on more advanced economies and provided the economic basis for Indian businessmen's attitude towards foreign collaboration.[115]

Yet, within the limits of these handicaps, the Indian capitalists had acquired much strength since the War. Although the control of Europeans on traditional industries (jute, tea, coal) changed little,[116] Indian enterprise played an increasingly larger role in import-substituting industries like cotton, cement and paper. In the 1930s despite the drastic fall in total Indian incomes the industrial sector as a whole fared well, and even recorded some growth. The external terms of trade moved against India; imports were cut off and local manufacturers increased their share in the internal market; the internal terms of trade moved in favour of industry; urban real incomes rose, and demand for industrial goods probably expanded. Even in the rural sector, real incomes fell less than the fall in prices would suggest, principally because food became cheaper. Rural demand was also maintained through the dishoarding of gold and through increased borrowing.[117] Moreover, the Ottawa Agreement helped to maintain Indian incomes. From 1933–34 the

[115] See in this connection A. K. Bagchi, *Private Investment in India 1900–1939* (1972), p. 199. Cf. Michael Kidron, *Foreign Investment in India* (1965), pp. 19–26.

[116] Bagchi, *Private Investment in India*, pp. 192–5; Kidron, *Foreign Investment in India*, pp. 3–11.

[117] See Bagchi, *Private Investment in India*, pp. 89–90.

depression began to lift, and industrial activity received an impetus.[118]

Besides, the political strength of the Indian capitalists had grown with the strengthening of the nationalist movement. They now wished to press for the recognition of their sphere of economic influence. In the condition of the 1930s they saw little danger in negotiating an economic agreement with Great Britain. Indeed they saw some advantages in such an agreement. They were aware that the products in which Britain would now cherish 'preferences' did not by and large compete with Indian goods. British industrialists were eager to arrive at a new system of specialization of production within the Empire, with the U.K. concentrating on capital goods and superior technology products. Furthermore, aware that the British and the Indian governments were eager to ensure India's export markets, the Indian industrialists felt their bargaining position to be strong in bilateral negotiations.

One may ask why, given British industry's relative backwardness in the era of the third industrial revolution, Indian industrialists did not look elsewhere for collaboration. First, it could be said that at a time of growing movement towards self-sufficiency and bilateralism in the world, Britain probably provided the most reliable market for India's exports. Secondly, the continuity of long established connection between British and Indian industry had obvious advantages. But perhaps the most important factor was political. For although the Indian capitalists had gained in political strength with the strengthening of the nationalist movement they were not quite confident of their ability to control the state apparatus; they were afraid that an all-out political struggle might reduce their chances of establishing their hegemony and were in favour of a gradual transfer of power by the British. Thus, in the early 1930s the Indian capitalists had been torn between their desire to get the best terms possible from the negotiations over constitutional reform, and their fears about the consequences of political agitation. To keep agitation under control, they encouraged government to associate Gandhi and the Congress with the constitutional settlement and encouraged the Congress to adopt a more conciliatory approach.[119] The Congress and the FICCI were not at all happy with

[118] Between 1933 and 1939 the total paid up capital of Joint Stock Companies rose by about 12%; Indian joint stock Bank deposits rose from Rs 66.2 crores in 1931 to Rs 108.6 in 1937; new assured business of India insurance companies increased from Rs 17.8 crores in 1931 to 41.7 crores in 1937. See S. Subramaniam and P. W. R. Homfray, *Recent Social and Economic Trends in India* (1946). Industrial employment also increased at a high rate. See N. S. R. Sastry, *A Statistical Study of India's Industrial Development* (1943), Ch. II esp. pp. 20–2, and pp. 40–1, and C.I.S.D., *Large Scale Industrial Establishments in India, 1931–1937.* (Biennial).

[119] Thus in 1934 while N. R. Sarkar (President of the FICCI) railed against the

the terms of the 1935 Act but the FICCI was ready to submerge its dissatisfaction and help make the constitution work.[120] Moreover, governments and businessmen in both Britain and India were increasingly ready to see agreements among businessmen as one important way of removing issues of economics from the field of politics. The negotiations for a new trade agreement provided the opportunity for a useful entente. If Indian businessmen were to refuse to negotiate such an agreement it would most certainly have raised the cry of anti-British discrimination, resurrected the question of constitutional safeguards (and there were many in Britain who had never reconciled themselves to the compromise of 1935), swung the Congress back into full action, and thus revived and perhaps even increased, the dangers of the early 1930s.

But in their efforts to find a way to disentangle business activities from the disturbances of political agitation, Birla and his followers hoped to enlist the acquiescence, if not open support, of Congress. Mody and those who had helped negotiate Ottawa had bypassed the Congress with disastrous results. This strategy of Birla and his allies, however, placed important constraints on their actions as 'unofficial advisers'. They needed to come away with an agreement which would be acceptable to the Congress, specifically to Gandhi. To improve the chances of Congress acceptance they needed to keep on the right side of the Congress and strengthen the 'right wing' within the Congress (which to them meant Gandhi). They also wished to commit the 'right' to accept ministerial office in the provinces under the new reforms. Around this time the capitalists were particularly worried about the growth of socialism and its possible capture of Congress. From about the middle of 1933 the labour movement had revived and the socialist and communist

shortcomings of the Government's economic and political policies, he was careful to note that all was not as he thought it should be among the nationalists themselves. He considered that 'in examining the Civil Disobedience Movement' one ought not to rely completely on its 'saintly originator' but ponder deeply about the possibility of the movement getting into the hands of those who advocated revolution ... As businessmen we cannot risk the creation of an atmosphere of national confusion and disintegration ... This is the simple and understandable position of Indian businessmen'. He appealed to Gandhi to follow a path such that 'every man who loves his country will have an opportunity to make some contribution ... Do not exclude us by taking a route we cannot follow or prescribing methods we cannot use'. *Annual Register*, I, 1934, 451–2.

[120] Before the Constitution of 1935 was ready, 'nationalist' business opinion was bitterly critical of the devices to retain British control in India. But they had begun to clear the way for accepting whatever they got. Thus while the President of the FICCI derided those who were willing to work the new constitution even before all its contents were known, he was himself at pains to extol the virtues of expediency. 'Political tactics often necessitate the adoption of several weapons at the same time ...', he rationalized, 'tenacious loyalty to a given method ... may become a handicap to political progress ... A river in its course to the sea encounters many obstacles. If it encounters a hill ... it circumvents and continues. So should it be with our politics'. *Ibid.*

led AITUC had begun to gain strength.[121] In rural areas, peasant movements grew.[122] The Congress Socialist Party's (formed in 1934) bid to control the Congress with the support of peasants' and workers' organizations created grave misgivings among the industrialists (and landlords).[123] Many were panic-striken and in 1935 Mody formed his 'Progressive Party' to combat the 'socialist menace' and to work the constitution. In mid-1936 Jawaharlal Nehru's speeches appalled and frightened the industrialists. Men of Mody's hue issued a 'manifesto' against Nehru and socialism. Thakurdas also signed it. But Birla saw, and succeeded in impressing his 'caste men' that the capitalists' bet lay in remaining with the Congress in order to strengthen the hands of the 'right wing'. They could fight the battle against socialism more successfully if they remained within a Congress movement which not only was amenable to their ideas but also achieved ministerial power in the provinces and could then use the instruments of the state to contain disorder.[124]

When the 'socialist menace' receded and the Congress decided to accept office, Birla was delighted. Even without office Congress had become an important factor in the class considerations of the industrialists. Congress had come to be recognized as a political force strong enough to arbitrate in conflicts between employers and workers. Once in office, the Congressmen were also custodians of the law and order cherished by the industrialists. Thus it became vital for Birla and his allies that the appropriate elements should dominate the Congress, and imperative that the industrialists do everything possible to promote (and nothing that might undermine) these appropriate elements. This imperative imposed certain restrictions on the industrialists' ability to

[121] The number of Trade Unions increased and their membership multiplied. For figures see C. Revri, *The Indian Trade Union Movement: An Outline History 1880–1947* (1972), p. 233; See also Bagchi, *Private Investment in India*, pp. 142–3.

[122] In the mid 1930s the growth of Kisan Sabhas was phenomenal, particularly in the U.P., Bihar and Andhra Pradesh.

[123] Vallabhai Patel had confided to Thakurdas that not everything was right within the Congress party. Thakurdas to Birla, 31 July 1934, P.T. MSS 126.

[124] As Birla wrote to Walchand Hirachand (one of the signatories of the Manifesto): 'I must say you have been instrumental in creating further opposition to capitalism. You have rendered no service to your caste men'. He criticized the shortsightedness of the signatory businessmen and urged that the best strategy was to 'help' men within the Congress 'who are fighting socialism'. 'It looks very crude for a man with property', admonished Birla, 'to say that he is opposed to expropriation in the wider interests of the country . . . Let those who have given up property say what you want to say. If we can only strengthen their hands we can help everyone'. Birla to Walchand, 26 May 1936. See also Birla to Thakurdas 18 April and 1 June 1938, P.T. MSS 177. For a detailed study of the response of the Capitalists to the developments in this period, see Bipan Chandra, 'Jawaharlal Nehru and the Capitalist Class, 1936', *Economic and Political Weekly*, X, 33–5, Special Number (1975).

press for their own economic interests; they could not afford to seek a
trade agreement which, however suitable for themselves, would prove
politically unacceptable to Gandhi and the Congress. This was particularly true regarding an agreement with Lancashire. The Indian industrialists were agreed that Lancashire was no longer competitive, that the
Tariff Board would most probably grant her the reduction in duty she
desired, and that therefore they might as well make a bargain regarding
Indian raw cotton. The idea of a pact with Lancashire was, however,
opposed to Gandhi's creed. Commercially a pact with Lancashire was
now quite acceptable. Politically it was still very difficult.[125]

Negotiating the New Agreement

In November 1936, the Board of Trade set out its initial proposals for the
new agreement. The principal aim was to obtain for every item of
interest to British trade favourable access to the Indian market. They
proposed that the arrangements made by Lees–Mody and embodied in
the Supplementary Agreement about cotton duties and the offtake of
raw cotton should be confirmed and that the catalogue of preferences for
British goods in the Indian market as established at Ottawa should be
confirmed and if possible extended.[126] The Indian reaction to these
proposals was hostile. The 'unofficial advisers' pointed out that 'a
correct understanding of the denunciation of Ottawa would have made
it apparent to them that the intention of the Legislature was that the
matter should be reopened more to restrict the preferences enjoyed by
the U.K. than to extend them'.[127] The Government of India also
objected because the Board of Trade's proposal would reduce Indian
revenues by Rs 3 crores, and joined with much of British commercial
opinion in thinking that it would be necessary to forego many of the
desirable preferences in order to secure the 'goodwill' required to make
any agreement a proper success.[128] The Board of Trade's shopping list

[125] Gandhi (and the 'right wingers' in the Congress) was regarded by Birla as 'his
man' not because Gandhi was the capitalists' 'henchman' or 'tool' (as Benthall once
described him. Benthall Diary 10 April 1936, Benthall MSS 12), but because the
practical and ideological limits to his politics were eminently suited to the objective
interests of the capitalists.

[126] See L/E/9/1124, especially Note by E. J. Turner, 18 November 1936.

[127] Report of the 'Unofficial Advisers', No. II, 9 December 1936. The 'Unofficial
Advisers' reports have been consulted from various Files in P.T. MSS.

[128] The Government of India pointed out that grant of preferences on the scale
demanded was impossible since 'we cannot accept any appreciable loss of revenue . . .'.
The point was accepted without further comment by the B.T. See GOI to S/S, 26
December 1936; S/S to GOI, 14 February 1937. Copies in P.T. MSS 182.

of preferences was quickly whittled down. HMG was not particularly happy about this, but still saw the point of making concessions on the question of preferences in order to get a good deal for Lancashire. By early 1937 it was clear that the negotiations would fall into two parts. On the one side was the matter of exchanging preferences —for British goods in the Indian market and for Indian goods in the British market— and the principles of bilateralism and imperial economic cooperation which stemmed from such exchanges. On the other was the question of cotton—the extent to which the duty on Lancashire imports into India would be lowered, and the amount of Indian raw cotton which Britain would guarantee to take in return. It was soon clear that the cotton question would form the crux of the negotiations, while concessions on the question of preferences would serve merely as bargaining counters aimed at smoothing the path towards a settlement of the cotton issue.

Britain still had good political and economic reasons to protect Lancashire's interests. As far as Indian commercial opinion was now concerned, Lancashire was an inoffensive competitor in the Indian piecegoods market. But the political implications of any concession to Lancashire were still dangerous. The political history of the cotton duties cast a heavy shadow across the logic of commercial bargaining.

The Board of Trade hoped to evade these difficult political overtones by reviving the strategy of direct negotiation between the businessmen of India and Lancashire. A Lancashire delegation met with the 'unofficial advisers', conceded the 'absolute right of Indian industry to be superior in the Indian market', and argued that a trade agreement which stimulated India's overall trade and thus raised Indian purchasing power would enable Lancashire to supply for 'consumption which would not take place otherwise than as a result of Indo-British economic cooperation'. At these negotiations the Lancashire men held out for a reduction of duties from twenty to eleven per cent, and the 'unofficial advisers' replied that this was unacceptable.[129] Yet in fact both sides were already working privately and independently on the assumption that a level of duty around 15 per cent would be about right. These talks between Lancashire and the 'unofficial advisers' reached no agreement, but the door was left open for future negotiations.[130]

[129] See Note on Meeting between the Indian 'unofficial advisers' and Lancashire representatives held at the B.T., 24 July 1937, Proceedings, India Section, 24 July 1937 pp. 107–16; 'unofficial advisers' report No. 8, 31 July 1937.
[130] For Lancashire's willingness to settle for a 15% duty see Zetland to Linlithgow, Pvt Letter, 23 May 1936, Linlithgow MSS 3. On the Indian side, Thakurdas felt that if HMG agreed to the 'unofficial advisers' proposals in every other respect, and if Lancashire agreed to buy one lakh bales of raw cotton it would be worth reducing the import

The Indian 'unofficial advisers' were very aware of the political constraints on the freedom to negotiate. As R. G. Saraya, a businessman closely involved in these affairs pointed out, given 'the jubilation with which the assumption of office by the Congress ministries is received, it is probable that any concessions given to Lancashire will be looked upon as a sign of weakness, and result in unpopularity for the Indian advisers' with the Congressmen. In these circumstances there was a possibility of an agreement being accepted by Congress only if it could be shown that 'for a concession worth, let us say 16 annas, they [the 'unofficial advisers'] have brought back something worth 17 annas'. It was worth while, moreover to bid for this '17 annas'. The awkward position of HMG and the GOI was only too clear. As Saraya pointed out: 'to the extent India is a debtor country to the U.K., the U.K. will suffer at least as much as India by breaking off the negotiations'. Saraya drew attention to a further factor which put the U.K. government in a weak position. In the atmosphere of impending war and increasing trade demand for raw materials, the U.K. was unlikely to forego the assurance of a number of commodities from India. 'Hence the position of India', wrote Saraya, 'is very strong and a threat to break off negotiations should not frighten. . .'.[131] Political calculations necessitated, and the U.K.'s awkward position enabled, the Indian businessmen to put up a stiff front. The only satisfactory *quid pro quo* was a guaranteed offtake of 8 lakh bales of Indian raw cotton rising to one million bales in the future, and a surrender by the U.K. of preferences worth £10,500,000 and guaranteed unrestricted free entry for Indian jute manufacturers into the U.K. market.

For the moment the vexed question of the cotton duties was put on ice while the two sides haggled over the extent of preferences and over the offtake of Indian raw cotton. The Board of Trade came some way to meet the Indian demand on these two topics. They agreed to surrender preferences in the Indian market up to a value of about Rs 4.5 crores, out of about Rs 18 crores gained at Ottawa which was much less than Indian demands—about Rs 14 crores (at 1935–36 values)—but rather more than the Board of Trade had originally offered.[132] They also began to

duty to 15%: 'Kasturbhai and Birla think that a reduction . . . [to 15%] will do no harm at all.' No concession to Lancashire could mean no Agreement while another Tariff Board enquiry in 1939 could give greater preference 'by the backdoor'. See Note by Thakurdas, 31 July 1937; Note by R. G. Saraya, 11 August 1937. P.T. MSS 201.

[131] Note by R. G. Saraya, 11 August 1937. P.T. MSS 201.

[132] See CAB 24/271 C.P. 219 (37) 'Indian Trade Negotiations', Memo by President, B.T. 25 September 1937; CAB 23/89 35/37 10, 29 September 1937, (37) 15, 9 October 1937; Note by President, B.T. 30 September 1937 for the Indian delegation, delivered on 9 October, P.T. MSS. 183.

work seriously on the old idea of the Lees–Mody pact that Lancashire's demands might best be secured by offering a suitably attractive *quid pro quo* over raw cotton. Moreover this strategy held a good chance of driving a wedge between different sections of Indian business opinion— namely between the cotton growers and merchants on the one hand, and the industrialists on the other. To improve the chances of securing such a deal, the Government of India used the opportunity presented by the resignation of two of the 'unofficial advisers'[133] to appoint in their place Professor W. Roberts who had good connections with raw cotton interests and the Maharaja of Parlakimedi who was a representative of the Indian cotton growers.[134] The Government of India also suggested that the level of preferences which the U.K. would surrender should be raised to Rs 9 crores.[135] These concessions, the officials in Delhi believed, should be attractive enough to lead quickly to an agreement.[136]

Oliver Stanley, President of the Board of Trade, thought they were already going too far. 'I should be prepared', he wrote in a memorandum for the Cabinet, 'in order to avoid the consequences of failing to reach agreement with India to . . . sacrifice preferences on trade worth something between 6 and 7 crores but even that I regard as being very difficult to justify on purely commercial grounds . . . [It] would be extremely difficult to induce Parliament to endorse such an agreement'. He was therefore prepared to see a breakdown of the negotiations and let 'India . . . become a foreign country for our custom purposes'.[137]

[133] E. C. Benthall left to attend to his business affairs and Dr Subbarayan to take up a portfolio in the Madras Cabinet.

[134] These two gentlemen stood forth as champions of agricultural interests and strongly argued for concessions which would be 'considered by the U.K. to be attractive enough for her to increase her purchase of Indian agricultural products . . . or at least to maintain them at their present level'. Minutes of Meetings of 'unofficial advisers' 2 December 1937, and Minutes of Meeting with the Commerce Member, 3 December 1937, P.T. MSS 187.

[135] This figure did not include the 'differential duties' which gave preference to U.K. cotton and steel goods.

[136] Zafrullah Khan's (the Commerce Member) optimism was based on his discussions with Frederick Whyte of the B.T.; Birla's own discussions with officials at the B.T. gave him the impression that the gulf was too wide. Grigg shared this impression and remarked: 'Frederick Whyte is a bloody fool'. See Birla to Thakurdas, 4 January 1938, P.T. MSS 181(4). See also Note of Discussion on 18 February between Zafrullah Khan and Horace J. Wilson, 19 February 1938, PREM. 1/290.

[137] CAB 24/276 C.P. 40(38) 'U.K.–India Trade Negotiations', Memo. by the President B.T. 18 February 1938. See also W. B. Brown to Thakurdas 26 February 1938 informing the latter that Indian proposals were unlikely to be accepted readily. 'I can see great difficulties for a minister in commending to the House an agreement based on the present proposals'. P.T. MSS. 181 (V).

But the India Office, the Treasury, British business representatives and many of Stanley's own staff quickly pointed out that Britain could not afford to march away from the negotiating table in a huff. First there was the whole question of imperial economic cooperation. Businessmen and officials were convinced that the long-term interests of British commerce demanded the conclusion of trade agreements along these lines. Secondly, there were the immense difficulties Britain faced because of her weak bargaining position *vis-à-vis* India. She could not retaliate against Indian intransigence by refusing to import Indian products since most of these were raw materials required by British industry. In the Cabinet itself it was admitted that if the negotiations foundered 'we could get the worst of the bargain, as India could buy elsewhere than in this country', while the U.K. would still be purchasing Indian raw materials. Thirdly, there was the question of India's sterling resources. Britain could not sensibly prejudice the chances of an agreement which would ensure that India acquired the sterling to meet her obligations to British exporters and investors. The Board of Trade was reluctantly manacled to the negotiating table. Horace Wilson of the Board of Trade reminded Chamberlain of 'the importance we attached, at Ottawa, to having an agreement with India; it is no less important now'.[138] The Cabinet agreed to accept the Government of India's compromise and forego preferences worth Rs 9 crores in the Indian market. Yet, while admitting the weakness of the British negotiating position in private, they maintained a haughty stance in public. The Cabinet announced that it accepted the Government of India's compromise 'with some reluctance in order to assist India' and in order to preserve 'goodwill'. They also insisted that their acceptance still depended on the conclusion of a satisfactory deal for Lancashire over the question of cotton duties.[139]

The Government of India did not tell the 'unofficial advisers' the details of the compromise on preferences which the Cabinet had approved. They merely gave the advisers an assurance that they could expect 'reasonable satisfaction' on this topic, and persuaded them to come back to the negotiating table and talk about the serious business of cotton. The question that most exercised the two key figures among the 'unofficial advisers', namely Birla and Kasturbhai Lalbhai, was the

[138] Note for the P.M. by H. J. Wilson, 'U.K.–India Trade', 19 February 1938; Treasury brief for the P.M., 18 February 1938, PREM I/290; Notes on Memo by the President, B.T. by A. Dibdin and C. Kisch, 22 February 1938, L/P/D/291; cf. I. Drummond, *British Economic Policy and the Empire 1919–1939* (1972),pp. 138–40.
[139] CAB.23/92, 10(38)8, 2 March 1938; Note by W. B. Brown, 3 March 1938, PREM I/290.

political orchestration of any agreement over cotton. They were perturbed by the attempts of the Government of India to bring in representatives of Indian cotton-growing interests and also to wheel in types like Homy Mody whose antecedents as far as international commercial negotiations were concerned were not exactly ambiguous. 'The government was trying', Birla commented, 'by indiscreet means to pack the delegation'. Such tactics, he feared, might result in an agreement which was overgenerous to Lancashire. Even more dangerously, they might prejudice the chances of gaining political acceptance in India for any agreement, even for one which was quite sensible in the view of Birla and his friends.[140] In the end Birla and Kasturbhai managed to make the Government of India appreciate the logic of this political sensitivity and to allow them to take the prominent part in the Indian side of the negotiations; they agreed to 'consult' the panel of representatives of millowners and growers.[141]

Even then there remained the difficult question of Gandhi's attitude towards a new trade agreement which was to include a settlement with Lancashire. Hitherto Gandhi had been characteristically vague and had left the 'unofficial advisers' dubious and perplexed. He had insisted that the political goal of the Congress was his primary concern,[142] but had never positively discouraged the Indian 'advisers' from proceeding with the negotiations for a new trade agreement. For example, in August 1937 he had written to Birla: ' . . . you do what is in the interests of India irrespective of the opinion of Congressmen. Rest assured that Congress will have to accept what is good for the country . . . '.[143]

Gandhi had in fact only cautioned Birla that 'since the Congress is the only popular institution, it is necessary that whatever agreement is reached should have the seal of the Congress . . . This would prove your integrity and sense of justice'.[144] Now when an agreement conditional upon a settlement with Lancashire was in sight the 'unofficial advisers' wanted Gandhi to state his position more clearly on the pact—prefer

[140] Birla to Thakurdas, 21 March 1938; Thakurdas to Birla and Kasturbhai, 18 March 1938, P.T. MSS 181 (V).
[141] See Thakurdas to H. Dow (Comm. Dept. GOI), 24 March 1938, Thakurdas to Zafrullah Khan, 3 April 1938, P.T. MSS 181 (V); Linlithgow to Zetland Pvt tel. 2 April 1938, Linlithgow MSS 17.
[142] 'Your viewpoint and mine are quite different . . . I cannot see any economic agreement independent of political issues'. He had, however, advised Birla to continue his efforts by concentrating on the economic aspects and added 'My opinion will probably coincide with yours'. Gandhi to Birla, 18 August 1937, C.W. LXVI.
[143] Gandhi to Birla, 25 August 1937, ibid.
[144] Gandhi to Birla, 18 August 1937, ibid.

ably in complete favour of it.[145] Birla reasoned with Gandhi: if the 'political point of view' prevailed and no agreement was made with Lancashire, she would most probably get a reduction in duty from the next Tariff Board enquiry 'without having to pay anything for it'; instead, if the reduction was conceded in return for a guaranteed offtake of Indian raw cotton it would be a bargain.[146] Moreover, it would be unethical for the Indian 'advisers', he pointed out, to refuse a settlement on cotton on political grounds 'after letting the Lancashire delegation come from five thousand miles'.[147] The doyen of the market place had chosen to moralize to the Mahatma. Thakurdas, too, pleaded with Gandhi.[148]

Gandhi appreciated these arguments. He would allow the 'unofficial advisers' to pursue the negotiations from the 'purely economic point of view', and as such, would not object if 'they honestly feel they can recommend a pact including one with Lancashire'. But he would not commit himself to political support for such an agreement. 'Do your best according to your lights and leave us to do our best according to the political light', were his final words to Thakurdas.[149] Clearly, it was the idea of supporting a pact with Lancashire which worried Gandhi most. He could not allow the Congress to compromise its creed and thereby lose its 'izzat'. As he had once remarked, 'the Congress has no other capital except its prestige'.[150]

Against this uncertain background the plenary negotiations opened in Simla in May 1938. The Lancashire side offered an offtake of 400,000 bales of Indian raw cotton rising to 700,000 bales within five years, in return for a fall in the duty on imports of textiles into India to 11 per cent. The Indian advisers replied with an insistence on an offtake of 750,000 bales rising to a million, and a figure of 15 per cent for the duty on cotton imports. Both sides decked their offers out with complex formulae for adjusting the level of tariff in the event of a severe drop in the volume of Lancashire's imports into India.[151] Neither side budged

[145] Birla to Gandhi, 17 April 1938; Gandhi to Birla (in Hindi), 20 April 1938, P.T. MSS 181(VI).
[146] As Birla put it: 'Purely from the economic point of view, we would not think of giving a free gift of 5%'. Birla to Gandhi, 17 April and 22 April 1938, *ibid.*
[147] Birla to Gandhi, 22 April 1938, *ibid.* If on political grounds there was to be no agreement, then Birla wanted the Congress to announce its position publicly. 'Only then', he told Gandhi, 'can the Indian negotiations save face . . .'.
[148] Thakurdas to Gandhi, 23 April 1938, *ibid.*
[149] Note by Thakurdas on conversation with Gandhi and Patel, 30 April 1938, *ibid.*
[150] Gandhi to Birla, 25 August 1937, *C.W.* LXVI.
[151] Lancashire's scheme of tariff reductions: the minimum revenue duty was assumed to be $7\frac{1}{2}\%$ and the maximum limit of tariff increases $17\frac{1}{2}\%$. To start with, this duty was to be reduced to 11%. If in any year imports from Lancashire fell below 333 million

much from the initial positions[152] and within days the negotiations had broken down.[153] The Government of India then drew out a compromise on its own initiative. It was not a particularly subtle compromise. They pitched their cotton duty at the level of the Indian demand (15 per cent) and the raw cotton offtake roughly at the level of the Lancashire demand (in fact 400,000 bales rising to 600,000). They also introduced even more complex formulae for adjusting levels of both duties and tariffs in the event of a severe alteration in the pattern of trade.[154] These were the best terms that Lancashire had been offered so far. The Board of Trade accepted the Government of India's compromise, and urged Lancashire to do so as well.[155] The 'unofficial advisers' remained very silent. When the Government of India then also revealed to them the exact terms of the Cabinet's earlier decision on the extent of preferences foregone (about Rs 9 crores), they formally disassociated themselves from the whole agreement. They realized that both the level of cotton offtake and the pitch of the cotton duty were too meagre even to secure Gandhi's acquiescence, let alone give Gandhi a chance of persuading other shades of nationalist opinion.[156]

The Agreement was approved by the Cabinet on 15 March 1939, and was signed five days later. It was not at all clear who had gained what. Stanley of the Board of Trade felt that it was unsatisfactory for Britain on

yards, the duty was to be reduced by $2\frac{1}{2}\%$. If in the following year imports continued to remain below 333 million there was to be further reduction by 1% only, since the minimum revenue duty was assumed to be $7\frac{1}{2}\%$. The duty would be increased by $2\frac{1}{2}\%$ only when Lancashire's exports to India exceeded 666 million yards. A. D. Campbell to Thakurdas, 19 May 1938, Annexure VII 'unofficial advisers' Report No. 13.

[152] Birla and Thakurdas countered the influence of the representatives of cotton growers (whose attitude they regarded as 'more a pleading for Lancashire') by enlisting the support of other representatives of cotton growers like Prof. Aney and Bettigery from Bombay. Prof. Roberts complained that Birla prevented the circulation of his minute of dissent. See Note dealing with Note of dissent, enclosed with 'unofficial advisers' report No. 13; Birla to Thakurdas 13 June 1938, P.T. MSS 185 and 181 (VII).

[153] Linlithgow sympathized with his Lancashire delegates, found Thakurdas 'somewhat ashamed of himself' and suspected Birla of duplicity for plotting against a settlement. See Linlithgow to Zetland, Pvt letter 24 May 1938, Linlithgow MSS 5.

[154] The GOI's final terms: an immediate reduction of the duty to 17% on printed piece-goods and 15% on others. The duty was to be further reduced by 2% if U.K. exports fell below 350 million yards, and to be increased above 15% if they exceeded above 500 million yards. If Lancashire's offtake of raw cotton exceeded 750,000 bales, duty on 'prints' was to be reduced to 15% as well. CAB 24/278, C.P. 186, Memo by President, B.T. 'Anglo-Indian Trade Negotiations', 27 July 1938.

[155] Note by Horace J. Wilson of the B.T. for the P.M., 26 and 27 July 1938, PREM I/290; CAB 23/94 36(38)4, 28 July 1938; Proceedings, India Section, 2 August 1938, pp. 163–4.

[156] See Patel to Thakurdas, Tel. 2 September 1938, P.T. MSS 216; 'unofficial advisers' report No. 14, 5 September 1938.

commercial grounds but conceded that it made sense 'from the wider
political point of view'.[157] This assessment was patently false. The
Agreement shortened the list of goods on which Britain could secure
preferences at Ottawa, and to that extent might have been expected to
have secured 'goodwill' in India. Yet in fact it did not appear that any
such 'goodwill' had resulted. The Indian 'unofficial advisers' had disassociated themselves from the agreement, the Congress was hostile, and
the Indian Legislative Assembly unceremoniously threw out the Agreement. The Agreement had to be introduced by Viceregal certification
rather than by consent. The fact that the Agreement could be introduced by an imperial executive fiat was hardly evidence of a flood of
'goodwill'. If the Agreement was still made in the face of such opposition, the reasons can hardly be political.

On the face of it the Agreement looked something like a triumph for
the Indian side. India had retained the preferences in the U.K. market
secured at Ottawa, reached an agreement on raw cotton exports, and
reduced the level of preferences for British imports into India.
Meanwhile, the British seemed to have done rather badly. They had
apparently lost many of the preferences gained at Ottawa, and had
achieved only a limited reduction in the cotton duties. But in reality,
India's gains were not as substantial, while Britain had managed to
secure the most important of her aims while making relatively unimportant concessions. India's goods secured preferences in the U.K. market
only on the same terms as other imperial goods and thus faced severe
competiton. The bilateral agreement restricted India's ability to establish trade links with other countries. Britain meanwhile had sacrificed
preferences in the Indian market mainly on goods which were so
competitive that they had no need of preferential assistance, or on goods
which were so uncompetitive that they would not benefit from preference anyway. On those goods where preferences were of crucial importance to their competitive position in the Indian market, preferences
had mostly been retained; 47 per cent of Britain's exports to India were
hereafter covered by preferences.[158] Moreover, the Agreement laid the
foundations of bilateralism and ensured that India would get the sterling to pay her way in the City. All through the negotiations from the
depression onwards this point had loomed large in Britain's efforts to

[157] CAB.23/98, 15 March 1939.
[158] For information and analysis of the effects of preference on India's exports and
imports see B. K. Madan, *India and Imperial Preference* (1939), pp. 228–39, esp. Table L
III, p. 229. For the importance attached to goods on which preference was retained see
W. H. Wilson, *British Empire: A Concise Handbook of the Markets of the British Empire* (1938),
pp. 102–8.

gain a trade agreement with India. Finally, Lancashire had got most of her pound of flesh. Right up to the eleventh hour of imperial rule, Lancashire had managed to manipulate the imperial connection, in the face of strong nationalist opposition, to gain a favoured position in the Indian market. As a whole, the negotiations may not have resulted in much political 'goodwill', but they had achieved some measure of commercial cooperation and financial security. India might have gained, but Britain certainly had not lost.

* * *

The complex negotiations leading up to the Indo-British Trade Agreement of 1939 illustrate some significant features of colonial economic relations in their penultimate phase. First, the relative decline of the Lancashire cotton textile industry did not, as some have argued, lead to a concomitant decline in its political clout. It retained its capacity to influence British policy and to mould the Indian economy, though the needs of imperial finance had tended to take a higher priority than Lancashire during times of crisis. Secondly, the 'fiscal autonomy' which Britain had conceded to India after the First World War did not indicate that colonial economic control was being substantially weakened, or that India was moving into the position of Canada or Australia. Britain had to give something in order to retain its essential interests, and fiscal autonomy was a technique to gather support, rather than a milestone to decolonization. Finally, though some British and Indian businessmen were capable of working for common interests, business and politics could not be separated. In the early 1930s those who tried to isolate economic issues from the political world failed because they had bypassed the Congress. The strategy failed again in the later 1930s because the businessmen concerned now had to remain on the right side of Congress.

Modern Asian Studies, **15**, 3 (1981), pp. 575–602.

Colonial Rule and the Internal Economy in Twentieth-century Madras

CHRISTOPHER BAKER

University of Cambridge

THROUGHOUT the colonial period, the government played a substantial role in structuring India's foreign trade and in moulding the economy of the great port cities and their immediate hinterlands. Once Company and government had started to prise themselves apart in the early nineteenth century, however, the colonial rulers adopted a very haughty attitude towards the working of the internal economy. The development of internal production and trade would of course be deeply affected by the imperial connection, but the colonial government refused to admit responsibility and was careful not to be drawn into active intervention. The transition from colonial rule to independence did not mark a sharp break between this era of laissez faire or minimal interference in the internal economy, and an era of 'development' or constructive intervention. Indeed, it is more likely that a reluctant slide into economic management during the latter part of the colonial period helped to speed the colonial rulers along their course of retreat; any attempt to tamper with the mechanisms of the internal economy opened up the colonial government to contradictory pressures and threatened to expose many of the weaker links in the mesh of colonial command.

There are now several studies of the colonial rulers' increasing difficulties in the early twentieth century in managing India's external economy, in balancing imperial interests against the demands of India's nascent class of big businessmen, and in coping with the problems involved in the growth of factory industry. These studies contribute to a rather scattered literature which argues that the crucial theme of India's history in the early twentieth century is the fractious story of the relations between the state (colonial and then independent) and big business, and the political bargain which eventually resulted. Yet to concentrate on this one area of economic management, on the tip of the Indian economy, should not mean to ignore the sprawling bulk of the

0027-749X/81/0406–0904$02.00 © 1981 Cambridge University Press

economy lower down. Here, too, there was a story of growing economic management with all its attendant difficulties. Similarly, to see the post-colonial state as an arena dominated by the lions of big business and by other equally powerful and ferocious animals, in which other classes figure only as manacled slaves or devoured christians, is certainly an unnecessary and ultimately mystifying simplification.

Big business formed a relatively small part of the Indian economy, albeit a very important small part. Both the colonial rulers and their nationalist successors had to deal with the other parts as well. The mass of small producers were not unimportant, inert, negligible. This essay traces the history of the colonial government's intrusion into the more mundane and tawdry parts of the Indian economy roughly from the first world war onwards. It argues that it is important to understand the logic of this intervention in order to analyse the role of the later colonial state and its legacy to its successors. The essay deals with the Madras Presidency, where there were fewer big businessmen than in the other major areas of India and where they were less powerful and coherent as a class. Much of the material is drawn from the Tamil districts, but it is necessary to shuffle uneasily between these localities, the provincial government, and the imperial umbrella in Delhi. The focus is fixed mainly on food and cloth, the two main items of internal consumption, and the systems of production and trade which they involved. The first section of the essay sketches out the forces which were pushing and pulling the colonial government into a greater role in the management of the internal economy. The second section traces the government's response. The third briefly reviews the consequences of this history in terms of the ideas and aims which the colonial rulers willed to their successors.

I

After the first world war, there were three sorts of pressure being exerted on government to take a more active role in the internal economy. The first and most articulate represented an extension of the 'drain theory' of the late nineteenth century and the 'swadeshi movement' of the early twentieth. The proponents of these ideas pointed out ways in which government structured the Indian economy to suit British interests, and argued that policies should be reversed in order to assist Indian ones. The variant of these theories popular after the first world war dwelt on two specific items. First there was the matter of government spending on imperial items, notably the notorious home charges and the Indian army. Such expenditure was seen both as a naked exploitation of the Indian economy, and as a means by which the Indian tax-bill was increased to the detriment of capital accumulation and the growth of internal demand. Secondly there was the question of the management of the external economy, particularly the rupee ratio and tariff protection. Critics argued that government deliberately kept the rupee over-valued in order to help (largely British) imports to penetrate the Indian market, and demanded a devaluation which would aid Indian goods both in the home and foreign markets. As part of the same train of thought, they also demanded protective tariffs to assist India's nascent industries.[1]

These arguments reached a new pitch during the depression of the 1930s when the fall in prices exaggerated the burden of taxation, the world-wide drift towards protection raised Indian expectations for a new tariff policy, and the maintenance of the rupee's high value could be seen as a deliberate device whereby Britain 'exported' many of the effects of the depression from Britain to India.[2] But these theories acquired not only new forcefulness in this period, but also new supporters. Originally they had been voiced in the leading commercial and industrial cities of India—particularly Bombay and Calcutta—and from the 1905–08 swadeshi campaign onwards had acted as the spearhead of Indian big business's inroads into the world of colonial politics.[3] But from the mid-1920s, slightly modified versions of these ideas were echoed by rural interests as they began to feel the effects of falling prices and falling demand in the international economy. This was important. Since the turn of the century the British had come to rely more and more on the 'landed interest' to provide a loyal and conservative counterweight to the restless truculence of urban India.

In Madras in 1931 it was not some ambitious industrialist or economic-nationalist ideologue who entered a minute of dissent on the government's Economic Depression Enquiry Report in order to criticize government and the Imperial Bank for trying to combat the effects of the slump with policies of tight money and 'sound finance' rather than with attempts to provide fiscal protection and to stimulate demand. Instead it was one of the province's leading landowners and loyalist politicians,

---

[1] The development of these ideas can be seen in books and periodicals, particularly the *Indian Journal of Economics*.

[2] P. S. Narayana Prasad, 'World depression in India', *Indian Journal of Economics*, XVI (1935–36).

[3] See, for instance, R. K. Raj, *Industrialization in India: Growth and Conflict in the Private Corporate Sector 1914–47* (Delhi, 1979); A. D. Gordon, *Businessmen and Politics: Rising Nationalism and a Modernising Economy in Bombay, 1919–1933* (New Delhi, 1978).

the raja of Bobbili.[4] Lower down the scale of the rural wealthy the reaction was not dissimilar. In 1933 the landowners of the deltaic district of Tanjavur coupled a demand for remission of land revenue with a demand that the relationship between the rupee and sterling be severed since it 'adversely affects the interest of the vast majority of Indian agriculturists'.[5] In 1938 the Tirunelveli District Landholders Association argued that the continued depression of agricultural prices would be overcome only if government was prepared to manipulate tariffs, railway rates and the currency.[6] An individual Tirunelveli landowner set out his own murky view of the relationship between his class interest, the fate of the international economy, and the mediating role of government in this way:

Some of the residents of this village are taking out leases of land in other parts of the country . . . The persons who enjoyed such leases were making a net profit of about Rs 3000 a year. For more than a year they have not been making any profit at all. The market price of every agricultural produce has been affected by the exchange policy of Government. If gold currency is adopted in this country, or if the rate of exchange is made to adjust itself to the market value of silver and gold, then this loss of income will not have been brought about. The serious consequences of this policy can easily be gauged when it is remembered that the annual rent paid by these lessees exceeds Rs 1 lakh every year. If a similar loss is caused by act of God, the people will easily bear it with resignation. But there cannot be any justification for the Government of an agricultural country to adopt any policy which will reduce their income in money value.[7]

The class which the British had pulled into the centre of the political stage in the Montagu-Chelmsford reforms was now aping the ideas of the very people it was supposed to counterbalance.

The second sort of pressure exerted on government was less theoretical but only a little less articulate. It came from those who felt they were at the frontiers of economic expansion and economic transformation and who wanted the assistance of the state in their endeavours. There were pockets of such entrepreneurial initiative scattered throughout the regional economy. In many different instances and in many different

[4] *Report of the Economic Depression Enquiry Committee* (Madras, 1931), copy in Proceedings of the Board of Revenue [BP] 1662 dated 28 May 1931 (all references to government files indicate files of the Government of Madras held in the Tamilnadu Archives).

[5] A. Srinivasa Iyengar forwarding resolutions of the Mannargudi Landholders' Association on 26 November 1933 in Revenue G.O. [Rev] 314 dated 13 February 1934.

[6] Tirunelveli District Landholders' Association, 4 July 1938, in Rev 2217 dated 31 August 1938.

[7] R. Sivarama Ayyar in *Madras Provincial Banking Enquiry Committee* (Madras, 1930) written evidence vol. II, p. 335.

ways, fledgeling small-scale capitalists came up against the deadweight of the old order and then petitioned the government for the kind of assistance which only the state could provide. A handful of examples should convey the variety and intensity of this sort of petitioning.

To begin with there were those who simply begged government to provide a framework of laws and institutions appropriate to the growth of a capitalist economy. From at least the turn of the century, traders and producers begged government to assist the growth of a structure of banking appropriate to the sorts of business carried on in the region. There were banks which served the export houses and the European business community, and government was urged to make these facilities available to traders, producers and would-be industrialists upcountry.[8] At the same time there was a constant murmur of frustration at the government's failure to draw up a legal code and to provide a structure of courts which would enable commercial institutions to get full protection under the law and would enable commercial disputes to be settled quickly, efficiently, and with some degree of predictability.[9] As more merchant capital was sunk in the expansion of commercial agriculture in the early twentieth century, there were demands that government provide a better legal framework for such investments. Much of this pressure focused on the question of land law since land was not only the most expensive asset involved in agricultural production but also the most usual collateral for rural investments of all kinds. In Madras it was notoriously difficult to secure from the courts the validation of a title in land. The courts refused to recognize the *patta* land-deeds issued by the revenue department; they took anything from two years to infinity (with an average between five and ten years) to bring a suit concerning a land-title to any conclusion; in the absence of good rules about documentary evidence the results of such suits were hopelessly wayward; and the procedure for enforcing the decrees from such suits was notoriously slack.[10] Merchants, financiers and rural borrowers constantly blamed the poor state of land law for the stickiness of the rural credit market and for the high rate of interest in rural lending. The difficulties involved in litigation meant that most rural loans were effectively not secured, and the existence of such risk boosted

[8] Complaints were voiced before all the main commissions; see the volumes of evidence of the Indian Industrial Commission 1916–18, the Royal Commission on Agriculture 1926–28, and the Banking Enquiry Committee 1930.

[9] See David Washbrook's article in this volume.

[10] G. F. F. Foulkes, *Local Autonomy* (Madras, 1937–38); *Report of the Madras Survey and Land Records Committee* (Madras, 1947); J. Shivashanmugham Pillai, *Legislative Protection for the Cultivating Tenant and Labourer* (Madras, 1947).

the rate of interest.[11] The Nattukottai Chettiars, the most prominent bankers of the Tamil districts, cited the land law as the principal reason why by the late 1920s they had withdrawn virtually all their capital from southern India and taken it to Calcutta, Ceylon, and southeast Asia.[12]

Next there were demands for government to provide the necessary infrastructure for economic expansion. Government built riverine irrigation works and port facilities in the mid-nineteenth century, railways in the late nineteenth century, roads and hydroelectric plants in the early twentieth. But these expenditures represented only a small part of the government budget and there was a constant demand that the proportion should be increased. Moreover there was a growing pressure on government to spend its meagre resources in ways which were specifically designed to help the expansion of internal commerce and industry. Landowners pressed for investment in irrigation projects tailored for cash-cropping, rather than the flush irrigation systems in which the Madras public works department specialized and under which mainly food could be grown. Government did not immediately respond to these demands and when it finally began boring wells on a large scale in the 1940s it was amazed at the extent of the demand. When it then made available a handful of war-surplus pumps, it was further surprised at the eagerness with which commercial farmers snapped up these relatively expensive items of agricultural investment and demanded permission to import more. Industrialists and commercial farmers pressed for more road-building, more electricity generating projects, more commercial irrigation.

Finally there were calls to government to assist in the transformation of local society into forms which would better suit the aims of capitalist growth. In the 1930s there was a spurt of investment in factory industries. It was impelled forward by the conditions of the depression which reduced the attractions of investment in rural commerce, occasioned some protection of the home market, and drove some of the most vulnerable members of the accelerating rural population to seek new employment in industry. The plentiful supply of labour was particularly important and encouraged investment in industries which were pretty labour intensive; most of the new factories were sited in the upcountry towns, or even in quite small villages, in order to take

[11] M. S. Natarajan, *The Capital Market of the Madras Presidency with Special Reference to its Evolution and Indigenous Institutions* (Calcutta, 1936); V. Krishnan, *Indigenous Banking in South India* (Bombay, 1959).

[12] O. R. M. M. S. M. Sevaga Chettiar in *Madras Provincial Banking Enquiry Committee*, vol. IV, p. 243; M. Ramanathan Chettiar in *ibid.*, pp. 160–3.

advantage of the pool of desperate rural labour. It was important for the industrialists to secure this labour at the cheap price which, they believed, its plentifulness warranted. Through the decade, the eagerness of the factory-owners to push down the real cost of labour advanced in parallel with the quickening pace of migration into the towns. In the cotton-mills, which formed the largest single block of new factories, wages were cut during the price-fall of the early 1930s, and held down when prices began to move upwards from 1935; while then in the late 1930s the mill-owners introduced 'efficiency' schemes designed to get more value out of each labourer.[13] By 1937–38 the work-force in the cotton-mills, sugar factories and other new enterprises protested through strikes.[14] Quickly the owners invited government to step in to restrain labour and to help negotiate the sort of wage-rates which the owners believed the glutted labour market could stand. The government was persuaded to erect a system for settling industrial disputes, to call in the police to quell strikes, to organize commissions to fix wage-rates on a province-wide basis, and in other ways to act as the personnel department of the new industries.[15]

Such events were not confined to the new factory industries but were echoed in parts of the agrarian economy. Here, too, there appeared in places to be a glut of labour. From the late nineteenth century the plantations of Ceylon and Malaya and the rice frontier in lower Burma had drawn off much of south India's excess population to the point in the 1920s when in any one year something like a million Tamilians were labouring abroad. The early years of the depression choked off most of this migration and caused a net return of migrants for the first time in half a century. There were sporadic reports that 'customary' wage rates were being forced down, but more importantly there were instances of attempts to revolutionize the methods of employing labour. Where once cultivators had preferred to take on permanent or annual labourers and to pay them even in the slack season in order to be sure of having hands during the peak periods of planting and harvesting, it was quickly becoming possible to dispense with such burdensome arrangements and to rely on hiring from the growing pool of casual labour. From the mid-1920s, labour gangs began to appear on the scene. With the spread

[13] Public Works and Labour Department G.O. PWL 854-L dated 7 April 1934; Development Department G.O. Dvt 2059 dated 23 August 1938; Dvt 869 dated 19 July 1933; Dvt 989 dated 11 April 1938.
[14] *Madras Labour July 1937–October 1938* (Madras, 1938).
[15] Dvt 2059 dated 23 August 1938; Dvt 2532 dated 12 October 1938; Dvt 2792 dated 8 November 1938; Dvt 208 dated 24 January 1939; see also D. Arnold, 'Labour Relations in a South Indian Sugar Factory 1937–9', *Social Scientist*, VI, 5 (1977).

of motor transport, they could circulate round the different agrarian regions taking in different cycles of planting, weeding and harvesting. Such gangs were not in evidence everywhere, but were particularly prominent in certain areas of commercial agriculture where the cultivators could appreciate the economic logic of going over to this form of labour usage.[16] Naturally enough, the appearance of gang labour provoked protests among those groups who had come to rely on employment as tied labourers. In the early 1940s the *pannaiyal* tied labourers in the central parts of the Kaveri delta were naturally dismayed when their *mirasidari* landowners started to use labour trucked in from neighbouring dry tracts, and then to deny the *pannaiyals* the harvest bonus which was a major part of their annual payment, secured at the point of the agricultural calendar when their bargaining position was normally at its best. Some *mirasidars* dispensed with their *pannaiyals* altogether. The protests which followed resulted in the first ventures of the region's communist party into rural organization, and the main demand of the *pannaiyals* and communists was that the *mirasidars* be forbidden to truck in the labour gangs. The *mirasidars* invited the government in to restrain the communists and help them construct the free market for labour which they believed was in their own best interests.[17]

The desire to derive increased profits from commercial agriculture occasioned moves not only against unreconstructed labour systems but also against 'traditional' forms of land control. Much of the protest against the system of *zamindari* estates—a protest which swelled to a climax in the early 1930s—originated among the tenant groups in some of the most commercial tracts which lay under *zamindari* tenure. These tenants resented the fact that the *zamindars* diverted some of the profits of their own enterprise, and they also complained that the *zamindars* were even worse than government at providing the irrigation, transport and other forms of infrastructure for agricultural growth. In some parts the *zamindars* actively tried to prevent the spread of commercial agriculture in their estates because it tended to create over-mighty subjects among the tenantry.[18] There were similar protests against negligent rentier control in parts of the *ryotwari* region, particularly during the 1940s in the tracts watered by the Periyar and Kaveri rivers.

[16] See C. J. Baker, *The Tamilnad Countryside: An Indian Rural Economy 1880–1955* (Oxford, forthcoming). ch. 3.
[17] Rev 2014 dated 7 November 1945; Dvt 4685 dated 23 December 1946.
[18] See the evidence volumes of the *Report of the Madras Estates Land Act Committee* (Madras, 1938), especially Part II, Tenants Memoranda, and Irrigation Reports from Zamindars.

Here government encouraged tenants to grow an extra crop of rice to help counteract the national shortage of grain. The tenants seized the opportunity to claim that they need not pay any extra rent to their landlord for the crop since all the decisions had been made and all the inputs found by government and tenant without the intervention of the landowner. Once they had established this significant precedent, they soon began to argue that the distribution of profits from agriculture should reflect the distribution of entrepreneurial initiative and capital input, not some customary system of shares, and asked government to help them negotiate with the landowners to have rents abolished or reduced.[19] Thus in different parts of the region, entrepreneurial cultivators were trying to get help from government to clear away the flotsam of rentier ownership and the jetsam of tied labour systems so that they might make more rational uses of the supplies of land and labour available.

The third way in which government was being pressed to involve itself more in the internal economy operated not so much through petition and protest as through government's own concern for security and stability. Two matters steadily forced themselves on government's attention—increasing evidence of selective deterioration in the economy, and the increasing scale of social conflict.

The evidence of decline in agriculture was not properly appreciated until the 1940s when the demands of wartime obliged government to worry about supplies of food. They were then to discover that the production of food had been diving steeply downwards for something like thirty years. The *per capita* production of the dry grains and pulses which were the staple food of the poor was cut in half in that time, while the region's production of rice crawled slowly upwards at a slower rate than the growth of the population. Southern India came to depend on an increasing import of southeast Asian rice which never made up for the shortfalls in local food production.[20] Meanwhile the fragile state of the urban economy became obvious in the 1930s when the spurt of town growth swelled the slum quarters and shanty towns on the outskirts of Madras City and the other major towns. In the 1870s it had been reckoned that an eighth of the provincial capital's population consisted of slum-dwellers, but a revised calculation in the 1930s raised that

[19] Rev 2870 dated 27 November 1947; Rev 2299 dated 30 September 1947; Rev 2014 dated 7 November 1945.
[20] S. Y. Krishnaswami, *Rural Problems in Madras: Monograph* (Madras, 1947); B. Natarajan, *Food and Agriculture in Madras State* (Madras, 1953); Dvt 253–6 dated 9 June 1947; BP 1373 dated 2 August 1944.

proportion to a third.[21] The interrelationship between this form of urban growth and the decline of agriculture was emphasized in the 1940s. The urban population accelerated still further when government provided food rationing in the towns and large numbers of the rural poor fled from the insecurity of the countryside to take advantage of these doles. In the early part of the twentieth century, the smaller market towns in south India had been growing rather faster than the bigger cities and industrial centres. In the 1930s and 1940s, this position was dramatically reversed. The attraction was partly the government's rice-doles, but more significantly the service employment which was provided by the professional communities (particularly government officials) in the cities, and also work in the petty handicraft and artisanal industries. Handloom weaving, rolling the cheap cheroots known as beedies, tanning, and certain kinds of metalwork and woodwork, were the usual resort of the poor of both town and country in hard times.[22] These industries were organized as putting-out systems and workers needed virtually no skill or capital to enter the industry, although employment was very insecure and wages below subsistence level. These industries formed the most rapidly growing part of the urban economy after the first world war, despite the contemporary growth of factory industries. Such industries flourished on rural decline, since they expanded on the flow of cheap labour from the deteriorating country-side. The tanning, weaving and beedi-rolling industries of Madras City, the handloom workshops of Salem and Coimbatore, the tanneries of the upper Palar towns, the metal workshops of Tanjavur and Kumbakonam, and the dyeing and weaving industries of Madurai drew in the rural poor in the 1930s and 1940s. The number of handlooms at work, which must act as a proxy for the number occupied as weavers and as a rough gauge of the growth of the petty industries as a whole, tripled between 1920 and 1955 according to official counts.[23]

This picture of economic decline, relieved by occasional flashes of insistent capitalist advance, provided the setting for social tensions and political conflicts. On the one hand there were conflicts created by the attempts to transform established systems of labour control and land management; there were widespread agitations in the *zamindaris* in the early 1930s, strikes in the factory industries in the middle of the decade,

[21] J. Dupuis, *Madras et le Nord du Coromandel; étude des conditions de la vie Indienne dans un cadre géographique* (Paris, 1960), p. 519.
[22] This fact is brought out strongly in Ma. Po. Sivagnanam, *Enathu Porattam* [Tamil—My Life's Struggle] (Madras, 1974), esp. pp. 31–4.
[23] B. S. Baliga, *Compendium on History of Handloom Industry in Madras* (Madras, 1960); K. S. Venkataraman, *The Handloom Industry in South India* (Madras, 1940).

and wrangles over the use of land and labour in the wet tracts in the early 1940s. All these incidents caused public disorders which demanded the attention of government. On the other hand there were protests from those who knew they were becoming economically less secure. There were occasional grain riots in the countryside,[24] but generally these were few and far between. Rather it was those who fled the countryside and stood on the edge of the precipice of the urban economy who served as the most sensitive monitor of economic decline. On any occasion of uncertainty about the immediate economic future, brought on by intimations of a slump in trade, an unusual kink in the price curve, or the effects of a bad harvest, the putting-out capitalists who ran the petty industries would cut off their advances, choke off production for as long as the market was uncertain, and make their labourers idle. That was part of the logic of a putting-out system—that the capitalist should not be saddled with plant and an imperative to maintain continuous production—and the weaving masters and beedi-financiers followed the logic rigorously. Every tremor in the economy thus sparked off a minor urban crisis, particularly in the big towns where the artisanal industries were concentrated (and also where government could most easily see the results). In 1925, 1930, 1934, 1936, 1940, 1941, 1942, 1948 and 1952–53 there were instances of distress, riot and disorder among weaving populations in the Tamil towns. During the worst of these the weavers attacked grain traders and looted bazaars, became embroiled in battles with the police, and wandered about with begging bowls. In the early 1930s and early 1940s, the weaving riots became associated with the Gandhian campaigns of Civil Disobedience and Quit India, only with some local differences of detail. The weavers often picketed shops selling foreign cloth with great enthusiasm and, in astute attempts to improve the market for their own products, set alight to such shops with their stocks (and sometimes their owners) inside.[25] In the mid-1930s the artisan towns of central Tamilnad also provided the seed-bed for the growth of the Self-Respect movement in its most radical and proto-socialist phase, and for the growth of other left-wing organizations.

These scattered examples of riot and conflict did not add up to an overwhelming tide of disorder, and the connections with nationalist or socialist political organizations were inconsistent and sporadic. Madras was still fairly quiet as far as Indian provinces went in this period. Yet the colonial government was gradually being persuaded that it must

[24] D. Arnold, 'Looting, Grain Riots and Government Policy in South India 1918', *Past and Present*, 84 (1979).

[25] See, for example, BP 484 dated 18 February 1942; Rev 1320 dated 16 June 1942.

take a greater role in the management of the internal economy or be prepared for more serious consequences. How, then, did the colonial government react to this pressure from reasoned argument, political petition, and social disorder?

II

Up to the inter-war period, government maintained a precise view of the legitimate extent of its involvement in the internal economy. Government could and should provide certain facilities like communications and irrigation works but should not be seen to be tampering with the market. The troubles caused by the great famines of the late nineteenth century, and the opportunities offered by the expansion of the world markets for primary produce, made government quite keen on the idea of expanding the agricultural economy but did not force government to overstep her self-imposed limits. Government was happy to sponsor research and to import various bits of production technology which might turn out to be useful. These ventures were not always successful. One enthusiastic Governor of Madras (Sir William Denison) imported a jumble of English agricultural machinery and established an experimental farm where some of the local gentry were allowed to play with these contraptions harmlessly and quite inconclusively.[26] Government also encouraged a European entrepreneur to import a Whitney cotton gin, but it soon had to be abandoned since 'eight strong men could scarcely clean as much daily [with the gin] as ten or twelve feeble old women or children could clean with the churka [a hand-driven mangle arrangement]'.[27] Government research stations began trying to hybridize and acclimatize new strains of crops and here there were some signal successes—notably the Cambodia and karunganni cotton strains, Mauritius groundnut, and the Coimbatore series of sugar-canes. In the early twentieth century a government textile institute managed to devise a form of fly-shuttle appropriate to local handlooms and to popularize this important bit of string and elastic and other technical innovations in weaving.[28] Government also had some success introducing innovations in leather production through its own experimental tannery.

[26] Krishnaswami, *Rural Problems*, 126–35.
[27] J. T. Wheeler, *Handbook to the Cotton Cultivation in the Madras Presidency* (Madras, 1862), p. 33.
[28] A. Chatterton, 'The Weaving Competitions in Madras', *Indian Textile Journal*, IX.

In all these endeavours government limited its responsibility to providing tools and facilities which others could use. It left the fate of these facilities and innovations to the workings of the marketplace, which were considered sacrosanct. Some government officials tried to point out that this was a very short-sighted view. Alfred Chatterton, for instance, agitated for the Madras Government to become much more closely involved in producing and marketing industrial goods. The only agrarian expert among officialdom in the south, Frederick Nicholson, argued that the market hardly worked in a just or efficient manner in the sphere of rural trade and rural credit, and urged government to take a more active role in upcountry finance.[29] Nicholson suggested that the government might consider sponsoring co-operative societies and this turned out to be a brilliantly appropriate solution which enabled government to take some form of action on pressing economic problems yet still to stay theoretically clear of any direct involvement in the mechanics of the economy.[30] Co-operative credit societies were to be started under government tutelage but they would, at least in theory, be self-sufficient and autonomous. In the first third of the twentieth century, the notion of the 'co-operative' became a panacea which government applied to all internal economic problems which swam unavoidably into view and which seemed to stem from some distortion of the market. Such problems were blamed on heinous 'middlemen', and some form of co-operative was prescribed as the cure. The poverty of handloom weavers was traced to the role of the master weavers and yarn merchants, and weavers' co-operatives were set up as a replacement. Low prices for farm produce were attributed to profiteering traders, and a number of co-operative marketing societies were begun in the 1920s. The exploitation of urban casual labour led to a move to found co-operative labour unions. Complaints by government servants about high prices in the urban bazaars led to the foundation of consumer co-operatives.[31] The impact of these institutions was very limited, and the pretence that they were truly co-operative and independent of government was always pretty thin. Yet the device allowed government to appear to act to overcome economic difficulties while at the same time retaining its pose of laissez faire.

From the First World War onwards the illusion that the workings of

[29] F. A. Nicholson, *Report Regarding the Possibilities of Introducing Land and Agricultural Banks into the Madras Presidency* (Madras, 1895–97).

[30] Nicholson advocated co-operatives, but several other things as well.

[31] See the *Annual Report on the Working of the Madras Co-operative Credit Societies Act*; B. V. Narayanaswamy Naidu, *The Co-operative Movement in the Madras Presidency* (Annamalainagar, 1933).

the market were somehow benign and therefore sacrosanct became steadily more difficult to sustain. Instabilities and disadvantages imported from a beleaguered world economy were too dramatic to be ignored. Yet even when the depression of the 1930s undercut prices, wrecked overseas trade, and caused confusion in the region's commercial and financial institutions, the Madras government responded not by setting out counteracting policies but rather by elaborating a 'natural' theory of the depression which was aimed to excuse government of any responsibility for cause or cure. According to this theory, the depression was an inevitable retribution for the years of rising prices and improving markets; farmers, traders and money-lenders had enjoyed thirty fat years and they should not now be surprised if they faced the same number of lean ones.[32] The Director of Agriculture in Madras expanded the theory to argue that the fall in prices was a result of over-production brought about by the successful expansion of agriculture in recent years and attributable in good measure to the triumphs of his own department. 'There is nothing that Government can do in this', he concluded, 'it is entirely left to the people to take to the cultivation of any product they desire'.[33] His departmental officials went even further in their analysis, and brought in echoes of the 'middlemen' theory, and an injured response to growing political pressure, to bolster up the notion of natural economic retribution:

A great deal of money has been invested in land, particularly in wet land, by people who are not cultivating ryots, and who mostly belong to a class which is specially vocal in representing its grievances. The Government consider it inevitable that much of the land brought under cultivation during the period of high prices will go out of cultivation with the fall in prices. This cannot, and indeed should not, be prevented.[34]

Within a decade of these arguments about over-production the same government would be lamenting that the region had a chronic deficit of foodgrains.

The depression slowly undermined the defences around the government's complacency. It became ever more difficult to maintain an awed and respectful view of the processes of the market when it was clearly the market which was causing all the trouble. Against the background of the depression, government launched into an attempt to find out how the Indian economy worked—something government had not been so bothered about since the early days of colonial rule. At first, most of the

[32] See, for example, Rev 41 (Confidential) dated 6 January 1934.
[33] Dvt 2046 dated 8 November 1930; Dvt 1299 dated 28 June 1930.
[34] Rev 41 (confidential) dated 6 January 1934.

initiatives came from the Government of India which was rather more sensitive to the political ramifications of the depression than was the provincial government in Madras. A series of commissions set out to investigate different aspects of the Indian economy. The Indian Industrial Commission, appointed during the instabilities of the latter part of the first world war, had established the precedent for large subcontinental economic investigations conducted through interviews with as many interested persons as possible. In the late 1920s this was followed by the Royal Commission on Labour, the Royal Commission on Agriculture, and the enormous Banking Enquiry which delved not only into banking and money-lending but also into the types of production and trade which lay behind them. From 1930 onwards the Government of India began firing off telegrams to the provincial governments asking them to report on the local impact of the depression. But Madras was experienced in deflecting missives from Delhi. The enquiries were passed on to Collectors who, believing that to report any difficulties in their districts would serve as a slur on their own competence, returned answers of overwhelming complacency. Fort St George gleefully precised these and despatched them to Delhi.[35] When the Government of India's enquiries became tiresomely regular, the Secretariat in Madras appointed an Economic Advisor specifically with the task of compiling the deadening replies to Delhi. When he pointed out that he found it difficult to find suitable figures with which to lard his reports, the Government of Madras also appointed a Statistical Officer. This gentleman immediately told government that its colossal effort at collecting statistics provided almost no material useful for assessing economic trends, and shortly the two of them were shuffled off to some gloomy nether reach of Fort St George and left to their own devices.[36]

Gradually the pressure from Delhi, local protests about land taxes, the chaotic state of the local money-market, disorders among zamindari tenants and handloom weavers, and the dangerous state of government's own revenues forced Madras officials to take some action. At first they merely joined in the Government of India's attempts to gather economic information. In 1931 Madras appointed a Depression Enquiry Committee;[37] in 1934 initiated an enquiry into production and

[35] Rev 765 dated 1 April 1931; BP 3315 dated 10 November 1930; BP 2880 dated 4 October 1930; BP 1662 dated 28 May 1931.
[36] Rev 1752–3 dated 14 August 1931; Rev 227–8 dated 30 January 1932; Rev 1687–8 dated 9 August 1932; Rev 1293 dated 24 July 1933; Rev 2532–3 dated 22 December 1932; Rev 9 dated 3 January 1933.
[37] *Report of the Economic Depression Enquiry Committee.*

trade in rice;[38] in 1935 appointed an official to follow up the Banking Enquiry with another survey of the credit market;[39] and almost every year instituted an investigation into the economics of handloom weaving.[40] Then in the second half of the decade Fort St George moved from research to legislation and executive action. A series of debt Acts set up special courts to scale down arrears of debt.[41] In 1937 government established the first regulated market (for groundnuts) under an Act passed in 1933. Another Act defined the hinterlands of cotton markets and restricted transport between marketing regions. A government order modified railway rates in an attempt to assist the local grain trade. Yet such moves remained few and tentative, and the inexperience of government in such matters qualified the effectiveness of such innovations as the debt conciliation boards. Some of the ragged edges of the internal economy were treated to some cosseting and to some regulation, but intervention was still strictly limited. It was only the special conditions of wartime which triggered off dramatic change.

There were two different reasons why the war precipitated government into a much greater involvement in the internal economy. First, Britain was looking on India as a source of certain war materials and thus had a direct interest in the efficiency of production. Second, the exploitation of the Indian economy for the war effort aggravated many of the structural problems which had been building up over previous decades.

Britain counted on India to provide armed men, a base for operations in the eastern theatre, food for the troops in the middle and far east, and various supplies such as cloth for uniforms and leather for boots. This meant that government was intent on diverting supplies of certain very basic consumption goods—notably the two biggest items of mass consumption, food and cloth—away from the home market towards the commissariat. There was some expansion of Indian production to meet this extraordinary new demand (particularly in cloth), but nowhere near enough to cover the amount diverted to the army. At the same time, the disruption of maritime trade reduced the inflow of many other consumption goods into India. The combined effect of wartime requisitions and reduced imports meant far fewer goods in the market and an inevitable inflationary result. In the case of food, which had been

[38] C. R. Srinivasan, *Report of the Rice Production and Trade in the Madras Presidency* (Madras, 1934), copy in Dvt 322 dated 2 March 1935.
[39] W. R. S. Sathyanathan, *Report on Agricultural Indebtedness* (Madras, 1935).
[40] Baliga, *Compendium*.
[41] B. V. Narayanaswamy Naidu and P. Vaidynathan, *The Madras Agriculturists' Relief Act—A Study* (Annamalainagar, 1939).

imported into India to cover the increasing local deficit over the past half-century, the stopping of imports from southeast Asia had a specially dramatic effect. Shortages let to hoarding, speculative trading, spurts in prices, and distress.

Britain agreed to pay for most of her wartime needs in India, but could neither afford to pay immediately nor make satisfactorily secure arrangements for payment while the war was on. Government therefore made its purchases by printing rupees against credits held in London, and did not immediately dare raise taxes to siphon an equivalent sum of rupees out of the pockets of people in India. Between 1939 and 1945, while the supplies of consumer goods in the Indian market were substantially reduced, the supply of money quintupled.[42] The result was a massive inflation which distorted the Indian economy and invited enormous social and political difficulties. Those at the bottom of the economic heap simply could not get access to the reduced supplies of goods. In real terms they were deprived; in many places they starved; and in Bengal many of them died.[43] At the other end of the scale, astute capitalists could make massive profits by hoarding, by playing the rising market and, particularly, by supplying the goods in demand both by the army and the local consumers. Government was obliged to intervene in an attempt to control the worst effects of these distortions. It had to try to maintain the supplies of goods to the poorer parts of the population, and particularly supplies of food to the destitute of the towns. It had to attempt to forestall the social conflicts brought on by deprivation or by the divisive effects of inflation. And it had to attempt to control the profiteers and to ensure that the economy produced the goods which government needed, rather than the goods which were merely the most profitable. These wartime imperatives drove government into a completely new world of economic management.

In the case of the two major items of mass consumption—food and cloth—the story was much the same. In 1941 prices shot upwards and government felt bound to intervene. Its initial intention was merely to follow the pattern of the 1930s—to tidy up the loose ends of the market but generally leave well alone. Yet after these first timid steps of intervention, government found itself on a slippery slope which carried it all the way down to market control.

[42] A. R. Prest, *War Economies of Primary Producing Countries* (Cambridge, 1948); B. R. Tomlinson, *The Political Economy of the Raj: The Economics of Decolonization in India* (London, 1979), ch. 3.

[43] A. K. Sen, 'Starvation and Exchange Entitlements: A General Approach and its Application to the Great Bengal Famine', *Cambridge Journal of Economics*, I (1977).

When food prices rose, the Madras government first reacted by setting up machinery to tell the grain market what to do. In early 1942 it set up Price Control Committees which issued licences to traders and published lists of fixed prices which everyone ignored. Later in the year it sent out officers to attempt to monitor stocks of grain. After a poor harvest in the winter of 1942–43, and after Bengal had started sliding towards a major catastrophe, government began plans to move food from surplus to deficit areas on an all-India scale. At first this meant that the Government of Madras issued contracts to merchants to move grain from one place to another. When this proved unsuccessful government moved another tentative step forwards; the merchants still worked on contract and put up their own finance, but government officials in the surplus districts were given the task of providing them with the grain. The next move was to add a new cadre of Grain Movement Officers to ensure that once the Grain Purchase Officers had found the grain the merchants would move it to the right market according to the terms of their contract. Then came a cadre of Food and Loading Inspectors to check the grain at the rice mills and railway stations, and then Marketing Assistants and Agricultural Development Officers to check the quality at purchase and retail points. Next government established its own transport fleet and built its own storage godowns. Finally, between 1943 and 1946 government dispensed with the merchants altogether and put up the capital itself. Meanwhile, at the other end of the marketing chain, the Madras government had set up a system of 'informal rationing' in the major cities in June 1943. Again the aim was to 'manage' the free market by forcing established traders to work to government's directions under licence. When this did not work, strict rationing on a card system began in Madras City in September 1943 and gradually spread until by mid-1946 government reckoned that all the province's inhabitants who did not produce their own supply of food were on some form of rationing scheme. To supply this system, government had to abandon the notion of purchasing grain from cultivators and introduce compulsory requisitioning instead. In October 1944 the Madras government ordained that all the rice crop beyond that portion required by the cultivator for seed, revenue, and subsistence could if necessary be commandeered by government. When the 1945–46 harvest turned out disastrously, government moved this machinery into operation and set out to monopolize the entire trade in grain above the level of the village. The surplus was acquired on the threshing floor by the revenue staff, stored in the government's set of seventy-nine godowns, transported by the Civil Supplies Unit fleet of

212 vehicles, and distributed through countless ration shops to 42 million people.[44]

In 1942 government had believed that attempts to control the grain trade would be 'not likely to yield results comparable to the panic they would create'.[45] In the next four years the grain trade was brought under a bureaucratic monopoly. In 1942–43, the Madras government sank no capital at all in the grain trade; in 1946–47 it put up Rs 291.4 million. In 1942 food administration took up half the time of one official; in 1946 there were fifteen thousand food officers. In 1942 food administration cost government virtually nothing; in 1946–47 it swallowed a quarter of the provincial budget.[46] 'One of the largest businesses in the country', noted one official, 'was being run by a government department staffed by general administrators'.[47]

The story in the textile trade was similar if less dramatic. In 1942 a Yarn Commissioner was appointed to issue licences to dealers and to oversee the trade in yarn and cloth. In mid-1943 the mills were obliged to produce accounts of input and output and to allow government to monitor their stocks. By 1944 government was issuing directives to the mills to make certain sorts of yarn and cloth, attempting to direct the movement of all stocks of yarn and cloth through a system of ration cards, franking all bales of cloth, and fixing retail prices.[48] In the cases of both food and cloth, government had taken over the market. Of course government was not entirely successful and a flourishing black market grew up in parallel with the spread of controls. Yet this was a deliberate attempt to supersede the hopelessly distorted market mechanism by bureaucratic management. Meanwhile the textile case also included the second feature of government's new intrusion into economic management—the imperative provided by the threat of social conflict.

The workers in the petty industries, and particularly in handloom weaving, were more than just an occupational group. Weaving and

[44] Agricultural Economics Research Centre, University of Madras, *Measures of Food Control, Procurement and Controlled Distribution of Food and their Effects on the Agrarian Economy* (Madras, n.d.); H. Knight, *Food Administration in India 1939–47* (Stanford, 1954); *A Survey of Procurement and Rationing of Food in the Madras State*, compiled by I. R. Jones (Pudukottai, 1951).

[45] Linlithgow to Amery dated 26 December 1942 in N. Mansergh (ed.), *The Transfer of Power 1942–7: Volume III* (London, 1971), p. 224.

[46] B. Govinda Row, 'Some Aspects of Economic Controls in India during the War', *Indian Journal of Economics*, XXIV (1943–44); *Measures of Food Control*; Dvt 4524 dated 16 November 1945; Dvt 2589 dated 3 July 1946; Dvt 631 dated 14 February 1945; Natarajan, *Food and Agriculture*, pp. 19, 39, 41; Dvt 2461 dated 25 June 1945.

[47] A. D. Gorwala, *The Role of the Administrator, Past, Present and Future* (Poona, 1952).

[48] N. C. Bhogendranath, *Development of the Textile Industry in Madras (up to 1950)* (Madras, 1957), pp. 75–86; Baliga, *Compendium*, pp. 65–81.

similar jobs acted as a form of social security for the poor. The workers in these industries were the marginal men of Tamilnad's economy. The distortions of the 1940s made them especially insecure. In 1941 yarn prices began to rise and the putting-out capitalists reacted by choking off production for as long as the future of the market remained unclear. Matters came to a head in the principal weaving district, Salem, where a sixth of the population of the district town depended on weaving and where in the winter of 1941–42 virtually all of them were destitute. The Collector set up a rice dole and when he found it had nine thousand customers decided to take more ambitious action. He took over the role of the putting-out capitalists and put the weavers to work. Fort St George was already worried about the sums being spent on outdoor relief in the province's many weaving centres and rather incautiously agreed to allow the Collector of Salem to use government funds to make advances to the weavers. The weavers sensed government's inexperience as a textile entrepreneur and turned out shoddy cloth for government wages as quickly as they could. When yarn prices then started to fall in mid-1942, the capitalists moved back into business and quickly flooded the market with cloth which was better and cheaper than that piling up in the government godowns. Government tried to get local merchants to submit tenders for their cloth, but without success. Then it set up its own retail depot, but the returns would not even pay the rent. It offered the cloth at a discount to government servants' consumer co-operatives, but aroused no interest. It invited the Government of India to take the cloth away for military use but the offer was declined. It finally got rid of the stocks by giving them away free to refugees from Burma. Fort St George quickly killed off similar schemes which were creaking into operation in other districts.[49] Thus ended Madras's first little venture into state capitalism.

Yet the handloom industry now had a charge on government's attention and for the rest of the war government officials were involved in the handloom business. The Handloom Weavers' Provincial Co-operative Society was reorganized so that it became in effect a department of government using government capital to produce handloom goods mainly for war supplies. Government negotiated a deal with the major spinning firm, Harveys, to fix the prices at which yarn would be made available to handloom weavers throughout the province. Government established Collective Weaving Centres which amounted to government handloom factories and which were much more closely regulated than the earlier Salem relief scheme. By 1944

[49] BP 937 dated 11 April 1942; Rev 1809 dated 17 August 1942.

every handloom capitalist had to have a ration card to get yarn; by 1945 government had fixed quotas for the production of different goods, divided up the textile market between handlooms and mills, and laid down fixed rates of profit for producer, financier, middleman, and retailer. By the end of the war the handloom industry was working substantially on government capital, for a market protected by government, at bureaucratically fixed rates of wages, prices and profits.[50]

The attempts to minister to the handloom weavers also illustrate the third aspect of intervention; government was becoming involved not only in policing and managing the market, but also in financing and directing production. This had an obvious importance in industries producing strategic supplies, and also in consumer industries such as textiles where both employment and availability had important social ramifications. But it also extended to agriculture. From 1942, government became steadily more involved in telling farmers what to grow, and helping them to find the necessary inputs. At first government was merely trying to discourage cultivation of those non-food crops like groundnuts and short-staple cotton which had lost their export markets because of the disruption of shipping.[51] Later it started to encourage farmers to cultivate more food crops. Under the Grow More Food campaign initiated in 1943, government became involved in supplying many of the important inputs for agriculture, and in forcing cultivators to accept governmental decisions about how and what they should cultivate. In five years, the Government of Madras spent Rs $5\frac{1}{2}$ crores on this campaign and this sum dwarfed expenditure on agriculture in previous years. The effect in terms of increased production was small, largely because of the unhappy coincidence of a string of bad seasons. But the effect on government organization was dramatic. Whereas the agricultural department had once limited its activities to technological experimentation and a little propaganda work, it was now involved in procuring and distributing seeds, manure and agricultural implements, and its officials began to spend a lot of time actually talking to the region's rural population.[52] In the space of two years the official role of the village headman had been turned upside down and he had begun his transformation into an agency of development; 1,456 agricultural societies had been founded in the localities and these served as the final

[50] Baliga, *Compendium*, pp. 65–81, 85, 102.

[51] BP 386-M dated 9 September 1942; BP 97-M dated 22 June 1942; BP 289-M dated 15 August 1942; BP 237-M dated 4 August 1942; BP 117-M dated 26 June 1942.

[52] Rev 238 dated 6 February 1945; Dvt 409 dated 1 February 1947; Dvt 229 dated 21 January 1947; BP 1030 dated 11 July 1945; Krishnaswami, *Rural Problems*, pp. 143–4.

links of a new chain of bureaucratic involvement in the countryside.[53]

In a short time government had discarded all its watchwords about intervention in the internal economy. Even in 1941–42 government believed that it should not and could not tell people what to produce, and could only promote disaster by trying to tamper with the market too drastically. But if the special conditions of the war were the occasion for this precipitate slide into economic management, the causes of these developments must properly be sought in more long-term trends. The war had done no more than exaggerate the trends of growing economic deterioration and social conflict over the past generation and force the colonial government to abandon its reluctance to respond to them. Thus after the war had ended, it proved difficult to disentangle the government from the network of controls. As far as textiles were concerned, the restoration of export markets promised to drain away local supplies so that in 1946–47 government imposed tighter controls over production and distribution than ever before. Between December 1947 and February 1948 government dismantled many of the controls on the textile trade, but left the scheme of yarn rationing in operation and, after prices climbed by two hundred per cent in the next six months, re-imposed licences, profit ceilings and other market regulations.[54] In 1948–49 the market settled down and most of the controls were relaxed, but government was far too deeply involved in the handloom business to step back completely. In one decade the number of weavers connected to the Provincial Co-operative, which was effectively a government-run production and sale organization, had quadrupled to the point where it included almost a third of the weavers in the province. Government had a direct financial interest, as well as a political concern, in maintaining the industry. Government resolved to buy at least a third of its own textile requirements from the handloom industry, started to promote handloom exports, continued to exert some control over the supply of yarn, and dictated a market-sharing agreement to the mill and handloom sections of the industry.[55] Decontrol of the grain trade was similarly incomplete. It was tried in 1947–48, and again in 1955–56; each time it survived one good harvest but at the first sign of poor rains, prices soared and controls were re-imposed. At the end of the war, a government enquiry musing on the future of food production and trade in India had concluded: 'In our

[53] Krishnaswami, *Rural Problems*; Natarajan, *Food and Agriculture*; C. W. B. Zacharias, *Madras Agriculture* (Madras, 1950); BP 1030 dated 11 July 1945.
[54] Baliga, *Compendium*, pp. 81–5.
[55] *Ibid.*, pp. 81–5, 102.

view, a policy of laisser faire in the matter of food supply and distribution is impossible in the future.'[56]

Indeed the war ended amid a number of resolutions that government intervention should in fact swell rather than atrophy. In 1942 government had decided it must abandon its fears about social engineering in the countryside and abolish the zamindari system as, among other things, a necessary preliminary to any serious effort at developing the economy of the countryside. The project was put on the shelf for the duration but was taken up again soon after the armistice. Meanwhile from 1944 government also began thinking for the first time about enacting legislation to modify systems of tenancy and labour usage in the countryside. In June 1944 the Government of India announced its intention to launch a ten-year plan to increase Indian agricultural production and commissioned a report on the technological aspects.[57] By 1946–47 the horizon had been lowered to five years in the first instance, but the Government of Madras was already at work drawing up a list of projects and plotting a massive expansion of one thousand new officials in the agriculture department. The major purpose of these plans was that government would increase its level of investment in agriculture, would undertake more of the responsibility of supplying agricultural inputs, and would extend the network of regulated markets.[58] In factory industry, the argument for increased government intervention came from the mouths of the factory-owners themselves, even the expatriates aware that the government they were inviting to intervene would shortly be national rather than imperial. In 1945 an executive of Binnys, the biggest European textile concern in the south, argued that the future of his industry must depend crucially on government assistance and cited four main areas. First, the industry needed more supplies of the long-staple cotton required for better quality cloth and government would have to encourage cultivation of the suitable varieties of cotton plant. Second, textile machinery had been overworked during the war and needed replacement, but it would be difficult to import replacements since the industrial nations would obviously retool their own industries first. Thus government would have to start up a new machine-tool industry. Third, both immediately before the war and again immediately after, the main industries in the region including textiles had been racked by labour troubles and the

[56] *Famine Enquiry Commission Final Report* (Madras, 1945), p. 45.
[57] Rev 238 dated 6 February 1945; W. Burns, *Technological Possibilities of Agricultural Development in India* (Lahore, 1944).
[58] *Ibid.*; BP 1030 dated 11 July 1945.

industrialists wanted government to continue to serve as their personnel managers. Finally there was a need for 'extensive Government measures of an anti-cyclical character designed to prevent those fluctuations in economic activity which have hitherto been accepted almost as if they belonged to the order of nature'.[59] European entrepreneurs in India had been usually known for their extreme attachment to laissez faire, yet here was a leading executive of one of the oldest and largest companies in the south, on the eve of the transfer of power to Indian hands, arguing for greater state intervention in his own industry. The reasons for the rapid slide into state intervention in the economy lay not just in peculiar conditions of wartime, but in the history of economic deterioration and imperfect capitalist development over the previous generation, and in the political pressures which that period produced.

III

The history of that period had also moulded many of the notions which dictated the course of state intervention. Through the first half of the twentieth century government received more and more petitions for assistance from those who wanted to instil more capitalist rationality into some part of the region's economy and who felt that they needed the help of the state to clear away the obstacles strewn in their way by the past. The petitioners wanted government's help in providing both an appropriate legal and institutional environment for capitalist growth, and also specific measures of assistance to encourage and assist accumulation. Sporadically government had seemed to respond to these petitions. The Ricardian basis of nineteenth-century rural adminis-tration seemed to favour commercial growth in agriculture. In the aftermath of the First World War the imperial government recognized that it might be useful if India had a more competent industrial sector.[60] In the 1920s some government officials in Madras argued that it was time government began to design irrigation schemes specifically geared to commercial agriculture.[61] But in the end the support from the colonial state for such endeavours was very half-hearted. Even in agriculture, where there seemed to be an enormous potential for

[59] Note from B. W. Batchelor in Dvt 840 dated 2 March 1945.

[60] C. J. Dewey, 'The Government of India's New Industrial Policy, 1900–1925: Formation and Failure', in C. J. Dewey and K. N. Chaudhuri (eds), *Economy and Society: Studies in Indian Economic and Social History* (New Delhi, 1978).

[61] Board of Revenue note dated 5 April 1940 in Rev 1355 (Confidential) dated 20 June 1942.

producing raw materials needed by European industry, the colonial government did little to encourage or channel commercial enterprise. In industry the rulers retained a lingering conviction that any encouragement to Indian commerce would occasion some damage to British interests. More particularly, there was a conviction, which grew in parallel with the forces demanding greater state intervention, that the colonial state could not afford to put its shoulder behind a capitalist transformation of the Indian economy since the social and political consequences of such a transition would easily overwhelm the tenuous bonds of the colonial state. Thus the colonial government prevaricated. As time passed and economic deterioration fuelled social tensions, then the perils of change became even more frightening. In its last generation the colonial government sank into a role of guardians of the old order. One or two examples should make clear the logic and implications of this role. When the Nattukottai Chettiar bankers told the Banking Enquiry in 1930 that the absence of good commercial and land laws obstructed the growth of commercial production, the Madras official on the Enquiry commission argued in retort that he thought this was a thoroughly good thing; the south Indian peasants would be safe only as long as they were shielded from the market by the chaos of the Anglo-Indian legal system.[62] In the early 1930s, the Madras Government's textile expert began to set himself up as the defender of petty handicraft industry in the face of competition from the factory and the production line. He argued quite explicitly that the handloom weavers *deserved* protection against the factory weaving sheds and automatic looms because there were more handloom weavers than there were factory employees and because the handloom weavers so patently stood on the lip of the dustbin of economic history; and he further argued that they *needed* protection just because they were less efficient than the factories.[63] His views eventually gained support and shaped government policy towards the textile industry, because economic decline was making the handloom weavers a more and more pressing social and political problem. The logic of its own survival also dictated the government's policy towards agricultural growth. By the time government began to sponsor agricultural expansion in earnest in the mid-1940s, it had forgotten its earlier notions of promoting commercial production; its priority was now clearly food. The major aim of the

[62] See the exchange between H. M. Hood and M. Ramanathan Chettiar in *Madras Provincial Banking Enquiry Committee*, vol. IV, pp. 160–5.

[63] D. H. Amalsad, 'Note on Protection of Hand Spinning and Handloom Weaving Industries' dated 27 August 1938 in Dvt 2106 dated 4 September 1940.

agricultural plans from the Grow More Food campaign onwards was to help the small farmer to grow more rice by slightly modified versions of age-old methods. Government was convinced that its efforts at increasing production would have the best chance of success if they occasioned the least possible change to established methods of production.

Thus by Independence the trajectory of government intervention had been plotted out. The state was to be the protector of the small and traditional producer rather than the armourer of the large and novel. Of course on an all-India scale the ideology of development drew the Independence government into a policy of promoting heavy manufacturing. But this ideology was never allowed free rein. For the most part government sponsored the extension of large-scale industries in fields which were relatively remote from the existing economic base. Any enthusiasm for a revolutionary change in the economy was constrained by the government's awareness of its responsibility for holding up the precarious pieces of the economy. The quality of the government's attitudes was revealed on occasions when government was asked to make a decision to sponsor one sort of production rather than another, and a couple of examples will serve as illustration. In the aftermath of the war, several of the region's spinning mills contemplated deploying their wartime profits to install a power loom section and correspondingly applied for licences to import the appropriate machinery. Government refused these permissions. It argued that it was inappropriate to spend scarce resources of foreign exchange to build up industrial units which would put handloom weavers out of work. Instead the Madras government induced the Government of India to promulgate a nation-wide order reserving the production of several sorts of cloth to the handloom.[64] Further, from the mid-1940s government was pulled into arbitrating disputes over the organization of cultivation in the Kaveri delta. Entrepreneurial farmers asked for assistance to do away with the burdens of rentier ownership and tied labour so that they might rationalize the system of production. Rentier *mirasidars* and *pannaiyal* tied labourers protested and begged government to protect the old order. Eventually in the early 1950s the Madras government passed a series of Acts and ordinances designed to preserve the system of tied labour and to shore up the remnants of *mirasidari* privilege. The Pannaiyals Protection Act gave the tied labourers legal protection against replacement by hired labour gangs. Over the next two decades legislation on land ceilings and on rentier holdings was devised around the image of a small, patrimonial, resident landholder employing

[64] Baliga, *Compendium.*

share-croppers or tied labourers.[65] While of course this legislation was not an unqualified success, village studies conducted in the Kaveri delta in subsequent years indicated that while many of the old generation of rentier *mirasidars* were squeezed out by the combination of agitation and legislation, they were quickly succeeded by upwardly mobile tenants and lesser landlords who quickly fell into the same pattern of management of land and labour which had characterized their predecessors.[66]

*   *   *

In southern India in the early twentieth century there were many examples of entrepreneurs trying to push forward a capitalist economy against the weight of the old order and appealing to government to lend them necessary assistance. It is widely recognized that in nineteenth-century Europe, governments were in general willing handmaidens of economic growth and often pushed forward the construction of an environment suitable for the growth of capitalism way in advance of the demand. The response of the colonial régime was much more restrained. It was equivocal in its attitude to economic growth and fearful of the political consequences of any severe socioeconomic transformation. It prevaricated against the hopeful petitioners for state assistance and delayed intervention until a time when it was required not by the optimistic promise of future prosperity, but by the pessimistic fears of impending disaster. This fact lent to the style of intervention and to the framing of development policies a distinctly cautious and conservative tone.

Those writers who portray the major business and landed interests as the principal influences on the conduct of the post-colonial state are obviously right as far as they go. But it is important to analyse the qualifications and limitations placed on the state's responses to pressures from these 'hegemonic' interests. That requires a closer look at the state, and a rather more comprehensive view of the classes in Indian society. The post-colonial state was, as Hamza Alavi put it, 'over-developed' by virtue of its foreign creation, and thus particularly powerful in

---

[65] K. S. Sonachalam, *Land Reforms in Tamilnadu: Evaluation of Implementation* (Delhi, 1970).

[66] A. Béteille, *Caste, Class and Power: Changing Patterns of Stratification in a Tanjore Village* (Berkeley and Los Angeles, 1965); E. K. Gough, 'Caste in a Tanjore village', in E. R. Leach (ed.), *Aspects of Caste in South India, Ceylon and Northeast Pakistan* (Cambridge, 1960); J. P. Mencher, *Agriculture and Social Structure in Tamilnadu: Past Origins, Present Transformations, Future Prospects* (Durham, 1978).

comparison to the leading agrarian and industrial classes which were comparatively 'under-developed'.[67] In his analysis of Pakistan, however, 'the state' is soon reduced to a handful of bureaucrats and military officers. In India, which did not experience such a break in the transition from colonial rule to national independence, the state must be seen as a rather more elaborate force. The colonial era had lent the state a certain remoteness and a certain purposiveness. Since one of the main aims of the colonial government was to minister to the interests of an external force—namely Britain—it had worked hard to steer clear of any cloying attachment to indigenous social forces. Even when the drift into closer economic management demanded the construction of more alliances and alignments, the state maintained much of its earlier aloofness and easily translated the deceptive protestations of laissez faire into the smooth talking of development. The state maintained a confidence in its own superior wisdom, and a conviction about the importance of its own freedom to manoeuvre. Yet the relative autonomy of the state was also the cause of its relative weakness. The battery of repressive powers masked a lack of administrative competence. The ability to avoid cloying engagements meant the impossibility of making powerful alliances. The culture of nationalism did only a little to solve this problem.

Meanwhile, for as long as India's economy remained sluggish, the mass of the population would be the small producers of town and country. Big business and the landed interest might indeed be 'hegemonic' classes, but neither they nor the state could ignore the sanctions of distress or disorder possessed by the majority. The readiness of the state to respond to the demands of the powerful would always be balanced against an awareness that the maintenance of the state depended on the survival and on the tacit consent of the many. Of course big business and the landed interest were also fearful of social disorder. But the state did more than act as their policeman and mediate their mutual feuds. It also curbed some of their ambitions and channelled some of their energies, in the vain hope that India could be 'developed' without undermining the brittle props which supported the weighty lower levels of her fragile economy and fractious society.

---

[67] H. Alavi, 'The State in Postcolonial Societies: Pakistan and Bangladesh', in K. Gough and H. P. Sharma (eds), *Imperialism and Revolution in South Asia* (New York and London, 1973). It should be noted that Alavi limits his study to Pakistan and Bangladesh and mentions that the greater political undertow in India makes it a very different case.

Modern Asian Studies, **15**, 3 (1981), pp. 603–647.

Workers' Politics and the Mill Districts in Bombay between the Wars

RAJNARAYAN CHANDAVARKAR

University of Cambridge

BETWEEN the wars, the development of a labour movement in Bombay reflected a growing polarization in social and political relations in the city. This period, which saw an intensification of social conflict, also witnessed changes in the character of industrial action. Until 1914, strikes in the cotton textile industry were largely confined to particular departments and mills; increasingly after the war, they were coordinated across the industry as a whole. Rising prices and unprecedented profits which accompanied the post-war boom led to the demand for higher wages supported by two general strikes. In the mid 1920s, as the industry's markets slumped, attempts to cut wages were once again strongly resisted. With a slight improvement in their fortunes in the later 1920s, the millowners introduced 'rationalization' schemes; for the workforce this meant more work, less wages and higher chances of unemployment. Between April 1928 and September 1929, two general strikes crippled the industry for about eleven months, and the extension of these schemes and a further round of wage cuts led to another strike wave in 1933–34. Apart from several one-day closures, eight general strikes occurred in the industry between 1919 and 1940. The impact of this militancy was felt not only in other occupations in Bombay but also in other industrial centres, such as Sholapur and Ahmedabad. As Bombay became the scene of militant working-class action in India, its labour movement, under communist leadership since 1928, acquired an explicitly political direction.

Yet even as strikes were coordinated across several mills, no stable trade union growth occurred until the mid-1920s; subsequently, the unions remained weak, vulnerable and often ineffective. To some contemporaries, this suggested the existence of concealed sources of leadership within the working-class communities;[1] to most, it indicated

---

[1] After the 1919 general strike, the Government of Bombay believed that 'while the workers had no accepted leaders' the conduct of the dispute 'appeared to indicate the probability of some controlling organisation'. J. Crerar, Sec. to Government of Bombay

0027-749X/81/0406-0904$02.00 © 1981 Cambridge University Press

the malign intervention of the political agitator. More recently, our historiographical common sense has been overtaken by such notions as the political immaturity and rural passivity of Bombay's workers. Historians have thus been concerned with the 'survival' of the 'pre-industrial' characteristics of the workforce, rather than their rationality within an industrial context. The traditional loyalties of the working class, in this view, obstructed the development of 'modern' trade unions. These accounts have assumed that the development of labour politics in Bombay can best be understood in the light of existing models of an 'early' factory labour force. In the context of the Bombay textile industry, this remains a problematic assumption. It is not satisfactory either to portray a factory labour force which had been in existence for about half a century by 1918[2] as if it was in a 'nascent' state of formation, or to analyse its history as if it were in transition towards the product of another historical experience, or indeed to measure its development against some universal paradigm of 'class'.

It is perhaps by focusing too exclusively on the sphere of the workplace, by confining their model of social consciousness to what was reflected by trade union development, that historians have overlooked the extent to which workers were active in the making of their own politics. The dynamic of labour politics in the inter-war years, in one view, was the struggle between politicians, attempting to mobilize labour, and their traditional leaders, the jobbers in the cotton mills.[3] The motive force behind labour militancy is thus located outside the realm which workers controlled: their political (and moral) choices, it would appear, were consistently being made by others. In such a view, the history of the working class becomes interchangeable with the history of their leaders, trade unions and political parties. As a result, the impact of labour militancy upon the development of labour politics in Bombay between the wars has been neglected; instead, the emphasis has

---

[GOB], to Sec. to Government of India [GOI], Home, Delhi, 7/15 February 1919, in Bombay Confidential Proceedings, vol. 46, 1919, India Office Library [IOL], London. This riddle of leadership bemused the *Bombay Chronicle*, too, in 1924 when it commented: 'it is absurd to suppose that the men are lacking in leadership . . . it is clear that there is good sound leadership among them somewhere.' *Bombay Chronicle*, 21 February 1924.

[2] The first cotton mill was built in 1856, see M. D. Morris, *The Emergence of an Industrial Labour Force in India* (California, 1965), p. 17.

[3] R. Newman, 'Labour Organisation in the Bombay Cotton Mills, 1918–1929', unpublished D.Phil. thesis, University of Sussex 1970; D. Kooiman, 'Jobbers and the Emergence of Trade Unions in Bombay City', *International Review of Social History*, vol. xxii (1977), pt 3, pp. 313–28. Morris attributes the growth of labour militancy to 'the role of the middle-class intellectual appearing in his first full-blown opposition to British rule', in *Industrial Labour Force*, p. 180.

rested upon the role of the nationalist and communist agitator and the role of the jobber, the agent of labour recruitment and control.

However, the weakness of trade union organizations did not prevent Bombay's workers from mounting an effective and sustained defence of their own interests. To understand the development of the perceptions and actions of Bombay's workers, therefore, we need to examine not only the social relationships of the workplace but particularly the context in which workers lived outside it. Since the earliest inquiries into the conditions of factory labour in Bombay, the interconnection between the spheres of workplace and neighbourhood have been frequently mentioned; but its implications for industrial politics have surprisingly remained neglected.

Customarily, the heterogeneity and cultural sectionalism of the working class is identified with the neighbourhood; yet in Bombay it provided an indispensable base for industrial action. Far from being herded peacefully by their jobbers and neighbourhood 'leaders', workers often acted to constrain them. The momentum of industrial action was not merely provided by men of prominence; sometimes it was maintained against them. Without organization and action in the neighbourhood, it is doubtful whether the general strikes could have been sustained. At the same time, the conduct of industrial action in the public arena of the street and the neighbourhood necessarily generalized the disputes of the workplace, at times brought workers into conflict with the state and created an explicitly political dimension for their struggle. While it would be misleading to portray Bombay's workers as a 'revolutionary proletariat' or indeed to play down the important tensions and antagonisms between them, it is in terms of the political culture of the working-class neighbourhoods that the scale of industrial action and the ascendancy of the communists can be explained.

I

From the late nineteenth century, a distinctly working-class district began to emerge in Bombay. Already in the 1850s, an official investigator had noticed the growing social and cultural distance between the mass of the population and 'the educated and more influential classes (whether Native or European) of our community'. 'The principal acquaintance of these [influential] classes with the Native Town' he wrote, 'is generally formed by traversing the Kalbadevee or Girgaum bazaar roads, in going from the country to the

Fort, or from the Fort into the country; and of all the densely peopled districts lying *behind* these great thoroughfares, they generally know as little as they do of the interior of Africa.'[4] The inception of industry added a further dimension to the city's social geography. An overwhelming majority of the cotton mills came to be situated in the three wards to the north of the old 'native town'. Increasingly the working classes, fairly evenly dispersed in the native town of the mid-nineteenth century, crowded into this area. By 1925, 90 per cent of the mill workers lived within fifteen minutes' walking distance of their place of work.[5] To its inhabitants, this area came to be known as Girangaon, literally the mill village. As the labour movement gathered momentum between the wars, Girangaon ceased to be a mere geographical entity; rather it came to represent an active political terrain.

The physical structure of the working-class neighbourhoods imparted a certain public quality to its social life. The landscape of the mill district was dominated by ramshackle, jerry-built chawls packed closely into the land between municipal thoroughfares. A survey conducted in 1921 discovered that 27 per cent of the population in Parel and 33 per cent in Umerkhadi lived in rooms containing six or more persons.[6] Another investigation conducted in the mid 1930s found over 35 per cent of families of 'untouchable' workers sharing a single room with at least another family, while over 63 per cent lived in a single room.[7] 'Every sixth person in the city,' it was reported in 1939, 'lives in conditions which are prohibited even by the existing antiquated law'.[8] The extent of overcrowding brought about by high rents, housing shortages and low wages, meant that the inhabitants of the chawl spilled over into the courtyard of the wadi and the street.

The importance of the street did not derive simply from the fact that men lived on it. Street life imparted its momentum to leisure and politics as well; the working classes actively organized on the street. Thus, street entertainers or the more 'organized' tamasha players constituted the

[4] H. Coneybeare, *Report on the Sanitary State and Requirements of Bombay* (Bombay, 1855), p. 2; Selections from the records of the Bombay Government, new series, vol. XI.

[5] *Labour Gazette*, vol. IV, no. 7 (March 1925), pp. 745–7. This survey was based on a sample of 1,349 male and 715 female mill hands.

[6] J. Sandilands, 'The Health of the Bombay Workers', *ibid.*, vol. I, no. 2 (October 1921), pp. 14–16.

[7] G. R. Pradhan, 'The Untouchable Workers of Bombay City,' unpublished M.A. thesis, University of Bombay, 1936.

[8] *Report of the Rent Enquiry Committee* (Bombay, 1939), vol. I, p. 9. The committee noted pertinently that the minimum space required by the Bombay Jail Manual for a prisoner was double that which was stipulated as permissible under the Bombay Municipal Act of 1888. It also reported that 256,379 people lived in rooms occupied by six or more persons and 15,490 lived in rooms with at least twenty others, see pp. 7–9.

working man's theatre. The street corner offered a meeting place. Liquor shops frequently drew their customers and gymnasiums their members from particular neighbourhoods.[9] Social investigators continue to be bemused that, when asked to give 'an account of their leisure time activities', the vast majority of workers 'could not be specific and said that they pass time roaming, which they consider a mode of relaxation.'[10]

The pleaders' offices, which proliferated along the streets of the mill district during the 1910s, were focal points of organization in industrial and political action; some also became important centres of social activity. 'There is a constant stream of mill hands to these offices,' noted the police commissioner in 1914, 'which in the evening especially become a regular "rendez-vous". Here the millhand gets into touch with the Brahmans or Marathas, who read the vernacular newspapers to them, and not infrequently incite them to go on strike.'[11] With the 'professionalization' of trade unionism in the 1920s, the methods of recruitment and publicity continued to be reminiscent of the modes of the street entertainer. S. H. Jhabvala, admittedly one of the most 'professional' publicists of labour's cause, and an official of nearly twenty unions in 1929, thus described his own recruiting drive:

I would stand at the end of the street when the factories were whistled off and would cry 'Ye who are fallen and miserable, come ye here and I shall help you out of the slough of distress'. A few letters were scribbled on behalf of the distressed individuals, posted by me to their employers and God helps those who help themselves, strange enough a couple of them were solved, and the poor illiterate flocks thought that I was a good instrument for the redress of their evil lot . . . Often I ventured to take a yellow-robed saint with me who attracted a larger crowd. Mr. Ginwalla managed to pay him eight annas per day, because he rolled in wealth and had no issue. He [the saint] sang Mahratta songs and I afterwards gave a dose of unionism . . . The result was that in a short time flocks of people, man [sic], women and children anxiously waited for me to hear some of their grievances and to get them solved.[12]

In its contrasting political style, the communist Girni Kamgar Union sustained the political momentum of the working class neighbourhoods

---

[9] For a description of the social life of the mill districts in this period see Parvatibai Bhor, *Eka Rannaraginichi Hakikat*, as told to Padmakar Chitale (Bombay, 1977).

[10] K. Patel, *Rural Labour in Industrial Bombay* (Bombay, 1963), p. 150.

[11] General Department, Order no. 3253/62-Confl; 15 May 1917 in Bombay Confidential Proceedings (1917), vol. 25, p. 15, IOL.

[12] Proceedings of the Meerut Conspiracy Case [henceforth MCC], statement by S. H. Jhabvala, vol. II, non-communist series, pp. 786–7. The fact that the Bible—as Jhabvala told the Meerut court—was 'one of my daily readings' perhaps explains his prose style.

by holding regular processions and public meetings—at times, these were an almost daily occurrence. Their public commemorations of notable events in the socialist tradition—from the birth of Marx to the death of Parashuram Jadhav, a worker killed in police firing during the 1928 strike in Bombay—were sometimes well attended, and at all times contributed to the pageantry of political activity.

Although these forms of social behaviour can be identified with the neighbourhood, they cannot be considered in isolation from the context of work. The separation of workplace and neighbourhood was more evident in the cotton textile industry than, for instance, in the smaller artisanal workshops;[13] yet in the textile industry as well these two social spheres were inextricably connected. Nowhere is this to be seen more clearly than in the role of the jobber, who straddled the boundaries between workplace and neighbourhood. Usually promoted from the shopfloor, the jobber was delegated vast powers over the workforce. So as to enable him to discipline labour effectively, management allowed him considerable discretion in the employment and dismissal of workers—the ultimate weapons of labour control. In return, the millowners expected their jobbers to keep production going: in other words, to maintain an adequate supply of labour, to resolve disputes between workers and to ensure industrial peace. The execution of these functions was complicated by the fact that the day-to-day demand for labour varied, partly because of absenteeism and partly in response to market fluctuations, which determined the counts of yarn to be spun or the type of cloth to be woven and thereby governed the amount of labour required by management. Each mill employed a sizable proportion of its workers on a casual, daily basis. Across the industry as a whole, this was estimated at 28 per cent of the average daily employment.[14] So every jobber had to maintain connections with potential badli or 'substitute' labourers to meet fluctuations in the daily demand for labour.

It was, therefore, integral to the jobber's managerial functions that he should acquire and maintain connections outside the workplace. To recruit and discipline workers 'with success', recorded the Gazetteer, the

[13] For the organization of the handloom weaving workshops in the city see R. E. Enthoven, *The Cotton Fabrics of the Bombay Presidency* (Bombay, 1897). The separation of workplace and neighbourhood in the mill district also had its physical aspect. The mill compounds resembled fortresses in the mill district, protected by high walls, iron gates and sentries equipped with lathis.

[14] Labour Office, Bombay, *General Wage Census, Part I; the Perennial Factories: Report on the Wages, Hours of Work, and Conditions of Industry in the Textile Industries (Cotton, Silk, Wool and Hosiery) in the Bombay Presidency (including Sind), May 1934* (Bombay, 1937), p. 20.

jobber is 'bound to have a following of men and boys who usually live in the same neighbourhood and often in the same chawl as himself.'[15] Burnett Hurst, in his study of the condition of wage-earners in Bombay in the 1920s, observed that the jobber 'endeavours to acquire an influence over his friends and acquaintances who live in the same or neighbouring chawls. He lends them money, advises them on family affairs and arbitrates in disputes. When labour is required, he uses the influence so gained and is generally successful in procuring hands.'[16] Later evidence, however, suggests that this picture of close neighbourhood control must be modified. Jobbers did not always live in the same chawls as their workers, and workers from a single mill did not usually live together.[17] There can be little doubt, however, that the jobber's power within the workplace rested upon his connections outside, and that at least some jobbers actively invested in the development of a following and a network of power and influence. What Ambalal Sarabhai said of the jobber in Ahmedabad could equally apply to Bombay: 'He becomes a jobber if he has friends and relatives in important positions in the mills and is also a favourite of the head of the department; the chances of his becoming a jobber entirely on his own merit are very few.'[18]

Not all jobbers sought to build these connections; but few could ignore them altogether. They attempted to establish themselves at influential points within the material structure of the neighbourhood. Frequently, they acted as rent collectors, sub-lessors and occasionally even as landlords. They sometimes helped to organize the khanavalis or boarding houses which catered specially for groups of single workers. They also lent money on their own account and more often guaranteed loans. Indeed, loans guaranteed by a jobber could be obtained at discounted rates of interest.[19] They sometimes ran liquor shops and

[15] *Gazetteer of Bombay City and Island*, compiled by S. M. Edwardes (Bombay, 1909), vol. I, p. 493.

[16] A. R. Burnett-Hurst, *Labour and Housing in Bombay: A Study in the Economic Conditions of the Wage Earning Classes in Bombay* (London, 1928), pp. 46–7.

[17] Bombay Disturbances Enquiry Committee, 1938 [henceforth BDEC] oral evidence of Dhaku Janu Lad, pp. 103–5; Mathura Kuber, p. 499, Daji Sakharam, p. 507 and several others in GOB, Home (special [sp]) file 550(25) III B of 1938, Maharashtra State Archives [MSA]. Such evidence should modify the widely accepted picture of the jobber's awesome *personal* control, which has tended to neglect the institutional basis of his power.

[18] *Royal Commission on Labour in India*, [henceforth *RCLI*], Evidence, Bombay Presidency (including Sind), 1929–31 (London, 1931), vol. I, pt i, written evidence, Seth Ambalal Sarabhai, Ahmedabad Manufacturing and Calico Printing Co. Ltd, p. 277.

[19] Proceedings of the Bombay Provincial Banking Enquiry Committee, 1929–31, file

gymnasiums, and were often active in the organization of religious ceremonies and festivals. Their authority at the workplace and the influence they acquired outside made them valuable members of chawl committees and caste panchayats as well as useful allies for politicians at various levels. These high-flying connections, deriving from their position at work, in turn enhanced their value within the neighbourhood. This range of activities did not, however, simply establish the jobber as a provider. His services to the community as well as his disciplinary function at the workplace placed him in a situation of potential conflict with the workers.

For the millowners, in turn, the jobber's connections outside the workplace increased his value as an agent of discipline. These connections were usually based on the caste, kinship and village ties of the jobber. Recruitment through the jobber ensured that the cultural diversity of the workers was brought into the workplace; consequently, the jobber served as an impressive bulwark against combination and provided a useful mechanism for strike-breaking. Significantly, it was when working-class militancy began to complicate the jobber's task of disciplining labour that the millowners grew concerned about the efficiency of his role in production and in the mid-1930s took steps to modify their methods of recruitment.

Workplace and neighbourhood were brought into relation with each other not only by the methods of labour recruitment but also by the uncertain conditions of employment. Periods of unemployment and chronic under-employment were commonly experienced by many mill workers, and even the 'permanent' jobs, which were held in high esteem, offered little security. Not surprisingly, workers organized outside the workplace to hedge against their narrow and fluctuating margins of survival. These informal welfare systems, or arrangements for mutual assistance, were based on their immediate social connections. Not only did migration occur within these connections of caste, kin and village, but workers also relied upon them to find work and housing, and turned to them in periods of distress. For instance, groups of single male workers, often from the same village, would rent a room together. As residents left, their friends and relatives who had moved to the city were also given a share.[20] This practice has inspired thought about its

12 c, Replies to the questionnaire ... submitted by the Currimbhoy Ebrahim Workmen's Institute, MSA.

[20] See Patel, *Rural Labour in Industrial Bombay*, p. 72. The most noted example of such organization was the 'clubs' established among the Goanese in Bombay. They were financed by subscription and operated as a welfare system, giving preference to the unemployed among them, see *RCLI*, Evidence, I, i, The Bombay Seamen's Union, p. 293.

anthropological significance: the re-creation of villages within the city or the recourse to traditional ways of life. However, it probably bears a simpler explanation: that this was an obvious response to housing shortages and high rents.

In 1936, one social investigator noted 'the fact that distant relations, with a view to finding a job in Bombay, come and live with their relatives here.' But he also suggested the double-sidedness of this dependency when he reported that workers 'find it very difficult to pay the rent ... and therefore ... they keep sub-tenants. ... People cannot generally afford to have one room per family.'[21] Such arrangements fulfilled a reciprocal need: newly-arrived migrants had a place to stay and contacts through which to find work; the more established residents were able to meet their living costs, renew their rural ties, fulfil family obligations and even extend their sphere of influence in the city. The importance of these social arrangements was reflected by the fact that, as far as housing was concerned, 'the neighbourhood of persons of one's own circle is sought'.[22] It is the political consequences of these interconnections between workplace and neighbourhood that the rest of this essay will explore.

II

If the social patterns of the neighbourhood cannot be abstracted from their material context, nor can they be portrayed as if they were devoid of political conflict. Not only in devising strategies for living but also in industrial and political action, workers had to act across the boundaries of workplace and neighbourhood. As spheres of social action, workplace and neighbourhood are frequently assumed to exert opposite pressures on the development of workers' perceptions and actions. At the workplace, it is said, economic factors assert their primacy in the conflict between capital and labour and the lines of class antagonism are clearly drawn. The social patterns of the neighbourhood, on the other hand, are cast in the image of villages transplanted to the city: here, workers appear to be the prisoners of their traditional loyalties. Yet time and again the urban neighbourhoods belied this image and the mill district became a militant, and at times, even an insurrectionary centre.

The image of the urban neighbourhood as composed of villages ruled by their headmen derived its plausibility from the informal welfare

[21] Pradhan, 'The Untouchable Workers', pp. 7–12.
[22] *Report of the Rent Enquiry Committee*, vol. I, p. 20.

systems operating in Bombay. Undoubtedly, these welfare systems created opportunities for some people to establish themselves as patrons and providers. But it would be misleading to portray their power as if it ran in a single direction. A closer examination of these relationships between neighbourhood 'leaders' and their 'followers' suggests the limits of political command and indicates the social basis for collective action.

The jobber, the dada or neighbourhood boss, the graindealer, the landlord, the moneylender, each acquired an impressive degree of influence in the course of their daily commerce. Yet few neighbourhood patrons were able to escape the constraints imposed upon them by the social and political demands of their clients. Their continued command of resources depended on their ability to fulfil the moral and material expectations of the neighbourhood. For instance, if the jobber's position at the workplace was based, as we have seen, on his influence within the political and economic structure of the neighbourhood, he was also constrained by this interdependence. Since his strength derived from the social and commercial ties he established with his workers, he had to remain receptive to their needs and responsive to their demands. It was when his patronage was extended to the wider organization of credit, housing and recreation that it was exposed to greater competition from rival jobbers as well as other neighbourhood patrons. Landlords, moneylenders, brothel-keepers and graindealers no less than workers could choose between jobbers. The interdependence of his position within the workplace and the neighbourhood meant that a jobber had to extend as far as possible the ambit of his control, unavoidably weakening his own lines of defence. Like all neighbourhood patrons, he had to compete not only for clients but also for the favour of those more powerful than himself, from employers and trade unions to politicians and minor officials.[23]

[23] Of course these relationships were not stagnant. Between the wars, the jobber's authority at the workplace diminished. This was partly because the growth of labour militancy made it increasingly difficult for him to reconcile the demands of his men with the imperatives of management. As the jobber's influence at work declined, it became more necessary and, at the same time, more difficult for him to entrench himself within the neighbourhoods. It was probably the case that, by the late 1930s the jobber's position became less crucial to political and commercial advance in the neighbourhood. The extent of the jobber's decline should not, however, be exaggerated. In the mid-1930s, the Bombay Millowners' Association, in response to the declining efficacy of the jobber, introduced schemes to revamp the system of labour recruitment and control in the industry. However, individual mill managements remained the jobber's last defender. At the level of the individual mill, the jobber still retained his uses for management. Ineffective in countering industry-wide action, the jobber attempted to entrench himself in the neighbourhood in order to dominate more completely the politics of the particular mill. At this level, BMOA schemes to control the jobber met

By virtue of their place within the credit structure of the neighbourhood, shopkeepers and graindealers also commanded considerable
influence and some became desirable political allies.[24] In their case, too,
their ability to do favours for people from their neighbourhood was
central to their own business interests. Often, they were pressed to
finance various social and political activities from festivals to strikes. The
expenditure involved was sometimes considerable. For instance, it was
reputed that, during Mohurram, mohollas spent between Rs 100 and Rs
400 to erect a tabut and carry it out in procession. Every street where a
tabut was being prepared would also arrange for a maulvi to deliver the
waaz up to the tenth day of the month. For his description over five
nights of the martyrdom of Husain, the maulvi was paid between Rs 30
and Rs 100. These expenses were met—as was common to all religious
observances—by the subscription of local residents. During Mohurram,
it was said, 'youths preceded by drummers and clarionet players,
wander through the streets, laying all the shopkeepers under contribution for subscriptions.'[25] Often these shopkeepers were non-Muslims.
The shopkeepers had paid their dues—often, no doubt, with reluctance
—because it was expected that they would. The relationship was more
one of obligation than of enforcement. It was only when the arrangements of the ugarani, the collection of funds for the tabut levied by each
moholla, broke down that its operation became evident to the state. For
this reason the violence of the arrangement was most noticeable to the
police commissioner who wrote in 1911 that the money was 'extorted—
there is no other word for it—from Marwadi and Bania merchants, who
are threatened with physical injury unless they subscribe liberally.'[26]

The first decade of the twentieth century was a sensitive period for the
conduct of the Mohurram festival.[27] As the state intervened in this
sphere, local shopkeepers discovered the language in which they could

with considerable initial resistance from some of its own members. For a summary of the
BMOA schemes to control badli hiring and the jobber system in general see the *Report of
the Textile Labour Inquiry Committee, vol. II, Final Report* (Bombay, 1953), pp. 337–50;
BMOA, *Annual Report* (1935), pp. 27–9 and BMOA *Annual Report* (1936), pp. 37–40.

[24] BDEC, oral evidence, Ravji Devakram in GOB, HD (sp) file 550 (25) IIIB of 1938,
pp. 277–9, MSA.

[25] *Gazetteer of Bombay City and Island*, vol. I, p. 185.

[26] Commissioner of Police, Bombay to Secretary, Judicial Department, Bombay, No.
545-C, 20 January 1911, reprinted in S. M. Edwardes, *The Bombay City Police 1672–1916:
A Historical Sketch* (London, 1923), Appendix, p. 198. Edwardes' account of Mohurram
related largely to areas of the city outside the mill district. But some of these relationships
described for these areas were equally applicable to the mill district.

[27] See J. Masselos, 'Power in the Bombay "Moholla" 1904–1915: An Initial
Exploration into the World of the Indian Urban Muslim', *South Asia*, no. 6 (1976), pp.
75–95.

614 RAJNARAYAN CHANDAVARKAR

complain about the payments they had hitherto been obliged to make.
The desire of the city police to intervene could find justification in the
'extortion' of which shopkeepers complained; at the same time, this gave
the shopkeepers the means by which they could rid themselves of the
burden imposed by these enforced payments. These complexities—and
especially the expectations of the neighbourhood—can be illustrated by
the outcome of a complaint lodged by some Marwadi merchants at
Pydhoni police station that they were being harassed and assaulted by
Muslims of the Bengalpura Moholla. When the police warned the
'leaders' of the moholla not to continue these extortions, 'this was
treated as a grievance and Latiff himself had the impertinence to come
to the Head Police Office and complain that "the police were not
assisting the collection of funds".'[28]

A similar picture of service, obligation and reciprocity emerges from
the role which shopkeepers played in the conduct of strikes. Without
their long-term credit, the general strikes which lasted between a month
and six months would not have been possible. During the 1919 general
strike, for instance, even as the mill workers were out in the streets, most
of the shops in the mill areas remained open.[29] This was at an early stage
of the strike. Prolonged strikes often placed immense pressure on local
credit arrangements. During the general strike of 1928, which lasted six
months, workers had to turn to their lenders of last resort, reputed to
charge the highest rates of interest: the Pathans. The Pathans' attempts
to recover their loans was one important reason for the communal riots
of February 1929.[30] During the general strike of 1940, the *Bombay
Chronicle* reported that the cheap grain shops, offered to workers when
they demanded an increased dearness-of-food allowance following the
price rises which accompanied the outbreak of war, were unacceptable
because they 'cut away the credit which workers had so far been
enjoying with other grain merchants. In times of disputes between
workers and employers, Bania grain dealers allow credit to workers to
the extent of five or six months.'[31] These were vital connections; even in
times of industrial and political peace they could not be ignored; in
moments of conflict, they were indispensable.

If the local shopkeeper was a figure of considerable importance, it was
crucial to cultivate his protection and his patronage. For shopkeepers it
was their ability to fulfil these functions that defined their local

[28] Edwardes, *Bombay City Police*, Appendix, p. 198.
[29] *Bombay Chronicle*, 13 January 1919.
[30] *Police Report on the Riots in Bombay, February 1929* (Bombay, 1929); *Report of the Bombay Riots Inquiry Committee* (Bombay, 1929).
[31] *Bombay Chronicle*, 7 February 1940.

importance and drew them into more exalted political connections. During the one-day strike of 7 November 1938, Tukaram Laxman, determined to go to work, turned to the bidi or tobacco shop, when he was stopped by strikers: 'I requested the bidi shopkeeper to send me to work. I said "Mama, anyhow see that I get to work." Then the Bidiwalla asked the [presumably his] motor driver who was nearby to take me to my mill.'[32] On the same day, however, several grain shops were 'looted'. Baijnath Bahadur complained that strikers entered the shop in which he worked, removed the gunny cloth covering the grain, ate the grain and ran away.[33] The Police Commissioner described the looting of a shop near the Worli Chawls in similar terms: 'The shopkeepers were arguing with these people. The crowd seemed to treat the whole affair as a joke. They would just pick up a handful of grain and throw it.'[34] The apparent festivity with which these shops were looted concealed the underlying tensions in the relationship between shop-keepers and the residents of the neighbourhood.

The dada—essentially, a title for a neighbourhood leader—fascinated and repulsed contemporary observers. For the dominant classes of the city the dada symbolized the 'roughness' of industrial politics. Burnett Hurst described the 'dada' as 'a hooligan, who lives by intimidation. He is both lazy and dangerous.'[35] In public discourse, neither the employers' nor the workers' organizations cared to be connected with the world of the dada even though they operated within it. Anti-communists used the term to describe the following of communist unions; communists used it to signify strike-breakers. During the investigations which followed the communal riots of 1929, Hindu and Muslim witnesses used the term in connection with the rival, rather than their own community.[36] In fact, 'dada' was a term of respect. Although, in public, everybody tried to dissociate themselves from 'dadas', as one trade unionist pointed out, 'I know personally that Dadas like to be called Dadas.'[37]

The dada was not a special kind of working man. Several workers established themselves as dadas by participating in crucial neighbour-

[32] BDEC, evidence of Tukaram Laxman, in GOB, Home (sp) file 550 (25) III B of 1938, p. 517 MSA.
[33] BDEC, evidence, Baijnath Bahadur in GOB, Home (sp) file 550 (25) III B of 1938, p. 639 MSA.
[34] BDEC, evidence, W. R. G. Smith, Commissioner of Police, Bombay, in GOB, Home (sp) file 550 (25) III B of 1938, p. 1049, MSA.
[35] Burnett-Hurst, *Labour and Housing in Bombay*, p. 49.
[36] Bombay Riots Inquiry Committee, 1929 [henceforth BRIC], oral evidence, Balubhai Desai, file 8, and A. R. Dimitimkar and S. Nabiullah, file 7, MSA.
[37] BRIC, oral evidence, G. L. Kandalkar and V. H. Joshi, p. 71, MSA.

hood activities such as the running of gymnasiums or rent collection. In the course of their activities, the dadas became, as V. H. Joshi, an official of the Girni Kamgar Union put it, 'agents dealing in working people.'[38] The metaphor is instructive of the dada's vulnerability to the ultimate sanctions of neighbourhood politics: social and, in reality, commercial boycott. If the dada was 'an agent dealing in working people', he could not alienate his clientele. This was why 'the dadas left to themselves cannot harm a mass of people.'[39] For this reason dadas could be engaged against strikers least during periods of solidarity and most when they were in some ways least needed, at times of working-class vulnerability.

The scale of a dada's activities was determined by his social connections and the base from which he was able to operate. Some, like Keshav dada Borkar, dominated the whole area of Ghorapdeo for several decades; others were small men, neither recognized nor respected in the next chawl. In a sense, dada was properly a reputation rather than a status—a reputation for physical prowess or for getting things done. The dada, said Balubhai Desai, 'is a person who has got this reputation of controlling the hooligans by rendering services to the hooligans and protecting them, giving grain to them and really of course controlling them . . . . some of these Dadas are rich.'[40] Their ability to exert this control depended upon their facility in providing such services. They did not always fight themselves, but they could mobilize men to do their fighting and in any case their leadership depended upon the belief that they were capable of fighting. In order to protect their followers they had to have the means to pay surety for those of their men who were arrested 'and help in any other way they can.' It was only 'in that way they collect the hooligans'.[41] To build up and maintain a following a dada needed influential friends and patrons; but to catch the eye of the great, let alone achieve a following, he needed to cut a figure on the street corner and in the chawl. Such prominence was often achieved through the leadership of a gymnasium. These gymnasiums, where wrestling contests were held and where men trained in stick play, proliferated in the mill district. Their cultural and political role will be examined later in this essay. What must be stressed here is that they formed an important part of the dada's domain. It was here that dadas served their apprenticeship and it was through these gymnasiums that

[38] BRIC, oral evidence, G. L. Kandalkar and V. H. Joshi, file 16, p. 69, MSA.
[39] *Ibid.*, p. 61.
[40] BRIC, oral evidence, Balubhai T. Desai, file 8 p. 29–31, MSA.
[41] *Ibid.*, p. 29.

they often built their reputations. According to V. B. Karnik, the prominent trade union leader of the 1930s,

every gymnasium used to have, say, two dozen or three dozen or sometimes even a much bigger number of students and those students were under the control of the gymnasium—that is the dada who taught at the gymnasium. And that dada could utilise his students in any way that he liked . . . . Every party tried to get the support of one dada or the other.[42]

The extent to which workplace and neighbourhood overlapped and the roles of jobber and dada could be combined were indicated by Dhaku Janu Lad, a jobber in the Bombay Cotton Mill. He had been prevented from going to work during the one-day strike of 7 November 1938. His less prominent brother had, however, managed to enter the mill. Because his brother had not returned when the first shift should have ended, Dhaku Janu walked to the mill to see whether he needed help. Crowds of strikers who had failed to stop some workers entering the mills, now decided to prevent them from leaving instead. The police might escort the workers out of the workplace, but they could not extend this service to their doorsteps. For this reason, it was unsafe for the workers to leave the mill. When Dhaku Janu approached the mill gates, 'those who were working in the mill went up to the Manager as soon as they recognised me.' The Manager sought the help of the police to escort the workers out of the mill, and Dhaku Janu Lad took two separate groups of workers to their rooms.[43] The provision of this kind of service was among the most crucial demands made upon dadas and jobbers. They acted as informal guardians of a public order and morality which they interpreted, sometimes arbitrarily and enforced without an excess of decorum.

The material conditions which made informal welfare organization necessary for most workers also created nodes of power and influence in the neighbourhood. The struggles waged around the jobber, the grain-dealer and the dada indicate the reciprocity of these power relations. As people got together to meet their social needs, their actions defined the extent, and the limits, of social control. It is important to turn from the institutional basis of dominance in the neighbourhood—arising from its material structure—to the patterns of association which occurred within them. The collectivities fostered by the conduct of religious festivals, especially in the earlier twentieth century, and the gymnasiums of the

---

[42] Interview, V. B. Karnik, April 1979.
[43] BDEC, evidence, Dhaku Janu Lad, GOB, Home (sp) file 550 (25) III B of 1938, pp. 103–17, MSA.

mill district reveal how social behaviour itself provided a basis for political mobilization.

The relationship between these collectivities and politics is difficult to determine. Of course, the fact that men were brought together to crack a pot during the Gokulashtami, carry Ganpati to the sea or dance with the toli bands at Mohurram did not mean that they could then be frog-marched into politics. The observance of some religious occasions, such as the Ganpati festival, had an explicitly political content and others, like Mohurram during the early years of the twentieth century, began to reflect social antagonisms, invited the intervention of the state and were dragged into the public domain.[44]

The associations which emerged in the conduct of religious obser-vances became the focal points of community sentiment and rivalry. The internal structure and organization of the melas—the companies of dancers at Gokulashtami—provide further insight into the complex interplay between leaders and followers. Participation in a mela some-times depended upon the payment of an entrance fee, a monthly subscription and contributions to the general expenses of the mela. Before being admitted to the mela, each entrant had to take an oath in which he swore not to divulge its secrets to any other mela and not to join its opposing or rival party even if he severed his connections with his own. Group loyalty was a central feature of these melas. The leader of the mela was afforded considerable respect, usually being a man of some local prominence, and it was expected that the members of the mela would remain strictly obedient to him. But the leader had to manage the mela, protect its interests and was held personally responsible for mak-ing all the necessary arrangements on the day. His continued leadership depended upon satisfying his team.[45]

In their organization, leadership and group loyalties, these associ-ations resembled street or neighbourhood gangs. As one observer of the toli bands which danced at Mohurram wrote:

Each street has its own band to parade the various quarters of the city and fight with bands of rival streets. If the rivalry is good humoured, little harm accrues; but if, as is sometimes the case, feelings of real resentments are cherished, heads are apt to be broken and the leaders find themselves consigned to the care of the police.[46]

[44] See R. I. Cashman, *The Myth of the Lokamamya: Tilak and Mass Politics in Maharashtra* (California, 1975), pp. 75–97; Masselos, 'Power in the Bombay "Moholla"', pp. 75–95.

[45] K. Raghunathji, *The Hindu Temples of Bombay* (Bombay, 1900).

[46] Cited by the *Gazetteer of Bombay City and Island*, vol. I, pp. 187–8.

The dynamic of neighbourhood competition on such occasions lay in the reputation which neighbourhood leaders, especially the dadas who led these gangs, were seeking to gain or conserve. These rivalries were part of the permanent social relationships of the neighbourhood, not the product of spectacular occasions alone.

Like the great festivals, the gymnasium was an important, albeit less public, focus of working-class culture. The akhada or gymnasium was not necessarily a place which the 'respectable' abjured. Sir Purshotta-madas Thakurdas announced proudly that he had trained at one in his youth and that he now sent his grandson to an akhada. Balubhai Desai, the Congress politician, claimed in 1929 that he still attended an akhada. It was, however, he added, an akhada only for 'decently behaving gentlemen', and he chose it because it was the only gymnasium in Bombay with machines 'for reducing fat which I am taking advantage of.' A more common feature of gymnasiums, however, was lathi-play. Those who trained in akhadas thus acquired a special skill. Balubhai Desai applauded its use as a form of self-defence. 'A lathi', he said, 'can give you protection if you are surrounded even by 50 people and you can escape unscathed.'[47] But akhadas were not associated with physical culture or self-defence alone. Young men, brought together at a gym-nasium, skilled at fighting and trained in the use of lathis, had consider-able potential for political mobilization, and frequently provided a basis for neighbourhood action. As social centres, gymnasiums could also become focal points of political organization. According to the moderate labour leader, Syed Munawar, 'akhadas and teashops were the rendez-vous of riff raffs and hooligans . . . those were the best places for them to meet.'[48] During the communal riots of 1929, they were again identified as sources for the organization of violence. Indeed, one witness argued that the Muslims had been put at a disadvantage in the riots by the decline of the Muslim dada 'since the Mohurram taboot processions in Bombay were stopped more than 15 years ago, and since the closing of the Muslim talimkhanas.'[49]

Gymnasiums were also pulled into industrial action, on both sides, by strikers and management alike. Some workers, by virtue of being dadas, could deploy the gymnasium members in support of a strike, while the management recruited strike breakers from their ranks. The role of the gymnasiums in political mobilization is more easily identified than the part they played in industrial action. Political pamphlets and the

[47] BRIC, oral evidence, Balubhai T. Desai, file 8, pp. 69–71, MSA.
[48] BRIC, oral evidence, Syed Munawar, file 3, p. 279, MSA.
[49] BRIC, oral evidence, A. R. Dimtimkar and S. Nabiullah, p. 271, MSA.

reported speeches of strike leaders often claimed that gymnasiums were being used in strike breaking. But it is extremely difficult to document the relationship between gymnasiums and mill managements. Obviously, strike breaking could offer gymnasiums a means of earning an income; the greater their income the better equipped they would be in relation to other gymnasiums, the more effective in attracting members and perhaps the more successful in the contests arranged between them. It is easy to see that strike breaking could become an activity essential to the success of some gymnasiums. From the point of view of the jobbers or the management, importing the hired strength of a gymnasium to settle scores on the shopfloor was not always advisable, nor often necessary. It was only when the employer 'became desperate and wanted to see that the mill started again,' when he felt he had exhausted all other options, according to V. B. Karnik, the Royist labour leader,

that he would get hold of a dada and recruit some strike breakers . . . . it all depended upon the market; if there was demand for cloth then he was anxious to re-open the mill; if there was no demand for cloth then he was not so keen: if the mill remained closed for a week or ten days or even a month it did not matter to him.[50]

There is as yet little available evidence on the organization and working of gymnasiums. Such evidence as exists suggests that the organization of some gymnasiums could be extremely elaborate. For instance, the Hanuman Vyayam Shalla was founded in 1912 by a certain Narayan Rao. By 1928 it claimed branches in parts of the city as dispersed as Vajreshwari, on the outskirts of Bombay in the neighbour-ing Thana district, and Bhoiwada in the heart of the mill district, apart from its headquarters in Prabhadevi. In January 1928 it acted as host to a contest between fifty other gymnasiums from all over Bombay. This particular occasion involved over 150 wrestling bouts and the collection amounted to over Rs 2,500. It was likely that a lot of money would pass through gymnasiums; no doubt, competition for their control could be fierce. Elections were held to decide the constitution of the committee. Gymnasiums sometimes even advertised their elections in the Marathi press, notifying their members of the time and place at which they would be held, and announcing how they could establish their qualification to vote. The candidates were sometimes men of considerable importance. In the case of the Shri Samarth Vyayam Mandir, the nationalist campaigner, Dr N. D. Savarkar, offered himself as a candidate.[51]

[50] Interview, V. B. Karnik, April 1979.
[51] Nava Kal, 6 January 1928.

It was as much a mark of prestige for gymnasiums, as it was for chawl committees and neighbourhood leaders, to be able to invite eminent people to their great occasions. When the Hanuman Vyayam Shalla held its contest in January 1928 it invited S. K. Bole, founder of the Kamgar Hitvardhak Sabha and, in 1928, Vice-President of the Bombay Textile Labour Union, to preside at the function. S. K. Bole, it was reported, gave the gymnasium a handsome donation.[52] Because of their obvious importance in political mobilization, politicians and trade unionists did not treat such connections lightly. Indeed, their political relevance enabled gymnasiums and their dadas to form alliances at exalted levels, which, in turn, then became an important factor in their position within the neighbourhood.

The tensions and conflicts within the working class were most obviously manifested in the neighbourhood; but here, too, the solidarities of labour politics were forged. Political experience in this arena was formed, in part, by the struggle to constrain and at times direct neighbourhood leaders. Power and control in the neighbourhood entailed a set of shifting relationships in which dominance was achieved and limited through negotiation, manoeuvre and sometimes violence. As the neighbourhood was increasingly brought into the sphere of industrial and public politics as well, it shaped the development of the political consciousness and political action of the working class.

III

Social relationships in the neighbourhood increasingly impinged upon industrial politics. This was partly because material conditions limited the possibility of organization at the workplace. In an overstocked labour market, employers were well placed to defeat workers' combinations and at times even exclude them from the workplace.[53] Consequently, if workers were to demand better conditions, fight wage cuts or protect employment levels, it was imperative that they organize in the neighbourhood as well. The arcane procedures and legal niceties of collective bargaining were never far removed from the baser negotiations of the street.

In dealing with labour unrest, mill managements employed the usual

---

[52] *Ibid.*

[53] One mill manager told B. Shiva Rao, 'For every one who goes out of this gate there are nine more waiting outside who would be grateful for the wages I am paying.' B. Shiva Rao, *The Industrial Worker in India* (London, 1939), p. 55.

forms of repression, as well as some novel ones. Workers who participated in trade-union activity were less likely to be promoted to more
responsible and lucrative posts. They were obvious candidates for
retrenchment after an industrial dispute or during a recession. They
were also vulnerable to discrimination in the allocation of machinery or
the distribution of raw materials. As the Social Service League pointed
out, 'Complaints about victimisation of workmen taking a prominent
part in the trade union movement are frequently heard.'[54] Trade
unions—particularly those which did not meet with the employers'
approval—could neither collect subscriptions nor hold their meetings in
the vicinity of the workplace. By choosing with whom they would
negotiate, by choosing between rival unions or factions, employers could
deal with their most favoured workers and thus strengthen the organizations they approved of while attempting to destroy those they considered
dangerous. Such action was by no means confined to the textile industry; however, both within and outside it, these measures were most
effective when the conditions of employment were casual and the level of
skill low.

Significantly, although the millowners failed to combine across the
industry in order to control production when their markets slumped,[55]
they were able to coordinate impressively in dealing with industrial
action. As early as 1893, the millowners had circulated the names of
strikers among themselves.[56] As conflict in the textile industry intensified between the wars, their efforts grew more vigorous. By the mid 1920s
the Sassoon group, for instance, was employing agents to spy upon the
meetings and organization of their workers as well as to take down and
translate such speeches as were made.[57] Each mill had in its Watch and
Ward department its own organized force for coercion. The superintendent of the Watch and Ward department at the Sassoon mills was 'a well
known boxer' called Milton Kubes. When asked how he had collected
the speeches he claimed to have done in 1928, Kubes said, 'I have got my
own secret service'.[58] The millowners were also able to mobilize their
own brigades for political action. In opposition to the Red Flag Union, it
was said, the millowners 'post their own pickets, publish leaflets, hand-

---

[54] *RCLI*, Evidence, Bombay Presidency, I, i, written evidence, The Social Service
League, p. 445.
[55] Dissatisfaction in this regard was often expressed in the speeches of the chairmen of
the Bombay Millowners' Association at their annual general meetings; see, for instance,
the BMOA, *Annual Report* (1934), Chairman's speech, p. ii.
[56] BMOA, *Annual Report*, 1893, p. 16.
[57] BRIC, oral evidence, Milton Kubes, file 5, p. 241–3, MSA.
[58] *Ibid.*, p. 201.

bills and keep watch and ward inspectors.' The object of the pickets 'is to help the loyalist workers to go to work . . . and to see that they are not molested. . . . They simply move around in the chawls, post themselves as pickets in front of the mill gates, and advise willing workers to go to work and if any of their workers are molested they go to their rescue.'[59] To organize such pickets, millowners relied upon their jobbers either to mobilize the support of their workers against the strike or to encourage anti-strike alliances in the neighbourhood. By the mid 1930s, they had become more systematic in keeping an eye on trade union activities, reporting on workers' meetings and sharing information with each other. Indeed, this political intelligence was embodied in the monthly report of the labour officer of the Bombay Millowners' Association to its committee. It was also made available to the police as well as to official inquiries into strikes, disturbances and seditious conspiracies, and seems to have been treated largely as unproblematic evidence.[60]

In addition, the millowners were increasingly able to call upon the assistance of the state. Fearful of the infiltration of class struggle into nationalist agitation and concerned at the spread of support for the communists among Bombay's workers in the late 1920s, the provincial government grew increasingly ready to intervene in industrial disputes. From the late 1920s, the government constructed a legal framework for the conduct and settlement of disputes, sent more police to the mill gates during strikes to restrict picketing and control 'intimidation', and prose-cuted the communist leaders of the labour movement more readily for incitement or conspiracy. The presence of the state was most evident, however, in the form of the police when they supervised pickets or escorted blacklegs to work. Introducing the Prevention of Intimidation Bill in 1929, the Home Member of the Bombay government recalled his memories of the general strike of that year for the benefit of the Legisla-tive Council:

One of the most remarkable sights it has ever been my fortune to view was a long procession headed by mounted police, followed by foot police and then by a hollow square with women workers in the middle and the workmen around them on all sides. The procession was wound up by more armed police and another party of mounted police. As they marched along the road, the street corners and points regarded as dangerous were guarded by still more police. Day after day these men and women were thus escorted to their work and away from it in complete security. These measures continued so long as they were necessary. As the number of men at work increased and the danger of their

[59] BRIC, oral evidence, Syed Munawar, file 3, p. 269, MSA.
[60] BDEC, evidence, extracts from the monthly reports of the Labour Officer, BMOA, in GOB Home (sp) file 550 (25) III of 1938, pp. 173–245, MSA.

being overawed by strikers decreased the police precautions were gradually relaxed.[61]

These were formidable obstacles against which to conduct a strike; they could scarcely leave the forms of industrial action, let alone its possibility, unaffected.

This structure of dominance within industrial relations, ranging from the economic sanctions available to employers at the workplace to the political means of repression outside, was often sufficient to smother any sustained resistance from the workers. For one thing, industrial action necessarily placed jobs in jeopardy. Moreover, unless workers were able to effect a fairly complete strike, they stood little chance of negotiating their demands with management, let alone achieving any concessions. When the state intervened, workers were placed under greater pressure to devise means by which they could prevent their jobs being usurped by 'blackleg' labour. It shifted the focus of action to the neighbourhood where social pressure as well as force could be deployed to maintain an offensive. Workers' combinations, excluded from the workplace, were forced to act in the social arena outside. The disputes of the workplace were brought into the street. Patterns of association developed in the neighbourhood were integrated into the conduct of industrial action. Managements were, at times, also active in forging anti-strike alliances in the neighbourhood, but unless workers had been able to constrain and immobilize these alliances, they would have been able to offer little effective resistance. As the neighbourhood itself became an arena of industrial conflict, workers used their social connections outside the workplace in two ways: first, as a material base and second, for varying degrees of direct action.

Neighbourhood social connections, indispensable to the daily life of workers, influenced the possibilities of their collective action. How long workers could remain on strike was governed by the extent to which they could draw upon the material resources of the neighbourhood and especially upon the credit they were able to mobilize. If through participation in a strike a worker risked his job, his willingness to strike would to some extent be influenced by his chances of finding another job, and for this he depended upon his neighbourhood connections. Industrial action sometimes even brought into play the rural connections of the workers. M. S. Bhumgara, formerly manager of the Khatau Makanji Mills, explained in 1931 that it was upon workers who had lost all connections with the land that 'the millowners generally depend to break the strike as these people have no home to return to and hence

61 *Times of India*, 8 August 1929.

they are the worst sufferers at such times.'[62] Those workers who could fall back upon their village connections were often the most resilient in industrial action.[63] Migrants with strong rural connections were expected to be less concerned, perhaps even less conscious of their economic interests in the city than urban proletarians with nowhere else to turn. In this case, however, it would appear that migrants with the strongest rural connections could also be the most conscious of their 'urban' interests and most active in their defence.

Strikers, trade unions and the political parties also had to rely upon the pressure which they could bring to bear upon the community as a whole in confronting strike breakers. Their actions were based partly on their own strength of numbers, partly on the alliances which they could effect within the structure of neighbourhood power and partly on their ability to publicize and thereby discredit workers and jobbers, dadas and gymnasiums involved in strike breaking. It was sometimes said of the communist-led Girni Kamgar Union that it hired 'mavalis and badmashes', literally 'roughs', to stop workers crossing the picket lines or to 'intimidate' blacklegs in their chawls.[64] But most unions did not have money for such enterprises. They were probably most capable of hiring dadas when their membership figures rose dramatically and their subscriptions permitted them a few luxuries, as for example during some general strike. Yet at such times, the militant mood of the workers was often enough to enable them to dispense with these extravagances. On the other hand, as V. B. Karnik put it, if 'usually it was the strikers themselves who used to take the lead in organising this type of defence' against organized blacklegs, 'sometimes some of the strikers may themselves be dadas.'[65]

One of the achievements of organization—especially the extensive organization which the communists were able to build up after 1928—was that unions could deal with dadas in an attempt to contain their hostility or negotiate their support. From 1928, the Girni Kamgar Union maintained a list of dadas in the mill district and invited workers to contribute to it.[66] *Kranti*, the union's official organ, published the

[62] *RCLI*, evidence, Bombay Presidency I, i, written evidence, Mr M. S. Bhumgara, p. 499.

[63] In January 1928, during the strike wave which finally launched the general strike, the police observed: 'The strikers were determined not to work the new system and are gradually leaving for the native places by the coasting steamers and trains after receiving their wages'. Bombay Presidency Police [henceforth BPP], *Secret Abstracts of Intelligence* [*SAI*], 1928, no. 3, 21 January, para. 61.

[64] BRIC, oral evidence, S. K. Bole, file 3, p. 217, MSA.

[65] Interview, V. B. Karnik, April, 1979.

[66] BRIC, oral evidence, G. L. Kandalkar and V. H. Joshi, file 16, p. 71, MSA.

names of 'loyal' workers, which meant their jobbers and escorts as well.[67] Workers, too, were involved in making the identities of strike breakers public, and, indeed, moral outrage was repeatedly expressed at their deeds at meetings and through leaflets. For instance, the residents of a wadi sometimes held public meetings at which local dadas were forced to explain and justify their actions. Blacklegs were often brought to strike meetings and humiliated. On 31 May 1928, two blacklegs were arrested by workers and brought, their faces blackened with soot, to Nagu Sayaji's Wadi, the communist stronghold in Prabhadevi. There, the communist leader, S. A. Dange, lectured them on the treachery which blacklegging involved. Dange was later arrested for his part in this episode, but was released on bail when the two workers failed to pick him out in an identity parade.[68]

Often, strike breakers suffered social boycotts. Their names, particularly those of collaborationist head jobbers, were read out at strike meetings. Indeed, during the general strike of 1940, these lists of names were sent in with so much enthusiasm that it embarrassed the leadership. The secretary of the Council of Action for the conduct of the strike, R. S. Nimbkar, had to advise speakers not to read out these names as they were not always correct and 'were sent sometimes on account of personal grudge.'[69] Men and women going to their mills were taunted. Strikers would, it was said, call out to somebody on his way to a mill: 'He is a *malik*'s son, that is why he is going so faithfully to work.' Such action, said Kandalkar, presenting hostile evidence against the communists who had jockeyed him out of power by the late 1930s, 'no doubt caused some embarrassment to the workers who were going in for work . . . being put to shame in the presence of their brother workmen naturally annoyed them.'[70] That moral pressure could be effective emphasizes the ambiguity inherent in the behaviour of some 'blacklegs'. Although the effect of working during a strike was clearly to contribute to its defeat, it would be misleading to assume that when workers crossed the picket lines they simply signified total opposition to industrial action, or revealed thereby an undeveloped social consciousness. Several contradictory pressures, both moral and material, for as well as against action, operated throughout the conduct of a strike and governed workers' options. Indeed, it was for this reason that moral pressure, which often

[67] BRIC, oral evidence, S. K. Bole, file 3, p. 247, MSA.
[68] MCC, statement by S. A. Dange, pp. 2447–8.
[69] Commissioner of Police, Bombay, Daily Report, 6 April 1940 in GOB, Home (sp) file 550 (23) C-I of 1940, p. 83, MSA.
[70] BDEC, evidence, Girni Kamgar Union, Bombay (Kandalkar) in GOB, Home (sp) file 550 (25) III of 1938, p. 431, MSA.

entailed some degree of physical coercion as well, could be effective at all: it found an ideological resonance in the public morality of the neighbourhood.

At the same time, moral pressure and public embarrassment, however effective, were not always enough. Throughout the 1930s, communist leaflets highlighted the causes of unemployment and argued the case for an identity of interest in the long term between the jobless and the workers in an attempt to deter 'blacklegs', while maintaining a steady, moralizing attack against 'blacklegging'.[71] Notions of morality and justice—or more clearly injustice—infused the most direct and physical forms of public pressure. At a meeting called to propagate the one-day strike of 1938, Lalji Pendse said that 'some goondas have beaten our volunteers' and called upon those children of workers who trained at gymnasiums to 'teach a good lesson to these dadas.'[72] Towards the last stages of the 1940 general strike, the Council of Action of the Bombay Provincial Trades Union Congress had to deal with the exertions of Mane Master. At a meeting on 31 March 1940 a communist worker, Khaire, said that,

Mane Master was defaming the Marathas and blackening the face of the Great Shivaji by conducting on the one hand the Shivaji Gymnasium at Bhoiwada and on the other hand trying to break the strike. This Mane Master who was a member of the Maratha League had blackened the face of the Marathas and was himself a blot on Maratha society and as such they should break his legs.[73]

It was sometimes necessary as well as possible for strikers actively to picket particular neighbourhoods, road junctions and even inside their chawls. For instance, during the 1938 strikes Madanpura was picketed so effectively that the Simplex Mill reported that its 'jobbers complained that they were not allowed to leave the moholla.' The experience of the Simplex Mill was by no means exceptional; workers from the New Great Eastern Mills, who lived in Kamathipura, and from the Madhavji Dharamsi Mills suffered a similar fate.[74] The efficacy of such action depended upon the particular political circumstances of each neighbourhood. As S. K. Patil, the brain behind Congress organization in Bombay city in the 1930s and general secretary of the Bombay Provin-

---

[71] See leaflets collected in GOB, Home (sp) file 543 (46) of 1934 and 543 (46) pt I of 1934, MSA.
[72] BDEC, confidential statement submitted by the Bombay Millowners' Association in GOB Home (sp) file 550 III of 1938, p. 315, MSA.
[73] Commissioner of Police, Bombay, Daily Reports, 1 April 1940 in GOB, Home (sp) file 550 (23) C-I of 1940, p. 21, MSA.
[74] BDEC, confidential statement submitted by the BMOA, Annexure B-I in GOB, Home (sp) file 550 (25) III of 1938, pp. 317–43, MSA.

cial Congress Committee, explained it, not all strikes or meetings could
be broken:

the breaking activities can succeed only in certain areas. Even in the labour
area, there are spheres of influence. If you go to a sphere other than your own, it
is easier for them to break up a meeting, because they have a larger following
round about. That is not possible everywhere.[75]

The fact that several mills of the Sassoon group continued to work on 7
November 1938 was attributed to perhaps the most significant dada in
Bombay between the wars, and a Congressman, Keshav Borkar. 'The
peculiarity about those mills,' said Deputy Commissioner of Police,
U'ren,

is that they are in the area which is looked after by Keshav Borkar. He was
naturally against the strike . . . . It is quite obvious that by virtue of the fact that
he holds sway in that area, the Red Flag Union did not think that they could get
much success there . . . . The mere fact that he was the headman of that area, I
think, was sufficient for the Red Flag volunteers not to bother with that area.[76]

The balance of power in the streets was clearly a crucial factor in
determining the geography, and sometimes even the possibility, of
political action.

Another common response to the structure of control which workers
had to face was to impose pressure at the most vulnerable point of most
strikes: the jobber. In 1928, strike breaking jobbers were hounded out of
their neighbourhoods. S. D. Saklatwalla of the Tata group of mills
informed the Fawcett Committee that one jobber had 'to change his
place of residence twice because they [workers] once found that he had
entered the mill and . . . they were therefore persecuting him. He said he
changed his residence although he had to pay increased rent.'[77] In one
case reported in 1938, Jaysingrao Bajirao, a head jobber of the winding
department related how during the one-day strike of 7 November,
workers waited in batches of ten to twenty until 11 p.m. at night 'in
order to assault me if I ventured to go out of the mill gate.'[78]

It was because workers were often most effective in political action
beyond the workplace that the millowners preferred the state to
intervene in the conduct rather than the settlement of strikes: for

[75] BDEC, oral evidence, S. K. Patil in GOB, Home (sp) file 550 (25) III B of 1938, p.
401, MSA.
[76] BDEC, oral evidence, Mr U'ren, Deputy Commissioner of Police in GOB, Home
(sp) file 550 (25) III B of 1938, pp. 681-3, MSA.
[77] Bombay Strike Enquiry Committee. 1928-29, Proceedings [henceforth BSEC],
vol. I, p. 121, MSA.
[78] BDEC, oral evidence, Jayasingrao Bajirao in GOB, Home (sp) file 550 (25) III B of
1938, p. 553; see also the evidence of Dhaku Janu Lad, p. 105, MSA.

instance by deploying the police to prevent picketing not only at the mill gates but also in the neighbourhood.[79] Ten years later, the millowners continued to argue a similar case: but more explicitly and with increased vehemence. During general strikes, 'the collection of crowds in streets and thoroughfares near the mills should certainly be prevented', urged the Bombay Millowners' Association, 'as otherwise free access by employees to their place of employment becomes impossible.' Such access was a necessary precondition for taking blacklegs into the workplace and maintaining production. Preferably, they argued, pickets 'should be confined to peaceful conversational persuasion and they should not be permitted to shout slogans or use abusive language or better still they should not be allowed to speak at all.' They were particularly emphatic that picketing at the workers' 'place of residence' should be made a criminal offence, for 'it is precisely this type of picketing that is most desirable to prevent.'[80]

The intimidation of 'ordinary workers' by 'strikers' often explained to the millowners as well as the Home Department why political agitators and their allies were able to shut down their mills. Clearly, intimidation by itself did not explain the solidarity of a strike, as, for instance, the Bombay Millowners' Association believed it did;[81] at the same time without 'intimidation' it was impossible at times to conduct a strike. In public discourse, intimidation simply meant that union bullies threatened to beat those who went to work. Undoubtedly, the sanction of physical force lay behind most forms of 'political' pressure in the neighbourhood. But intimidation was not conducted only by such 'professional' groups. It was more usual for workers who favoured a strike to act in their own chawls to prevent their fellow residents from going to work. Since their own jobs were in the balance, it is unlikely that their actions needed to be instigated or organized for them. One jobber described the working methods of those who canvassed for the 1938 strike: 'Usually five or ten men are real workers, they approach people but these five or ten people are followed by a large crowd.'[82] When union bullies acted successfully in their self-conscious role as bullies, they appear to have done so with the aid and approval of the chawl.

As intimidation became a subject for public debate, workers began to

[79] BMOA, *Annual Report*, 1928, Chairman's speech, AGM, p. iii.

[80] BDEC, BMOA answers to the questionnaire in GOB, Home (sp) file 550 (25) III of 1938 pp. 141–5, MSA.

[81] BMOA, *Annual Report*, 1928, Chairman's speech, AGM, pp. v–vii; BMOA, *Annual Report*, 1933, Chairman's speech, AGM, p. v.

[82] BDEC, oral evidence of Dhaku Janu Lad, in GOB, Home (sp) file 550 (25) III B of 1938, p. 105, MSA.

use it to their own advantage. One millowner told the Bombay Riots Inquiry Committee, 'I have had certain talks with groups of work people, and I have questioned them: "Why don't you come forward and report these people [who intimidate] to the police?" They say "if we do so, we are marked men." '[83] However, there was an underside to the picture presented by the employers and the state. As N. M. Joshi argued, workers used intimidation as an excuse to remain on strike. 'It may be that there was intimidation on your part,' he told S. D. Saklatwalla, during their negotiations after the 1928 strike, 'and so the men could not tell you the truth.'[84] Similarly, K. F. Nariman, the populist Congress leader, pointed out that the intimidation of which workers claimed to be the victims was often fictional. 'Sometimes what happens is this', said Nariman,

The mill hands do not want to go to work for reasons which they believe exist. When somebody on behalf of the millowners asks them 'Why don't you go?' they have not got the courage to say that they do not want to come [to work]. They say that they are intimidated and so we [sic] do not come. They narrate their grievances to the Union. If anybody who commands their confidence asks them the question they would narrate their grievances.[85]

By pleading intimidation as their excuse for industrial action, workers attempted to establish their bona fides as loyal employees and thus to ensure they were given back their jobs.

We have already seen that workers could exert some pressure on their jobbers in a variety of ways and it was by no means customary for its culmination to be violent. Although there was no positively definable point at which the jobber's position would be entirely rejected, it was essential for him to bend with the political temper of the mill district, to know when he should act with the workers and when he should act against them. It was particularly in the face of mass action, effectively orchestrated by a powerful trade union, and extending to more than a single mill, that the limits of a jobber's power were exposed, and that employers appeared vulnerable without the physical potency of the state. In periods of working-class solidarity, the jobber's opposition or his participation in victimization could lead to the desertion of his men, moral opprobrium from the community and the severance of the social and commercial ties upon which his position rested. At such times, working-class action to neutralize hostile neighbourhood alliances of all kinds was most successful. It is not intended to suggest that the ability of

[83] BRIC, oral evidence, J. Addyman, file I, p. 85, MSA.
[84] BSEC, vol. I, p. 122, MSA.
[85] BRIC, oral evidence of K. F. Nariman, file 6, p. 89, MSA.

Bombay's workers to resist their employers or shackle their neighbour-hood leaders was by any means equal or uniform. Their place within the material as well as the muscular structure of the neighbourhood registered differences between workers; some were plainly better equipped than others to absorb or counter their antagonists. Nor can it be said that there was any linear development in the balance of power between the 'forces' for or against the labour movement, let alone that these forces in their entirety remained consistently on either side of the divide. Clearly, the success of the Girni Kamgar Union enabled it in 1928 and 1934 decisively to alter the existing political balances of the neighbourhood, and it was probably the case that working-class action was in general most effective when the union was able both to protect workers at the mill and coordinate their action in the neighbourhood.

The permanent social relations of the workplace, and of the industry, pushed strikes which began within the limits of the workplace into the wider arena of the neighbourhood. As workers attempted to cope with the limits which this structure of control imposed upon them, para-doxically their actions acquired an important political edge. Conven-tionally, we should consider a strike, as a form of industrial or even political action, as an event which related directly to the workplace and concerned particular groups of workers. However, as industrial action was forced into the public sphere, into the streets and neighbourhoods, the effects of industrial disputes were generalized. In this wider context, the parochial disputes of a mill or a group of mills were placed before the mill district as a whole. By being placed in the wider arena of the working-class neighbourhood, each individual strike became an essen-tial part of the collective experience of Bombay's workers. As a result, the apparently limited nature of industrial disputes became essential to the process by which the social experience and the social consciousness of the working class as a whole was forged.

IV

It has already been argued that the social exchange of the neighbour-hoods shaped the perceptions of Bombay's workers and influenced the forms of industrial action. But its ramifications were wider still. It exercised an important influence upon the character of workers' politics in the public domain. From the late 1920s onwards, the communist-led Girni Kamgar Union became the dominant force in the politics of the mill district. Not only was the GKU the only union to achieve a more or less permanent presence in industrial politics but it also led every general strike in the industry after 1928. Throughout much of this period, it was subjected to considerable repression by the state. In the early 1930s, the Bombay Millowners' Association withdrew its recognition of the union; in 1934, along with other communist organizations it was declared illegal. As a result, the Girni Kamgar Union was at times incapacitated. But it was a measure of its achievement that although it was subjected to severe repression and its members to victimization and disfavour, it was repeatedly able to reassert its ascendancy. 'Had it not been for certain measures', the police commissioner admitted in 1935, referring to the Meerut arrests and the passing of such repressive legislation as the Criminal Law Amendment Act and the Bombay Special Emergency Powers Act, 'the communists would no doubt have become a positive danger by this time.' For, although its activities 'have been paralysed to a great extent by the internment of active communists . . . [and] they have comparatively few leaders and organisers . . . the subterranean activities of the Communists are not effectively kept in check by the measures adopted by the Government from time to time.'[86] As late as 1940, Bombay was still considered the 'nerve centre of Communist agitation in India.'[87] Not only did the communists survive this repression, but they also succeeded in creating an active political tradition: in the 1930s, their office became a landmark in the mill district and rival unions competed to adopt the name of the Girni Kamgar Union.[88]

The spread of support for the communists reflected changes that were occurring within the political culture of the working-class neighbourhoods, changes which were the outcome of growing conflicts, both in the workplace and outside. In the process, tensions within the working class and between mill workers were exposed. It is not intended to suggest that the intervention of the communists heralded the dawn of working-class unity. However, it is also clear that from the late 1920s onwards, an impressive community of political sentiment formed around the communists. As Syed Munawar, the 'moderate' trade union leader, said in 1929, 'Communistic principles have captured the minds of textile workers to a great extent in the Parel area.'[89] For the mill workers in particular, the Girni Kamgar Union created the possibility of a sustained political expression.

[86] Commissioner of Police, Bombay, to Secretary, GOB, Home (sp) Secret no. 3757 B, 8 August 1935 in GOB, Home (sp) file 543 (77) of 1935, p. 77, MSA.
[87] Departmental note in GOB, Home (sp) file 543 (42) of 1940, p. 16, MSA.
[88] During the 1930s, three unions adopted this name.
[89] BRIC, oral evidence, Syed Munawar, file 3, p. 267, MSA.

The place which the communists came to occupy in the mill district was partly the result of the nature of their intervention in industrial politics. It has already been argued that material conditions as well as the employer's policies made workers' combinations vulnerable at the workplace. This meant that trade unions had to maintain an effective presence in the neighbourhood; at the same time, it also meant that they were excluded from the area of the daily social relations of the workplace and forced to operate often at a level removed from the thrust of working-class action.

The tension between trade union organization at the level of the individual mill and at the level of the whole industry was crucial to the determination of the politics of the textile industry. The system of labour control based upon the jobber, worked best at the most parochial level. At this level, what mattered was the extent to which jobbers, acting within the context of the neighbourhood as a whole, were able to resist or incorporate pressures from the workforce. At this level, too, trade unions were most easily rendered ineffective. As long as a significant proportion of jobbers and workers were not connected with a particular union, there was little need for the employer to recognize its existence, and even when a trade union acquired any considerable influence amongst his workers, an employer could discipline or at worst dismiss some of them as a warning to the rest. It was at a more general level that trade unions operated, making alliances with jobbers and then representing their case to management, to the Millowners' Association and to government when necessary. Significantly, the first trade unions in Bombay were essentially pleaders' offices where grievances were heard and services, such as the writing of leave notices and the drafting of petitions, were provided.[90] Yet, to operate successfully at this more general level, it was obviously essential to establish more than an ephemeral presence at the workplace.

The major problem which trade unions faced was their inability to act at both levels. Most trade unions were constrained by this intermediary position. As intermediaries who built upon their jobber and neighbourhood connections, they were better placed to mediate in the workers' disputes than to lead them. Trade unions, like the Kamgar Hitwardhak Sabha, the Social Service League and the Bombay Textile Labour Union never became company unions, but nor were they free to champion the workers' cause. Following the momentum of workers' action could bring them directly into conflict with jobbers and other

[90] See Confidential Proceedings of the Government of Bombay, 1917, vol. 25, pp. 15–19, IOL.

neighbourhood patrons. It could also invoke the displeasure of the state and of the employers, whose benevolence and trust was vital to their political survival. For it was their influence in ruling circles which made these unions valuable allies for the workers and the lesser leaders of the neighbourhood. 'Had the millowners been a little more sympathetic towards the Union,' the representatives of the BTLU mused upon the fate of their own organization, 'the success it had achieved would have been more substantial and the Union would not have required to go through the agonies it went through after the 1928 strike.' It was 'only recently', the union argued in the aftermath of the communist-led strikes of 1928 and 1929, 'when an undesirable element has entered the trade union fold that the employers have begun to talk in terms of sympathy towards the unions.'[91] Their political alliances inhibited them in advancing the workers' interests and thereby also restricted their membership. At least, by force of habit, these unions were better placed to act as advocates when they had no clients than as spokesmen when they had no audience.

Not only their material interests but also their conception of their own role in relation to workers limited the efficacy of their leadership. Organizations like the Kamgar Hitwardhak Sabha and the Social Service League were concerned mainly with social work and the 'uplift' of the poor. They were, as the Labour Office reported, less trade unions than 'associations for the welfare of their members.'[92] Their aim was to rescue workers from the depths of ignorance. In response to low wages, they suggested more education; as a solution to bad housing conditions, they tried to teach workers hygiene; faced with poverty they advocated thrift. Their strength lay in speaking on behalf of the poor; in active struggle, they often disintegrated.

It is against this background that the intervention of the communists in the labour movement in 1927–28 was significant. It marked a radical transformation in the style and content of trade union leadership. The communists entered the labour movement in 1927 through the Girni Kamgar Mahamandal, a trade union founded and organized by jobbers and mill clerks during the 1924 general strike. Since 1927, rationalization schemes had been introduced into certain mills. Although their object was efficiency, these schemes increased workloads, created the possibility of greater unemployment and induced among the mill

[91] *RCLI*, evidence, I, i, written evidence, the Bombay Textile Labour Union, p. 353. The outcome of these agonies was that by 1931 the Union's membership figure stood at 56 and was to fall further to 20 in 1938; see *Labour Gazette*, 'Principal trade unions in the Bombay Presidency', *passim*.

[92] *Labour Gazette*, vol. II, no. 7, March 1923, p. 26.

workers 'a genuine fear of less wages.'[93] As strikes followed these changes in work practices from mill to mill, it became apparent that individual resistance, however determined, was doomed. As N. M. Joshi put it later, 'a strike in one mill does not and will not succeed. If there is discontent on a large scale there must be a general strike. Then only the grievances have some chance of being redressed.'[94] Between August 1927 and April 1928, strikes occurred in 24 mills.[95] Under the impact of this political determination among the workers, the leadership of the labour movement vacillated.

The only significant pressure in favour of a general strike came from the communists; but they were still incapable of carrying the Girni Kamgar Mahamandal with them. To lead a strike when the workers' mood was militant offered the communists an invaluable opportunity of establishing organization among the workers. Moreover, unlike the other unions, the communists of the Bombay Labour Group had two advantages. First, they attributed a positive value to industrial action, for larger purposes than the immediate conflict, in developing the political and revolutionary consciousness of the working class. At the same time, their enthusiasm was not as yet weighted down by neighbourhood or even jobber connections which they would have to defend. The Girni Kamgar Mahamandal and the Bombay Textile Labour Union, on the other hand, with more established political connections were hesitant to risk their linkages in a strike liable to fail. As the strike wave spread across the mill district, both groups were faced with the danger of being outflanked by the communists. Tensions between the two rival courses of action dominated the affairs of both these unions. By March 1928, the Girni Kamgar Mahamandal divided and one of its founders, Mayekar, was expelled in a dispute over the control of funds.[96] 'What happened in this strike,' as Dange said later, 'was that the rank and file was forcing the lead on the organisation.'[97] This general strike lasted for six months. The intensity of class consciousness which was expressed in the period was never perhaps to be repeated.

The linkages which were forged in this strike placed the communists firmly in control of the GKM and enabled them to dominate trade union politics. They were now forced to confront the problems posed by the structure of industrial relations. The initiative taken by the

[93] Departmental note in GOB, Home (sp) file 543 (10) E Pt D of 1929, p. 25, MSA.
[94] BSEC, vol. I, p. 71, MSA.
[95] MCC, statement submitted by S. A. Dange, pp. 2413–15.
[96] MCC, examination of Arjun A. Alwe, p. 961; BPP, SAI, 1928, no. 20, 19 May, para. 793; GOB, Home (sp) file 543 (18) C of 1928, MSA.
[97] MCC, statement submitted by S. A. Dange, p. 2424.

communist leadership in reflecting working-class militancy enabled them to establish their political presence at the level of the industry as a whole. To consolidate this support, it was imperative for the Girni Kamgar Union, as it was now called, to penetrate the level of the individual mill. This was precisely what occurred in the following months. The general strike of 1928 had ended on the basis of an agreement that the rationalization schemes would not be extended until the committee of inquiry appointed to investigate the dispute had reported. Between October 1928 and March 1929, 71 lightning strikes occurred as mill workers resisted victimization or zealously ensured that the agreement was not breached. The Girni Kamgar Union's intervention in these disputes had, as Dange put it, a 'magical' effect upon organization.[98] On 30 September 1928, the Girni Kamgar Union had a membership of 324; by the end of that year, they boasted 54,000 members.[99] The organizational achievement of this period was the mill committees which sprang up throughout the industry. Workers from each department elected representatives to the mill committee. At the same time, the Girni Kamgar Union opened several centres within the mill area for the enrolment of members and the collection of subscriptions, but especially to establish and extend connections with the workers of their neighbourhoods. These centres supervised the work of mill committees in their area. The members of a mill committee would contact their centre as soon as a dispute arose in their department or their mill. Each centre elected a committee, which in turn elected a managing committee for the Union as a whole and to whose decisions it remained subordinate. The committee of each centre was elected by the most effective unit of the union machine: the mill committee.[100]

The representatives elected onto the mill committee were responsible for the organizational tasks of the union in their department. They enrolled members and collected subscriptions; they acted as watchdogs of the workers' interests; they formulated grievances and approached management to negotiate settlements; and if this brought them no joy, they approached the union, or more frequently in practice, proceeded to strike. In this way, they brought the union to that microcosmic level of the individual mill and department from which it had so effectively been excluded in the past. While it was their ability to intervene at this microcosmic level which enabled the Girni Kamgar Union to gain such

[98] *Ibid.*, p. 2507.

[99] *Report of the Court of Inquiry into a Trade Dispute Between Several Textile Mills and their Workmen* (Bombay, 1929), p. 11.

[100] See BRIC, oral evidence, file 5, Milton Kubes, pp. 209–13, MSA.; see also MCC, statement submitted by S. A. Dange, pp. 2498–537.

formidable support and create such an extensive organization, it was precisely their strength across the industry as a whole which prevented the millowners from excluding them from the politics of the workplace. 'We are helpless,' complained Sir Manmohandas Ramji in 1929, 'If we dismiss a man who is a member of that union, the question of victimization comes in, and we create a strike. If today my mill is working partially and I suspect a man who belongs to that union and try to dismiss him, there will be a strike next morning.'[101] The strength of the Girni Kamgar Union across the industry enabled it to protect its members as well as advance their interests at the level of the mill.

The mill committees linked, and operated at the junction of, the workplace, the neighbourhood, the mill and the trade union head-quarters. But the mill committees of 1928–29 did more than this—they also became 'parallel organs of supervision and control' in rivalry with the jobber and constraining his freedom of action. In 1928–29, they sometimes seemed to give substance to Dange's claim that the Girni Kamgar Union 'overthrew the power of the jobbers and the head jobbers.'[102] Through the mill committees, workers gained access to the union offices. The result was to give meaning to the union as an alternative source of patronage, extending from the workplace and the neighbourhood to the union headquarters, which operated at a level well beyond the jobber's reach. Their presence forced jobbers to choose between making an alliance with the union to preserve their position with the workers and risk managerial disfavour, or else to ally with the management to break the mill committee and isolate the union. As the union penetrated the workplace, it brought new complexities to bear upon the jobber's function of labour control.

However much the mill committees checked the jobber's power in the short term, it did not, contrary to Dange's claim, overthrow him.[103] At times the union leadership even found itself attempting to defend the jobber against the opposition of workers. At a public meeting to elect the mill committee for the Kohinoor mill, on 24 November 1928, one section of the workers pressed for the exclusion of the head jobber of the weaving department and his six men. Dange and Alwe advocated restraint: they argued that it would not be practical to exclude men of influence, especially those who had the backing of their department. They suggested a compromise in the form of a resolution to warn that those who opposed the majority opinion of the mill committee or ignored

[101] BRIC, oral evidence, file 2, Sir M. M. Ramji, p. 367, MSA.
[102] MCC, statement submitted by S. A. Dange, p. 2514.
[103] *Ibid.*

union policies would be removed.[104] To attack the jobber, it was clear, the union would have to proceed with care. In the short term, it was arguably sufficient and perhaps only possible, to constrain him. The mill committee could not overthrow the jobber; but their failure meant that as the union's position across the industry weakened, the jobbers were able to reassert themselves.

In 1929, the Girni Kamgar Union, by leading another general strike, built upon the momentum established in the previous year and then exhausted it. Already, the arrests and imprisonment of its most important leaders created chaos in the union's organization. In 1930, G. L. Kandalkar, its new president, declared his support for the Congress and carried an important section of the union into the nationalist fold. In the face of growing unemployment in the industry, the millworkers' militancy was seemingly diluted. As the overarching trade union organization grew weaker, its relationship with the mill committees grew more tenuous. The weakening of the bond between the mill committee and the union or a decline in the activism of the union made it easier for the jobber to turn the mill committee into yet another institution around which to consolidate his power. However, where they survived, mill committees formed a core of shopfloor organization, through which the Girni Kamgar Union could rehabilitate itself.

To some extent, the organizational basis of 1928–29 was revived during the strike wave of 1933–34; moreover, it was diversified and extended more formally to the neighbourhood. The Millowners' Association emphasized the vital role of the union's chawl committees in the conduct of the general strike of 1934.[105] In December 1937, the police noted the fact that the organization of the union integrated both workplace and neighbourhood. 'They have gone to great trouble,' it was reported, 'to establish "communist cells" in mills and industrial concerns, and in addition they have appointed Chawl Committees to influence the workers still further.'[106] Although the communists could not re-create their achievement of 1928–29, these changes enabled them to absorb the growing repressive pressures at the workplace and, at the same time, to maintain their presence in the neighbourhood.

The reassertion of the communist ascendancy out of the doldrums of the early 1930s occurred through industrial action, in the strike wave of 1933–34. This militancy forced choices upon workers, jobbers as well as

[104] MCC, vol. 10, Marathi Exhibits, Girni Kamgar Union Minute Book, Public Meetings, pp. 6–7.
[105] BDEC, evidence, extract from monthly report of the Labour Officer, BMOA, August 1935, in GOB, Home (sp) file 550 (25) III, of 1938, p. 181, MSA.
[106] GOB, HD (sp) file 546 (13) B (1) of 1937–38, p. 7, MSA.

other trade unions. In 1934, when the communists attempted to persuade the Council of Action, composed of the representatives of several unions, to support a general strike, 'quasi-communists such as Alwe and Abdul Majid felt they had to come in or be pushed aside' and the Royists 'in order not to lose such influence with the workers as they had, felt impelled to join in and pose as communists.'[107] That the communists were able to exert such pressure on the other unions in 1934 suggests the extent of their recovery. That they recovered at all was due to the powerful base and the political sympathy they had created in 1928–29.

It was probably their stance of continued opposition to the employers and the state which established for the communists their place within the political culture of the neighbourhood. The communists came to be identified as the only political group untainted by their association with the state, for instance by nominations to provincial and central legislatures, to royal commissions, and even to ILO conferences. This enabled the communists to present themselves as the one political group in the labour movement which acted in the interests of the working class alone. When asked why the Girni Kamgar Mahamandal had permitted the communists to enter and work in the union although it had recently rejected the leadership of the 'outsiders' of the Bombay Textile Labour Union, Arjun Alwe, President of the GKM, replied: 'we believed to be true the fellow-feeling which they exhibited towards the workers.'[108] After 1928, the communists' exertions in the workplace and neighbourhood served to confirm, at least for some workers, this assessment.

Between the wars, the state intervened increasingly in the working-class neighbourhoods. The effect of this intervention was not universally to antagonize workers. Legislation was passed to protect trade unions and govern working conditions, to grant maternity benefits and to provide compensation for injuries and even to ensure the prompt payment of wages. The police were known to arbitrate in labour disputes and occasionally even to ensure the payment of overdue wages.[109] In practice, however, there was little life in the new legislation; and the police, the most immediate point of contact between workers and the state, appeared increasingly as the most organized of the repressive forces which confronted the working class. Indeed, police action during strikes defeated pickets and aided blacklegs and in the

[107] W. R. G. Smith, Commissioner of Police to R. M. Maxwell, Secretary, GOB, Home (sp), no. 3035 L, 20 June 1935, in GOB, Home (sp) file 543 (48) L, pp. 99–101, MSA.
[108] MCC, examination of Arjun A. Alwe, 12 August 1931, p. 972.
[109] See, for instance, Edwardes, *Bombay City Police*, Appendix, p. 197.

process contributed to the suppression of workers' demands and the destruction of their organizations.

Moreover, as conflicts between national and imperial interests were increasingly articulated in the political domain, they helped to clarify the relationship between the workers and the state. During and immediately after the first world war, the living conditions of most workers, characterized by rising prices, high rents and general scarcities, worsened considerably. Grain prices rose almost immediately after the war began, and the government had to take active measures to prevent food riots. The opening of labour camps in Dadar in 1917 and the work of military recruiting officers led to considerable tension within the working-class neighbourhoods of Bombay.[110] The impact of the first world war upon workers was to reveal to them that the Indian economy was 'now influenced by international factors.'[111] Imperialism signified another force which governed their conditions of life but over which they had no control. Several factors clarified these perceptions. First, the millowners were closely identified with the social rituals of a foreign ruling class. Second, the nationalist campaigns of 1917–22 stirred people's minds and involved a racial self-assertion. It could affect the way in which workers related to their Anglo-Indian and Parsi supervisors who were closely associated with the British rulers. Third, the economic campaigns of their employers also sharpened the lines of conflict between Indian workers and an imperial state. Indeed, at certain points, the state appeared to be the cause of their worsening economic conditions and of their industry's problems.

Although the millowners were perceived by the workers as being socially associated with this ruling imperial culture, their attempts to confront the long-term depression in the industry's fortunes brought them into conflict with the state. When the Government of India refused to abolish the excise duty on Indian mill production, the Bombay millowners cut wages by eleven and a half per cent. This wage cut led to a general strike. Indeed, when in the face of the threat of prolonged working-class action, the Government abolished the excise duty, the millowners restored the wage cut. Similar connections between the economic policies of the colonial state and the worsening conditions of the industry and its workers were made by the capitalist class during its

[110] 'Statement relating to the disturbances in the City of Bombay in April 1919', in Bombay Confidential Proceedings, 1920, vol. 53, pp. 13–27 IOL; 'A Report from the Commissioner of Police, Bombay to the Government of Bombay Concerning Political Developments before and during 1919' in Curry Papers, Box IV, item nos 54 and 55, Centre of South Asian Studies, Cambridge; BPP, SAI, 1917, no. 29, 21 July para. 794.
[111] MCC, statement submitted by S. A. Dange, p. 2404.

currency campaign of 1927–28. Within the labour movement it appeared as if both the Government of India and the capitalists were arguing opposite cases while professing the interests of the working class, and that both posed as the guardians of labour in order to promote their own particular interests. It was said that while the government's case for a higher exchange ratio rested upon the contention that a lower ratio would depreciate wages and lead to serious strikes, the capitalists argued that in order to function at the higher ratio they would be forced to reduce wages.

It was not merely at one remove that workers were forced into confrontation with the state. Their economic struggles also brought them into political arenas. In the immediate post-war period, a pattern of resistance and surrender to wage demands had established itself. Its consequence was to make the power of combination and the effectiveness of industrial action increasingly clear. During the 1920s, as the millowners organized across the industry to influence the policies of the state, their Association began to affect the management of individual mills. As the level of the individual mill and the industry were integrated, workers, too, had to act across the industry to press their demands. As strike activity occurred on a larger scale, negotiations were conducted at more elevated levels. The mill manager no longer conducted the case for the management alone; the centralizing initiatives of the Millowners' Association became increasingly important. The state intervened less through the office of the police commissioner and increasingly from Government House. The mutuality of workers' interests became more evident and their conflicts with the state occurred at new levels. A general strike, a matter of industrial politics, could entail visible forms of class confrontation: from the police escorting blacklegs across the picket lines to the work of an arbitration court headed by a High Court judge or a civil servant, whose rulings were perceived to be unjust.

To a large extent, the political experience of the working class was constituted in relation to the state; this relationship in turn influenced the development of their political consciousness. For instance, the police impinged upon the conduct of a strike in various ways. During the general strike of 1928, police reporters attended workers' meetings; policemen supervised pickets at the mill gates and attempts were made to restrict their number to two;[112] and when picketing was carried into the neighbourhoods, the police presence extended to the chawls as well. At a meeting at the communist stronghold of Nagu Sayaji's Wadi in Parel on

[112] *Ibid.*, pp. 2438–9; BRIC, oral evidence, K. F. Nariman, p. 87, MSA.

1 June 1928, according to the police reporter's account, Dange reminded his audience, 'the police have no right to come to your room without a warrant. . . . Even if he comes in the room with uniform but is not armed with a warrant, you can consider him a thief. . . . You must protect your own chawl.'[113] The opinion was being more readily expressed that, in general, the police had shown greater solicitude for the millowners than for the strikers.[114] For many people, the police came to represent not the guardians of the law but the long arm of tyranny. 'Many things are not reported to the police out of fear,' said one observer, who also noted that 'Hindus . . . always avoid to go to the courts and police.'[115]

The Borkar riot which occurred on 11 December 1928 in support of the communist leaders, two months after the general strike had officially ended, showed how in a single moment the levels of neighbourhood and industrial and public politics could be combined. The origins of the riot dated back to the split within the old Girni Kamgar Mahamandal in March 1928, when Mayekar was expelled from the union. Finding his old bases of support being pulled away from under him, Mayekar came to lean upon his friendship with Keshav dada Borkar, gymnasium owner and neighbourhood boss of Ghorapdeo. Borkar's terrain at Ghorapdeo became Mayekar's last refuge. Throughout 1928, Mayekar now isolated within the labour movement opposed the communists with the help of Borkar, and attempted on several occasions to break up their meetings. 'For six months and more,' reported Horniman's *Indian National Herald*, 'the leaders of the communist led Girni Kamgar Union were repeatedly disturbed by his unwelcome presence which at once acted as a disintegrating factor on one section of the workers and an infuriating phenomenon on the other.'[116] The effect of Mayekar's intervention 'through his friend Borkar',[117] at several communist meetings was interpreted very differently by left-wing sympathizers and by the police. While the police commissioner reported that frequent complaints were received that they were 'seeking to stir up trouble at the communist meetings . . . but no serious clash occurred',[118] the *Indian National Herald*'s version was that the communist leaders 'went to the length of even dissolving crowded meetings', to avoid confrontation.

[113] GOB, Home (sp) file 543 (18) C of 1928, MSA.
[114] BRIC, oral evidence, W. T. Halai, file 5, p. 81, MSA.
[115] BRIC, file 6, oral evidence, Dr P. G. Solanki, p. 165; see also, file 16, oral evidence of G. L. Kandalkar and V. H. Joshi of the Girni Kamgar Union, pp. 65–7, MSA.
[116] *Indian National Herald*, 7 December 1928.
[117] Letter, Commissioner of Police, Bombay, to Secretary, GOB, Home, Bombay no. 5395 L, 13 December 1928, in GOB, Home (Poll) file 265 of 1928, MSA.
[118] *Ibid.*

Indeed, at practically every meeting the leaders exhorted the men to remain restrained in the face of provocation.[119] If the Mayekar–Borkar alliance had been able to create a riot, this would have provided the police with the kind of opportunity they sought to take further repressive action. During the strike, Mirajkar had told a strikers' meeting at Kalachowki on 2 August 1928 that

our strength lies in unity and peace. On Monday attempts are [sic] made to disturb our peace with the use of lathis. If they use their lathis we can also retaliate in the same way; but as we want to win the struggle, we must keep peace. If we disturb peace, lathis and guns will be used and under that threat they will try to put men into the mills. But our men are firm and they already know the knavery of the millowners. They [strikers] have already resolved not to fall prey to the hirelings of the millowners.[120]

On 11 December 1928, a message was received at the Girni Kamgar Union office, calling for their assistance in connection with a dispute at the David Sassoon Spinning and Manufacturing Mill at Ghorapdeo— the heart of Borkar's territory. The communist leader R. S. Nimbkar, P. T. Tamhanekar, Govind Kasale and a few others who went to investigate found the complaint to be false. As they left the mill, Nimbkar and his associates were set upon and attacked by Keshav Borkar and a gang of about 20 men. Complaints lodged at the local police station, however, 'of course failed to trace the assailants.'[121] The following morning workers from the David Sassoon, Morarji Gokuldas, Moon and Shapurji Broacha mills did not resume work, out of sympathy for their bruised leaders. At a meeting of the Girni Kamgar Union at Poibavdi that morning Kasale who had taken the brunt of the attack displayed his wounds. Clearly the temper of the meeting was highly charged. Plain clothes policemen in the crowd were identified and assaulted.[122] Within minutes, about 500 workers set off towards Borkar's house, 'with the intention presumably of settling accounts with him. He got intimation of their advance and left his house.'[123] By the time the crowd reached Borkar's house they were estimated to be more than three thousand strong. The contents of his house were pulled onto the street and a bonfire was lit. His furniture and cooking utensils were

[119] *Indian National Herald*, 7 December 1928. Mayekar, claimed the paper, only 'masquerades as a labour leader and is, in fact, alleged to be an agent of the Criminal Investigation Department.'

[120] GOB, Home (sp), file 543 (18) C of 1928, MSA.

[121] MCC, statement submitted by S. A. Dange, p. 2522.

[122] Telegram, Police Commissioner to Secretary, GOB, Home (sp) no. 5368 L, 12 December 1928 in GOB Home (Poll) file 265 of 1928, MSA.

[123] Letter, Commissioner of Police to Secretary, GOB, Home, Bombay no. 5395 L, 13 December 1928, in GOB, Home (Poll) file 265 of 1928, pp. 41–5, MSA.

damaged; the house was ransacked, the tiles on his roof were removed and thrown away; his gymnasium was wrecked.[124]

As the morning wore on, mill after mill was brought out on strike by workers who gathered at the gates and stoned the premises until those who had remained inside the mill were locked out by the management. The police were alerted and brought into action: the result was riot. By the time Inspector Klein of Bhoiwada Police Station met the crowd on Suparibagh Road, they were according to him armed with sticks, bamboos, iron rods, gymnastic paraphernalia and 'obviously bent on mischief'. With a small force and awaiting reinforcements, the police attempted to stop this crowd by throwing a cordon across the road. The result was that the police were routed. Crowds appeared from every direction and hemmed the police in on all sides, while 'stones were also being thrown from the rooms and windows of the neighbouring houses.' When Klein fired with his revolver, the crowd 'held back slightly but came on with renewed vigour.' The constables began to climb into the police lorry and Klein failed to 'force them to stand fast.'[125] His deputy was set upon by the crowd and badly beaten. Klein was forced to take refuge in a nearby building while 'the mob furiously attacked the house from outside.'[126] The police lorry had to be chased by Superintendent Spiers, who noticed it hurtling away from the action.[127] Spiers returned to the scene of action, fired into the crowd, 'drove the rioters helter-skelter off the roads', and rescued the brave if battered Klein.[128] However, several features of this riot must be noted. First, the nature of the police intervention had the opposite effect to what was intended: for instance, the attempt to stop the crowd with an ineffective cordon at first, and later by the show of a pistol, and an attempt by some constables to snatch away the red flag which some workers were carrying aggravated the situation.[129] Second, five workers died in the riot, four of them from bullet wounds. 'We must put an end to the idea prevailing in police circles,' one newspaper reporter wrote indignantly, 'that human life is so cheap that it can be wantonly destroyed on the slightest

[124] Report of H. C. Stokes, Inspector, Byculla Police Station, D. Division in GOB, Home (Poll) file 265 of 1928, pp. 13–15, MSA; *Times of India*, 21 December 1928.
[125] Report by Inspector Klein, Bhoiwada Police Station to Superintendent of Police, E. Division, Bombay in GOB, Home (Poll) file 265 of 1928, pp. 21–5, MSA.
[126] Letter of Commissioner of Police, Bombay, to Secretary, GOB, Home, Bombay no. 5395 L, 13 December 1928 in GOB, Home (Poll) file 265 of 1928, pp. 41–5, MSA.
[127] Report by W. D. R. Spiers, Superintendent, E. Division, in GOB, Home (Poll) file 265 of 1928, pp. 27–31, MSA.
[128] Letter Commissioner of Police, Bombay, to Secretary, GOB, Home, Bombay no. 5395 L, 13 December 1928 in GOB, Home (Poll) file 265 of 1928, pp. 41–5, MSA.
[129] *Indian National Herald*, 7 December 1928.

provocation.'[130] However, it must be taken as an indication of popular anger and determination that the crowd withstood considerable police firing and returned to counter attack, 'with renewed vigour.' Third, the 'mob' on the streets was neither undifferentiated nor, in its response, exceptional to working-class sentiment. As the police commissioner noted, 'I am told by the officers that the stones were being hurled not only by the rioters on the road, but by mill hands who were in the rooms of houses adjoining the road. These stones could not have been obtained on the road itself and it appears to me that the strikers were out yesterday for mischief and had brought the stones with them.'[131] Yet the scene of action—Suparibagh Road—was one of the main thoroughfares through the mill district. If we are to believe that 'this strike was mainly brought about by those (communist) leaders and was done very secretly and in a well organized way,' we must also believe that this conspiracy involved a vast proportion of the Bombay working class. Significantly, what began as an expression of protest on an impressive scale against the anti-union activities of Borkar and his men, culminated in a full-scale battle with the police.

While it was by supporting the militant tendencies within the neighbourhood, and through their apparent refusal to collaborate with employers and the state that the communists staked their claim to be the party of the working class, this claim was not always accepted. In the early 1930s, for instance, their refusal to associate with the Congress and their attempts to lead their constituents—exhausted by the strikes of 1928–29 and faced with the threat of unemployment—into battle once more cost the communists membership, neighbourhood allies as well as political sympathy. The support for the communists was not a simple fusion of shared antagonism towards the capitalist class and the state. Clearly, the Girni Kamgar Union brought to trade union politics a fresh concept of the conduct of working-class politics, and in contrast to the condescension of the vacuous sermons of improvement of the early labour organizations, a new concern with the daily issues of working-class life.[132] These departures in trade union leadership arose, in a sense, from necessity. Faced with exclusion at the level of the individual mill,

[130] Ibid.

[131] Letter, Commissioner of Police, Bombay, to Secretary, GOB, Home, Bombay no 5395 L, 13 December 1928 in GOB, Home (Poll) file 265 of 1928, p. 45, MSA.

[132] Their leaflets, fly-sheets and public meetings dealt with such questions as jobber tyranny, methods of wage calculations, the shortcomings of 'efficiency' schemes which increased workloads without improving machinery, the use of the rotation of shifts to weed out troublesome workers and the causes of unemployment. See, for instance, the communist fly-sheets and leaflets collected in GOB, Home (sp) file 543 (46) of 1934 and file 543 (46) Pt 1 of 1934, MSA.

the communists lacked the resources—essentially the good will of the state and the employers—to renew their linkages through patronage. To function as a trade union at all, the Girni Kamgar Union had to intervene energetically in the disputes of individual mills and build up enough support across the industry to prevent the employers from disregarding them. In one sense, the price of survival itself was militancy. However, this brought them into immediate conflict with the state. The conduct of a strike, which required organization and action in the neighbourhood, carried workers into public forms of confrontation and shaped their political consciousness.

*   *   *

'In recent times,' K. F. Nariman was to say in 1929, 'a new spirit of organization and class consciousness has come into existence among our labouring classes.'[133] But it is difficult to estimate the impact of this class consciousness upon other competing social identities amongst Bombay's workers. It would be misleading to suggest that the response of Bombay's workers to the growth of industrial action and the communist ascendancy in labour politics was in any sense uniform. The possibilities of action varied with their village connections, their position in the neighbourhood and their bargaining power in the workplace. For instance, weavers, working in the most profitable and rapidly growing sector of the industry, and protected by their level of skill, formed the most militant section of the workforce; while Mahars who manned the unskilled jobs in spinning departments or north Indian workers, whose lines of supply from their villages were weak, were more easily contained. The predominant cultural influence within the labour movement was exercised by Marathas from Ratnagiri and Satara. 'Labour activity in Bombay', Jhabvala was to say, considering his isolation, 'is largely Mahratta in its nature. The leaders must be conversant firstly with the Mahratta language, secondly with Mahratta habits of life and with a good deal of social outlook upon life that is Mahratta partly in its character.'[134] On the other hand, after 1929, Muslim workers were probably increasingly alienated from the labour movement in Bombay, partly no doubt as a consequence of increasing communal tension within national politics.

[133] *Times of India*, 8 August 1929.
[134] MCC, statements made by the accused, non-communist series, examination of S. H. Jhabvala, p. 756. This comment must also be read in the light that Jhabvala by his own admission 'knew very little Mahratti' and was, when he spoke these words, apparently isolated within the labour movement.

Many of these cultural differences were developed into political conflicts and sectarian rivalries by the actions of the employers and the state. As we have seen, the jobber system operated along the lines of these cultural divisions; it not only facilitated strike breaking but also could, if necessary, enable employers to replace one group of workers with those of another caste or religion. Indeed, the communal riots of 1929 began during a strike when Hindu workers tried to stop Muslims from going to work.[135] It is probable that industrialization, far from dissolving caste, strengthened its bonds. The cotton textile industry did not depend upon the perpetuation of these bonds, but it profited greatly from their use. Caste should, therefore, be seen less as a cultural condition whose primacy was being challenged by the emergence of 'class' than another important tension embedded within a class context.

This essay has attempted to depict a network of social relationships out of which the working class experience was formed. It was in the neighbourhood that the classic picture of the Indian working class, bound immutably by their changeless past, their powerless present and their hopeless future was most apparent. Yet the neighbourhood, which was integral to the relationships of the workplace, became an important base for industrial and political action. It was here, where tensions within the working class were played out, that the solidarities of class also received their most public expression.

[135] Memorandum by Director of Information, Government of Bombay, 3 May 1929 in GOB, Home (Poll) file 344 of 1929, pp. 113–15, MSA.

Modern Asian Studies, **15**, 3 (1981), pp. 649–721.

Law, State and Agrarian Society in Colonial India

D. A. WASHBROOK

University of Warwick

PERHAPS the most intransigent problem in the recent history of Indian society remains an adequate understanding of the processes of social change which took place under colonialism. As the continuing controversies within, as much as between, the traditions of modernization theory, Marxism, and the underdevelopment theory make plain, the Indian historical record is peculiarly difficult to grasp with conventional sociological concepts. In the study of Western European society, a focus on the evolution of legal ideas and institutions has proved a useful entry point to social history.[1] The law may be seen to represent a set of general principles through which political authority and the state (however constituted) attempt to legitimize the social institutions and norms of conduct which they find valuable. As such, its history reflects the struggle in society to assume, control or resist this authority. Its study should help to reveal the nature of the forces involved in the struggle and to suggest the implications for social development of the way in which, at any one time, their struggle was resolved. The condition of the law may be seen to crystallize the condition of society. This, of course, could be said of any governing institution. But where the law becomes uniquely valuable is in that, because of its social function, the struggle around it is necessarily expressed in terms of general statements of principle rather than particular statements of private and discrete interest. At the most

Versions of this paper were read to the Commonwealth History Seminar, University of Cambridge, March 1978 and to the annual conference of the Political Science Association, University of Warwick, April 1978. I am extremely grateful for subsequent help, advice and encouragement to Drs Anil Seal, Christopher Baker, Christopher Bayly, John Lonsdale, Tom Tomlinson and Robin Okey. Responsibility for any of the nonsenses, however, is entirely my own.

[1] For example, R. Tawney, *The Agrarian Problem in the Sixteenth Century* (London, 1912). More recently, J. Goody (ed), *Family and Inheritance* (Cambridge, 1976); E. P. Thompson, *Whigs and Hunters* (London, 1975). The following essay does not necessarily pick up any of the themes raised in these works. The differing historical and historiographical contexts of Indian study make straight translation invalid. It merely also uses the law as a focus on society.

0027-749X/81/0406-0904$02.00 © 1981 Cambridge University Press

fundamental level, these principles demarcate the rules on which the contending parties seek to build their versions of society and provide useful clues to their wider, often undisclosed, positions. Study over time of their relative successes, failures and compromises, and of the nature of their evolving relationships, may throw into sharper relief the more significant movements in the historical process. Of course, for the law to fulfill this wider analytical purpose, it is not possible to study it only in the courtroom. It is essential to trace the arguments and forces displayed there back to their various origins and consider their situation in the general social context. But the courtroom may not be that bad a place to try to re-assemble them and consider their implications for India's social history.

What follows represents an attempt to look at the conundrum of colonial India from the angle of the law, especially with regard to the nature of effective property right in land. One of the few points of common agreement among historians is the preponderant significance of agrarian relations in the structure of Indian society. The land remained overwhelmingly the single most important source of wealth and the base of production. While, however, there may be a consensus on the role of the land, views of its legal (and social) context under colonialism are much more divergent. On the one hand, some historians have tended to assume rapid and radical change, under the influence of 'Westernization' or 'capitalism', and to imbue the intruments of the law with great power, to break up village solidarities and to establish 'bourgeois' dominance over the peasant economy.[2] On the other, different historical perspectives have emphasized the continuity of 'traditional' and 'feudal' elements in the law and have questioned whether it was ever very effective in establishing its authority.[3] To add to the confusion, although a third view has shown the law to have consisted of an eclectic mixture of the new and the old, the effective and the ineffective, it does not seem to have found very adequate explanations of

[2] For example, B. S. Cohn, 'From Indian Status to British Contract', *Journal of Economic History* (XXI), 1961; R. Kumar, *Western India in the Nineteenth Century* (London, 1968), chs 3–4; H. Alavi, 'India and the Colonial Mode of Production', *Socialist Register 1975* (London, 1975).
[3] For example, S. and L. Rudolph, *The Modernity of Tradition* (Chicago, 1967), ch. 3; B. S. Cohn, 'Structural Change in Indian Rural Society 1596–1885', in R. E. Frykenberg (ed.), *Land Control and Social Structure in Indian History* (Madison, 1969); B. S. Cohn, 'Anthropological Notes on Disputes and Law in India', *American Anthropologist* (LXVII), 1965; C. A. Breckenridge, 'From Protector to Litigant', *Indian Economic and Social History Review* (XIV), 1977; B. S. Cohn, 'Some Notes on Law and Change in North India', *Economic Development and Cultural Change* (VIII), 1959.

the resulting compound.[4] In these circumstances, it may be best to go back to basics and to consider the social implications of the colonial legal system as it first developed out of the conquest of Bengal in the late eighteenth century. Section II of this essay examines the logic of property right in the context of the early colonial state. This context, however, was historically relative and contingent. By the middle of the nineteenth century, Indian society was becoming subject to a very different set of pressures which necessitated new relations on the land and confronted the law with new problems. Section III traces the evolution of property right against this background. By the second decade of the twentieth century, a further sea-change was in progress, ultimately taking India to decolonization and independence. Section IV considers the meaning of the raj's final phase through the legal developments of this period. By looking constantly at the relationship between the law and its historical milieu, we may be able to understand better not only its effects on society but also, and more critically, the forces in society which moulded it.

By convention, the British raj emerged out of the political relations of Bengal in the middle of the eighteenth century. The East India Company, until then a mercantile/warrior institution operating (albeit with great independence) within the structure of the pre-colonial state, began to assume the formal responsibilities of government and to develop its own principles of state-craft. These principles, especially with regard to the rule of law and the nature of property right, usually are seen to have received their clearest expression in the Permanent Settlement of 1793, which also laid the foundations of the Anglo-Indian legal system.[5] First, a judiciary was set up independent of the executive institutions of the state and acting as a check on them. The law defined and protected the private rights of subjects against all-comers, including the encroachments of the executive itself. Among these private rights was that to property: the legal subject was guaranteed enjoyment of all his posses-

---

[4] For example, J. D. M. Derrett, *Religion, Law and Society in India* (London, 1968); E. Whitcombe, *Agrarian Conditions in Northern India* (California, 1972), ch 5. It is perhaps unfair to challenge Derrett's legal history to provide explanations of colonial policy. But, as we shall see, his suggestions that British conservatism with regard to family law flowed from a desire to avoid disruption and to save money may not be entirely adequate. Whitcombe's excellent analysis of the legal confusion of North India at the end of the nineteenth century is accompanied by no clear attempt to explain the phenomenon either in terms of colonial designs or in a context of pressures on the colonial authority. She appears to understand it as a product of administrative incompetence and the social disruption caused to Indian society by colonial land policy.

[5] P. Spear, *A History of India* (London, 1965), Vol. II, ch. 8; J. Furnivall, *Colonial Policy and Practice* (Cambridge, 1948).

sions free from external interference. Second, to facilitate economic relationships between propertied subjects, the public law developed a number of conventions. The sale of property for value was held always to be valid. A vendor could not subsequently claim it back. Contracts for debt and services were held to be binding and enforcible at law on the property of the party who failed to meet his obligations.[6] These conventions, as much as the notion of an independent judiciary itself, have been taken by many historians as indicative of the wider philosophical perspective represented in the settlement. They are regarded as part of a scheme for the transformation of Indian society under principles drawn from British Whig political and European Physiocratic economic theory.[7] The scheme centred on promoting the commercial and economic development of Bengal by emancipating the individual from the dead hand of the state (and the land from the weight of taxation) and encouraging him to accumulate private wealth and property through the market. It was stamped by a philosophy of 'possessive individualism'. To accomplish it, the revenue demand of the state on the land was limited, rights to ownership of the land were separated from rights to collect revenue on it and the role of the state in the economy was cut back to the simple preservation of law and order. The Permanent Settlement envisioned a society whose prosperity was underpinned by a free market in all commodities, including and especially land.

What, however, seems to be very much less noticed is that, parallel to this enunciation of the principles of the 'public' law, the Bengal authorities also attempted to define the bases of the 'private' or 'personal' law of their subjects. This definition rested upon jurisprudential principles sharply contrasting with those in the public domain and implied a quite contradictory vision of the future. Whereas the public law had the intention of enlarging and safeguarding the freedoms of the individual in the market place, and was to be made by statute and the courts in the light of equity and policy, the personal law was meant to limit the sphere of 'free' activity by prescribing the moral and community obligations to which the individual was subject, and was to be made by the 'discovery' of existing customary and religious norms.[8] Its purpose was to keep society in the structure of relations in which the colonial authority had found it and to construe the moral problems of the present against standards taken directly from the past.

As the personal side of the law has been investigated, so its subtle,

---

[6] Derrett, *Religion*, chs 9, 12.
[7] R. Guhar, *A Rule of Property For Bengal* (Paris, 1963).
[8] Derrett, *Religion*, ch 8.

conservative implications for the development of society have become clearer. These consisted not only of obstructions to change in the future but also of reversions to long dead or unfashionable conventions. Initially, the courts looked to the scriptures for guidance on domestic and social norms and rested heavily on the interpretations of pandits for the Hindu law. These interpretations reflected a Brahminical view of society, which saw its structure in terms of immutable religious principles. Under their influence, the personal law recognized and validated the caste system and the varna theory of social order.[9] It also applied a theological definition to the concept of the family and to the proper basis of relations within it.[10] With the support of British power, the Hindu law expanded its authority across large areas of society which had not known it before or which, for a very long period, had possessed their own more localized and non-scriptural customs.[11] On those sections of society closest to the regulating authority of the colonial power (mainly the upper echelons involved, in one way or another, with the higher institutions of state), the effects of the Hindu law seem to have been considerable. There is evidence that processes bringing about nuclear family formation were set into reverse;[12] that discretionary and voluntaristic elements in family relations were suppressed by enforced prescription;[13] that the position and independence of women declined.[14] The rise of the Hindu law was one of many developments of the period which made the nineteenth century the Brahmin century in Indian history (and perhaps helps to explain why the twentieth century was to be the anti-Brahmin century).

From its very beginnings, then, the Anglo-Indian legal system was distinctly Janus-faced and rested on two contradictory principles with

[9] A useful account is provided in S. and L. Rudolph, *Modernity*, ch. 3.

[10] Derrett, *Religion*, ch. 12.

[11] However, in the Punjab, which was annexed very late, *de facto* community custom provided the basis of personal law. Moreover, there always remained significant provincial disparities in the interpretation of the Hindu law. These, in part, reflected resistances thrown up by the differing customary conventions of the provinces. Within Hindu law, of course, there was room for caste custom but this was legitimated by scripture.

[12] T. Raychaudhuri, 'Norms of Family Life and Personal Morality among the Bengali Hindu Elite, 1600–1850', in R. van M. Baumer (ed.), *Aspects of Bengali History and Society* (Hawaii, 1975). Raychaudhuri does not formally relate this reversion to the legal context, nor indeed to any context at all. But its timing coincides with the establishment of the Anglo-Indian Hindu law and reflects its norms.

[13] K. I. Leonard, *Social History of an Indian Caste* (California, 1978), chs 7, 10.

[14] For example, see L. C. Stout, 'Hindu Law, Customary Law and Statutory Social Reform: The Hindu Widow Remarriage Act XV of 1856', paper read at International Symposium on Imposed Law, University of Warwick, April 1978.

different social implications. If the public side of the law sought to subordinate the rule of 'Indian status' to that of 'British contract'[15] and to free the individual in a world of amoral market relations, the personal side entrenched ascriptive (caste, religious and familial) status as the basis of individual right.[16] Strangely, this paradox seems not to have been grasped by the official mind of the early raj. There appears no awareness of a contradiction between the two parts of the law and no concern that rigid Hindu social tradition might stand in the way of free market economic enterprise. Such disinterest, however, certainly did not reflect the practical irrelevance of the Hindu law to the context of property relations in the market. In a large number of ways, its conventions interfered with the rights of the individual to possess, acquire, use and accumulate property, especially land. The legal definition of the family, for example, was taken from a religious principle which emphasized the almost infinite jointness of a kindred.[17] Members of a family were recognized to have rights to shares in, and maintenance from, its collective property, which naturally restricted the rights of other members to use that property. Under various schools of law, sons might constrain the activities of their father, and brothers of one another; prospective heirs and beneficiaries might invalidate alienations of their patrimony for other than religious purposes; an heir might insist upon partition of family properties against the wishes of other heirs or, conversely, the joint-family might prevent the division required by one of its members; vendors of, or foreclosed debtors who lost family property, might be sued for their share of its value by other members.[18] Private property rights were, in effect, deeply entangled in the relations of the Hindu joint-family and very much influenced by its norms. While with regard to 'movable' property, from the earliest period of Company rule an easy accommodation proved possible between the demands of the market for property exchange and transfer and those of the personal law for constraint on individual freedom, the same was

[15] B. S. Cohn, 'From Indian Status'.

[16] Cohn's generalizations about the Anglo-Indian law seem very suspect. Status determined the body of personal law to which the individual was subject. As these bodies differed, the law cannot be said to have treated individuals on an equal basis. Moreover, personal law rights clearly interfered in certain types of contractual relations. Cohn's dichotomous frame of reference appears to derive from an over-zealous use of the tradition/modernity paradigm. Here, as perhaps universally, its eclecticism obscures more than it reveals.

[17] Derrett, *Religion*, ch. 12.

[18] *Ibid.* The precise terms of these restraints varied by provincial and caste custom and by legal school (Dayabhaga or Mitakshara). Also, see W. H. Morley, *An Analytical Digest of All the Reported Cases Decided in the Supreme Courts of Judicature in India* (London, 1850), esp. pp. 38–44; 478–87.

certainly not true of immovable property such as land. The public law rules concerning the validity of sale for value and the enforceability of debt contracts tended to stick fast on the question of hereditary ancestral landed property. The rights of the purchaser of land (or its acquirer in honour of a debt) against those of the family of the vendor (or foreclosed mortgagee) remained exceptionally unclear and confused until the very end of the nineteenth century.[19] In these circumstances, it may not be surprising that there is little evidence of an active market in land other than that created by forced sales for revenue defalcation (over which the law, in any event, had no direct competence).[20]

But it was not only with regard to the Hindu family that the principles of the personal law affected market relations. Social prescriptions derived from the caste system could interfere with property right: where it could be shown that local customs had denied access to land or a trade to members of a particular community, they might find legal as well as practical obstacles placed in their path if they tried to precipitate change.[21] The law also validated (or at least had no competence to invalidate) the inegalitarian conventions of the tax system, which laid differential rates of assessment on the properties of different castes, with obvious implications for the value of property when transferred.[22] The extent to which different communities were subject to different bodies of law posed a further limit to market activities. Before the coming of legislation to regulate the affairs of companies, members of different communities who entered into property-owning business partnerships

[19] Whitcombe, *Agrarian Conditions*, ch. 5.

[20] Especially in Northern India, these forced sales of, essentially, revenue right were very considerable in the early nineteenth century. But it has long been questioned how far they necessarily involved the transfer of possession. Moreover, their incidence was declining in the second third of the century. See, B. S. Cohn, 'Structural Change'; E. T. Stokes, *The Peasant and the Raj* (Cambridge, 1978), chs 1, 5. Of course, the lack of formal evidence of a 'voluntary' land market does not mean that one did not exist outside the regulation of the law. But, as we shall see, general conditions make it unlikely: except in densely populated, highly irrigated regions, land as a commodity had little value.

[21] Especially in the towns, much litigation seems to have derived from inter-community disputes about rights to locate houses, conduct businesses, etc. In general, the law attempted to arbitrate these in the light of 'traditional' practice. But usually, this meant denying the innovatory group the right to compete with the established group. In a society in which caste and religious status were intimately bound up with economic activities, a preserved tradition was a strong barrier to market freedom. For an example from the earliest period of British rule, see P. A. Roche, 'Caste and the British Merchant Government in Madras, 1639–1749', *Indian Economic and Social History Review* (XII), 1975; for a later example, see R. L. Hardgrave, *The Nadars of Tamilnad* (California, 1969), ch. 3.

[22] The civil law was held to have no competence in the adjudication of taxation matters and subjects possessed no legal defence against inequitable state practices.

could find that a death or enforced dissolution trapped them in a hopeless confusion of overlapping jurisdictions. The preference of merchants and traders to operate through connections of kin and caste did not reflect only a cultural peculiarity.[23] The structure of the law made extra-communal relations dangerous in practice.

More significantly, however, as the framework of the Bengal legal system started to be imposed on other provinces, the personal law's concept of property as a trust rather than a right began to spread rapidly across what had been considered the domain of the public law and to affect, especially, landed relations. In one sense, which raises questions about the real purpose even of the Permanent Settlement, this possibility had been implicit in the original formulation of land law. It had been no intention of the Bengal Permanent Settlement to sweep away the 'traditional' and 'customary' rights which agricultural tenants possessed in the lands whose proprietary title had been given to zamindars.[24] Theoretically, the claims of underproprietors to a species of property right in the land were recognized. However, the settlement notably failed to define what these rights and claims were and left the courts the impossible task of discovering them. As the Permanent Settlement spread to parts of Upper and Southern India, more care was taken to define tenants' rights which qualified the titular landholder's absolute possession of his property.[25] In areas of non-zamindari settlement, other forms of community 'trust' were built into land law. In parts of Northern India, village bhaiacharas (brotherhoods) were recognized as possessing a kind of corporate property right which allowed them to pre-empt the land sales of any of their individual members.[26] In parts of South India, the same notions of corporate possession limited individual rights of alienation in certain types of co-sharing mirasi tenure.[27] Many grants of land (inams) reflected the social status and public roles of their

[23] The role of caste and kinship in mercantile activities is explored in C. A. Bayly, 'Indian Merchants in a Traditional Setting' in C. Dewey and A. Hopkins, *The Imperial Impact* (London, 1978). Bayly also notes the existence of powerful supra-kinship mahajan organizations among the business community. These, however, seem to have played only a regulating and arbitrational role. They were not property holding corporations.

[24] See Spear, *History*, ch. 8.

[25] T. Metcalf, *Land, Landlords and the British Raj* (California, 1979), ch. 3; for South India, see 'Proceedings of the Special Committee on the Permanent Settlement', Madras Revenue Records, special series 1800–04, India Office Library, London.

[26] E. T. Stokes, *The English Utilitarians and India* (London, 1965), ch. 2.

[27] Morley, *Analytical Digest*, p. 450.

The law also could insist on redistributing lands between shareholders. See D. Ludden, 'Mirasidars and Government in Nineteenth Century Tinnevelly District', paper read at Conference on Intermediate Political Linkages in South Asia, University of California, March 1978.

holders.[28] They could not be freely transferred or alienated and did not represent marketable forms of landed property.

The contradiction between the individual freedoms supposedly supported by the public law and the social constraints strongly imposed by the personal law was, then, very deep and greatly coloured the nature of effective property right. As the law evolved in the first half of the nineteenth century, it tended to favour the principle of community trust at least as much as that of private property right.[29] In reflection of the contradiction, the courts recognised two different species of property in which owners had different kinds of right: 'individual' property which could be possessed and used freely and 'ancestral' property which was subject to encumbrance and the claims of the family. However, the balance of the law was inclined to favour the latter at the expense of the former. It was held that if an individual received any substantial help in his business activities from members of his joint-family, then all his business profits were joint-family property and fell on the ancestral side of the line. In South India at least, this was carried so far that if a lawyer, civil servant or other member of the 'learned' professions had received support from his family during his education, then his earnings throughout his career belonged to them rather than himself.[30] The conventions of land law also suggest the extent to which the 'community', not only the individual, was an object of the law's concern. In those mirasi tenures which allowed a collective veto on individual alienations, it was sometimes held that all shareholders had to give their consent before the sale was valid.[31] The more closely is the Anglo-Indian law's 'freedom' of property scrutinized, the more limited does it seem to become. The avowed intention of the Bengal authorities to subject India to 'a rule of

[28] In some provinces, the amount of land under inam tenure was enormous. In early nineteenth-century Madras, it varied across the districts at between about 12 and 40 per cent.

[29] It should be noted that, of course, the Anglo-Indian law notion of the 'community' was not necessarily the same as that of the régimes which it replaced nor that which its subjects easily recognized. In general, it excluded lineage and cross-caste neighbourhood ties and included an expanded sense of family and caste obligation. We are not arguing that the law genuinely preserved 'tradition' but only that it protected institutions of supra-private right. Some of the problems in interpretating legal change, and indeed change under the raj, may be due to careless assumptions drawn from modernization theory that all British change, by definition, functioned towards the private and individual principles. For a discussion of these problems in the context of Punjabi society, see T. G. Kessinger, *Vilyatpur 1848–1968* (California, 1974), chs 1, 6.

[30] Derrett, *Religion*, ch. 12; the law, of course, did permit privately earned property to be used at the individual's discretion and to be kept apart from ancestral property. But, in these circumstances, it is hard to see how much could be privately earned.

[31] Morley, *Analytical Digest*, p. 450.

property' which would promote economic development through the operations of an open market was not realized either in the legal system which they themselves provided or in its subsequent development in other provinces. The large gap between practice and theory naturally raises questions about whether this was ever the serious intention of early colonial rule at all. An examination of the institutions of the law confirms the suspicion.

In the first half of the nineteenth century, if the British were trying to bring society's property relations under the regulation of statute and the courts, it can only be said that they were not trying very hard or with much consistency. In spite of the initial popularity of the Company's courts,[32] their number in the mofussil of Bengal and Madras was reduced.[33] Stamp fees to bring a suit were pushed up to prohibitive levels: it cost Rs 1,000 in initial court charges to start an action on property worth only Rs 50,000.[34] The courts were denied the necessary machinery to enforce their own decrees with the result that the great majority of suits for the execution of decrees already obtained were 'infructuous'.[35] The Company state paid scant attention to the quality of the judiciary, which tended to consist of civil servants largely ignorant of the law but too incompetent to be given other duties, or passed retirement age and too impecunious to live on their pensions.[36] No reforms were made in trial procedures which had been set up originally in haste and optimism. The possibility of a near-limitless number of appeals prolonged litigation interminably, while the insistence on British conventions of evidence (especially documentary evidence) was unreal in the context of a largely illiterate society and put much potential business outside the reach of the law. Yet nothing was done to improve the situation and Indian property rights were left to be safeguarded by a legal system which could take up to fifty years to resolve a

[32] In most provinces, the first response of Indian society to 'Company law' was extremely positive. In fact, in Bengal it could only be described as prodigious. In 1813, 160,313 original suits were instituted, of which only 62,787 were contributed by Calcutta. See *Minutes of Evidence taken before the Select Committee on the Affairs of the East India Company*, Vol. IV, pp. 538–41. Parliamentary Papers (XII), 1832.

[33] Zillah courts had their competences reduced to suits worth less than Rs 5000 and their numbers cut back. *Ibid.*, Appendices 2,6.

[34] See J. B. Norton, *The Administration of Justice in South India* (Madras, 1853).

[35] *Ibid.* The problem of enforcing decrees is raised in Cohn, 'Structural Change', and P. J. Musgrave, 'Landlords and Lords of the Land', *Modern Asian Studies* (VI), 1972, and 'Rural Credit and Rural Society', in Dewey and Hopkins, *Impact*.

[36] Norton, *The Administration*. This incompetence showed itself repeatedly in the use by the lower judiciary of British precedents, which were not admissible under the terms of the Anglo-Indian law. The appeal courts probably overturned more judgements for this 'cardinal' error than for anything else.

contentious case or which could order the re-trial six times of a suit for property worth Rs 6.[37] Corruption was smugly admitted to be rife at all levels of the law but, and in sharp contrast to the revenue system, no systematic moves were ever contemplated against it. Prior to the granting of the Company's 1853 charter, the condition of the law became a *cause célèbre* and attracted a large pamphlet literature.[38] If only a small part of J. B. Norton's carefully documented attack on the Madras legal system was true, there would still be more than sufficient to sustain his challenge that South India existed outside the rule of law.[39]

In these circumstances, it may not be surprising that the courts were not always used for their 'proper' purposes in seeking the speedy resolution of disputes. Often, they were seen by litigants merely as a convenient place in which to bury 'bad' cases for years at a time, which might be lost if heard before unofficial panchayati tribunals.[40] This state of affairs, and the tendency which it reflected to refuse acceptance of initial court rulings and to prolong litigation by every means available, have been associated with a supposed innate litigiousness in the Indian character or with a supposed cultural haitus between the values of Indian litigants and those enshrined in the 'Western' legal system.[41] But

[37] As an example, the Sivaganga zamindari in Madras went into litigation in 1832 over a series of, admittedly complex, inheritance and debt suits, Judgement was finally delivered by the House of Lords in 1896. See Norton, *The Administration*, for a long list of débâcles.

[38] Besides Norton, see P. Khan, *Revelations of an Orderly* (Benares, 1848).

[39] See also, J. B. Norton, *Reply to a Madras Civilian's Defence of the Mofussil Courts in India* (London, 1853).

[40] The extent of 'informal' arbitrational procedures in Indian society, to supplement the inadequacies of the Anglo-Indian law, remained enormous and provided the real institutional support to property right. This was true to a considerable degree even in urban metropolitan society. See Bayly, 'Traditional Merchants'; J. Dykes, *Salem: an Indian Collectorate* (London, 1853). In the countryside, it was even more true and various types of authority, ranging from dominant caste panchayats to paternalistic zamindar, lineage leader, local notable and village officer justice were available.

[41] Cohn, 'Some Notes' and 'Anthropological Notes'. The view that there was (is) a 'problem' in the way that Indians litigate and that it derives from the peculiarity of their culture in relation to that reflected in the law, which Cohn assumes without demonstrating, was shared by the British bureaucracy who had their own reasons for not wanting to be subjected to extensive checks from the judiciary. Cohn, and a number of other legal sociologists, appear to have 'objectified' colonial prejudices into the bases of social scientific problematics. For alternative views on the sources of Indian litigation, see R. L. Kidder, 'Courts and Conflict in an Indian City', *Journal of Commonwealth Political Studies* (XI), 1973; O. Mendelsohn, 'The Pathology of the Indian Legal System', *Modern Asian Studies* (forthcoming). There are two further difficulties with the Cohn 'dualistic' conception of the law, not merely for the Company period but generally. It assumes without demonstrating that the law is not extensively used for prevarication and harassment in the 'West' and that nineteenth-century British law, which provided the Western part of the Indian experience, was itself devoid of status-based, non-contractual notions of obligation. Neither assumption seems sound.

it must be asked what precisely were the Western values embedded in this extraordinary legal apparatus and whether Indian litigants were using it irrationally or rationally to its absurd specifications? If, after sixty years of experience in which they had come to know only too well the deficiencies of the courts, the Company government still attempted no remedy, it may be more reasonable to suppose that they were quite content with the apparent abuse of the law and intended it to be used in no other way than it was, and as its institutional structure suggested it should be. Outside Bengal, where the vagueness of the original Permanent Settlement and the lack of an alternative state apparatus fuelled a continuous expansion in litigation, [42] the system was used remarkably little, especially for disputes about land. As late as 1850 in the whole of Madras, for example, only 64,500 suits were instituted for property worth just Rs 73.5 lakhs; in N.W.P. at the same time, the figures were 69,500 suits for property worth Rs 67 lakhs. The number of suits involving land titles were 4742 and 7279 respectively. [43] Most of the suits concerned debts and bonds and, while some of these undoubtedly were connected with the security of land, most seem not to have been but representative of commercial transactions within mercantile 'metropolitan' society. [44] For provinces with populations of upwards of 25 million, based upon modes of petty commodity production which gave them perhaps 3–5 million claimants to land rights of various sorts, these statistics hardly bespeak a situation in which the law was very active in resolving disputes and securing rights to property. Nor, of course, do they bespeak a society to be noted for its overindulgence in litigation. In effect, they suggest that it would be extremely misleading to conceive the Company's purpose or effect as creating a 'free' market economy in land sustained by the rule of law. The courts scarcely engaged the issues of landed property and hence could not impose market forms upon it, even

[42] By 1829, the Bengal courts were trying to hear upwards of 190,000 cases a year worth Rs 6 crores in property values. *Minutes of Evidence . . . Select Committee* (1832), Apps 2,6. The expansion never slowed down, and reached proportions of some three-quarters of a million cases a year a century later. Bengal, however, was always exceptional in having, as a result of the Permanent Settlement, no real revenue administration to provide alternative channels between government and society. One suspects that the general view of Indian society as exceptionally litigious derives, in part, from a tendency to read the whole of India in the light of Bengal's peculiar problems. This certainly is the case in J. Furnivall, *Colonial Policy*.

[43] *Report from the Select Committee on Indian Territories*, Appendix, *P.P.* (x) 1852, pp. 608–95.

[44] This is suggested both by the fact that the heaviest centres of litigation by far were the courts of the major metropolitan centres rather than the small, semi-rural district towns and by the large participation within them of the 'higher level' financial community involved in the finance of government and trade.

had they seriously wished to (which, as we have seen, is doubtful). Landed relations were not re-constituted (at least on 'modern') lines by the Anglo-Indian law nor was the reproduction of the agrarian base a function of interactions in the market place regulated by the law.

These negative points, however, leave us with two very large questions still unanswered: what was the nature of the Company state and how were rights in land effectively defined? With regard to the first, the more carefully is it examined, the more does the Company state appear to be a continuity of the 'ancien régime'[45] and the less a revolutionary 'liberating' government. The key to the radical part of the Bengal programme had been the fixing of the land revenue in perpetuity and the withdrawal of government from management of the economy. Only on the completion of these policies could ownership rights in land meaningfully be separated from revenue rights and capital come to compete freely for commodities in the market. But, of course, over most of British India, the land revenue never was fixed in perpetuity, while even in the permanently settled areas its initial incidence was so high that generations passed before it ceased to be massively burdensome.[46] Moreover, the Company dismantled very few of the monopolies which it inherited from its predecessors and greatly strengthened some—as in opium. Early colonial India operated under a 'state mercantilist' form of economy in which the institutions of the 'ancien régime' were made more efficient, brutalized and bastardized but, significantly, not dissolved. The land revenue, for example, continued to absorb a very high proportion, perhaps 40–50 per cent, of production and thereby to

[45] This raises questions, which can hardly be tackled here, as to the character of pre-British state systems. The issue has been much clouded by the analytical conventions of structural-functional anthropology and the political interests of Nationalists which, together, once presented a picture of rural harmony and equilibrium. Much recent work, however, has begun to challenge these images, at least for the eighteenth century. By the 'ancien régime', the author means a state system strongly influenced by Islamic traditions of political centralization, extracting considerable quantities of surplus from the agrarian base and, in the eighteenth century if not earlier, undergoing a commercialization of its institutional forms. His reading derives from such sources as I. Habib, *The Agrarian System of Mughal India* (Bombay, 1962); F. Perlin, 'Of White Whale and Countrymen', *Journal of Peasant Studies* (V), 1978; D. Singh, 'The Role of the Mahajan in the Rural Economy of E. Rajasthan during the 18th Century', *Social Scientist*, 1974; P. Calkins, 'The Formation of a Regionally Oriented Ruling Group in Bengal, 1700–1740', *Journal of Asian Studies* (XXIX), 1970; K. Leonard, 'The Hyderabad Political System and its Participants', *Journal of Asian Studies* (XXX), 1971; H. Mukhia, 'Illegal Extortions in . . . Eighteenth Century Eastern Rahasthan', *Indian Economic and Social History Review* (XIV), 1977; Stokes, *Peasant*, ch. 3; J. F. Richards, *Mughal Administration in Golconda* (Oxford, 1975), chs 2, 8.

[46] See, for example, B. B. Chaudhuri, 'The Land Market in Eastern India 1793–1940', I and II, *Indian Economic and Social History Review* (XII), 1975.

remain the prime determinant of the value of land.[47] Land values
hinged on protection and privilege from the weight of taxation: they
were created in the various village offices, zamindaris, inams and
specialized tenures which, on the basis of status or political function,
conveyed rights to avoid or apportion the revenue.[48] Landed property
was not emancipated from the political institutions of the state. Nor, in
many ways, was commerce. Company monopolies sat across most of the
more valuable areas of commerce and influenced all of the others. The
principal profits of trade came from working and financing the salt,
abkari and drug mahals. Until the 1830s, the Company also possessed
an important stake in the textile trade and posted extra taxes on those
textile merchants and producers who did not serve it.[49] Finance, too,
was dominated by the state's fiscal institutions. 'Banking' often meant
little more than financing the land revenue system or moneylending and
moneychanging to facilitate state operations.[50]

In these circumstances, with an 'open' market hardly existent, it was
inevitable that the state should take direct responsibility for the organization of production and the reproduction of the agrarian base. Political
influence and force were used to establish favourable conditions for the
production of various commodities such as indigo, opium, tea, coffee
and sisal.[51] Military coercion was applied liberally to support the
dominance of those playing intermediary roles in the revenue system
and to help them collect revenue and maintain the peace. The Company's claim to have 'demilitarized' society was strictly a half-truth.
While removing arms from the rest of society, it kept its own army closely
involved in 'civil' affairs.[52] Groups of sepoys and auxiliaries attended
the day-to-day operations of the bureaucracy. The qualities which they
brought to economic relations are well caught in such documents as the
Report of the Madras Torture Committee (1855) which found physical
intimidation and violence to be routine elements in the revenue system.

[47] Obviously, the actual fertility of the soil and its irrigation context played a role in
determining land's relative economic value. I mean here the relative value of the 'social'
property right created in it.
[48] For an interesting discussion of the role of revenue shields in the pre-British period,
see Stokes, Peasant, ch. 2.
[49] Through 'loom' and 'moturpha' taxes.
[50] For North India, see C. A. Bayly, The Local Roots of Indian Politics (Oxford, 1975),
ch. 3.
[51] For the coercion involved in the indigo system, see R. Guhar, 'Neel Darpan: the
Image of a Peasant Revolt in a Liberal Mirror,' Journal of Peasant Studies (II), 1975.
[52] For example, until the 1840s in most provinces, civil engineering and public works
were departments of the military. The first two generations of Company raj represented
a military occupation.

Very importantly, political force also was used to keep labour tied to the land and to coerce production for the market. The cash demand of the land revenue naturally obliged farmers to grow crops for exchange. In addition, the early settlements in many areas forced farmers to pay revenue on land whether they wished to cultivate it or not.[53] Equally, the Company recognized various types of serf and (before 1843) slave relations of labour and threw its weight behind their maintenance.[54] Its officials seem to have spent much of the early nineteenth century setting up serf-catching patrols and chasing runaways in order to bring them back to their masters.[55] The Company also tried to discourage the custom of hijrat and to prevent the physical movement of the peasantry to avoid revenue and rental exactions.[56] Forms of labour compulsion, validated by, and resting on, the support of the state, played a large role in the relations of production of the period.

Effective rights to landed property were forged in relation to this state apparatus. Obviously, as revenue demand was central to the value in land, the revenue department's distribution of privileged tenures and offices was of fundamental importance. The patronage of the revenue system tended over time (and Western theories of political economy notwithstanding) to be allocated to those in the agrarian structure capable of performing the services which it required, of extracting surplus and continuing production.[57] Ability to perform these services depended very much on the proclivities of the inherited social organization of production, which acted to mould effective rights. The precise nature of this organization varied enormously across the different Indian regions. But, in general terms, it could be characterized as consist-

[53] This was most obviously true of the early ryotwari settlements, see N. Mukherjee, *The Ryotwari System in Madras* (Calcutta, 1962), chs 3, 5, 10; but, by implication, it was also true of the heavy settlements initially laid on zamindars.

[54] In part by recognizing such relations as valid by tradition, in part by doing nothing to disturb the authority of those who commanded labour, in part by commanding labour itself on a caste differential basis and, occasionally, by re-inforcing the authority of 'masters'. For accounts of dependent agrarian relations, see D. Kumar, *Land and Caste in South India* (Cambridge, 1965); B. Hjelje, 'Slavery and Agricultural Bondage in the Nineteenth Century', *Scandinavian Economic History Review* (XV) 1967. J. Breman, *Patronage and Exploitation* (California, 1975), ch. 4.

[55] Especially in areas where labour shortage was acute. See D. Kumar, *Land*, ch. 5; also report of Collector of Bellary in 'General Report of the Board of Revenue', Madras Revenue Proceedings Nos 1345–46, 4 January 1821, I.O.L.; Breman, *Patronage*, p. 63.

[56] Collector of Bellary, *ibid.*; for the continuing possibilities of physical movement to avoid revenue exactions in Western India, see Stokes, *English Utilitarians*, ch. 2.

[57] An excellent account of the pragmatism of settlement practice is contained in J. Rosselli, 'Theory and Practice in North India', *Indian Economic and Social History Review* (VIII), 1971; also see R. E. Frykenberg, 'Village Strength in South India', Frykenberg, *Land Control*.

ing of corporate, kin-related patterns of land settlement shaped over a long period by attempts of the state to reduce their autonomy and by the penetration of the caste system, both of which created internal social and political differentiation.[58] The Company state, following its predecessors, tried to latch onto this differentiation, where it could find it, and turn it into the dominance which could be used to extract surplus. The early raj re-inforced the authority of local leaderships (headmen, vatandars, small zamindars, single family mirasidars, malghuzars, etc.) and subvented caste-based privileges (through inams and differential rates of assessments).[59] In some cases, it failed to find significant differentiation within the kin-body but was obliged to elevate it in its entirety .to privilege over outsiders (bhaiachara, co-sharing mirasi tenure, etc.). The key feature of the process, however, was that although the state partially drew out these elements of potential dominance, it neither controlled nor created the context from which they came and in which they remained half-situated. In consequence, actual rights to possess and use the land remained part-conditioned by this context and dependent on the customs and norms of the local agrarian community. These customs and norms (institutionalized in the authority of panchayats, lineage leaders, caste and religious deference, etc.) played at least as large a role in determining the relationship of society to the land as did the granting of state privilege in the first place. In fact, the exact character of, and safeguards to, rights in the land continued, as before, to reflect the condition of a political struggle between the state and the agrarian community for control over production and surplus.[60] Access to the land and rights to its use were squeezed out and distributed in the course of this struggle. The British settlement of the land rested upon a

[58] See Perlin, 'White Whale'; Stokes, *Peasant*, chs 2, 3; B. Stein, 'Integration of the Agrarian System of South India', in Frykenberg, *Land Control*, for Vijayanagar and Muslim periods.

[59] In the turbulence of the early days of, especially, ryotwari settlement, claims sometimes were made that an egalitarian settlement had been made, and occasionally enthusiastic Collectors responded to the claim. However, the élitism of even this, the most direct, form of settlement can be seen in such statements as: 'It never was intended that the Ryotware [*sic*] settlement should go lower than the landholders and Meerassidars; it never could have been meant that their cultivating sub-tenants should be immediately included in the engagements with the Circar.' 'General Report . . . 1820', MRP Nos 1441–47, 4 January 1821, IOL.

[60] This never was, and never had been static, and it is no part of the case for continuity outlined here that groups currently possessing land did not suffer under the British. There is evidence, especially from North India, that a few 'resident' cultivating groups were dispossessed. Metcalf, *Land*, ch. 3; Stokes, *Peasant*, chs 3, 6, 7. But the process dispossessing them derived from the politico-revenue system in ways which were not new to British rule. Once again perhaps our judgement of colonial novelty has been made difficult by assumptions about a prior stasis.

series of political deals, flexible and changeable, which offered and withdrew revenue privileges to intermediaries situated between itself and agrarian society and trying to play roles which satisfied, in some measure, the demands of both.[61]

In spite, then, of its frequent avowals to the contrary, the Company state was not bent on creating a free market economy sustained by the rule of law. It did not, at least willingly or consciously, dismantle the ancien régime's revenue system and institutions of economic management. Indeed, it worked them more intensively than they had ever been worked before. Its effective revenue demand was much higher than that of previous régimes (prior to the 1820s by intent and, thereafter, by 'accident')[62] and bore more heavily on the value of land. It reduced several of the investment and re-distributive functions of the old state system (takkavi, maintenance and extension of irrigation works, etc.) and increased the use of force to secure surplus and the continuation of production. Against this background, its elaboration of a legal system which treated and protected landed property as if it existed at a remove from the state, as a private subject's right, was pure farce (and plainly regarded as such by the mind of local administration). But what brought the Company to abandon so completely the revolutionary elements in the Bengal settlement and to continue a state system of whose inutilities late eighteenth century Anglo-Indian statesmen had been only too aware?

The elements of continuity in 'the first century' of colonial rule frequently have been seen to derive either from fears which the British possessed that, by disturbing the bases of religious and traditional authority, they would unleash revolt against their rule or from administrative and political weaknesses which made them dependent on ill-controlled collaborators.[63] These constraints on action obviously existed and cannot be dismissed. However, they may have been less severe than is often supposed and, of themselves, do not explain very adequately the Company's activities. It is clear, for example, that colonial rule did

[61] If the penalty for failing to meet British demands was loss of revenue rights and offices, the penalty for failing to protect local subsistence and security needs was migration and occasionally revolt.

[62] Even the Company admitted that, prior to the 1820s, its revenue demands had been exorbitant and had created chaos. In most provinces, it thereafter set about lowering and regularizing payments. However, from the late 1820s to the 1850s, most parts of India underwent a serious depression in grain prices and the Company's cash demands may not, in the end, have been much lower in real terms although expanded cultivation helped them to be met.

[63] For example, Derrett, *Religion*, chs 8, 9; R. E. Frykenberg, *Guntur District 1788–1848* (Oxford, 1965), conclusion.

disturb the bases of religious and traditional authority. There was support, overt and covert, for Christian missionaries;[64] relationships between Hindus and Muslims were placed on a drastically different basis;[65] the Brahminization of the Hindu law represented a real revolution in domestic and social mores, which was pushed through in the face of considerable opposition.[66] Moreover, the struggle on the land produced many casualties among the 'traditional' élites.[67] If the Company could afford to take these risks, which served no coherent purpose of its own, why should it not have attempted to restructure society along lines in which it claimed to see positive value? Equally, the weakness evidenced in the Company's relationships with its indigenous collaborators can easily be over-estimated and misunderstood. Occasionally, the state did show an ability to change the groups from which it drew its intermediaries, and regularly to change individuals within the groups.[68] More significantly, whatever the limitations on control, these collaborators were producing for the Company higher levels of surplus extraction than any previous indigenous state had enjoyed. What both of these formulations may miss is consideration of the general forces restricting the freedom of the Company to reconstruct society and manipulate the various types of collaborator available to it. It was the pressure of these forces which dictated, more precisely, the degree of innovation which the early colonial state could make, and they can only be understood by taking a wider view of the content.

Two particular aspects of the context in which the Company had to operate seem especially important. First, there was the military imperative. Throughout the first third of the nineteenth century, and for longer in some provinces, the Company was still trying to establish its rule by force of arms and was engaged in continuous military activity. This placed an enormous drain on state resources and had to be met by maximizing tax yields.[69] Second, there was the problem of organizing the production and marketing of high value crops, from which both the government and its various commercial partners took profit, in econo-

[64] See, for example, T. Metcalf, *The Aftermath of Revolt* (Princeton, 1965), chs 1, 2.
[65] Especially in Bengal.
[66] As in South India, articulated by such civilians as J. H. Nelson. See Derrett, *Religion*, ch. 9.
[67] For example, among some of the Rajput warrior clans of North India. See R. G. Fox, *Kin, Clan, Raja and Rule* (California, 1971), chs 3, 5; Stokes, *Peasant*, ch. 3.
[68] In both Bengal and North India, for example, the social composition of revenue rights' holders showed some tendency to move from a basis in the 'warrior' to the 'mercantile' and 'bureaucratic' élites. Sales for default and occasional bureaucratic purges also moved individuals around.
[69] See Rosselli, 'Theory'.

mic conditions of land plenty and labour scarcity. Although the land: man ratio varied enormously across India, and some scrub regions of the interior had scarcely been populated at all, there are strong grounds for believing that the eighteenth and early nineteenth centuries were periods of demographic crisis even in the wealthier and traditionally more developed tracts. There is evidence that the wars which followed the weakening of Mughal power devastated several of the centres of prosperity in Northern and Central India, while the struggle between the Company and Mysore had serious effects on South India. Moreover, cyclones and famines at the close of the eighteenth century destroyed cultivation in the rich lands down the East Coast. Bengal may have lost a third of its population in the 1770s and, in coastal Andhrapradesh, the productive capacity of many estates was thought to have declined by four-fifths during the 1790s.[70] The initial settlement reports of the Company in most provinces make mention of extremely favourable rates of taxation being offered by zamindars and village leaders to attract paikasht or pykari wandering cultivators to their lands; and contain many suggestions that, compared to heights achieved more than a century before, the extent of cultivation was low.[71] Circumstances of land plenty and labour shortage, of course, limit the possibilities of subordinating labour and peasant production to the market.[72] Both have easy and continuing access to the means of subsistence and can retreat. Their engagement will depend heavily on the level of rewards, compared to the subsistence risks, available in the market. But, in the context of the Company state, this was not high. The weight of state taxation, the depressed condition of the market between the late 1820s and the 1850s and the constant climatic threat to subsistence all restricted the appeal of 'voluntary' production for market exchange, at least on anything approaching the scale required by the Company and its allied mercantile capitalist interests.

It is very difficult to see how the early Company raj could have coped with these twin imperatives in any other way than it did. Without a high revenue yield and close political management of the economy, it would have risked military defeat, bankruptcy and internal collapse. But while the land revenue was heavy and the institutions of management remained in place, there was clearly little scope for free market relations to develop. The relationship between this situation and the social continuities reflected in the raj's structure lies, of course, in the extent to

[70] See 'Special Commission on Permanent Settlement'.
[71] For example, see *ibid.*; also 'General Report . . . 1820', *passim*.
[72] See J. Goody, *Production and Reproduction* (Cambridge, 1976).

which the Indian régimes which the Company replaced had faced very similar problems and had already designed state institutions to cope with them. The British inherited the cash demand revenue system, which coerced market production, and the various political deals with local notabilities and peasant corporations (symbolized in inam grants, village offices, corporate tenures, etc.) which continued production and maintained the revenue flow. They took over a state system well-adapted to its environment. Although they appear to have contemplated innumerable alternatives, and tried a few, as soon as difficulties were encountered they inevitably came back to their inheritance. Ultimately, the Company's governing strategy may best be understood as adapting to its own ends the state structure which it had been bequeathed in order to raise its efficiency (which meant cheapening its costs by substituting force for patronage wherever possible). Its opportunities for qualitative innovation were strictly limited.

Against this background of a state-dominated economy and an agrarian society in which the possession of land was a function of the political system, the Anglo-Indian law begins to take on a different set of meanings. Its main purpose, so far from protecting the private rights of subjects, may be better seen as providing a range of secondary services for the Company, both as 'state' and as 'shield' for European business interests, which helped to translate political power into money. While the extraction of primary production and its insertion into the market was accomplished by the apparatus of the state, that apparatus itself had become thoroughly penetrated by capital. Following and extending tendencies which had arisen in the eighteenth century, state rights in monopolies, in the currency and in the revenue system had been put out to competitive tender (the difference between pre-colonial tax farming and the colonial fast turnover market in zamindari titles being perhaps more notional than real).[73] Mercantile capitalists bid against one another for what amounted to the right to work state institutions for their own profit. In consequence, a great deal of private capital was tied up in the business of government. It was clearly essential for the state that this capital be kept in motion and that commercial transactions affecting its finances be secured. The cost of market anarchy at the level of the state was declining tax yields and liquidity problems of its own.

[73] For comments on the growth of tax-farming and state commercialization in the eighteenth century, see H. Furber, *John Company at Work* (Harvard, 1948), chs 6–8; Calkins, 'The Formation'; Perlin, 'White Whale'. In some regions, commercial principles had penetrated the revenue system down to the village level and village offices and rights to share in dominant community assets were bought and sold. See also Ludden, 'Mirasidars'.

AGRARIAN SOCIETY IN COLONIAL INDIA

Motion and liquidity were both facilitated by the conventions of the public law, especially in relation to the parallel Hindu personal law. In fact, the rules regarding sales for value and the honourability of 'fair' debts and 'reasonable' contracts created a bailiff's paradise. At least with regard to movable property, these rules were held to be superior to the constraints of the Hindu law. A sale for value was valid even if the vendor had sold ancestral property to which he had no private title; debt commitments had to be met, if necessary also from ancestral property which the debtor had no right to mortgage in the first place. The Hindu law offered no shield to responsibilities undertaken by the individual in the market place.[74] But what this meant was that the assets of the entire joint-family were standing as security for the liabilities of each and everyone of its individual members. Liability was vastly extended and assets could always be found to service any debt. Thus the wheels of commerce were kept turning and, as the ultimate creditor in a vast range of transactions, the state was well secured. The Anglo-Indian law also helped European capital to penetrate the sphere of Indian finance. Prior to the law's establishment across India, European capital had been in a distinctly difficult position outside the courts of the presidency towns and dependent upon Indian justice for its security. Now it could relate to indigenous business on more than equal terms. Not only was there likely to be racial sympathy between the 'white' higher judiciary and British mercantile interests, but the personal law of Europeans gave them distinct advantages over Indian rivals. Whereas their Hindu debtors stood liable to the full extent of joint-family assets, they themselves could be liable for no more than their personal fortunes.[75]

The practice of the Anglo-Indian law cannot be divorced from the political structure of the colonial state. It never achieved the autonomy from 'the executive' which the late eighteenth century Bengal authorities proposed for it. The law functioned in the main to regulate the relations of urban commercial groups in the interests of the colonial power. Its concern with 'traditional' social forms, while no doubt reflecting a genuine desire to avoid social disturbance, also aided the collection of debt, which was of more than passing importance to an essentially extractive state. While these forms did very little to free the market entrepreneur in Hindu society, this hardly mattered for the open market was not operative in the agrarian base and was directing neither its

[74] Derrett, *Religion*, chs 9, 12.

[75] The relative freedom of European businessmen, compared to the restraints on Indian entrepreneurship, created a species of legal 'dualism' not essentially dissimilar to that to be found in Dutch Indonesia or, later, in colonial Africa.

production nor reproduction. These were left to the ebb and flow of political relations stemming from the conjuncture of state and local corporate institutions. In effect, the first phase of colonial rule subjected India less to the rule of property and law than to that of bureaucratic despotism and state monopoly.

From the middle decades of the nineteenth century, property law began to undergo a set of profound changes. The incidence of litigation rose sharply and cases concerning disputes about landed property (including its relations of tenancy, rent and debt) became very much more common.[76] To cope with the new pressures, the legal system was both expanded and streamlined by the imperial government. The number of courts was increased, the appeals procedure was foreshortened and the formal costs of litigation were reduced.[77] Agrarian society now was placed in much closer contact with the concepts and practices of the Anglo-Indian judiciary, and given far better access to its institutions and powers. The period from the Mutiny to the First World War was the great age of civil litigation in India and, if ever the rule of law was established, it was in these years.

Behind the new circumstances of the law, it is possible to see important changes in the socio-economic and political contents. First, the general increase in population was reaching levels at which it reversed the relationship between man and the land.[78] Land itself was becoming scarce and the object of more intense competition, which existing customary and state institutions had difficulty in containing. Labour was becoming more plentiful and being pushed into a 'natural' position of subordination. These conditions increased the use value of land and reduced the need for 'artificial' political instruments to secure its utilization. Second, the rural economy came out of its long depression and passed into a period of growth which lasted, broken only by the occasional and regional famine, until the 1920s. Grain prices rose steadily,

[76] For example, by the later nineteenth century, the number of suits instituted in Madras and U.P. was running at an annual average of over 200,000. See *Reports on the Administration of Civil Justice* by the various provincial governments, annual series. Bengal, by this time, had broken through the 600,000 a year barrier.

[77] Details of the changes are contained in the *Reports on . . . Civil Justice* 1862–65.

[78] The point of crisis, of course, was reached at different times in different places. Bengal may have reached its own limits as early as 1860; parts of Southern India continued to expand to the 1920s. As with all the generalizations in this essay, this one is a loose aggregate hiding many local variations. But the turn of the century has been noted as a watershed in the history of North, Central and parts of South India. See D. Kumar, *Land*; Stokes, *Peasant*, ch. 11; W. Neale, *Economic Change in Rural India* (Yale, 1962), ch. 8; R. Ray, 'The Crisis of Bengal Agriculture', *Indian Economic and Social History Review* (X), 1973.

while railways and steam shipping helped to open out the production of the interior to wider opportunities in the world market. And third, the state fell back from its roles of dominance over, and management of, economic activity. Its monopoly controls weakened and progressively lost their significance. Over a long period, Parliament had chipped away at them for, while no doubt serving well those interests which could gain contracts and licenses, they operated at the expense of those which could not. Further, the declining value of several of the old staples, such as opium, together with the expansion of commerce in areas outside state control, reduced the weight of the residual monopolies (in salt and abkari) in the overall economy. The transfer of governing authority from the Company to the Crown in 1858 symbolized the final part of the transition from mercantilist monopoly to free market competitive economy. More significant than the liberation of commerce, however, was the easing of the land revenue burden. Established in an era of stagnant and even declining prices, the land revenue systems of British India allowed for revision of the cash rates of assessment only every twenty-five to thirty years (if at all). The price rise caught out the raj and it never managed to devise a means of keeping land revenue rates even close to inflation. The gaps between resettlements were too long to permit any kind of forward planning and tridecennial revenue revisions provoked fierce displays of political resistance which often obliged compromises and reductions. Between 1880 and 1920, the proportion of total government receipts represented by the land revenue fell from 43 per cent to 23 per cent.[79] Estimates of the fall in real value are difficult to make. But, in South India at least, the weight of the land revenue in relation to the value of agricultural produce may have declined by as much as two-thirds between 1860 and 1920.[80] It was this which marked the real 'property' revolution in the Indian state. It combined with the growing profitability of agriculture and scarcity of land to give land a much greater exchange value, independent of the revenue assessment, and it weakened the political authority of the revenue bureaucracy over the distribution of effective property rights.

The new context established the basic conditions which made a

[79] These figures refer to gross income from taxation not gross government revenues. *Finance and Revenue Account of the Government of India for the year 1880–81* (Calcutta, 1882), pp. 4–5; *ibid., 1921–22*, pp. 3–4.

[80] The average assessment per acre of cultivated land (regardless of type) rose only from Rs 1.7 to Rs 2.1. Grain prices rose by at least an average of 120 to 180 percent, depending on type; and much land was converted from the low-yielding dry grains to high-value cotton and groundnut. See *Reports on the Settlement of the Land Revenue in the Districts of the Madras Presidency*, Annual series.

competitive market economy possible. However, if the logic of that economy was to grip the agrarian base, it was essential that the law change both its role and its social biases. The growing distance of the state from the sources of production left it up to the 'free' interplay of class forces to sustain production for the market and to reproduce labour on the land. As in all competitive capitalist societies, it would be the job of the law to regulate this interplay and to provide the political instruments of class domination, which secured production and reproduction. The new role expected of the law, however, cruelly exposed the contradiction currently within it between the 'public' and 'personal' principles. Now that the institutions of state mercantilism were in decline, the constraints on property relations imposed by the Hindu joint-family and corporate- and status-based forms of landholding were no longer functional to colonial needs. Indeed, they stood in the way of Indian capital coming to develop the very active entrepreneurial duties now expected of it.[81] If the conditions implied by the new context were to transform agrarian society, the sphere of 'amoral' market relations assigned to Indian capital must needs be greatly expanded. Indian property relations would have to undergo very much the same kinds of change as British property relations during the transition to advanced market capitalism: concepts of community trust and moral obligation would have to weaken in favour of the freedom of the individual.[82] The price of these developments not taking place would be to leave society without the means of responding to its new situation. In fact, without the state to coerce market production any longer, it would be unclear what dynamic could lie behind the development of production.

To some degree, the law shouldered the enormous burden thrown upon it. It moved in various ways to beat back the frontier of the personal law and to disentangle private property rights from the institutions of the Hindu family and from the functions of ascriptive status and political office. In the zamindari areas, the rise of competition rents put pressure on the vague and uncertain domain of landlord/tenant relations. In part, the law responded by strongly favouring the proprietorial side and creating intruments to improve rent collection and landlord control. Landlords were helped to distrain defaulters' properties, eject at will at the end of leases and raise their rents.[83] Elsewhere, community

[81] That is to say, entrepreneurial in the commodity and export trades, where indigenous banking capital did most of the local spadework for both the state and British business. There was, of course, no expectation of an active industrial role.

[82] See Tawney, *Agrarian Problem*; also A. Harding, *A Social History of English Law* (London, 1966), chs 11, 12.

[83] This was the ostensible purpose of the various Rent Recovery Acts of the 1860s.

rights of veto on private land alienations became increasingly difficult to enforce at law; while even some intra-familial constraints, such as the theoretical check on fathers of sons, fell into desuetude.[84] In the market, a variety of measures made land more easily transferable. 'Traditional' usury laws were weakened; where still uncertain, the right to acquire ancestral land to meet the unrepaid debts of individual joint-family members was strengthened;[85] the growth of registration departments and documented property title improved land's legal security and freed it for exchange from prescriptive social encumbrance.[86] Much land locked up in status- and role-specific inam tenure became converted into freehold private property which could be used and alienated freely.[87] The revenue system progressively dropped caste differential rates of assessment, which had created artificial land values which were difficult to realize through sale. Finally, various property-holding public trusts, such as temples which had been directly supervised by the state, were turned into semi-private corporations responsible only to the courts. As the law assumed a role of far greater centrality in the property regulations of society, so it began to alter its character and to conceive the rights involved in property much more in terms of private ownership and use. Several pre-existing areas of moral and social constraint were reduced in scope. The transition to a competitive private capitalist social system was emergent.

Or so it might seem. Yet a closer look begins to raise questions about the slowness and timidity of the process and, indeed, to catch sight of a remarkable counter-movement against it. Progress in dismantling the Hindu law was greatly hindered by the 'assumption' of the law which took place in the 1860s[88] and by the determination with which the Government of India maintained the ban on religious and social interference. The first measure restricted what little flexibility the judiciary may have possessed to manoeuvre between different scriptural authorities and pandits' interpretations to innovate. The 'assumption' now fixed the norms and relations of Hindu ethics and left society to try and

[84] Derrett, *Religion*, ch. 12; on the individualization of 'community' mirasi rights in the period 1862–77, see Ludden, 'Mirasidars'; on Punjab, see Kessinger, *Vilyatpur*, chs 1, 6.

[85] Whitcombe, *Agrarian Conditions*, ch. 5.

[86] *Ibid.*

[87] In South India, for example, this was the principal purpose of the Inam Commission, which completed its work in 1869. See *A Collection of Papers relating to the Inam Settlement of the Madras Presidency* (Madras, 1906).

[88] From 1864, the Anglo-Indian law 'assumed' its knowledge of Hindu ethics to be adequate and dismissed its pandits. Interpretation thus became fixed. Derrett, *Religion*, ch. 9.

accommodate itself to the pressures of the epoch with mores frozen in the Vedic age (or what nineteenth-century jurists thought was the Vedic age). The ban on religious and social legislation prevented reform even when the need was obvious and the support strong. The rigidity of the law and the state's determination to preserve its version of 'tradition' are well seen in the 'Gains of Learning' agitation in South India. In spite of strong pressure from the educated élite to redraw the line between 'individual' and 'ancestral' property in order to allow at least professional earnings to be regarded as individual property, the law was unmoved until the 1930s. More than twenty legislative Bills were sent from Madras to Calcutta and New Delhi but they all came back.[89] There was, in the end, remarkably little movement to contract the vast sphere of right allowed to the joint-family nor was there much easing in the caste proscriptions of certain types of market activity. Indeed, with access to the courts becoming wider, the existing provisions began to have more serious consequences. Litigation to enforce rights to property in the inflated Hindu family seems to have become increasingly common; while the courts also made their presence felt by preserving the conventions of caste and religious deference against growing attempts to change them from below.[90]

But it was not only that the law stayed put. Through statute, it was advancing to develop new forms of constraint and prescription. The concept of occupancy tenure, validated on the grounds of tradition, came increasingly to qualify proprietorial right. From 1859, a mountain of tenancy legislation began to grow in all the provinces with permanent settlements, steadily extending tenant right and bringing the freedoms of the landlord under closer control. It represented the first stirring of that logic which, in North India, was to bring about a redistribution of property right from large zamindars to small holders and was to reach completion only at zamindari abolition in 1951.[91] The laws of contract with regard to indebtedness came under similar pressures. As land, rather than revenue rights, became valuable and the object of acquisition by capital,[92] so the legal conventions regarding contract went into reverse. The judiciary were instructed to examine the terms of mortgages and debt bonds in the light of 'fairness' (an increasingly ubiqui-

---

[89] See my *The Emergence of Provincial Politics* (Cambridge, 1976), ch. 5.

[90] On the widening of precedents in family and caste law, see Derrett, *Religion*, ch. 12; also Hardgrave, *The Nadars*, ch. 3.

[91] See Stokes, *Peasant*, ch. 9; Neale, *Economic Change*, chs 6, 7.

[92] These had not been totally separate before but the incidence of cultivators' dispossession as a result of changes in revenue right seems to have been small and unusual. In the years *c.* 1840–80, however, it is noticeable that sales of intra-village lands

tous if utterly vague concept of the period) and, more importantly, were empowered to reduce or abrogate at will the contractual stipulations of those which failed the test.[93] In several provinces, legislation carried this revision even farther and introduced prescriptive social identities into the market to outlaw certain actors. In Bombay, 'urban' moneylenders had their abilities to take land to meet debts severely curtailed;[94] while in Bundelkhand and the Punjab, a list of castes was proscribed from all additional acquisitions of land.[95] Not only 'the peasant' but also the 'landlord' could enjoy the special protection of statute. Most provinces developed Encumbered Estates and Court of Wards Acts which functioned as 'shields' to safeguard the properties of certain 'ancient and prestigious' families from loss for debt or other market irresponsibilities.[96] Although the legislatures certainly preferred to act on the basis of 'discovered' traditions (however fictitious), they need not necessarily do so. When special primogeniture provisions were applied to inheritance systems, there was no pretence that they represented anything other than innovations. Significantly, however, they were not applied generally to facilitate accumulation or even to prevent the fragmentation of peasant smallholdings, and they did not give individuals greater control over their property. They were applied only to 'ancient and prestigious' families to prevent their estates from being partitioned.

The conventions of the law, then, did not move very far or fast to accommodate the social imperatives of market capitalism. They served at least as much to shore up 'antique' social institutions and rights as they did to pave the way towards a society based upon individualism and competition. They confused the definition of property right and maintained the personal/public law contradiction. It would be easy perhaps to associate the slowness of 'progress' with the enervate and conservative qualities of agrarian society itself or with the weaknesses of the objective market pressures for transformation. Certainly, there were forces of resistance to change in rural society and, until perhaps the turn of the twentieth century, it was unclear how seriously Indian agriculture required structural innovations to make it market-worthy. However, to

for revenue default took place on a larger scale and that zamindars also were 'selling' the lease rights of defaulting tenants. Sometimes these lands fell into the hands of non-members of the agrarian community (such as moneylenders) who had revenue rights earlier.

[93] See, for examples, *Report on ... Civil Justice in Punjab*, 1868–69, and annually through the 1870s. This was also practice in Madras.

[94] As a result of the Deccan Agriculturists' Relief Act of 1879.

[95] See N. G. Barrier, *The Punjab Alienation of Land Bill of 1900* (Duke, 1966); also Stokes, *Peasant*, ch. 11.

[96] A. Yang, 'An Institutional Shelter', *Modern Asian Studies* (XIII), 1979.

emphasize these features alone would be to miss the fact that Indian society itself did contain a range of forces critical of the timidity of the law and demanding politico-legal changes more appropriate to market forms of capitalism, Large landholders frequently petitioned for improvements in their rights over property;[97] mercantile capitalists, such as the Nattukottai Chetties of South India, began to vote on the issue with their feet and to take their capital out of India in protest at legal insecurities and frustrations;[98] even the Congress took up the cause of the embattled creditor.[99] Moreover, the crisis in the agrarian economy at the end of the 1890s, when widespread famine coincided with the collapse of favourable exchange rates, indicated that, whatever else, agriculture remained seriously undercapitalized and had not attracted an adequate level of investment to its current needs. The case that the social and economic pressures for more radical change in agrarian relations were very weak is arguable at best. What is less contentious and much clearer, however, is that the raj itself was resisting these pressures and was concerned to try and hold up the existing agrarian structure.

The attitude of the colonial state towards a hypothetical capitalist transformation of agriculture was notoriously ambiguous. On the one hand, a great many of the imperatives towards competitive market relations emanated from its own activities. Although of declining weight, the land revenue demand continued to oblige production for the market and, until the twentieth century, to be the prime cause of exchanges in landed property rights (which now represented less tax collecting privileges than physical possession of, and access to, the land). The raj was also responsible for opening up the agrarian interior to deeper market penetration by building the railways and port facilities and sustaining the currency and credit systems of the colonial primary product exporting economy. In fact, its own finances depended critically on the success of this export (and the reciprocal import) trade and

[97] Such petitions were the main business of the various Landholders' Associations. It is clear that some large zamindars, contrary to their general image of feudal sloth, did try to run their estates on profit-maximizing lines and to invest in production and commerce. See Musgrave, 'Landlords', pp. 274–5; Stokes, *Peasant*, ch. 8; D. Kolf, 'A Study of Land Transfers in Mau Tahsil, Jhansi District', K. Chaudhuri and C. Dewey (eds), *Economy and Society* (Delhi, 1979).

[98] A leading Nattukottai Chetty gave the character of the legal system as the prime reason why his community preferred to work in South East Asia. *Madras Provincial Banking Enquiry Committee. Evidence*, IV, p. 243. Under rare favourable conditions 'banias' showed themselves capable of undertaking active development roles. See Stokes, *Peasant*, ch. 11, Kolf, 'A Study'.

[99] Especially in the wake of the Punjab Land Alienation Act.

it could not survive without the progress of market production. Yet, while needing and wanting economic growth in the primary sector, it set its face hard against most of the social changes which were corollaries of and facilitated that growth. The continuing conservative tendencies in the law can be traced mainly to the legislative activities, or inactivities, of the executive which refused to permit the courts to respond to the pressures on them for change.

Nor was it only by manufacturing laws that the state restricted the possibilities of the social development of market relations. It absolutely refused to build the 'modern' administrative structure necessary to underpinning such freedoms of the market as the courts were coming to provide.[100] The essential development of an efficient and centrally-disciplined police force, to protect 'legal' rights, safeguard the emancipation of the individual from community constraint and impose the rule of law, was neglected. The 'police' continued to be drawn from locally dominant (or warrior/criminal) castes and to be the agents of local agrarian élites. Equally, the bureaucracy notably failed to provide the courts with the facilities which would enable them to convey their jurisdictions to society. In spite of their new role and increased business, funds to sustain the courts and facilitate their use were kept painfully short. The expansion in the number of courts, especially in the rural areas, was slow; little executive machinery was afforded them so that, in most provinces, the proportion of their decrees which could be enforced was negligible; with the new weight of business, delays in obtaining legal arbitration remained enormous.[101] In effect, if the rule of law were meant to provide the social and political force driving the market economy, the raj was doing its best to see that it had little power.

The legal and political environment which the raj was creating for the operation of market forces and the penetration of capital remained contradictory. While not undermining the relations of the market or preventing capital entirely from engaging petty commodity production, it limited the social possibilities of development, failed to provide capital

[100] Many writers, including this one, have discussed the modernization of administration in the later nineteenth century. It was, however, a process initially confined to the nature of the state's own bureaucracy. Reflecting perhaps a continued antipathy to the rule of law, the executive did very little to centralize judicial authority or, critically, to re-build the police until much later.

[101] See *Reports on . . . Civil Justice* for the various provinces. In Madras, as an example, the average waiting time for a suit to be heard was 9–13 months, during which, if it were a debt-suit, interest could accumulate only at the rate of $6\frac{1}{4}$ per cent per annum, which was derisory in terms of the market rate of interest. Then, of course, the appeals procedure could begin. At all times, about two thirds of petitions for the execution of decrees were classified as wholly or partially infructuous.

with instruments to subordinate production and gave social groups resistant to the demands of the market much scope for manoeuvre. The clearest sign of the problem was the difficulty which large accumulations of capital, whether made during the mercantilist era in revenue and monopoly speculation or imported from outside, encountered in gaining direct access to, and control over, agricultural production. Adequate access and control, of course, meant having the ability to dispossess resident cultivators. Yet the biases of the law, the potential for prevarication contained in its processes and the lack of executive machinery to enforce decrees if won, made dispossession, at least by outsiders to the agrarian community, a parlous exercise.[102] The cost of this impotence, from the perspective of capital, was to reduce the pressures of competition at work in the market and the possibility of investment in the means of production. If landlords could not charge competition rents, what forces drove peasants to increase production? If they could not re-possess their tenants' lands, why should they invest in improving them?[103] If urban and mercantile capitalists did not possess the ultimate sanction of being able to seize their defaulting debtors' lands, how could they impose the rhythms of the market on production? Indeed, without this sanction, what kind of security was offered them to invest at all? A large gap was opened up and perpetuated between existing large accumulations of capital and the productive base. This had several implications for the character of both.

First, and, obviously, it tended to limit capital to relations of rentierism, commodity speculation and short-term usury. Profits of a kind could be made in these with less difficulty than in confronting the agrarian community for control of the land.[104] Second, capital was

[102] The continuing 'diffusion' of effective authority in late nineteenth-century North Indian society is the subject of Musgrave, 'Landlords' and 'Rural Credit' and also, 'Social Power and Social Change in the United Provinces 1860–1920', Chaudhuri and Dewey (eds), *Economy and Society.*

[103] The general failure of zamindars and other rentier proprietors to maintain, let alone improve, irrigation works was the cause of endless complaint in this period. As an example, see *Land Revenue Madras*, 1904–05, 'Report on Chingleput'.

[104] For reasons of analytical convenience, it is going to be supposed that a sharp break can be made between members of the agrarian community, involved closely in the processes of production, and members of a metropolitan community who were distinguishable from the agrarian base and lived (whether capitalistically or feudalistically) on the profits of rent, revenue and commerce. The author is only too aware of the difficulties involved in applying this 'break' to reality where, certainly in densely populated and irrigated zones, 'metropolitan' groups such as mirasidars, petty Rajput landholders and Brahmin service families held village lands. None the less, he feels that the distinction serves some purpose in highlighting differences in the social and economic constraints on the uses of capital among groups located differently in the social structure.

deflected from productive investment in agriculture and pushed towards other uses. Landlord profits tended to drift off into further rent rights and urban property speculation or into the maintenance of the luxury display which supported the politics of rentierism.[105] Mercantile profits either stayed in moneylending and commodity speculation or, before the growth of industrialization, found outlets overseas or in revenue rights. Third, one consequence of failing to subordinate the agrarian base to capital was to leave it vulnerable to the vagaries of nature and insensitive to market changes. This increased the risks for those capitalists who speculated in its commodities, encouraging them into diffuse, risk-splitting operations which avoided concentration and consolidation in single activities.[106] But concentration and consolidation were essential to lowering costs and raising efficiency. And fourth, all this left a large measure of control over production with the small-holding farmers and petty village landowners who laboured, or directed labour, on the land.

It was not, of course, that these groups were entirely incapable of increasing market production or of developing the forces of production. They had been involved in a market context, albeit one imposed through the revenue system and the state, for generations. Their various patterns of internal differentiation were underpinned, now that revenue privileges were losing their value, by profits made from commodity production and exchange. Their internal relations showed an increasing stress on the status given by wealth rather than genealogical descent or political office. The commercial capitalism encouraged by the growth of the colonial export trades and of internal commodity markets made an obvious impression on, and elicited an obvious response from, 'village' society.[107] It was rather that, in this context, there were severe limits on their ability to secure and qualitatively improve production on the land. First, for many small producers, a large part of the profits of production tended to be secured by moneylenders and market operators. While, and increasingly, larger producers may have done better and, indeed,

---

[105] Metcalf, *Land*, chs 11, 12. Among petty landholding 'service' groups, investment in education was another use for agricultural profits.

[106] For the extreme 'risk-context' of North Indian banking and mercantile operations, see C. A. Bayly, 'Old style Merchants and Risk', paper read at conference on risk in South Asian social and economic history, University of Pennsylvania, 1977.

[107] For examples, see my 'Country Politics: Madras 1880–1930', *Modern Asian Studies* (VII), 1973; D. Hardiman, 'The Crisis of the Lesser Patidars', D. A. Low (ed.), *The Congress and the Raj* (London, 1977); N. Charlesworth, 'Rich Peasants and Poor Peasants in Late Nineteenth-Century Maharashtra', Dewey and Hopkins, *Impact*; J. Banaji, 'Capitalist Domination and the Small Peasantry', *Economic and Political Weekly* (August), 1977.

acquired some of these profits from small neighbours, the surplus was
seldom of a kind to finance heavy fixed investments (other than wells).
The scale of production and landholding at this level of rural society was
not such as to generate sufficient private resources. Such resources would
have to be borrowed and, in the absence of cheap state finance, this
created a second problem. The risks of large-scale borrowing were
penal. Most of the markets served by Indian production were highly
volatile and difficult to predict. Moreover, the growing scarcity of land
(the means of subsistence) was starting to make it very precious. To
mortgage its future possession against an investment loan was to gamble
for very high stakes. Indian farmers showed an almost universal aversion
to long-term borrowing on the security of the land.[108]

And third, continuing community conventions, in part enforced by
the conservatism of the law but in part filling the social vacuum created
by the absence of the institutions of a modern state, constrained the
forms of entrepreneurial activity. Although, indeed, there was competition between farming families for the land, it was competition not
directly regulated by, or constituted in, the market. In tightly corporate
peasantries, such as the Jats of East Punjab and West U.P., the possibilities of capitalist exploitation were restricted by the reliance of all individual farming families on community panchayats and consensus. The
farmer who attempted to maximize his profits at the expense of his
neighbours by, for example, changing the customary terms of crop-
sharing rents or importing extra-local labour to work his fields, was
liable to incur heavy censure and sabotage.[109] In more hierarchic
communities, caste fellows and lineage relations might exercise a special
call on the patronage and protection of the wealthy. In general, local
landowners were expected to grow and store subsistence crops for a wide
variety of clients.[110] The restraints were not completely rigid: they left
room for a degree of market production and many were slowly being

[108] On risk-aversion in the context of Punjabi farming, see Kessinger, *Vilyatpur*, chs 4,
6. Needless to say, as a function both of the size of profits and the degree of risk,
propensity to invest (as in wells) varied considerably with the particularities of agrarian
conditions. In, for example, the cotton-belt of South India, a combination of particularly wealthy and large landholders together with a profitability in cotton hardly to be
equalled by local grain production promoted an expansion of well investment on a
considerable scale. In the 'wheat frontier' of the C.P., a similar scale of borrowings and
investments was in evidence. Both of these cases, however, seem exceptional.
[109] T. G. Kessinger, 'The Peasant Farm in North India 1848–1968', *Explorations in
Economic History* (XII), 1975.
[110] For example, see my *Provincial Politics*, pp. 74–8. On the general influence of the
need for grain storage against famine, see M. McAlpin. 'The Effects of Markets on Rural
Income Distribution in Nineteenth-Century India', *Explorations in Economic History*
(XII), 1975.

eroded over time. But they held back and made difficult a 'perfect' response to the market opportunities theoretically available to landowners and producers of agricultural commodities.[111]

The political and legal context in which the raj invited capital to work, was not very conducive to the development of the forces of production. It contained a series of restrictions on the social competition which, at least in Marxian theories of economic change, drive forward the revolution in the means of production. In India, the social groups already established on the land were being protected from the competitive threats of others both above and below them in the class structure. The tenancy and indebtedness laws, and the continuing chaos of the courts, kept landlord and mercantile capital at a remove from the productive base. Custom and conservative legal conventions guaranteed that members of 'dominant' caste communities of landholders would not be pressed by the land hunger of those from inferior statuses. Although competition within these communities, fuelled as much by demographic pressures as by anything else, was growing, it was unable to produce qualitatively significant results. As the state steadily withdrew the coercive pressures which, in the past, had whipped agrarian society into servicing the market and left the development of production to the 'free' interplay of class forces, so it was helping to create a class structure premised on perpetual economic stagnation.[112]

How and why did the late nineteenth-century raj get itself into this extraordinary position? Recurrent in the literature of Indian history are arguments that the maintenance of this 'quasi-traditional' agrarian base was of maximum utility to, at least, the British metropolitan economy and, possibly, to the Indian capital locked up in the systems of rentierism, moneylending and commodity speculation.[113] For the British, it produced a steady stream of cash crop exports at the price of very little effort. The stream not only carried forward government finances but

[111] Once more, of course, the degree to which these 'restraints' operated was a function of the local agrarian structure and its precise market context. These structures and contexts were given to wide variation and in some areas they permitted considerable agricultural expansion. But it remained quantitative expansion within the existing mode of labour-intensive, small-scale, family-organized production.

[112] We are beginning to become aware of how far the state apparatus of the ancien régime and early Company rule had not merely extracted surplus but also invested in the means of production through takkavi, irrigation and political protection. For examples, see Stokes, *Peasant*, ch. 3.

[113] For a classic statement, see R. and R. Ray, 'The Dynamics of Continuity in Rural Bengal', *Indian Economic and Social History Review* (X), 1973; also, by implication for the colonial period, H. Alavi, 'India and the Colonial Mode of Production', *Socialist Register* *1975*.

also, via international currency manipulations, helped metropolitan balance of payments problems. Within the Indian economy, it offered easy profits to ex-patriate business interests, who could use monopoly powers in the market to strip producers of most of the potential rewards, and to British industry, which need anticipate no rival industrialization in so 'backward' a context. For Indian capital, the situation also offered ample opportunity to profit from the peasantry. The law and the state validated rental relations and provided machinery to aid collections. The small scale of Indian farming, its distance from the market and need for short-term credit to pay revenue and finance seasonal operations, put creditors and men with power in the market in a very strong position and enabled them to manipulate the mechanisms of exchange to their own advantage. In effect, on this reading of the evidence, the colonial class structure appears perfectly functional to, and the paradigm creation of, both metropolitan and Indian capital. At costs kept low by lack of need to invest in the means of production and at risks kept low by their transference to the peasant producer, capital could enjoy an unproblematic profitability.

On a different reading, however, difficulties begin to appear. First, while indeed the exploitation of India was profitable to those metropolitan interests involved in it, the nature of this exploitation reduced their numbers and cut off many other metropolitan interests from sharing in it. Cotton manufacturers and import/export trading houses might do well but capital goods producers and finance capitalists found much less in the Indian economy to attract them.[114] Its structure was not functional to their operations and it remains to be seen why they should not have pressed the limited Indian 'establishment' for better access to India and have pushed for a greater development of the forces of production, on which their own profits depended. Second, the stagnation of the agrarian base left it vulnerable to the climate, and this risk was one which metropolitan and domestic capital both shared with the peasantry. Periodically, when famine struck, rents proved uncollectable, advances made to cultivators for their crops were lost, the import/export market collapsed and the state went into the red. True, the risk to capital was only bankruptcy whereas to the peasantry it was death. But, for all parties engaged, a seriously undercapitalized agriculture provided a context of constant danger.

But third, and perhaps most important of all, the logic of the market economy was developmental and that of this agrarian structure static. Both the international market and imperial systems, of which India was

[114] See R. Ray, *Industrialization in India* (New Delhi, 1979), ch. 1.

a part, were changing over time and making new demands on their components. The nature of Indian agricultural production limited the possibilities of its response. Until the turn of the twentieth century, this problem went largely unnoticed. A considerable quantitative expansion in agricultural output, as new lands were opened up by the plough and the well to petty commodity production, and artificially favourable export prices, caused by imbalances in the gold:silver ratio, gave the appearance of an agrarian boom. Thereafter, however, these conditions disappeared, and the real intractability of the agrarian base became clear. Several leading market regions (the wheat frontier in C.P., the Gujerat cotton belt) were badly hit by the famines of the 1890s and subsequently found it very difficult to get back their markets.[115] Changing methods of production in other parts of the world, mechanized agriculture in North America and fresh zones of peasant farming in South East Asia and Africa, threatened their competitiveness. Equally, changes in the nature of the metropolitan economies began to undermine the existing 'colonial' relationship with India and not to replace it. The modern chemical industry displaced the need for several tropical crops (such as indigo); the traditional imperial export industries (such as cotton) reached saturation point in their Asian markets; new patterns of multi-lateral trade between the developed economies stimulated capital goods production and turned metropolitan interests away from impoverished satellites.[116] The 'disengagement' between the colonial and metropolitan economies, which became obvious in the inter-war period, was already starting. The proportion of world trade in which India was involved declined steadily from the turn of the century.[117] And this decline, of course, marked a reciprocal shrinkage in the possibilities of metropolitan exploitation and profit. Nor was it only British capitalists who began to feel the strait-jacket of Indian poverty. The Boer War revealed to the British Parliament the extent to which the rising costs of modern warfare made its Indian military barracks useless. This imperial 'police action' simply could not be financed off Indian revenues, as had so many before.[118] Indian economic stagnation now

[115] For examples, see Stokes, *Peasant*, ch. 11; Hardiman, 'The Crisis'.

[116] The rate of increase in British cotton textile exports to India slowed noticeably from the 1890s. S. B. Saul has seen 1890 as the critical turning-point in the old British-dominated, colony-orientated pattern of world trade. S. B. Saul, *Studies in British Overseas Trade 1870–1914* (Liverpool, 1960), ch. 5.

[117] From about 4 per cent in 1900 to 2.5 per cent by 1939. The fall was steady and not merely a reflection of the depression of the early 1930s. See B. R. Tomlinson, *The Political Economy of the Raj* (London, 1979), ch. 2.

[118] See Committee of Imperial Defence, Minutes, 11 June 1903 and 5 August 1903, Cabinet Papers (CAB 2/1), Public Record Office, London.

began to hit the British tax-payer in the pocket, where it hurt most. By these years too, Indian rentier and mercantile capital was starting to be pinched. Landlords were failing to keep their rents in line with inflation and, in several provinces, were finding that the combination of occupancy tenure rights and complicated legal rituals was making it difficult for them to collect rents at all. In Bengal, the levels of effective rent collection appear to have collapsed;[119] while in West U.P., many petty zamindars were under the severest of pressures.[120] The signs of stress in the mercantile communities were unmistakable. The protections afforded to the agrarian community drove many professional bania groups out of agricultural finance and turned their roles over to wealthier members of the community itself.[121] A flood of mercantile capital made for better opportunities overseas, in East and South Africa and South East Asia.[122] A wave of bankruptcies, especially in the wake of the financial crisis of 1908, shook the financial structure of India.[123] Even European business houses started to increase the diversification of their operations in order to be less reliant on the commodity trades.[124]

By the early twentieth century, all was by no means well with the Indian agrarian economy. Metropolitan government and capital as much as Indian government and capital were encountering increasing difficulties in working it to their present needs, while the future looked dark. Yet, so far from responding to these imperatives by pursuing policies of structural change, the raj was inclined to do exactly the opposite. Every crisis was met by efforts further to defend the agrarian community and to shore up its antique mode of production. Both tenancy and indebtedness legislation reached the height of their popularity in the decade before the First World War; while conservationist co-operative credit and canal colony programmes speeded up.

The policy documents of the period, however, make it plain that the raj saw the agrarian problem much more in political than in immediately economic terms. Its policies of social conservation and peasant protection

---

[119] See R. and R. Ray, 'Zamindars and Jotedars: A Study of Rural Politics in Bengal', *Modern Asian Studies* (IX), 1975.

[120] F. C. R. Robinson, *Separatism Among Indian Muslims* (Cambridge, 1974), ch. 2.

[121] As has been argued for Western India by R. Kumar, *Western India*, ch. 6; Charlesworth, 'Rich Peasants'.

[122] The Nattukottai Chetties provide the clearest example. By the late 1920s, their overseas assets were thought to be Rs 60 crores. But Western Indian financiers were active in the opening up of East Africa and in the Natal sugar production economy.

[123] For the currency problems of 1907–08, see Tomlinson, *Political Economy*, ch. 1.

[124] Binnys of Madras, for example, went into cotton textile production; Parrys of Madras increased their hold on the alcohol distillation industry; in Calcutta, firms such as Andrew Yule speeded up their diversification into industries such as coal.

flowed from the fear that if competitive capitalist relations were allowed freedom to take over the countryside, the resulting conflict would destroy the raj's own institutions of government and political security.[125] On such an understanding, it clearly made sense to block the development of these relations and to hang on to its inheritance for as long as possible. The price of this strategy, which meant that the value of the inheritance would be dwindling, was lower than that of encouraging the capitalist process and risking the loss of everything. But there are two curiosities or paradoxes about this otherwise readily comprehensible position. The first is the extent to which British fears always ran far ahead of Indian realities. The raj was already paranoid about the consequences of the imminent capitalist transformation before any signs that it might be taking place appeared. It jumped at the shadows of small-scale and hardly novel riots between landlords and tenants or between moneylenders and their peasant debtors, as if they represented the silhouettes of a massive social drama being played out before it.[126] Moreover, it frequently misunderstood the nature of the political struggles actually taking place. Many of its conservationist policies pre-dated the problems they were meant to solve and thus killed in advance the development of the conditions to which they were supposed to be a response. Second, this strategy of protection represented a very strange way for any capitalist state, or at least state attached to capitalist metropolitan base, to behave. Leaving aside the ideologically-biased models of modernization theory, with their supposition of a smooth and 'osmotic' transition, all capitalist processes of development have involved (and continue to involve as part of their nature) political struggle, resistance and repression. The 'problem' faced by the raj was not unique to it but one of universal historical experience. However, it has been by no means universal for the political instruments of capitalist states to be used not to crush resistance but to protect and preserve the social bases from which it is arising. What would have been the consequence to Meiji Japan had its much larger and fiercer peasant and samurai rebellions led to an accommodation with, and freezing of, the Tokugawa social structure? Both the paranoia and the counter-intuitive behaviour of the raj need closer investigation for they may tell us something important about the peculiarities of the colonial context.

The consequences which the British Indian civil service, at various

---

[125] See, for example, Metcalf, *Aftermath*, chs 4–6; Barrier, *The Alienation*; Whitcombe, *Agrarian Conditions*, chs 4, 6.

[126] For example, see N. Charlesworth, 'The Myth of the Deccan Riots of 1875', *Modern Asian Studies* (VI), 1972; Stokes, *Peasant*, ch. 11; Musgrave, 'Social Power'.

times, claimed to fear most from a competitive capitalist conquest of agriculture were a decline in the land revenue, a link up between the wrath of dispossessed peasants and the emergent nationalist movement and a general collapse of political order leading to mass revolt.[127] Neither of the first two fears seems well-founded. It is unclear why mercantile capitalist landowners should have been any less able than peasants to meet the declining incidence of the land revenue, and evidence from a few areas where their penetration was considerable and had been attended by commercial development suggests precisely the reverse.[128] Where mercantile capital may indeed have interfered with revenue operations was where it was squeezing the peasantry dry through usury relations. But these relations were, arguably, as much a result of its inability to penetrate the productive process completely as of the degree of its existing penetration. It is also unclear, given the social character of the early nationalist movement, what kind of connection it could have made with a marginal peasantry being driven off the land. At most, this might have extended to propaganda (as in the Poona Sarvajanik Sabha). But, outside the Western-educated intelligentsia, most of nationalism's popular following seems to have come from urban commercial and mercantile groups who frequently were expressing frustrations at the limitations posed to their exploitation of the country-side by the raj (as over the Punjab Land Alienation Act). The third fear is the only one which seems to have substance. But the evidence that the threat was real is not strong. It was the shadow of the Mutiny rather than a cold examination of the facts, which turned the petty Deccan Riots into the justification for a far-reaching policy of peasant protection, and every act of bazaar violence into the augury of mass revolt. The tendency of the raj to over-dramatize the problem may be indicative of two significant features of Indian colonialism. First, a large part of the Indian Civil Service itself was, for whatever reason, opposed to a capitalist transformation of agrarian society and was fumbling for excuses to support its case. And second, the recurrent nightmare of the Mutiny suggests how extremely weak the raj felt its political and military position to be.

Both of these themes appear again in the logic which took the raj to opposing radical social change and in the contradictions which increasingly were exposed in its situation. Had the raj pursued a more aggres-

[127] Whitcombe, *Agrarian Conditions*, chs 4, 6; Metcalf, *Aftermath*, chs 4–6; R. Kumar, *Western India*, ch. 5.
[128] There seems to have been no revenue problem, for example, in the Namada valley during the wheat boom. See Stokes, *Peasant*, ch. 11.

sive set of capitalist policies, it would have needed a strong coercive arm. But where could this have come from? The obvious answer would seem the British Indian army, which absorbed over 40 per cent of the state's budget and stood as the awesome pillar of British might in South Asia. But, for these purposes, the army was wrongly constructed, geared to a different end and utterly useless. It was a wing of imperial policy worldwide and its principal roles were to defend the Indian frontier, maintain the Pax Britannica from Africa to China and protect international trade routes. It was no longer a domestic police force and, having an independent command structure, could not readily be engaged for internal purposes short of dire emergencies. The raj could not count on the army to face long-term civil dissidence and rebellion and, had it done so, one cost would have been the insecurity of the rest of the imperial system. Moreover, the army was particularly not a force which could have been deployed with safety against the North Indian countryside. It had become increasingly reliant on recruits from 'the martial races' of North India, whose own origins lay in the dominant peasant and petty landlord communities of the region.[129] Indeed, not only could it not be so deployed but its social character placed a set of counter-imperatives on the development of policy. Much of the Punjab Government's strategy of social conservation, derived from the need to maintain army loyalty by protecting and subventing the existing rural community.

Without the army, there was the police itself. However, as we have already seen, the later nineteenth-century police force was still deeply entangled in the networks of local level rural powers and, as such, could hardly be used to attack those powers and the social bases on which they rested. At the very least, a new type of centrally-directed police system would have had to be created. From the turn of the twentieth century, especially under Curzon's authoritarian promptings, such a system began to emerge. But it was held back by the eternal problem of cost, by the political resistance which it tended to provoke and by the difficulty of breaking down local loyalties.[130] By the time that police organization even began to approach its ideal, the political equation had altered and the police could not be used for an onslaught on the dominant village landowners of the countryside.

The question of the police provides a clue to a second dimension of the

[129] C. Dewey, 'The Rise of the Martial Castes: Changes in the Composition of the Indian Army, 1878–1914', paper read at conference on Social Stratification in India, University of Leicester, April 1977.

[130] For the police in South India, see D. Arnold, 'The Armed Police and Colonial Rule in South India', *Modern Asian Studies* (XI), 1977; also my *Provincial Politics*, ch 2.

problem. This concerned the enormous strength of the potential forces of resistance. In any initial confrontation with competitive capitalism, it was not so much the poor and the dispossessed who were going to be engaged and threatening revolt—or, if they were, the raj neither saw nor cared about them. Its advance palliative legislation did nothing for the landless and precious little for the two-acre ryot. Indeed, few of its processes and protections could be used if money and a degree of independence were not available. The archetypal occupancy tenant of the U.P. or peasant proprietor of the Punjab, whose interests were to be safeguarded, was conceived more as a substantial farmer than a marginal peasant. Rather, the serious resistance was imagined to come from the erstwhile dominant local-level elements in the mercantilist/revenue based political structure through which the ancien régime and its Company variant had operated. It was village community brotherhoods, mirasidars, inamdars, vatandars, pedda ryots and petty zamindars whose disaffection the British feared and which they tried to avoid. As early as the 1850s, when attempts in South India to resume inams had stirred the opposition of their substantial holders, the state had beaten a rapid retreat;[131] in the 1880s in Tanjore, when its revenue resettlement operations had touched mirasidar quick it had backed off and cut the revised rates of assessment.[132] The reasons for this sensitivity were cogent: these groups' influence over the entire agrarian base was strong and it was still being used to support many of the functions of government, such as revenue collection and the maintenance of the peace. Through influence over access to land, through the provision of employment and credit opportunities, through traditional ideologies of deference and through often extensive connections of caste and kinship, these land controlling groups could call out the countryside into sustained opposition or keep it stable for the raj. They made formidable enemies and, ultimately, could only be suppressed if the colonial authorities could come to build a different, an alternative, political structure which would distribute and validate the power of other classes in society. But where could the elements of a new class structure be found and would they work easily inside a colonial framework?

The answer, presumably, would have had to come from the social forces favourable to the expansion of capitalist relations. But, in the late nineteenth-century context, they were still weak, needed enormous support and opened out a further set of contradictions for the raj. Urban-based mercantile capitalists and large absentee landed pro-

[131] See *Papers on Inam.*
[132] See my *Provincial Politics*, ch. 1.

prietors, who had the resources and might have come to possess the incentives to play a new dominant role, seem to have exercised only the most contingent forms of authority over the village resident agrarian community. Their 'influence' has been seen to hinge on an ability to work through members of the local agrarian élite or to exploit cleavages within the community.[133] They tended to have little permanent standing or independent power in the rural areas and to be vulnerable to any closing up of the local community against them. If they became increasingly assertive and sought to take over direct control of the agricultural base, this closure could be guaranteed. They did not represent very promising material out of which to forge a new political system, certainly under the terms in which imperial collaborationist politics had to work. It would require a great effort on the raj's part, a massive elaboration of police and bureaucratic power, to push these interests down onto the foundations of production. But who would pay?

And there was a further problem. Would these groups be as prepared as the 'traditional' agrarian authorities they replaced to work within the framework of colonial rule? Ultimately, this question takes us to the general relationship between capitalism and nationalism, and indeed between capitalism and any particular political system, and lies beyond the scope of our inquiries. But there are good reasons for believing that, even if the development of Indian capitalism were compatible with some species of colonial rule, it was not the species then extant and its rise would have posed a threat to the current colonial establishment. First, given the constraints imposed by metropolitan dominance and the economic structure, it is very difficult to see how an expansion of Indian capitalist activity[134] could have avoided coming into conflict with existing metropolitan and ex-patriate business interests. The stasis of the economy meant that the rise of one group could only be at the expense of others: as Indian capital expanded its control over agricultural produce, it would necessarily run up against the dominant role currently played in the export, and some internal, trades by British capital. Moreover, challenges would be posed to the hegemony of British imported manufactures. Of course, this did not mean that an expanding Indian capitalism might not establish new links with different parts of the metropolitan economy (as to some degree happened later). But it did suggest that the present 'old India hands' would be squeezed, and their squeals were

[133] Especially by Musgrave, 'landlords' and 'Rural Credit'; also Charlesworth, 'Myth'.

[134] By this I mean an expansion beyond the confines of the 'middle-man' commodity trades, where it was confined, to the bases of production.

treated with some importance by the raj. Second, an expanding Indian
capitalism would necessarily have demanded a greater share of state
power and political authority. Again, there is no reason why this should
not have been accommodated within a continuing colonial context, but
it would not have been the same colonial context. In particular, the ICS
would have had to have shared power with Indians and granted Indian
politicians and bureaucrats a measure of equality. This, of course, they
regarded as anathema and struggled against down to the dying days of
the raj.[135] In the late nineteenth century, the mere suggestion offended
against widely-held theories about racial superiority and the British
civilizing mission. And third, the social values of the ICS were plainly
out of kilter with those of the groups from which emergent Indian
capitalists came (or were anticipated to come). It was the 'martial'
races, the 'yeoman' peasantry and the magnificent feudality whom the
late Victorian mind respected. The ethics of the moneylender and
Brahmin were held in a distinctly lower regard and the notion that the
interests of the latter should be developed at the expense of the former
was outrageous.[136] By a curious process of elision, whose logic is not easy
to follow, fears for the feudality and peasantry were then converted into
fears for the raj itself and it was argued that an Indian society dominated
by the bania and the priest would have no room for the Briton.

Whatever the wider possibilities of the situation, the prospects of an
active Indian capitalism, gnawing at the bases of the agrarian order,
displeased the civil servants and businessmen who composed the British
Indian establishment. They made their own interests and prejudices
synonymous with the fate of any raj at all. In view of their influence over
Indian policy, it may not be surprising that they managed to drive many
of the elements of a proto-Indian capitalism, especially on the land, into
opposition to themselves and thus to bring their prophesy of a connection between capitalism and nationalism to self-fulfilment. Blocked and
frustrated by the protective legislation, Indian business groups showed a
strong tendency to respond to the appeal of nationalism. In the Punjab,
the Land Alienation Act made the urban mercantile community
natural allies of the Congress; in Bengal, the twin pressures on the
bhadralogh of white racist businessmen in Calcutta and a favoured

[135] H. A. Ewing, 'The Indian Civil Service 1919–42. Some Aspects of British Control
in India', unpublished Ph.D. dissertation, University of Cambridge, 1980.
[136] These sentiments seem to have been particularly strong in North India, where the
feudal 'Oudh' policy was influential in the U.P. Secretariat and the more peasant
orientated 'Punjab' school held sway farther West. For discussions of the civilian
mentality, see Musgrave, 'Social Power'; C. Dewey, 'Images of the Village Community',
Modern Asian Studies (VI), 1972; Metcalf, *Aftermath*, chs 4, 5.

Muslim tenantry outside pushed their politics along an anti-imperialist course.[137] By the early twentieth century, when the case for structural change in the agrarian economy was becoming strong, it was less fantasy than fact that the social forces capable of advancing this change were those most vehemently opposed to the continuation of British rule.

The raj, then, was, or felt itself to be, in an acute dilemma. Having established a context for the capitalist development of agrarian society, it could see no way of allowing the corollarous social transformation to come about and survive. It therefore proceeded to obstruct the unfolding of the logic which it had set in motion in the first place. But all its problems stemmed from the perception that it needed to survive indefinitely in the shape which it had acquired by the late nineteenth century. This accorded with the interests of the narrow band of businessmen and bureaucrats currently holding the Indian jewel. But why should it have accorded with the interests of the much broader splay of interests in the metropolitan economy and government? Economic stagnation kept them out of potential markets, limited the opportunities for exploitation and, ultimately, improverished the empire.[138] The answer to this riddle may be that, within the terms of profitability set by the international market system, there was no way that metropolitan capital could have promoted a more significant development of the Indian economy, and the price of trying would have been the loss of the existing limited benefits. What India needed above all else and before appreciable movements in her economic structure would begin was a very large dose of infra-structural investment capital.[139] The deficiencies of the railway system, of irrigation facilities and of support services to production and commerce posed immense limitations to development. Yet where could the colonial state have found the resources for such a massive undertaking? It could hardly have got them by sequestering existing Indian assets. Such a policy would certainly have promoted political revolt besides dampening the existing precarious levels of demand. If it went to the money market, what profits and security could it have offered to pull capital out of its current uses? India had no great and valuable mineral wealth. She enjoyed few comparative advantages in production costs

[137] See Barrier, *The Alienation*; J. Broomfield, *Elite Politics in a Plural Society* (California, 1969); G. Johnson, *Provincial Politics and Indian Nationalism* (Cambridge, 1973).

[138] The question of the real benefits to advanced capitalist economies of impoverished colonial satellites was raised by G. Lichteim, *Imperialism* (London, 1961).

[139] This, at least, seems agreed by all the juxtaposed theorists of the colonial Indian economy. See A. K. Bagchi, *Private Investment in India 1900–1939* (Cambridge, 1972); and a review of this by M. D. Morris, 'Private Industrial Investment in the Indian Sub-continent 1900–39' *Modern Asian Studies* (VIII), 1974.

and her own markets were too small to warrant the re-location of existing international industries.[140] Most particularly, the many problems of her agrarian base made attempts to develop her agricultural production for international consumption questionable. The potential resistance of the dense Asian peasantry, the depth of ecological weaknesses and the need for many non-economic investments (for example, in transport to articulate the internal food-market) made the costs of development very high. It could hardly be that it was worth capital's while coping with these problems when the opening out of Canada, Australia, South Africa and South East Asia offered comparable commodities at much cheaper rates and less risk. In effect, there was nothing in India to attract the capital necessary to a fundamental transformation of the economy.

British colonialism's possibilities of exploitation were limited by two powerful sets of constraints. On the one side lay the structure of class relations built up in the previous epoch of state mercantilism, which was difficult to change and threatened serious revolt if disturbed; on the other lay the international market economy, whose competitive norms gave it only a peripheral interest in Indian production. In these circumstances, the narrow British establishment in India offered the metropolis the most that it could hope to gain. To reverse the time-honoured formulation, it was less British colonialism which was determining the structure of the Indian economy than that structure, in its class and international context, which was determining the forms which colonial, and metropolitan, exploitation could take. What the late nineteenth-century establishment offered was a free army, the import/export trades and guaranteed payment on the sterling debt. Even if these proved to be dwindling assets, it was clearly better to hold onto them for as long as possible than to back a futile gamble on a class transformation which could not be brought to completion but might just create disturbances in its wake powerful enough to break the raj and the bases of political order in India. 'Holding on', however, meant allowing the present establishment its head and the metropolitan government seems to have taken its prejudiced and self-interested understanding of Indian politics as gospel and given it freedom to suppress its enemies before they stirred.

The raj found itself in a situation in which it would have liked to stop history somewhere around 1880. At that point, it possessed a near perfect equilibrium between the development of the forces of production necessary to its economic needs and the solidity of the social and political

---

[140] R. Ray recently has argued that the colonial economy was not underutilizing supply factors to its existing demand capacity. Ray, *Industrialization*, ch. 3.

structures necessary to its security. The strong quantitative expansion in agricultural production and the temporary profitability of the new cash crop markets were enlivening the old mode of production without, as yet, threatening to dissolve it. There appeared to be room for accommodation between metropolitan (and indigenous rentier and mercantile) capital and the existing agrarian structure in the buoyancy of the economy. All could live together, in some kind of harmony, without contending for the bases of one another's social existence. The hope of this harmony, and balance, was fully expressed in the law. The apparent confusions and contradictions in its theories and procedures served to make it an intrument of compromise. In practice, it did not deal in absolute rights and wrongs, in property rights and exclusions. The tenancy and indebtedness legislation of the period sought to give the landlord his 'fair' rent without threatening the tenant's continued possession of his land and the creditor his 'fair' returns without pauperizing the debtor. The complex and long-winded procedures of the law, and the dependence of its executive machinery on local power structures, promoted out of court compromises and settlements.[141] The law pursued a modus vivendi between all the parties contending for the production of the land, helping capital to extract some level of profit from the agrarian community but obstructing it from a deeper social penetration. The civil law, in effect, was being used by the colonial state to maintain the class balance most suitable to its present purposes.

But, of course, history does not stand still and, certainly by the early twentieth century if not before in some areas, the bases of this balance were ceasing to exist. On the land, the rate of demographic increase was catching up with the possibilities of the quantitative expansion in cultivation and the favourable market conditions were on the turn. The inherited mode of production could no longer take as easily the pressures being imposed upon it from above; and the force of competition was starting to make landlord and mercantile capital increase the pressures. The conditions underpinning the raj's optimistic compromise were fast collapsing and its legal institutions, designed to foster harmony, were being used in the course of a class struggle no longer capable of being contained in these terms. The emergence of this struggle was reflected both in the huge increase in litigation and in the more rapid pace of legislative enactment in the years before the First World War. As the courts failed to hold the compromises required of them, the raj was attempting desperately to re-create through legislation the social condi-

---

[141] For discussions of the 'long' political process of which the law was but a part, see Whitcombe, *Agrarian Conditions*, ch. 5.

tions which economic change was destroying. Needless to say, the attempt did not work but rather exacerbated the sources of conflict. Capital and the agrarian community were in direct confrontation. By holding them together, without allowing either adequately to subordinate the other, the raj was sitting still while their antagonism intensified and perpetuated a framework which prevented its resolution. In the wake of the First World War it was to face the costs of its policies in the explosion of agrarian agitation, which attended the non-cooperation movement.[142] By the second decade of the twentieth century, the British Indian state was at a cross-roads. It could no longer maintain its precious balance from a laissez faire economic position and through mere manipulation of the civil law. It was obliged to re-think its strategy of imperial rule and look for some different answers.

In the period between the wars, three significant developments overtook the creation and definition of property rights in land. First, although the formal judicial apparatus continued to increase its sway over land disputes, it was changing its social character. Part of this change came simply from the Indianization of the judiciary but part, and politically the most important part, came from the devolution of the courts' authority to locally elected or appointed committees. In the late nineteenth century, some use had been made of local notables to sit on arbitration committees and many of the state's village officials had possessed petty judicial powers.[143] However, after the First World War, the movement to devolve the administration of the law became much more pronounced. In Madras by the late 1920s, panchayats elected by village landowners dealt with nine-tenths of all the officially recorded cases, and certainly the vast majority of petty disputes about land.[144] As we have seen, throughout the colonial era, unofficial and informal arbitrational procedures had always existed in rural society, supplementing and often being more effective than the jurisdictions of the British courts. What was happening now was that these procedures were being drawn up into the structure of the state and given a full legitimation.

Second, there was growing state regulation of the uses to which

[142] See D. N. Dhanagare, *Agrarian Movements and Gandhian Politics* (Agra, 1975); M. H. Siddiqi, 'The Peasant Movement in Pratabgrah 1920' *Indian Economic and Social History Review* (IX), 1972; W. F. Crawley, 'Kisan Sabhas and Agrarian Revolt in the United Provinces', *Modern Asian Studies* (V), 1971.

[143] For examples, see my *Provincial Politics*, ch. 4; in Bombay, under the terms of the Deccan Agriculturists' Relief Act (1879), village officials had been empowered to arbitrate in debt suits; in Punjab, the courts had long encouraged the use of appointed arbitrators, see *Civil Law* (Punjab), for example 1868–69.

[144] C. J. Baker, 'Madras Headmen', in Chaudhuri and Dewey, *Economy*.

property could be put and of relations in the market. Some of these interventions also had their origins in the previous period. Under the fiction of a special branch of 'revenue law', the bureaucracy had kept in touch with the administration of landlord/tenant relations and influenced the setting and collection of rents. Revenue law, however, had existed alongside the civil law and been dependent upon it for many of its sanctions. Defaulting tenants might be penalized at revenue law but they could lose their occupancy tenures, which would represent a species of property transfer, only by due process of the courts. But the domain of revenue law had shown a strong tendency to expand, especially towards the end of the nineteenth century and in the early twentieth century.[145] By the interwar period, it was dominant over litigation in the zamindari regions and effectively being used by the state to convert rental relations into a department of government administration. Rental rights and obligations were fixed down to increasingly small details and taken further out of the market context.[146] Equally, a number of provincial anomalies and gaps between theory and practice, which had kept the state at a remove from agrarian relations, were resolved to bring the administrative apparatus closer to society. In 1921 and 1930 respectively, Oudh and Malabar received tenancy legislation which gave them more effective occupancy right; the 'planter' problem in Bihar was largely overcome;[147] the ryotwari system in Western India finally broke through the residual corporate social forms blocking its penetration of the agrarian base.[148] Further, bureaucratic regulation of the overseas labour market tightened. This process had begun in North India in the 1890s and was extended southwards, to the large migrant labour flows to Ceylon and Burma, in the wake of the First World War.[149] In administrative theory, of course, British Indian government, even at the height of the popularity of laissez-faire ideology, implicitly had possessed strong powers of intervention in the market place. Now it was using them much more vigorously and purposefully than before.

Moreover, several crises of the period pushed it into invading areas which it always had claimed lay beyond its competence. In the food shortages at the end of the First World War, several provincial govern-

[145] See Whitcombe, *Agrarian Conditions*, ch. 5 for U.P.; revenue courts for the Permanently Settled estates reached Madras in 1908.

[146] See D. Rothermund, *Government, Landlord and Peasant in India* (Wiesbaden, 1978).

[147] S. Henningham, 'The Social Setting of the Champaran Satyagraha', *Indian Economic and Social History Review* (XIII), 1976.

[148] D. Hardiman, 'Peasant Agitation in Kheda District, Gujarat 1917–34', unpublished Ph.D. dissertation, University of Sussex, 1977.

[149] H. Tinker, *A New System of Slavery* (London, 1974), pp. 279–80; also my *Provincial Politics*, ch. 7.

ments found themselves having to step into the market in order to prevent not only economic dislocation but the threat of serious political violence. True, this intervention concerned itself only with the manipulation of transport and the purchase of foreign grain. It did not yet reach domestic retail.[150] But the pattern was set and the ideological objection to 'interference' in the market removed. During the next major food crisis of the Second World War, the state moved in on retail and took up a position whence it has seldom been able to escape. The inter-war problems of the Bombay textile industry provoked the state into a leap into the raw cotton market and into the direction of supplies.[151] The crisis of the depression proved another spur to intervention. The chaos of unrecoverable rents and debts left in its wake suspended the operation of the market over large parts of the rural economy. The raj, albeit too late to avoid the rise of major political protest, set up a series of Conciliation Boards to arbitrate disputes and passed debt cancellation legislation, both of which overrode the legal conventions of property right.[152] Finally, and very tellingly, the state found itself becoming involved in the relations of rural labour. It had always been desperate to avoid this involvement and to keep out of intra-village labour systems. Inadvertently, its property laws had implied both regulation and change: the claims of dependent labourers to shares in their patrons' product had never been recognized as a form of property right.[153] But, in practice, this implication had not been picked up by society to any great degree. The economic problems of the period, however, brought labour and landed property into greater confrontation over division of the social product and the law (backed by a more effective police) found itself supporting the landed interest in protecting property against the claims of labour.[154]

And third, the value in the possession of landed property began to revert directly to a function of the state system. This function, however, was very different from that under the old mercantilist state. First, the political benefits accrued not merely to those who held specific tax-shielded state offices but in general to the increasingly small proportion of agrarian society who held significant amounts of land at all. Making

[150] D. Arnold, 'Looting, Grain Riots and Government Policy in South India 1918', *Past and Present* (84), 1979.

[151] A. D. D. Gordon, *Businessmen and Politics* (New Delhi, 1978), ch. 3.

[152] C. J. Baker, *The Politics of South India* (Cambridge, 1976), ch. 3; B. R. Tomlinson, *The Indian National Congress and the Raj* (London, 1976), ch. 3.

[153] The precise legal understanding of dependent labour relations is difficult to assess. At times, it seems to have stressed the rule of the market but at times the rule of some species of custom. For an interesting case, see Kessinger, *Vilyatpur*.

[154] See, for examples, Arnold, 'Armed Police'.

explicit what inflationary trends and the rigidity of the land revenue system had made implicit since the middle of the nineteenth century, the raj consciously shifted the burden of taxation off landownership.[155] State finances became increasingly reliant on customs and excise duties and taxes on non-agricultural incomes, which fell most heavily on the urban and poorer rural sections of the population.[156] Land ownership itself was coming to include a privileged tax status. More than this, the raj also was redirecting income and capital towards landholders. To some degree, of course, it had been obliged to do this even in the late nineteenth century, especially where deep economic and demographic pressures were threatening the social balances which it sought. The imperatives towards social conservation, as well as economic gain, were represented in its programme for the punjab canal colonies, which was not costed on a strictly profit-making basis as were most irrigation projects and which was undertaken mainly to relieve population problems, threatening the bases of the 'traditional' agrarian order, in the East Punjab. The colonies were settled on social models which tried to replicate and perpetuate as far as possible (though with less than perfect success) the structure of landed society in the regions from which the immigrants came.[157] Equally, the initial and largely unsuccessful co-operative credit movement had provided a small amount of government funding in an effort to make agrarian society more self-reliant and less dependent on socially-threatening urban sources of finance. Between the wars, however, state activities to aid and subvent landowners became much stronger. In several provinces, the co-operative credit movement took off and, by the middle 1930s, was coming to provide at least the larger landowners, who could take advantage of it, with a privileged credit status and means of taking over local-level credit systems from 'outside' financiers.[158] As state proscriptions on the activities of 'professional' moneylenders and commodity dealers hardened, protected opportunities for landowners to increase their role in agrarian commerce also appeared.[159] The coming of tariff protection increased the profitability of some kinds of production at the expense of the consumer.[160] Moreover, through new sources of funding, greater

[155] See *Report of the Indian Taxation Enquiry Committee 1924–25* (Government of India, 1925), Vol. 1.

[156] *Ibid.* For example, about 15–20 per cent of state revenues came from the abkari excise which fell mainly on the cheap liquor drunk by the lower classes.

[157] See M. Darling, *The Punjab Peasant in Prosperity and Debt* (Oxford, 1925), ch. 7.

[158] B. L. Robert, 'Agricultural Co-operatives in Madras 1893–1937', *Indian Economic and Social History Review* (XVI), 1979.

[159] For examples, see my 'Country Politics'; also Tomlinson, *Political Economy*, ch. 2.

[160] Especially sugar.

resources were beginning to be pumped into agricultural development. Government experiments with export cash crops produced several notable successes: most particularly, the 'Cambodia' cotton strains which underlay the cotton boom in the extreme South.[161] Development agencies began, however falteringly, to consider the problems of agricultural profitability and, via the expanded competence of district and local boards, rural infra-structural services (particularly roads capable of carrying motor transport) were much improved.[162] The agrarian community, or at least the land-possessing members of it, were becoming net beneficiaries of the state.

Second, the devolution of the administration continued much beyond the judiciary and opened up a political process which gave certain members of the agrarian community 'legitimate' control over many of the ancillaries of agriculture. Administration of forest rights, irrigation and local markets was being transferred to committees whose members could enhance or diminish the value of land by their decisions. Doubtless, of course, informal political processes had been involved in these matters even when their control lay with the nationally a-political bureaucracy. But these changes formalized such processes and gave them the imprimatur of the state. As ecological and demographic problems increasingly beset agriculture, access to these ancillary facilities played a growing role in determining the profitability of production. It was an access now firmly in the hands of the dominant elements in the local agrarian community.[163]

These developments in the nature of property right and value in land make it plain that the colonial state was still concerned to protect the social bases of petty commodity production. But it was doing so in different ways which carried subtly different implications for the character of agrarian relations. It was no longer simply manipulating the terms of the civil law to provide some general shields from the potentially disruptive effects of mercantile and rentier capitalism. Much more, it was isolating the wealthier members of the landholding community and trying to establish positive relations with them, which could act as pillars of a new political system. Its strategy had several important consequences. It became more possible for the larger landowners to emancipate themselves from some of the constraints of community and custom. The new police protection afforded by greater bureaucratic penetration

[161] Baker, *Politics*, ch. 3.
[162] In Madras by the mid-1930s, for example, local boards and municipalities were handling 44 per cent of all government expenditure. Baker, *Politics*, ch. 2.
[163] See my *Provincial Politics*, ch. 4.

facilitated the movement in wage forms from patronage and dependency to casual labour. This movement had been progressing slowly from the later nineteenth century but now speeded up in the depressed agricultural conditions of the period.[164] It promoted a much clearer differentiation in the agrarian community between those with sufficient land to be full-time farmers and those without, dependent on labouring for a large part of their subsistence. The latter were pushed into a situation whence their relative share of the social product declined even faster than before.[165] Naturally, such a movement provoked fierce resistance from labour, manifested in a wave of riots and violence.[166] But better police coercion sustained the rights of property owners.[167] The new control gained by the upper echelons of rural society over the apparatus of the law also proved of positive advantage to them. It was less a case now of using the law as a defensive weapon to block out the encroachments of absentee zamindars and banias than of using it as a weapon of aggression to cement dominance within the local community. In the generation before independence, as afterwards, there was little contrast or contradiction between the notion of property right found in official panchayati tribunals and that in the higher courts of the law. The two were symmetrical and continuous, reflecting the symbiosis being achieved between the ideology of 'governance' and that of the village landowning class interest.[168] These legal and institutional changes, of course, were part of a much wider set of social and political changes overtaking India in these years. The devolution of the law and of agrarian administration was an aspect of the general devolution of political authority from the colonial bureaucracy to domestic politicians, from Briton to Indian, as the raj moved steadily, if for a long time unwittingly, to its demise. As the British hesitatingly withdrew, a new structure capable of articulating the political relations of a 'national' society was being forged. Political devolution both made possible and paid for the expansion of the bureaucracy and the interventionism of the

[164] It seems generally agreed by many writers that this period was critical in the weakening of 'traditional' labour relations, although explanations differ. See, for example, Breman, *Patronage*, ch. 5. Less often considered, however, are the political conditions which would permit what for many dependent labourers amounted to a considerable deterioration in, at least, their security and, frequently, their standard of living.

[165] See M. Mukherji, 'National Income', V. B. Singh (ed.), *The Economic History of India* (Bombay, 1965).

[166] See Baker, *Politics*, ch. 3; G. Pandey, *The Congress in Uttar Pradesh 1926–34* (New Delhi, 1978), ch. 6.

[167] Arnold, 'Armed Police'.

[168] For a discussion of the continuity between 'local' panchayati and higher judicial tribunals, see M. Galanter, 'The Aborted Restoration of Indigenous Law in India', *Comparative Studies in Society and History* (XIV), 1972.

state. The 'mixed' constitutions and partially representative provincial
governments of the inter-war years pushed and pulled the colonial state
to break with many of its nineteenth-century taboos. The ban on
religious and social legislation, for example, went by the wayside when
'representatives' of Indian society expressed a contempt for Anglo-
Indian 'tradition'. In the 1930s, the Madras intelligentsia at last won its
Gains of Learning Act and several of the caste impediments to social and
economic activities were removed. Equally, Indian political pressure in
the context of an increasingly powerful nationalist movement, capable
of offering practical solutions to the problems which the British blamed
on providence, drove the state away from its laissez faire postures and
into the market. Particularly important in the strengthening of the role
of the state was the acceptance of its authority by the local agrarian
community, some of whose members now were influential in its legislatures. The ability of the police and the administration to penetrate 'the
village' to a far greater degree than before reflected the extent to which
they were now being invited in by dominant local groups who had much
less to fear from political processes over which they had gained some
control. The political context of devolution and state building also was
reflected in the new patterns of resource distribution through the tax
system and of state aid to, and subvention of, parts of the economy. The
grasp of the colonial metropolis on the Indian economy was loosening
and the powers of the state were coming to be used to sustain a different
parallelogram of class forces.

Within this parallelogram, as before, one side was represented by
landed society. The other side, however, was of a very different character. The raj's balancing act in the inter-war years was much less concerned to hold together a quasi-traditional agricultural system of production with a mercantile/rentier capitalism than with a domestic
industrial capitalism. The other principal beneficiary of state subvention, protection and intervention was a sector of 'advanced' industry
painfully beginning to arise within the Indian economy itself. Through
tariffs, state contracts, infra-structural services, interventions in both the
commodity and labour markets and the political repression of labour,
the raj expressed a commitment to industrial development.[169] Of
course, given the constraint of scarce resources, the colonial state could
only subvent land and industry at the expense of other interests. Its

[169] Tomlinson, *Political Economy*, ch. 2; C. Markovits, 'Indian Business and Nationalist Politics 1931–39', unpublished Ph.D. dissertation, Cambridge University, 1978;
Gordon, *Businessmen, passim*; R. Chandavarkar, 'Between Work and Politics', fellowship
dissertation, Trinity College, Cambridge, 1979, chs 1, 2.

attempts at economic management plainly discriminated against three elements. First, the consumer, who had to meet the bills from higher taxes and pay higher prices for protected production. Second, commerce, especially at the local level, which was being taken over by state agencies and squeezed by state regulation of the market. Many of the larger and more significant 'indigenous' mercantile capitalist groups of the previous generation were finally driven back from agrarian commerce at this time and into industrialization or higher level finance.[170] The commodity trades were engrossed by the state and wealthier members of the agrarian community. And third, labour which was subjected to increasing repression in both agriculture and industry. State support for the rights of landowners against labour was matched by reciprocal support for the rights of industrial capitalists. Wage bills were cheapened by state-sponsored 'rationalization' programmes and policies to limit and moderate trades unionism.[171]

The emergence of Indian industrialization was the product of many causes. Doubtless, the growing political pressures of the nationalist movement played their part, making it more difficult for the British to maintain the political structure and 'open door' trade policy which had favoured the limited interests of the metropolis. But shifts in the international and domestic Indian markets already were destroying the bases of the old colonial relationship. Indian primary product exports stagnated and declined as a result both of the crisis in world trade and of their particular uncompetitiveness. The British metropolitan economy itself was turning rapidly towards new patterns of production designed to serve its own, and other developed countries', markets. A fundamental disengagement between the two economies was taking place, which left the old colonial policies bereft of a rationale. Moreover, strong forces were developing to create profitability in industrial investment in India. The decline of commerce and the commodity trades (as much overseas as domestically) released Indian capital and made the relatively lower rates of return possible in import-substitute industrialization attractive. The rise of Japan threatened Britain's ability to use the Indian open door and helped to bring tariff protection to underpin the profitability of industrial manufacture.[172] In these conditions, the colonial state could not ignore the needs of Indian industry and began to develop policies more favourable to it. Indeed, state finances were increasingly depen-

---

[170] Tomlinson, *Political Economy*, ch. 2; T. Timberg, 'Three Types of Marwari Firm', *Indian Economic and Social History Review* (IX), 1973; Baker, *Politics*, ch. 3.

[171] Chandavarkar, 'Between Work', chs 1, 2.

[172] Tomlinson, *Political Economy*, ch. 2.

dent upon its progress and, if the residual legacy of the raj (the army and the sterling debt) was to be maintained, industry must prosper to replace the income lost from the colonial trades and the protection of the countryside. The one remaining reservation was that industry's expansion ought to be directed away from a challenge to rival British manufacture wherever possible. The squeeze on labour costs in part stemmed from an attempt to improve Indian industry's profits without increasing its needs to compete more strongly for residual British markets.[173]

In the context of this shift in the structure of the colonial economy, however, the continued and re-inforced protection of agriculture becomes problematic. The old colonial structure, to which a quasi-traditional agriculture had been partially functional, was fast disappearing, while the industrial elements in the new configuration possessed very different rural needs. Indeed, the dysfunctions caused to industrial development by the condition of agriculture were very considerable. Between the wars, Indian primary commodity production not only lost foreign markets but significantly failed to respond to the new domestic imperatives upon it. In spite of the expanding demand for food crops, production of grain, on most readings of the evidence, remained static and India became ever more reliant on imports of foreign food.[174] Equally, with the exception of some specially protected commodities such as sugar, the increase in industrial crops was small.[175] Indian industry had to look to foreign imports for many raw materials which, theoretically, could have been supplied by its own economy.[176] Further, the social structure of the countryside restricted the level of market demand and limited industry's scope for expansion. The state's attempts to raise agricultural productivity through new in-puts and technological help were proving too little and too late to make much of an impact. But its social conservation strategy, of lowering tax demands, creating opportunities for landowners to increase their profits from commerce and reduced wage bills and offering community (or state) ancillary assets to the private political command of the wealthier farmers, was

[173] Chandavarkar, 'Between Work', chs 1, 2.

[174] Although the bases of its statistics have been challenged, G. Blyn, *Agricultural Trends in India 1891–1947* (Philadelphia, 1966), remains the most comprehensive survey of grain production in the inter-war period.

[175] Sugar acreage expanded by about 20 per cent in the 1930s. The other area of significant growth was groundnut which was coming to be used as a cheap source of vegetable oil. See D. Narain, *Impact of Price Movements on Areas Under Selected Crops in India, 1900–1939* (Cambridge, 1965). The failure of agriculture to respond to industrialization in the inter-war period naturally raises questions about how far agricultural stagnation previously had been the product of lack of industrialization.

[176] Especially raw cotton which was coming in large quantities from East Africa.

succeeding in easing the competitive pressures on agriculturists and enabling them to survive without change. The economic corollary of the state's agrarian policy was stagnation and the growth of industry was not part of any far-reaching process of economic transformation.[177] This situation hardly suited metropolitan interests. With the decline of the colonial trades, India's future value to Britain lay in the ability of the growth sectors in her economy to link up with new elements in the metropolis. The provision of finance capital and capital goods to Indian industrialization offered the promise of continuing profit from the empire. The restraints imposed by the protection of agriculture obstructed the realization of this promise. Indeed, the economics of empire in India became increasingly questionable. New markets failed to develop; the acute crisis in primary commodity production caused by the depression saw the metropolis having to bail out the cotton market and cover the stirling debt; and the 'modernization' of the Indian army was having to be paid for, in part, by the British tax-payer. If the 'old' colonial economy could not be held, there was precious little for Britain to exploit in the stunted national economy which was beginning to replace it.[178]

An 'agrarians' versus 'industrialists' problem, of course, is not at all unusual in the history of 'developing' societies. In most European countries, apart from Britain, industry found itself having to live with, and accord a measure of expensive favour to, agricultural producers. The difficulty in this case, however, was that the protected bases of the agrarian order were peculiarly incompatible with industry's progress. Except in a few parts of Northern India (Oudh, Bihar), the 'agrarian' interest did not reflect that of the large landholder and feudal aristocrat. Generally, the economic trends and legislation of the previous two generations had done their work and eased the feudality back to a distant rentier and pensioner role. And even in Oudh and Bihar, the events of the 1930s suggested that the real power of their talukdars and zamindars was below that assumed by British officialdom.[179] Over most of India, the agrarian interest represented that of wealthier, village-based landowners and members of the dominant castes. The significance of this was that, as in the previous 'colonial' economic structure, these agrarians had little ability to develop agriculture along lines suitable to

[177] There was no significant shift in the sectoral balance of the workforce across the period. See J. Krishnamurty, 'The Distribution of the Indian Working Force 1901–51', Chaudhuri and Dewey, *Economy*.

[178] See Tomlinson, *Political Economy*.

[179] For examples, Pandey, *The Congress*, chs 2, 6; G. McDonald, 'Unity on Trial.' D. A. Low, *Congress*.

the 'external' world of capital. In German industrialization, for example, the agrarian interest of the Junker aristocracy at least had been able to improve production by sponsoring large-scale farming and to drive labour off the land and cheapen its supply to industry.[180] It had provided some services to compensate for its protection. But here there was no scope for large-scale farming or cheapening production and labour. The organization of production tended to remain based around the use of family labour and to contain a high measure of local subsistence provision which kept production out of the market.[181] Although, indeed, the demographic increase guaranteed that labour was supplied from agriculture to industry, it is unclear that the latter gained much from the relationship. The commonly-made argument that Indian factory labour's continued access and relationship to the land reduced its costs to employers, by providing a hidden subsistence component, does not accord well with a great deal of the evidence. Full-time factory wages in, for example, the Bombay textile industry were relatively high due, on some accounts, to continued rural linkages which had to be bought out in order to stabilize the labour force.[182] Equally, the level of wage remittances back into the countryside seems so high that it is difficult to believe wages made no substantial contribution to the subsistence of the worker's family as well as himself.[183] In effect, it would be possible to argue the reverse of the 'cheap industrial wage' thesis. Remittances from industry cheapened the cost of agricultural labour by providing part of its subsistence. The returns to hired casual labour in agriculture appear so low that alone they could not have met the

---

[180] K. S. Pinson, *Modern Germany* (Toronto, 1954), chs 1, 6.

[181] The family farm model of production made famous by Chayanov and held in, for example, Kessinger, *Vilyatpur*, chs 3–5, to underlie Punjabi farming may imply too much decision-making independence to be widely applicable to other regions. Nonetheless, it seems true that, within different contexts of decision-making, the family remained the principal unit of labour organization and, in the absence of a fully articulated food-market, tried to provide a large part of its own subsistence needs. This appears to have held true generally until at least the early 1960s. See B. Dasgupta (*et al.*), *Village Society and Labour Use* (Delhi, 1977).

[182] D. Mazumdar, 'Labour Supply in Early Industrialization', *Economic History Review* (XXVI), 1973; on rural/urban wage differentials see L. Chakravarty, 'Emergence of an Industrial Labour Force in a Dual Economy', *Indian Economic and Social History Review* (XV), 1978.

[183] Recently, the point has been strongly disputed by G. Omvedt, 'Migration in Colonial India', *Journal of Peasant Studies* (VII), 1980. But the statistics she herself provides are not so easily dismissed. The sum of Rs 10.7 crores reportedly remitted to six North Bihari districts between 1915 and 1920 is very striking. In Gorakhpur by the 1890s, remittances through the post office alone came to more than the total land revenue demand of the district. I am grateful to Dr Peter Musgrave for this information.

reproduction costs of the workforce.[184] Moreover, the drag of rural connections pushed industry into developing a number of 'expensive' devices to retain and control its labour. There was no real basis for compatibility between industry and this protected agrarian base. It is striking that, for example, in both the Japanese and Russian experiences, where the nature of the social organization of agricultural production was somewhat similar, industrialization proceeded in concert with a squeeze on the peasantry, which took a high proportion of surplus from it to pay for infra-structural costs and attempted radically to alter its class character by engineering the emergence of larger capitalist farmers geared to the market.[185] In Indian industrialization the policies of the state were accented quite differently.

The antagonism between the agrarian and industrial orders was exceptionally deep and bitter in the Indian context. It showed itself in increasingly frequent breakdowns in market relations and in political confrontations. The agrarian interest naturally sought to push up primary product prices and, in the violently fluctuating economic conditions of the period, was provided with many opportunities to hoard and to threaten to starve out the towns. Urban grain riots, common enough occurrences in times of dearth, became a regular feature of the inter-war years even in non-famine conditions.[186] Supplies of important industrial crops, such as cotton and jute, also were subject to sudden local fluctuations and unforeseen leaps in price.[187] The agrarian problem was further manifested in the aid which the countryside provided in sustaining strike action in industry. Retreat to the village, and reliance on village resources to hold out against recalcitrant employers, were important weapons in the struggle of factory labour.[188] On the industrial side, the interest naturally lay in raising the price of necessary manufactured goods. The cloth market seems to have suffered from the same difficulties as the grain market and sudden shortages and leaps in the price of cloth were the occasion of much rural rioting.[189] Industrialists' attempts to beat down the price of factory labour also affected the countryside,

[184] For the declining share of the social product represented by agricultural wages, see Mukherji, 'National Income'. The chief problem may have been one of underemployment, for casual agricultural labour frequently was employed only seasonally.

[185] For examples, see R. P. Dore, Land Reform and Japan's Economic Development', *Developing Economies* (III), 1965; H. Willets, 'The Agrarian Problem', G. Katkov (ed.), *Russia Enters The Twentieth Century* (London, 1973).

[186] Especially in the 1930s, see Baker, *Politics*, ch. 3.

[187] For the problems of cotton, see Gordon, *Businessmen*, ch. 3.

[188] Chandavarkar, 'Between Work', chs 1, 2.

[189] See *Report(s) on the Administration of the Police in the Madras Presidency* (Annual Series), especially 1929–39.

reducing the flow of remittances to it. In effect, the articulation of the industrial and agrarian economies was beset with increasing problems and inclined to collapse into chaos and violence. It was in response to this that the state found itself having to intervene constantly in the market place and to set up its own bureaucratic apparatus to provide the regulation which conditions were preventing the market from supplying. The raj, of course, saw the problem entirely in terms of 'the middle man', the agent of commerce who stood between the producer and consumer and supposedly exploited both.[190] Its market interventions were aimed primarily against him and sought to establish a context of 'fair' competition in which, at least, industry and agriculture could live. But middle-men are constrained by the structures of supply and demand in which they work and over which they have limited control. The extent to which the raj was having to subvent both the farmer and the industrialist tells a different story. Stripped of their mutual powers to dominate each other politically, neither industry nor agriculture could hold their own in the market, be it state regulated or not. Both needed resources drawn, through tariffs, tax losses and state repression, from other sectors of the economy. The colonial state's ideology of the evil middle-man was merely an excuse designed to avoid confronting the much deeper structural problems of the economy, which were developing under its rule but which, for various reasons, it was unwilling to admit. To hold the two together and contain their natural antagonisms, the raj was having vastly to expand the competence of its own bureaucracy and to facilitate the increasing exploitation of society by privileged classes of landowners and industrialists. This exploitation was producing as little in the way of the development of the forces of production and the qualitative transformation of the Indian economy as it was in the way of benefits to a new metropolitan relationship. It functioned, in effect, to hold the economy still.

What lay behind the last balancing act of the colonial juggler and what purpose was served by sustaining so contradictory a structure? If the problematic element in the situation is seen to be the protection of agriculture, the immediate context of politics in this, the final, phase of the raj supplies some ready answers. In most provinces, policies favourable to the petty landowning interest were part of the colonial state's battle with nationalism; and in others, although its perception of the political struggle may have been different, it inadvertently created opportunities which this interest could take. In Bengal, Punjab and most

[190] The classic statement of the anti-middleman thesis is the *Report of the Royal Commission on Agriculture in India* (HMSO, 1928).

of Madras, the raj was inclined to identify nationalism with urban groups among the intelligentsia or commercial classes and to gear its programme of political devolution to exclude or weaken them.[191] This strategy had the effect of bringing dominant local-level agrarian groups into the legitimate structure of government from an early period and giving them a considerable measure of local power. It could hardly be that their loyalty and continued collaboration would survive the formulation of policies in the higher institutions of the state, which attacked their material interests by squeezing them in favour of industry. In provinces such as the U.P., matters were complicated by a nostalgia for the feudality. Although the plan of using a supposedly loyal countryside against a supposedly seditious town appears to have been the same, its execution broke down on the British belief that the larger landlords, whose relations with their tenants had been moved progressively to a basis of administrative rentalism and whose conflicts with their tenants had been filling the courts for nearly fifty years, were somehow the natural leaders of the rural community. This belief, and its realization in the constitution of dyarchy between 1920 and 1937, gave the structure of legitimate government to the zamindars and the upper level of village society to the Congress. Logic, however, prevailed in the 1937 election when, much to the surprise of the British, a Congress provincial government closely related to the upper tenant interest was returned to power and, here too, the state came to rest on entrenched petty landholding interest.[192]

In addition to the simple struggle with nationalism, the shock of the depression also created political imperatives to protect agriculture. The worst effects were felt by those most closely involved in market production and commerce. This tended to include at least the wealthier village landowners who invested in supra-subsistence cultivation, who indulged in commodity speculation and moneylending and who often had labour to pay from the sale of valueless crops. The slowness of state intervention to suspend tax (and zamindari rental) collections and, absurdly, even revenue resettlement operations, provoked a series of direct confrontations with the raj and suggested the serious possibility of a general political alliance between the 'coqs du village' and the Con-

[191] For Bengal, see J. Gallagher, 'Congress in Decline', *Modern Asian Studies* (VII), 1973; for the agrarian roots of the Punjab Unionist Party, see I. A. Talbot, 'The 1946 Punjab Elections', *Modern Asian Studies* (XIV), 1980; for Madras, see Baker, *Politics*, chs 2, 4.

[192] However, beneath the epiphenomenon of the dyarchic landlord governments, the process consolidating the position of the upper level of village tenants' landholders seems to have continued in U.P. as elsewhere. See Stokes, *Peasant*, ch. 9.

gress. Once again, and now in the pressing circumstances of a political emergency, the raj had reason to court the favour of petty landowning society. Its extraordinary willingness to do so indicates how far, by this time, its concern in India was just to hang on for as long as it could, even at the expense of stultifying economic development and the growth of a new 'neo-colonial' relationship with a progressive Indian industrial capitalism. As history closed in upon it, the raj's notion of survival became based on increasingly short-term expedients.

Yet the context of nationalist struggle does not provide all, or even very many, of the answers. One of the most remarkable aspects of the matter is the extent to which not only the British but also all the other important elements in the political system favoured the village landowning interest. The Congress came to consist of a mixture of precisely the same class interests as those pursued by the British in the cause of loyalism. The agrarian/industrialists alliance was fully reflected in its own membership and social policies. Moreover, although our information is not good, there seems little sign that industrialists themselves were deeply unhappy with the alliance and pushing either the Congress or the British to take a more aggressive line towards the archaic mode of petty commodity production, designed to force it into structural change. Indeed, the signs everywhere suggest a consensus on the need to serve the landowning interest, manifested in Gandhian nostalgia for the village community (which, whatever its mystical and romantic connotations, could now but mean the preservation of existing patterns of agrarian dominance) or in the anti-middleman ideology shared as much by the Congress as the raj[193] (which overlooked the structural question) or even in the workings of the devolved administration (which showed no indication of a difference in the notion of rights enforced by local rural and national bureaucratic authorities). The symmetry of dominant class opinion on the desired structure of Indian society, with its continued inefficient and theoretically obstructive agrarian base, is extremely striking.

Behind it, it is possible to see three patterns of development which drew the agrarians and industrialists into a symbiosis and which, for all their residual differences and antagonisms, made them inter-dependent. First, under their demographic and ecological/technological difficulties, dominant village groups had become very reliant on the existence of a context of industrialization to which they could relate. Earnings made in

---

[193] Most of the Congress provincial governments of 1937–39, for example, discussed further improvements in indebtedness and tenancy legislation although their brief period in office seldom allowed them to achieve much.

commerce, in work outside agriculture and in market production played an increasingly large role in the 'family' economies of farming groups.[194] Indeed, the economic structure of 'traditional' rural society was dependent upon a host of connections to, and subventions from, advanced capitalist development going on somewhere else. Had a revolt of 'the agrarians' actually succeeded in seriously damaging India's industrial bases, the price would have been the collapse of the agrarian structure itself. Here, then, there was room for compromise which the state could use to impose conditions on agriculture, which permitted the existence of some complementary industrialization. On the other side, the structure of the countryside, for all its obstructions, performed one service for industrial capital which was becoming increasingly critical: it provided political stability. Beneath the solid level of privileged village landownership, the conditions of the inter-war period were stirring up a maelstrom. Demographic pressures on the now fixed landed base had greatly increased the landless or virtually landless proportion of the population who were dependent on agricultural or migrant labour for their subsistence, who had been pushed out of local subsistence calculation and onto the precarious grain market for their food and who had borne most of the risks to life in the limited development of market production. In the 1920s and, especially, the 1930s, their situation was becoming impossible. Many sources of work in neighbouring agrarian economies collapsed, transport services (a major employer of casual labour) suffered from the commercial stagnation and market fluctuations threatened the continuity of their food supplies. The final straw perhaps was the great depression which, while temporarily providing them with relative wage bonuses, in the longer term set landowners to cutting their labour costs and to converting more rapidly from permanent and patronage-based to casual and short-term forms of labour exploitation. The rural poor were becoming a major problem and their frustations began to boil over into a series of agrarian riots and violent confrontations with their 'traditional' authorities.[195] At least one of the reasons why the colonial state began to devolve power to dominant village leadership groups and to support their authority with greater coercive force was to keep the lid on the potentially turbulent rural pot.

[194] In the upper echelons of the agrarian community, this showed itself less in 'labour' than in investment in urban and urban-related undertakings. For examples, see Baker, *Politics*, ch. 3; Tomlinson, *Political Economy*, ch. 2. Also, there was drift towards education and the professions, see my 'Country Politics'. In less hierarchic communities, however, even some of the more substantial farming families were now sending scions to labour elsewhere. See Kessinger, 'Family Farm'.
[195] Baker, *Politics*, ch. 3; Pandey, *Congress*, ch. 6.

710   D. A. WASHBROOK

The need for this support became particularly acute in the depression, when economic changes damaged the material bases of the networks of clientage which articulated the agrarian order and threatened the structure of social dominance within it. There was a danger that not only would the agrarian élite not be able to hold down the countryside but that some of its members might even join and sponsor an attack on the institutions of the raj which, through failure to respond quickly to the conditions of depression, was putting added pressure on the élite. The absorption of dominant village landowners into the structure of legitimate political (state) authority in the middle- to late-1930s greatly improved the means of maintaining social control in the countryside and added supports from the higher levels of the political system to shore up the institutions of local dominance which economic conditions were undermining. From the vantage point of the raj and of industrial capital, a preservation of petty landowning society guaranteed peace in the countryside and the possibility of continuing some kind of business. It might limit development in the longer term but it was cheaper in the short term than any conceivable alternative (such as welfarism or military repression) and promised to be a great deal more effective. On the understanding that its removal might produce conditions even less conducive to capitalist activity, industry could be brought to pay its price.

Beneath, then, the fundamental antagonisms between industry and this agrarian structure, there were lines of communication and possibilities for collaboration. It was these which the colonial state picked up in its devices of regulation and subvention. And once, of course, they were in place, a third reason for, and basis of, compromise emerged. Both industry and agriculture were joined together in enjoying a growing influence over the apparatus of the state. They were mutually dependent upon its powers and redistributions (of demand and wealth) for their prosperity and survival. The risks involved in taking their differences to the point at which they might threaten to break up the state and undermine its integrity were very great. They needs must compromise to preserve their alliance, for the price of its falling apart could be their mutual loss of authority and ability to use state power in the service of their own interests.[196]

The peculiar context giving property right and value to land in the interwar years, which was reflected in the legal developments of the

[196] For an analysis of the post-independence political economy, which stresses this 'contradiction' see P. Patnaik, 'Imperialism and the Growth of Indian Capitalism', R. Owen and R. B. Sutcliffe (eds), *Studies in the Theory of Imperialism* (London, 1972).

period, was the product of the agrarian/industrial alliance being brokered in the colonial state. The possession of land (or at least of significant quantities of it) was a function of the possession of political privilege. This privilege manifested itself in the way that existing village landowning groups were coming to control the policies of the state with regard to land and the administrative machinery distributing access to, and adjudicating rights over it. While, doubtless, dominant village groups always had possessed a considerable informal influence over the land, these developments legitimated their position and promoted clearer differentiation within ascriptive caste and kinship communities between the more substantial landholders, with access to the institutions of the emergent 'national' political system, and those without. As the British carefully bequeathed this agrarian political structure to India at independence, it was clear that no social revolution could follow the winning of 'freedom'. The class qualities of the new national political structure suggested major problems being stored up for the future. The possibilities of economic development in both agriculture and industry were bleak. After industry had taken over the manufacturing quota of the old metropolis, in what directions could it expand without putting pressure on its agrarian ally? Without some fundamental change in the nature of agricultural technology capable of being used within its social constraints, how could agrarian society significantly increase its output? The political structure seemed to contain in-built principles of immobility. Yet neither industrial capital nor the agrarian community could stand still: the one existed under competitive market pressures for constant accumulation; the other under demographic pressures to support ever higher numbers. Within the continuing structure of the state and the class alliance frozen into its operations, it appears possible to conceive 'progress' coming from only two sources. Industrial capital and the dominant agrarian élite might either improve their profits by increasing their mutual protection and acquiring an ever larger relative proportion of the static social product for themselves; or (and) they might combine to use their control of the state to increase the repression of labour and constantly cheapen its costs in production. Both are indicative of the dark legacy which nearly two hundred years of British rule left behind it, embedded in the form of the state and the contradictory structure of class domination in society.

To summarize, in each of these three phases of colonial rule in India, characterized by different constellations of social forces, the role of the law and the nature of the property right which it sought to uphold varied considerably. In the first phase of 'the mercantilist state', the influence of the Anglo-Indian law over the relations of production on the land was limited to a secondary function in maintaining the liquidity of capital within the apparatus of the state. Effective rights to land emerged, as under the ancien régime, at the point of conjuncture between the extractive institutions of government and the corporate organizations of agrarian society and reflected the status of the struggle between the two for control over surplus. With regard to the land, the courts merely validated the frequently non-market forms of property right required by the state in this struggle. Most of the courts' business seems to have concerned the relations of 'metropolitan' society and its 'movable' properties. Here the Anglo-Indian law strongly favoured neo-traditional types of property relationship and concepts of community trust. These presented an illusion of continuity which served the Company's political security. But they also facilitated the extractive operations of the state and European mercantile capitalists by extending liabilities and holding together property trusts to service debts. The key feature of the period, however, was that the state showed no real interest in making market competition, under the rule of law, the dynamic behind agrarian society, regulating its production and reproduction. Its own structure of political relations oversaw the development and continuity of production.

In the second phase of 'the high colonial' state, this situation had changed. Conditions of market competition now touched the agrarian base and the law was assuming definitions of property right more suitable to a 'free' capitalist context. Yet it clearly did not go so far as to establish a basis of equal and individualistic competition. The state was maintaining and manufacturing social prescriptions which limited the consequences of competition and was trying to keep control over the land in the hands of existing agrarian corporations. To conserve society in this way, while at the same time sustaining some market dynamic, the raj undertook a delicate balancing act. Its laws sought to guarantee a level of returns to mercantile and rentier capital but, at the same time, to restrict the pressures which they could exert on agriculture. The law of property now was meant to serve as an instrument of compromise and took on suitably confused and contradictory forms.

In the third phase of 'the incipient nation state' the basis of the compromise broke down. The definition and regulation of property right passed back directly to the state and the political systems and became increasingly subject to the operations of the criminal, rather than civil, law. Behind this lay attempts to build the wealthier members of the village landholder class into a dominant position, shared with large-scale industrial capital, in the state apparatus as it was progressively nationalized. The principal purpose of this position was to provide political stability over a countryside whose growing relative impoverishment was starting to threaten the possibilities of continuing capitalist business activity at all. Through each of these phases, we have used the law as a focus on the complex social and political forces at work in colonial India, on the problems posed by these (and by the international context) to the governing metropolis and on the consequences of the law's various resolutions for the continuing development of agrarian society.

What does this view of India's colonial history through the law have to tell us about the problems of historical and sociological conceptualization which dominate debates about the recent past? First, it may help to periodize the history of the raj rather more clearly. Our knowledge of the structural characteristics of the colonial régime at different times is not highly developed. On the one hand, there has been a tendency to treat 'British' rule as all of one piece, from the eighteenth to the twentieth centuries, and to pay insufficient attention to the very significant re-orientations in the relationship between state and society which took place over those two hundred years.[197] On the other, there has been a tendency to suppose a single break, from the time of the Mutiny, between an active and innovatory 'early' period and a conservative later phase.[198] This, however, seems facile, for the 'conservatism' took place in the context of qualitatively new socio-economic pressures and involved the elaboration of a qualitatively new form of state, while the activity of the earlier years masked continuation of 'ancien régime' state-craft. By situating the raj in the context of forces, both from within and without, which generated imperatives upon it, we may be able to grasp its structural evolution more firmly. This evolution is important not only if we wish to understand the 'colonial' but also the 'indigenous' side of Indian history.[199] It is very difficult to see how the development of Indian society is to be comprehended without reference to the precise economic and political pressures to which it was subject and which composed its immediate historical context.

Second, our perspective may help to dispel the images of British rule as monolithic and omnicompetent, which still are very widespread in

[197] This is implicit in, for example, Cohn, 'Notes' and 'Anthropological Notes'; and, for the period to 1885, in 'Structural Change'.

[198] Metcalf, *Aftermath*, chs. 4–6.

[199] This is not a distinction which the author finds meaningful but it is one stressed in much of the social history informed by American cultural anthropology. As far as the author is concerned, the raj was part of the same social field as its subjects.

assumptions about the colonial period. Again, by considering the pressures upon it, we can see the particular points of weakness and the deepening contradictions in the structure of the raj. These provide valuable information for construing its response to events, which, in comparative terms, often seems idiosyncratic. Of course, to suggest that colonial rule was weak might appear to suggest that its impact on Indian society was minimal. But this would be a false inference. Indeed, the greatest significance of the raj for Indian history may have lain precisely in the severity of its contradictions. These meant that it was unable to pick up the forces of capitalist development, which had been released partially as a consequence of its own actions, and support them politically in a programme of social transformation. The 'dynamic immobility' of the Indian economy reflected, and was constrained by, a 'dynamic immobility' in the social and political principles of later British rule. In effect, the colonial state proved a poor vehicle to convey the social imperatives of capitalist development, to the long-term cost not only of India but even of the metropolis itself.

And third, our view from the law also may raise questions about how the law itself should be conceptualized. Clearly, we have not treated the Anglo-Indian law as an autonomous field of sociological inquiry, whose norms and institutions can be separated from the wider context of society and analysed meaningfully in their own terms. Constantly, we have tried to relate the law to other aspects of the state and the developing class structure and have looked for its meanings in those relationships. There are two contextual justifications for this approach. First, the notional independence of the judiciary from the executive, proclaimed in the Permanent Settlement, was never realized. Colonial India had no independent legislature or written constitution to act as a check on the executive, which actually appointed the judiciary as part of the civil service and changed the law as it pleased. The supposed autonomy of the judiciary was an illusion, perpetuated by colonial legitimating ideology, and the law was a department of the executive. Second, undoubtedly the most important changes of the period were those emanating from the socio-economic context and progressively altering the nature of the value in landed property. It is very hard to see how rules for the protection of property may be understood apart from the conditions creating 'social' value in that property in the first place. One worry about the more conventional approach to the study of the law is that it tends to exclude both the state and the class dimensions and to proffer judgements of significance in terms of abstract sociological principles (which, if traced back, lead into the wilderness of Parsonian/

modernization theory speculation). This can be very misleading. It is not clear, for example, what should be made of the popular saw that the possession of land underwent a fundamental change during the colonial period from a function of political power and rulership to a function of 'economic' property ownership. While the forms of political relationship on the land indeed were given to change, effective access to land was not divorced from the functions of political power in the dominant caste and kinship 'corporations' of the locality and, increasingly, in the apparatus of the emergent nation state.[200] This abstraction of the law is suggestive of a species of ethnocentrism (or false universalism) which holds that the social role of the (formal) legal apparatus was the same in colonial India (and universally) as in the West where judicial autonomy was more highly developed and the class base of property ownership had become fixed in different ways much earlier. Moreover, from its Parsonian influence, it may represent a class-centric view too: the notion that, even in the West, access to property is a function of the economic rather than the political (class) system reflects 'pure' bourgeois ideology.

In addition to raising some questions about the historical interpretation of India's colonial experience, our perspective also may throw light on some problems of conceptualization involved in the analysis of social change. For analysts working within the framework of modernization theory, India's empirical record has proved a constant source of nightmare. It can be construed as a history of 'ongoing social modernization' only at the expense of a degree of blindness and eclecticism unusual even by the notoriously lax standards of modernization theory. The past and tradition have simply refused to go away as they should and only by a remarkable flight of fantasy can Indian social history be read as the growing replication of modern Western society, which the theory anticipated. To cope with the unpalatable facts of continuity and difference, the original theory has been twisted round in several interesting ways. Concepts of 'dualism' have been introduced to show that, for various reasons, modern Western society did not establish contact with the bases of Indian tradition. Somewhat mystical formulations of 'the modernity of tradition',[201] 'traditionalisation as a process of modernisation'[202] and 'the absorption of tradition into modernity'[203] have been

---

[200] This point is borne out in innumerable anthropological studies of the village context. For example, Kessinger, *Vilyatpur*, ch. 2.

[201] Rudolphs, *Modernity*, ch. 1.

[202] P. Brass, 'The Politics of Ayurvedic Education', S. and L. Rudolph, *Education and Politics in India* (Cambridge, Mass., 1972).

[203] M. Galanter, 'The Aborted Restoration of Indigenous Law in India', *Comparative Studies in Society and History* (XIV), 1972.

716 D. A. WASHBROOK

evolved to suggest that the Indian past conditioned and was a formative influence on the way that India modernized. Both of these twists, however, are empirically and logically unsatisfactory. Dualism now seems wrecked on critiques both from 'underdevelopment' theory and from 'empiricist' history. On the one hand, most of the obstructions and hiatuses which it postulates between the worlds of tradition and modernity have been shown to be illusory: 'modern' capital, for example, clearly reached the 'peasant economy' through the commercial and credit systems;[204] there is no evidence of a pool of 'surplus labour' holding back production;[205] peasants are 'rational' economic producers given the nature of the situation which they face, etc. On the other hand, many of the institutions which dualism understands to be 'traditional' (the village community, the extended family, etc.)[206] have been shown by historians to have assumed their character under colonialism no earlier than the nineteenth century and to have been the product of change. The difficulties with the 'modernity of tradition' formulations are more profound. The 'classical' theory of modernization elucidates, and therefore rests upon the assumption of, a fundamental transformation in the nature of human society. Tradition and modernity are qualitatively different and antithetical types of society defined as opposites of one another. Modernity emerges through the progressive destruction of its antithesis. Given the historical condition which the theory conceptualizes and the way that it conceptualizes it, it is not at all clear that arguments supposing a continuity and a sympathy between tradition and modernity can be logically contained within its paradigm. Such formulations implicitly deny the existence of the qualitative antithesis and transformation and thus wreck the theoretical foundations of their own concepts. They may continue to use the terms 'tradition' and 'modernity' but they have rendered them meaningless.

Although, of course, the view of society through the law taken above was not informed by the theory of modernization, nor the Parsonian epistemology behind it, nonetheless what was seen there may help to put these problems into perspective. The central difficulty with 'dualism' appears to lie in its assumptions that the state and market apparatus of colonialism were 'modern' in the technical sense (or 'Western' in the

[204] See A. G. Frank, 'The Development of Underdevelopment', *Monthly Review* (1966); as early as the 1820s, the fate of Indian cash crops such as indigo involved the fortunes of London finance houses, see C. A. Bayly, 'The Age of Hiatus', C. Philips and M. Wainwright (eds), *Indian Society and the Beginnings of Modernization* (London, 1976).

[205] M. Paglin, 'Surplus Agricultural Labour and Development', *American Economic Review* (LV), 1965.

[206] See Kessinger, *Vilyatpur*, ch. 2; Leonard, *Social History*, chs. 7, 10.

same sense), that they were trying to engage Indian society in a modernizing social transformation and that they were blocked by the intransigence (cultural, social, political) of Indian tradition. But at least the first two seem not to be warranted by the evidence of the law, or at best to be highly questionable. And once they are questioned, the significance of the third begins to disappear. Indeed, the preservation of certain aspects of Indian tradition (if that, indeed, describes the process we are examining) appears to be functionally related to the character of the colonial 'superstructure'. There is no dualism, no break, although it is clear that the nature of what the British inherited played a considerable part in determining what they decided to do with it. Looked at from this angle, the 'problematics' also shift, partially away from the qualities of the inheritance and onto the context influencing the colonial authorities.

This angle also helps us to put the 'modernity of tradition' formulation into focus. As Richard Fox has argued, part of its logical weakness lies in its insistence that the link between past and present, which determines what aspects of tradition are taken up into and condition modernity, is forged more out of the peculiar qualities of the past than the specific nature of the present.[207] In the arguments of S. and L. Rudolph, the important social functions of caste in 'tradition' provide the only clue to, and therefore presumably explain, why caste should play a prominent role in modernity.[208] Fox pointed out that this makes little sense, for the contextual pressures of the present, which the Rudolphs on a nexus between past and present but tries to understand its specificities in terms of the dynamics of a process of historical change. To make an old point, the real weakness of modernization theory is its our analysis of the law and the state may have highlighted some of the pressures leading to accommodations with, and sublations of, aspects of the inherited social structure in the new colonial design. But it may also have suggested that the specific characteristics of the past are themselves a pressure on the present. In effect, our analysis agrees with the Rudolphs on a nexus between past and present but tries to understand its specificities in terms of the dynamics of a process of historical change. To make an old point, the real weakness of modernization theory is its tendency to assume and not to demonstrate the dynamics involved in processes of historical change.[209]

[207] R. G. Fox, 'The Avatars of Indian Research', *Comparative Studies in Society and History* (XII), 1970.
[208] Rudolphs, *Modernity*, ch. 1.
[209] For an extended critique of the principles of modernization theory, see R. Bendix, 'Tradition and Modernity Reconsidered', *Comparative Studies in Society and History* (IX), 1967; D. Tipps, 'Modernization Theory and the Study of National Societies', *ibid.* (XV),

In the Marxist study of colonial India, the character of the mode of production has become an important focus of debate. The debate has been of major significance in developing a more sophisticated understanding of Marxist concepts and in reversing trends towards re-ification. But it still may not have gone far to resolving the historical problem, concerning the nature of agrarian change under colonialism, whence it started. Neither of the two most favoured formulations seems empirically sound. The argument, for example, that the relations of production in agriculture were becoming increasingly 'capitalistic', or adequate to the notion of capital, contains many difficulties.[210] It rests upon an implicit history of growing market production, land consolidation and wage labour. Yet if the existence of a considerable degree of (albeit 'coerced') market production in the pre-colonial period is taken into account, the qualitative increase under colonial rule may not have been very great[211] and, anyway, tended to come to a halt in many areas from the turn of the twentieth century. Equally, the evidence of any more than a marginal increase in the stratification of landholdings over the period 1850–1950 is not strong;[212] and while, certainly, the amount of wage labour in society increased, it is unclear that it was replacing rather than supplementing family-based units of production.[213] There was, of course, a considerable increase in the proportion of the population having no, or virtually no, land at all and dependent upon a precarious, casual wage labouring existence inside and outside agriculture. But this increase is suggestive more of a demographic than a qualitatively capitalistic dynamic. The other formulation, of a retained 'feudal' agriculture articulated to capital appears to fit empirical conditions rather better. But its weakness lies both in specifying the institutions through which the articulation took place and in explaining why capital functioned in this way. The recent argument of Gail Omvedt that colonialism perpetuated agricultural 'feudalism' in order to give European mine-owners, planters, and other capitalists in and around

1973; L. Shiner, 'Tradition/Modernity: An Ideal Type Gone Astray', *ibid.* (XVII), 1975.

[210] As in Banaji, 'Capitalist Domination'.

[211] See, for example, Habib, *Agrarian System*.

[212] See D. Kumar, 'Landownership and Inequality in Madras Presidency', *Indian Economic and Social History Review* (XII), 1975; Charlesworth, 'Rich Peasant'; Stokes, *Peasant*, ch. 9.

[213] Kessinger, 'Family Farm'. The strongest evidence of replacement comes from those areas in which, while land had been owned by locally resident village families, it had been leased out to sharecroppers. Here, the economic conditions of the 1930s seem to have started a trend which continued in response to land reform legislation after independence and in which the sharecroppers were evicted to be replaced by hired labour. But this represents a particular rather than a general case.

the South Asian economy a cheap labour force, whose subsistence costs were partially covered by toy-plot farming, is inadequate in many ways. It fails to establish that there were any special instruments forcing out migrant labour and preventing the development of agriculture: the raj did not possess the poll-taxes and bans on petty commodity production which the colonial régimes of East and South Africa used to develop migrant labour.[214] It fails to establish why the larger landowners, who were not dependent on short-term migrant labour and who held most of the land, did not develop a more progressive agriculture, or how indeed the existence of migrant labourers in the neighbouring economy affected them. And it fails to explain why it was in the interest of colonial capital to sacrifice the vast agrarian base of South Asia in order to service a tiny plantation sector, peripheral industry and such 'advanced' areas of production as Burma, Ceylon and the West Indies, where went most of the migrants.

Where perhaps the difficulties with both sides of this debate lie is in their adoption of functionalist and economistic approaches to the analysis of the relations of capital. Both appear to assume that the dominance of capital over the Indian economy, which colonial rule sustained, included a power to redesign the social structure entirely at will and to any specification optimal to an abstractly-conceived profitability. Neither side considers the implications and possible resistances of the inherited agrarian structure; neither considers the influence on possible economic activity of the need for a stable political base; neither puts the concept of profit (or rate of surplus value extraction) in a relative and competitive historical context; neither detects any contradictions in the relations and imperatives of capital. These are strange omissions, or contextual assumptions, for a history claiming to be informed by Marx. Our own analysis has tried to put these considerations back into agrarian history and to emphasize, again, that the relations of capital are not merely economic or material but also social and political, that they develop in definite historical contexts whose specificities cannot be assumed and that processes of historical change may best be understood in terms of the contradictions which arise within those relations. Whether or not we have adequately grasped the nature of the contradictions in this case, of course, is another matter and one which it is up to empirical research to decide.

[214] Omvedt, 'Migration'. Omvedt specifies only colonial instruments organizing labour for migration but not forcing it out in the first place nor deliberately preventing it from earning its living in other ways. Of course, this was because the colonial state did not need such instruments, as 'natural' conditions did its work for it. But this alters the meaning of the case.

Finally, colonial Indian history has been viewed through a range of theories of underdevelopment, which can be traced back to the earliest era of nationalist politics. These, whatever their theoretical foundation, share the common form of attributing India's poverty and economic stagnation to the operations of colonialism. One common difficulty with many of them, however, has been an adequate specification of the instruments and historical logic of the underdevelopment process. Several of the old theories, such as those of 'drain' or surplus extraction,[215] of monopolistic exploitation of commodity markets by European purchasing houses[216] and lack of sufficient infra-structural investment,[217] either do not stand up to scrutiny or raise more questions than they answer. Equally, neo-Marxist conceptualizations resting upon functionalist economist premises have been popular but are just as questionable as when presented in orthodox Marxist form.[218] These assume for the dominance of metropolitan capital the same absolute powers over social reconstruction. Yet if the colonial economy were a simple function of metropolitan dominance, then it must be presumed to have performed optimally to the needs of its metropolis. As we have suggested, this is a difficult presumption to make, at least without qualifying it in the light of the class structure and international market system, which would change its meaning.

Our own analysis could be said to fall within the range of underdevelopment theory, at least if that means seeing colonial rule as having had definite and negative consequences for the development of advanced capitalist forms of production. Where, however, it may differ from some other formulations for the colonial, although not the postcolonial, era is in emphasizing less the instruments of colonial exploitation than the class and state structures of colonialism in the creation of the conditions of 'underdevelopment'. Indeed, we have been inclined to see the specific forms of economic exploitation as determined by, in part, the class and state structures (and, in part, the logic of competition in the rest of the international market system). However, while this clearly does not removed any responsibility for India's condition from colonialism, nor suggest that Indian history would have been no different had there been no British empire, it does carry certain corollaries for the

[215] See K. N. Chaudhuri, 'India's International Economy in the Nineteenth Century', *Modern Asian Studies* (II), 1968.
[216] For the market stimulation caused by European cotton purchasing agents, see Banaji, 'Small Peasantry'; also Tomlinson, *Political Economy*, ch. 1.
[217] M. McAlpin, 'The Impact of Railroads on Agriculture in India', unpublished Ph.D. dissertation, University of Wisconsin, 1973.
[218] For example, Alavi, 'Colonial Mode'.

counterfactual against which underdevelopment should be understood. In a number of interpretations of Indian economic (especially indus-trial)[219] history from the late nineteenth century onwards, it is strongly implied that had India simply possessed a different, a national, state, she might easily have developed advanced forms of capitalist production and achieved a Japanese-style transformation. These interpretations are notable for excluding entirely from the context in which industrializa-tion is discussed any reference to the class or international contexts in which it is supposed to take place. Returning India to these contexts, the validity of this counterfactual becomes very questionable. While it may be reasonable to suppose that a hypothetical national India at this time might have developed advanced forms of production faster, it is more difficult to see how the resulting class strains could have been contained or how much support for the effort would have been provided by international capital (and, if none, then the class strains would have increased). While indeed British rule may be held to have made a difference, it is not clear that its alternative was Japan. There seem stronger grounds for thinking that, in context, a more actively state-backed attempt to promote a capitalist socio-economic revolution would have produced results closer to the Chinese experience. But it may, in the end, be better not to formulate at all problematics in the light of quite such complex counterfactuals.

[219] Bagchi, *Private Industrial Investment*.

For EU product safety concerns, contact us at Calle de José Abascal, 56–1°,
28003 Madrid, Spain or eugpsr@cambridge.org.

www.ingramcontent.com/pod-product-compliance
Ingram Content Group UK Ltd.
Pitfield, Milton Keynes, MK11 3LW, UK
UKHW042143130625
459647UK00011B/1161